Zenaide Alexeievna Ragozin

Media, Babylon and Persia

Including a study of the Zend-Avesta or religion of Zoroaster

Zenaide Alexeievna Ragozin

Media, Babylon and Persia
Including a study of the Zend-Avesta or religion of Zoroaster

ISBN/EAN: 9783337234232

Printed in Europe, USA, Canada, Australia, Japan

Cover: Foto ©Lupo / pixelio.de

More available books at **www.hansebooks.com**

MEDIA

BABYLON AND PERSIA

INCLUDING A STUDY OF THE ZEND-AVESTA OR RELIGION OF ZOROASTER

FROM THE FALL OF NINEVEH TO THE PERSIAN WAR

BY

ZÉNAÏDE A. RAGOZIN

MEMBER OF THE "SOCIÉTÉ ETHNOLOGIQUE" OF PARIS; AUTHOR OF "ASSYRIA," "CHALDEA," ETC.

London
T. FISHER UNWIN
26 PATERNOSTER SQUARE
NEW YORK: G. P. PUTNAM'S SONS
MDCCCLXXXIX

CLASSIFIED CONTENTS.

I.

PAGE

A NOTABLE RELIGIOUS SURVIVAL: THE PARSIS— ANQUETIL DUPERRON 1–16

§ 1. The Parsis, descendants of the Persians and followers of Zoroaster.—§ 2. The Parsis not heathens.—§ 3. Conquest of Persia by the Arabs.—§ 4. Oppression and conversion of the country.—§ 5. Self-exile of the Zoroastrians. —§ 6. Their wanderings and settlements in India.—§ 7. Principal tenets of their religion.—§ 8. Discovery of Parsi manuscripts.—§ 9. Anquetil Duperron and his mission.— § 10. His departure for India.—§ 11. Obstacles and hardships.—§ 12. His translation of the Zend-Avesta.—§ 13. He is attacked by William Jones.—§ 14. His mistakes and disadvantages.—§ 15. Eugène Burnouf, the founder of Eranian scholarship.—§ 16. Advance and results of Eranian studies.

II.

THE PROPHET OF ÉRÁN —THE AVESTA . 17–33

§ 1. The religions that have sacred books, and their demands.—§ 2. They claim to be supernaturally revealed.— § 3. The Veda and the Zend-Avesta—the sacred books of the Hindus and Aranians.—§ 4. "Zend-Avesta" a misnomer.—§§ 5, 6. "Pehlevi" the Persian language of the Sassanian period.—§ 7. Uncertainty and obscurity of most points concerning the Avesta.—§ 8. Ancient writers on Zoroaster.—§ 9. The "Gâthas" (songs) the oldest portion of the Avesta.—§ 10. Scant information on Zarathushtra (Zoroaster) in the Avesta.—§ 11. King Vishtâspa, the friend and follower of Zarathushtra.—§ 12. Loss of the greatest part of the Zoroastrian literature.—§ 13. Survival of some texts. The parts of the Avesta as we have it.—§ 14. The Bundehesh; its lateness and its contents.

III.

ARYAN MYTHS 34-55

§§ 1, 2. Impossibility of invention in a strict sense.—§ 3. Zarathushtra not an inventor, but a reformer.—§ 4. The Hindus and Eranians—sister nations of the Aryan or Indo-European race.—§ 5. The Airyâna-Vaêja, or first Aryan home of Eranian tradition.—§ 6. The Rig-Veda, the most ancient sacred book of the Aryan Hindus, and its indications concerning the religion of the primitive Âryas.—§ 7. The powers of nature—the gods of the Âryas.—§ 8. The Aryan sky-gods, Dyâus and Vâruna.—§ 9. The Aryan light-god, Mitra.—§ 10. The Aryan fire-god, Agni.— § 11. Aryan-dualism. Gods and demons, light and darkness, rain and drought.—§ 12. Aryan storm-myth.— § 13. Indra, the god of the thunderbolt.—§ 14. Vritra and Ahi, the cloud-fiends.—§§ 15, 16. Soma, plant, beverage and drink.—17, 18. Efficacy of sacred texts—Mantra—and of sacrifice.—§ 19. Grossness of some of these conceptions.—§ 20. Richness of Aryan mythical epos.—§ 21. King Yama and the Pitris.—§ 22. Aryan reverence toward the spirits of the departed—the Pitris.—§ 23. The Pitris pass into heroic epos.

IV.

ARYAN MYTHS IN THE AVESTA—THEIR ALLEGORICAL TRANSFORMATION . . . 56-94

§ 1. Enervating influence of the Indian climate on the Aryan population.—§ 2. Bracing and hardening influence of the soil and climate of Erân. The nature of Erân all in extremes.—§ 3. It intensifies the feeling of dualism, and develops the battle-myth almost exclusively.—§ 4. Spiritual transformation of Aryan myths in Erân.—§ 5. Ahura-Mazda, the supreme God and Creator, the successor of the

Aryan sky-gods.—§ 6. The sacred mountain and paradise of the Eranians.—§ 7. The heavenly sea, the celestial spring, and the tree of life and immortality.—§ 8. Anthropomorism subordinate in Eranian myth.—§§ 9, 10. Mithra, the successor of the Aryan Mitra, transparently mythical.—11. His spiritual transformation ; the god of light becomes the god of truth.—§ 12. His allegorical attendants : Victory, Obedience, Uprightness, etc.—§ 13. Allegory a distinctive feature of the Eranian mind.—§ 14. The Amesha-Spentas, or "Bountiful Immortals," and their allegorical character.—§ 15. The seven Amesha-Spentas and their functions.—§ 16. Ahura-Mazda is the first of them and has created the others.—§ 17. Atar—Fire—successor of the Aryan Agni.—§ 18. The Hvarenō, or "Kingly Glory."—§ 19. Tishtrya, the chief of stars and Eranian storm-god.—§ 20. The Fravashis, the successors of the Aryan Pitris.—§§ 21, 22.—Desire of the Eranian gods for sacrifice.—§ 23, 24. The Manthra, or sacred text, and the Ahuna-Vairya, and their power over the fiends.—§ 25. Angra-Mainyu, or the "Evil One."—§ 26. Yima, the successor of the Aryan Yama ; history in the Avesta.—§ 27. The fall of Yima.—§ 28. The Sagdid.

V.

THE GÂTHAS—THE YASNA OF SEVEN CHAPTERS, 95–112

§ 1. Mazdayasnians and Daêvayasnians.—§ 2. Zarathushtra's work.—§ 3. Early period of the Gâthas.—§ 4. The prophet's denunciations of the Daêvayasnians, or Fiend-worshippers.—§ 5. The Aryan, "Devas,"—gods—transformed into the Eranian "Daêvas"—fiends. "Ahura" and "Asura."—§ 6. Poetical prologue of the Gâthas.—§ 7. Proclamation of the new religion.—§ 8. Essence of Mazdeism : moral dualism.—§ 9. The hymn of questions.—§ 10. Simplicity and literalness of the Gâthas.—§ 11, 12. The "Yasna of Seven Chapters." Slight deterioriation in the spirit of Mazdeism ; formation and return to myth.—§ 13. The Mazdayasnian "Profession of Faith."—§ 14. Marriages between near relations.

VI.

MIGRATION AND FOREIGN INFLUENCES — THE VENDIDAD — HEATHEN REVIVAL — THE KHORDEH AVESTA 113–168

§ 1. Character of the Vendidâd.—§ 2. The three fundamental principles of the priestly legislation.—§ 3. Power of the priesthood.—§ 4. The Athravans and Zoroastrian sacrifice. §§ 5, 6. Holiness of an agricultural life.—§ 7. Care of the body enjoined; asceticism denounced.—§§ 8, 9. Exposing of the dead.—§ 10. The Dakhma.—§ 11. Questions on purity and pollution.—§ 12. Impurity of the Dakhmas.—§ 13. Treatment of corpses in winter.—§ 14. Sinfulness of burying a corpse.—§ 15. Impure creatures become clean by dying.—§ 16. On sickness.—§ 17. On thriftiness.—§ 18. The Nasu, or corpse-fiend. Rights of purification.—§ 19. Dangerous sinfulness of carrying a corpse alone.—§ 20. On physicians.—§ 21. Sacredness of the dog.—§ 22. Of the cock.—§ 23. Signs of nomadic life in the Vendidâd.—§ 24. 25. Turanian influences encountered by the Eranians in their westward migration.—§§ 26, 28. Traces of these influences in the Avesta.—§ 29. Hebrew affinities.—§§ 30–31. Puzzling penal legislation.—§ 32. The "Khordeh-Avesta." Heathen Revival.—§ 33, 34. The Chinvat Bridge, and the trials of the soul after death.—§ 35. High standard and beauty of Mazdeism. Its high place among religions.

VII.

THE LAST DAYS OF JUDAH . 169–185

§ 1. Affairs in Syria.—2. Necho II. of Egypt plans an invasion of Asia.—§ 3. His campaign in Syria.—§ 4. Battle of Megiddo, and defeat of Josiah of Judah.—§ 5. Battle of Karkhemish; defeat of Necho by Nebuchadrezzar.—§ 6. The Median and Babylonian empires.—§ 7. Submission of Syria.—§ 8. The prophet Jeremiah.—§ 9. First taking of Jerusalem by Nebuchadrezzar.—§ 10–13. Jeremiah's preaching and unpopularity.—§ 14. Destruction of Jerusalem.—§ 15, 16. The siege of Tyre. Nebuchadrezzar.

VIII.

LYDIA AND ASIA MINOR—THE BALANCE OF POWER IN THE EAST 186–222

§§ 1–3. The countries of Asia Minor independent of Babylon.—§§ 4, 5. Lydia. Kandaules and Gyges.—§ 6. Rock-tombs of Lycia.—§ 7. Languages of Asia Minor.—§ 8. The Hittite element in Asia Minor.—§ 9. Indo-European influences.—§ 10. Hellas, the Doric migration and Ionian colonies.—§ 11. Ionian colonies on the shore of Asia Minor. —§ 12. Mutual influence of the Greeks and Lydians.— §§ 13, 14. Invention of coinage by the Lydians.—§ 15. Aggrandizement of Lydia.—§ 16. Her wars against the Greek cities on the sea-shore.—§ 17. War between Lydia and Media.—§ 18. Battle of the Eclipse. Peace and intermarriages.—§ 19. Death of Kyaxares.

IX.

BABYLON THE GREAT—THE HOUSE EGIBI. 223–260

§ 1. Little durability of a balance of powers.—§ 2. Nebuchadrezzar's fear of Media.—His works of fortification. — § 4. The Median Wall.—§ 5. His constructions at Babylon.—§ 6. The great walls.—§ 7. The great bridge and the embankments. § 8. The new palace.—§§ 9, 10. The Hanging Gardens.—§ 11. The temple of Bel-Marduk.— § 12. Legends of Semiramis and Nitokris.—§ 13. Nebuchadrezzar's greatness.—§ 14. Herodotus' account of some Babylonian customs.—§ 15. Discovery of the banking house of Egibi.—§ 16. Long duration of the firm.—§ 17. Their archive of private transactions.—§ 18. Their business operations.—§ 19. Legal transactions in property. - §§ 20–22. Tablets of legal precedents.—§ 23, 24. Dignified and independent position of Babylonian women.—§ 25. Private letters.—§ 26. Reading-books, and children's exercise books. § 27. Late use of cuneiform writing in contract-tablets.

X.

MEDIA AND THE RISE OF PERSIA . . 261–288

§ 1. Astyages succeeds Kyaxares. His insignificance.—§ 2. Splendor of Median royalty.—§ 3. Columnar architecture introduced by the Medes.—§§ 4, 5. The palace at Agbatana. § 5. Uncertainty concerning the Medes.—§ 7. The Median tribes, Aryan and un-Aryan.—§ 8. The Magi—the priesthood of Media.—§ 9. Their probable un-Aryan origin.—§ 10. Their political power.—§ 11. The Persians. Uncertainty about their origin.—§ 12. Persia proper—its climate and productions. Character of the Persians—§ 13. The Persian tribes, Aryan and un-Aryan. Elam and Anshan. § 14. Reunion of the tribes under Akhæmenes. Beginnings of the Persian nation.—§ 15. The double line of the Akhæmenian house; the Anshan line, and the Persian line. § 16. The newly discovered cylinders of Nabonidus and Kyros.—§ 17. The Rock and Inscription of Behistûn.—§ 18. The early Akhæmenian house reconstructed from these documents.

XI.

KURUSH, THE KING, THE AKHÆMENIAN . 289–332

§§ 1, 2. Fall of the Median Empire.—§§ 3, 4. Herodotus' fabulous account of the birth and childhood of Kyros.—§ 5. Explanation of the account.—§ 6. Probable details.—§ 7. Extension of the Persian Empire in the East.—§ 8. Kyros' wise rule. Fusion of the Medes and Persians.—§ 9. The ruins of Pasargadæ, Kyros' royal city in Persia.—§ 10. Persian art, as shown in the monuments at Pasargadæ, imitated from Assyrian art.—§ 11. The balance of powers threatened by Kyros.—§ 12. Alyattes of Lydia succeeded by Kroisos.—§ 13. Kroisos prepares to make war against Kyros, and seeks alliances.—§ 14. His embassy and gifts to the Delphic temple.—§ 15. Beginning of the war.—§ 16, 17. The fall of Sardis and capture of Kroisos.—§ 18. Attempted self-immolation of Kroisos. His rescue from the pyre.—§ 19. Subjection of the Ionian cities and the rest of Asia Minor.—§ 20. First and unsuccessful attack on Babylon. Complete subjection of Elam. Susa one of the capitals of the Persian empire.—§ 21. The successors of Nebuchadrezzar at Babylon. Accession of Nabonidus.—§ 22. He indisposes the priesthood of Babylon. First and unsuccessful attempt of Kyros.—§ 23. The priesthood call in Kyros.—§ 24. The Jews support him.—§ 25. Surrender of Babylon and triumphal entry of Kyros.—§ 26. He conciliates the priests and delivers the Jews.—§ 27. Obscurity of his last years, and death.

APPENDIX TO CHAPTER XI. . . 333–343
The last discoveries at Susa.

XII.

KAMBYSES. 529–522 B.C. . . . 344–360
§ 1. Accession of Kambyses.—§ 2. His unfortunate nature and jealousy of his brother Bardiya.—§ 3. He plans the conquest of Egypt.—§ 4.—Preparations on both sides.—§ 5. Assassination of Bardiya.—§ 6. Battle of Pelusion and conquest of Egypt.—§ 7.—Kambyses' religious tolerance and mild rule in Egypt.—§ 8.—His reluctance to return and further campaigns.—§ 9. Tidings of an impostor personating Bardiya, and of a general revolt. Kambyses confesses his crime and puts an end to his life.—§ 10. Record of the event in the Behistûn inscription.

XIII.

DAREIOS I., THE SON OF HYSTASPES. 522–485 B.C.
FIRST PERIOD: CIVIL WARS . . 361–383
§ 1–3. Gaumata the Magian slain by the seven Persian princes. Accession of Dareios I.—§ 4. The Behistûn inscription on the subject.—§ 5. Dareios a Mazdayasnian.— § 6. The Persians not strictly followers of the Vendidâd.— § 7. Breaking out of the civil war.—§ 8. Revolt of nine provinces.—§ 9. Revolt of Media.—§ 10. Capture of the Median pretender.—§ 11. End of the civil war.—§ 12. Sculptures at Behistûn.—§ 13. List of nations.

XIV.

DAREIOS I. SECOND PERIOD: YEARS OF PEACE, 384–411
§ 1. Dareios' wise home rule.—§ 2. His system of taxation. § 3. Construction of roads, and institution of a postal ser-

vice.—§ 4. The Nile canal and uniformity of coinage.—§ 5. Susa and Persepolis.—§ 6. Great platform at Persepolis.—§ 7. Stairs at Persepolis.—§ 8. The palace of Dareios.—§ 9. The Hall of Hundred Columns.—§ 10. The audience-hall at Susa, in the Book of Esther.—§ 11. Buildings of Xerxes at Persepolis.—§ 12. Conjectures about the walls of the palaces.—§ 13. The royal tombs at Persepolis.

XV.

DAREIOS I. THIRD PERIOD: FOREIGN WARS. 412–433

§ 1. Dareios begins a series of foreign wars.—§ 2. The knowledge of the Greeks about Scythia.—§§ 3, 4. Herodotus' description of Scythia.—§§ 5, 6. Of the Scythians.—§ 7. Dareios bridges and crosses the Bosporus and the Danube.—§§ 8, 9. His campaign in Scythia.—§ 10. His retreat and return across the Danube and the Hellespont.—§ 11. Expeditions in India and Africa. Revolt and chastisement of the Greek cities in Asia and Thracia. Preparations against Greece.

INDEX 435

LIST OF ILLUSTRATIONS.

	PAGE
ARCHER-FRIEZE	*Frontispiece*
A PARSI GENTLEMAN (MODERN)	6
A PARSI LADY (MODERN)	7
PAGE OF THE AVESTA	29
PARSI IN PRAYING COSTUME	115
"PAITIDÂNA"	115
"KOSTI"	115
"ÂTESH-GAH," OR "FIRE-ALTAR" OF MODERN PARSIS	116
"ÂTESH-GAH," OR "FIRE-ALTAR"; SEEN BY ANQUETIL DUPERRON	117
SACRIFICIAL IMPLEMENTS USED IN PARSI WORSHIP	119
A "DAKHMA," OR "TOWER OF SILENCE"	127
ANCIENT "DAKHMA" NEAR TEHERÂN IN PERSIA	129
VIEW IN ÂUDERBEIDJÂN	143
VIEW IN ÂUDERBEIDJÂN	145
ASSYRIAN ALTAR	149
RUIN OF "ATESH-GAH" AT FIRÛZABAD	151
RESTORATION OF THE SAME	153
LYCIAN ROCK-TOMBS AT MYRA	190
LYCIAN ROCK-TOMB AT TELMESSUS	191
LYCIAN ROCK-TOMB AT TELMESSUS	192
FAÇADE OF LYCIAN ROCK-TOMB AT MYRA	194
ROCK-TOMB AT MYRA	195
RELIEFS ON THE SO-CALLED "HARPY-TOWER"	197

	PAGE
SEPULCHRAL MONUMENT AT XANTHOS	199
MODERN CONSTRUCTIONS IN LYCIA	200
GRANARY IN MODERN LYCIA	201
GRANARY IN MODERN LYCIA	202
ROCK-TOMB OF MIDAS	203
CITY WALL OF CNIDUS	205
STATUE OF THE ARTEMUS OF EPHESUS	208
RUINS OF THE TEMPLE OF DIDYMÆAN APOLLO	211
FRAGMENT OF ORNAMENT	213
EARLY AND LATE LYDIAN COINS	216
BRICK OF NEBUCHADREZZAR	232
HANGING GARDENS OF BABYLON	235
MOUNTAIN SCENERY IN MEDIA	237
PERSIAN AND MEDIAN FOOT-SOLDIERS	276
ROCK OF BEHISTÛN	283
SCULPTURES AND INSCRIPTIONS ON THE ROCK OF BEHISTÛN	285
GATE-PILLAR OF KYROS' PALACE	299
BAS-RELIEF REPRESENTING KYROS	301
TOMB OF KYROS AT PASARGADÆ	302
SUPPOSED TOMB OF KAMBYSES I.	305
LION-FRIEZE, IN GLAZED TILES, AT SUSA	335
DESIGN ON ARCHERS' ROBES	337
BATTLEMENTED STAIR PARAPET	338
ROYAL SEAL OF THE AKHÆMENIAN KINGS	339
WINGED BULL AT PERSEPOLIS	340
PERSIAN PILLAR—BASE AND CAPITAL	341
DOUBLE GRIFFIN CAPITAL	342
DOUBLE BULL CAPITAL	343
RUINED PALACE AT FIRÛZABAD	355
SASSANIAN ROCK-SCULPTURES	359
DAREIOS I. ON HIS THRONE	363
TOMBS OF AKHÆMENIAN KINGS	367

LIST OF ILLUSTRATIONS. xiii

	PAGE
DETAIL OF AKHÆMENIAN TOMB	371
BUILDING KNOWN AS " RUSTEM'S TOMB "	373
SASSANIAN SCULPTURE	375
SASSANIAN KINGS	377
MASONRY OF GREAT PLATFORM AT PERSEPOLIS	393
LION ATTACKING BULL	396
PARAPET OF STAIR, PERSEPOLIS	397
CARVED LINTEL OF WINDOWS AND DOORS	398
PALACE OF DAREIOS AT PERSEPOLIS	399
ATTEMPT AT RESTORATION OF SOUTH FRONT OF PALACE OF DAREIOS AT PERSEPOLIS	401
DAREIOS FIGHTING A MONSTER	403
DOOR OF PALACE OF DAREIOS, PERSEPOLIS	405
PILLARS OF THE HALL OF XERXES	407
GENERAL VIEW OF THE PALACE OF DAREIOS	409
SCYTHIANS AFTER A BATTLE	421
GREEK SILVER VASE, FOUND AT KERTCH	423

PRINCIPAL WORKS READ OR CONSULTED IN THE PREPARATION OF THIS VOLUME.

ANQUETIL, Duperron. ZEND-AVESTA : Ouvrage de Zoroastre, contenant les idées theologiques, physiques et morales de ce législateur, les cérémonies du culte religieux qu'il a établies, etc., etc. 2 vol. in 4°. Paris 1761.

AYUSO, Francisco Garcia. LOS PUEBLOS IRANIOS Y ZOROASTRO. Madrid, 1874. 1 vol.

BABELON, Ernest. HISTOIRE ANCIENNE DE L'ORIENT. 9me éd. 5th and 6th vol. Paris, 1887 and 1888. (Continued from Lenormant.)

BARTHOLOMÆ, Chr. ARISCHE FORSCHUNGEN. II. and III. Halle, 1886 and 1887.

BRADKE, P. v. DYÁUS ASURA, AHURA-MAZDÁ UND DIE ASURAS. Studien und Versuche auf dem Gebiete alt-indo-germanischer Religionsgeschichte. Halle, 1885. 128 pages.

DARMESTETER, James. THE ZEND AVESTA. Part I., The Vendîdâd. Part II., The Sîrôzahs, Yasts, and Nyâis. ("Sacred Books of the East." Series, vol. IV. and vol. XXIII). Oxford, 1880 and 1883. 2 vols.

——— ORMAZD ET AHRIMAN : Leurs origines et leur histoire. (Bibliothèque de l' École des Hautes Études ; 29e Fascicule.) Paris, 1877. 1 vol.

——— HAURVATÂT ET AMERETÂT : Essai sur la mythologie de l'Avesta. (Bibliothèque de l'École des Hautes Études ; 23e Fascicule.) Paris, 1875. 85 pages.

DELATTRE, A. LE PEUPLE ET L' EMPIRE DES MÈDES, jusqu' à la fin du règne de Cyaxare. Bruxelles : 1883. 1 vol.

DOSABHAI, Framji Karaka. HISTORY OF THE PARSIS. Including their Manners, Customs, Religion and Present Position. London, 1884. 2 vol.

DUNCKER, Max. GESCHICHTE DES ALTERTHUMS. 5th edition. 12th and 4th vol. Leipzig, 1880.

EVERS, Dr. E. DAS EMPORKOMMEN DER PERSISCHEN MACHT UNTER CYRUS: nach den neuentdeckten Inschriften. Berlin, 1884. 40 pages.

FERGUSON, James. PALACES OF NINEVEH AND PERSEPOLIS RESTORED. London, 1851. 1 vol.

FLOIGL, Dr. Victor. CYRUS UND HERODOT: nach den neugefundenen Keilinschriften. Leipzig, 1881. 197 pages.

HARLEZ, M. C. de. AVESTA: Livre sacré du Zoroastrisme traduit du texte Zend, accompagné de notes explicatives, et précédé d'une Introduction à l'étude de l'Avesta et de la Religion Mazdéenne; 2e édition. Paris, 1881. 1 vol.

——— LES ORIGINES DU ZOROASTRISME. (Extrait du Journal Asiatique.) Paris, 1879. Deux parties en 8°.

HAUG, Martin. ESSAYS ON THE SACRED LANGUAGE, WRITINGS, AND RELIGION OF THE PARSIS. 1 vol. Second edition.

HOVELACQUE, Abel. L'AVESTA, ZOROASTRE ET LE MAZDÉISME. Paris, 1880. 1 vol.

——— LE CHIEN DANS L'AVESTA. Les soins qui lui sont dus. Son éloge. Paris, 1876. 56 pages.

——— LES MÉDECINS ET LA MÉDECINE DANS L'AVESTA. 21 pages.

JACKSON, A. V. WILLIAMS. A HYMN OF ZOROASTER YASNA XXXI. Translated with comments, 62 pages; Stuttgart, 1888.

JUSTI, Dr. Ferdinand. GESCHICHTE DES ALTEN PERSIENS. Berlin, 1879. 1 vol.

KUHN, A. DIE HERABKUNFT DES FEUERS UND DES GÖTTER. TRANKES. First edition. 1 vol.

LENORMANT, François. LA MONNAIE DANS L'ANTIQUITÉ. Vol. 1st. Paris, 1878.

——— LES ORIGINES DE L'HISTOIRE, d'après la Bible et les traditions des peuples Orientaux. 2d vol. Paris, 1882.

MASPERO, G. HISTOIRE ANCIENNE DES PEUPLES DE L'ORIENT. 3d edition. Paris, 1878.

MÉNANT, JOACHIM. ZOROASTRE: Essai sur la Philosophie Religieuse de la Perse. 2d edition. Paris, 1857. 1 vol.

MEYER, Eduard. GESCHICHTE DES ALTERTHUMS. Stuttgart, 1884. Vol. 1st.

MILLS, L. H. THE ZEND AVESTA: Part III. The Yasna, Visparad, Âfrinagân, Gâhs, and Miscellaneous Fragments. ("Sacred Books of the East," Series, vol. XXXI.) Oxford, 1887. 1 vol.

MÜLLER, F. Max. CHIPS FROM A GERMAN WORKSHOP. New
York, 1876. 4 vol.
——— LECTURES ON THE SCIENCE OF LANGUAGE. New York,
1875. 2 vol.
——— BIOGRAPHIES OF WORDS AND THE HOME OF THE ARYAS.
London, 1888.
MYER. REMAINS OF LOST EMPIRES. 1 vol.
OPPERT, J. LE PEUPLE ET LA LANGUE DES MÈDES.
——— L' HONOVER : le Verbe Créateur de Zoroastre. (Extrait des
Annales de Philosophie Chrétienne, janvier, 1862.) 24 pages.
PLUTARCH. DE ISIDE ET OSIRIDE.
RAWLINSON, GEORGE. THE FIVE GREAT MONARCHIES OF THE
ANCIENT EASTERN WORLD. London, 1865. 3d and 4th vol.
——— HISTORY OF HERODOTUS, a new English version. London,
1875. 4 vol.
RIALLE, Girard de. AGNI, PETIT-FILS DES EAUX, dans le Véda et
l'Avesta. Paris, 1869. 16 pages.
SAYCE, A. H. THE ANCIENT EMPIRES OF THE EAST. London,
1884. 1 vol.
——— LECTURES ON THE ORIGIN AND GROWTH OF RELIGION, AS
ILLUSTRATED BY THE RELIGION OF THE ANCIENT BABYLONIANS.
Hibbert Lectures, 1887. 1 vol.
SCHRADER, Eberhard. DIE KEILINSCHRIFTEN UND DAS ALTE
TESTAMENT. 2d edition. Giessen, 1883. 1 vol.
SPIEGEL, Friedrich. ERÄNISCHE ALTERTHUMSKUNDE. 3 vol.
Leipzig, 1871, 1873, and 1878.
——— DIE ALTPERSISCHEN KEILINSCHRIFTEN. 2d edit. 1881.
UNGER, G. Fr. KYAXARES UND ASTYAGES. (Aus den Abhandlungen
der kön. Bayerischen Akademie der Wissenschaften, I Cl., XVI.
Bd., III Abth.) München, 1882. 85 pages.
VAUX, W. S. W. PERSIA, FROM THE EARLIEST PERIOD TO THE
ARAB CONQUEST. (Ancient History from the Monuments.)
1 vol.
VIGOUROUX, Abbé F. LA BIBLE ET LES DÉCOUVERTES MODERNES
en Palestine, en Égypte et en Assyrie. 4th edit. Paris, 1884.
4 vols.
WEST, E. W. PAHLAVI TEXTS. Part I. The Bundahis, Bah-
man Yast and Shâyast Lâ-Shâyast. ("Sacred Books of the East."
Series, Vol. V.) Oxford, 1880. 1 vol.
WHITNEY, Wm. Dwight. ORIENTAL AND LINGUISTIC STUDIES,
New York, 1873. 1 vol.

WINDISCHMANN, Friedrich. ZOROASTRISCHE STUDIEN. Abhandlungen zur Mythologie und Sagengeschichte des alten Iran. Berlin, 1863.

—— MITHRA: ein Beitrag zur Mythengeschichte des Orients, Leipzig, 1857. 89 pages.

Numerous works on Ancient India and Comparative Mythology; also pamphlets and essays by Sir H. C. Rawlinson, Th. G. Pinches, W. St. Chad Boscawen, H. Rassam, De Harlez, Spiegel, Hovelacque, Halévy, Girard de Rialle, E. Dieulafoy, and others, in Rawlinson's "Herodotus," the Encyclopædia Britannica, and various periodicals, such as "Transactions" and "Proceedings" of the Society of Biblical Archæology, the "Journal" of the Victoria Institute, the "Muséon," the "Babylonian and Oriental Record," the "Revue Archéologique," "Gazette des Beaux Arts," and others.

This volume will surely—and deservedly—be found fault with by critics on the score of inconsistent spelling of Oriental and Greek names. It is a defect very difficult to avoid in the present transition stage between the spelling sanctioned by old habit, though utterly incorrect and misleading, and the more faithful and rational transliteration which a finer scholarship is rapidly introducing. The author is fully conscious of this shortcoming, which, however, shall be thoroughly eliminated in a final revised edition.

Z. A. R.

PRINCIPAL DATES GIVEN IN THIS VOLUME.

BATTLE OF MEGIDDO (DEFEAT OF JOSIAH OF JUDAH BY NECHO II. OF EGYPT)	609	B.C.
BATTLE OF KARKHEMISH (DEFEAT OF NECHO II. BY NEBUCHADREZZAR OF BABYLON)	605	"
FIRST TAKING OF JERUSALEM BY NEBUCHADREZZAR	597	"
DESTRUCTION OF JERUSALEM AND BEGINNING OF CAPTIVITY	586	"
BATTLE OF THE ECLIPSE (BETWEEN ALYATTES OF LYDIA AND KYAXARES OF MEDIA)	585	"
DEATH OF KYAXARES	584	"
DEATH OF NEBUCHADREZZAR	561	"
FALL OF THE MEDIAN EMPIRE (ASTYAGES, SON OF KYAXARES, DETHRONED BY KYROS, KING OF ANSHAN AND PERSIA)	549	"
CONQUEST OF LYDIA BY KYROS	546	"
CONQUEST OF BABYLON BY KYROS AND END OF JEWISH CAPTIVITY	539	"
DEATH OF KYROS THE GREAT	529	"
KAMBYSES, SON OF KYROS	529–522	"
BATTLE OF PELUSION AND CONQUEST OF EGYPT	525	"
DAREIOS I., SON OF HYSTASPES	522–485	"
(522–515, CIVIL WARS; 515–508, YEARS OF PEACE; 508–485, FOREIGN WARS).		
BATTLE OF MARATHON.	490	"

xix

THE STORY OF MEDIA, BABYLON, AND PERSIA.

I.

A NOTABLE RELIGIOUS SURVIVAL: THE PARSIS.—
ANQUETIL DUPERRON.

1. AMONG the so-called heathen religions which still claim for their own more than one half of mankind, there is none of greater interest and importance than that of the PARSIS, more generally known under the graphic but misleading name of "Fire-Worshippers." It is certainly not from their numbers this sect derive that interest and importance, for in that respect they form an almost imperceptible unit in the general sum. The entire number of Parsis now living scarcely, if at all, exceeds 100,000, which represents about one in fourteen thousand of the earth's population. But, small as that fragment of humanity is, it is a chip from one of the world's noblest and mightiest nations, the PERSIANS of old, a nation which, though not extinct, and still counted as one of the greater political powers of the East, has degenerated beyond recognition under the

influence of foreign conquest, enforced change of religion, and mixture of races. And the religion which these exiled descendants of the ancient Persians have preserved along with purity of race and time-honored customs, is that of ancient Erân, the old and widely spread faith, the prophet of which, SPITÂMA ZARATHUSHTRA, was vaguely known and reverenced by the writers of Greek and Roman antiquity, as well as by the later scholars of Europe, under the name of ZOROASTER.

2. It is customary to sweep under the head "Heathen Religions" all except the three great Semitic religions: Judaism, Christianity, and Islamism, or the religion of Mohammed. It is doubtful how far so comprehensive a designation may be correct in individual instances. In that of the Parsis, at least, it appears decidedly rash, since they earnestly, emphatically profess the worship of the one true God, and a horror of any kind of polytheism—a form of belief which, surely, should win them a place among monotheists, as must be shown by a brief review of their religious tenets and practices.

3. It was in the year 641 A.D. that the Arab invaders, in the heyday of their fervor for the faith of which their prophet Mohammed had taught them to consider themselves the heaven-sent bearers, won the battle, (on the field of NEHAVEND, fifty miles from ancient Ecbatana), which changed the destinies of Erân, and turned its people, dreaded and victorious for four centuries under their last national kings, the SASSANIAN dynasty, into a conquered, enslaved, and for a long time ruthlessly oppressed and ill-treated

population. YEZDEGERD III., the last Sassanian king, was murdered on his flight, for plunder, and no effort was made to retrieve the lost fortunes of that terrible day, with which closed an heroic struggle of over eight years; the country's energies were broken.

4. It was but natural that the religion of the vanquished should be the first object of persecution at the hands of victors whose wars and conquests were all prompted by religious fanaticism. The Persian clergy were persecuted, their temples desecrated and destroyed, their sacred books likewise, and the faithful followers of the ancient national creed subjected to so many indignities and extortions as to make existence not only burdensome, but wellnigh impossible. They were made to pay ruinous extra taxes, were excluded from all offices, from all participation in public life, and, worst of all, very nearly deprived of the protection of the law, at all events systematically denied justice or redress whenever they applied for either against a Mussulman. Their property, their lives, their honor, thus were completely at the mercy of the insolent and grasping foreign rulers. From so many and unbearable ills, the only escape lay in embracing the faith of these rulers, doing homage to Mohammed, and abjuring all their own traditions, beliefs, and practices. By this one act they could step at once from the state of down-trodden slaves to a condition if not of equality with their masters, at least of well-protected subjects. It is no wonder that apostasy became ripe in the land. Compulsory conversion, however, is scarcely likely to be sincere, and we may take it

for granted that the first generations of new-made Mussulmans were so only in self-defence and in outer form. Not so their descendants. Habit and associations gradually endeared to them the faith in which, unlike their fathers, they were born and bred, and at the present moment there are no more zealous followers of the Arab prophet than the Persians.

5. But even at the time of the wholesale conversion of the country to Islamism, which was an accomplished fact in less than two hundred years after the conquest, great numbers preferred every hardship to apostasy. Only, as life under such conditions had become unendurable at home, the vast majority of these took the desperate resolution of going into exile, to seek some place of refuge in foreign lands, where they would be tolerated as harmless guests, and suffered to practise their religion unmolested. A small remnant only stayed, lacking the courage to sever all old ties and go forth into absolute uncertainty, and of this remnant the fate was most pitiful. "In the tenth century of the Christian era," says a distinguished modern Parsi writer,* "remnants of the Zoroastrian population were to be found only in the provinces of Fars and Kerman; and the reader will have an idea of the rate at which that remnant has declined even in recent times, when it is stated that, while about a hundred and fifty years ago it numbered one hundred thousand souls, it does not at present exceed seven or eight thousand."

* Dosabhai Framji Karaka, in his "History of the Parsis," London. 1884.

6. The self-exiled Zoroastrians fared better. After wandering for many years somewhat at random, stopping at various places, but not attempting any permanent settlement until they effected a descent on the western coast of India, they reached at last the peninsula of GUJERÂT (or GUZERAT), where they were hospitably received by the reigning Hindu prince, after they had agreed to some by no means onerous conditions: they were to lay down their arms, to give an account of the religion they professed, to adopt the language of the country, to conform to some of its customs. From this time forth and through several centuries the Zoroastrian exiles, who now began to be called Parsis, prospered greatly. Deprived of arms, and with no call to use them had they retained them, they settled into the thrifty, intelligent, industrious ways which characterize them at the present day. Agriculture and commerce became their favorite pursuits, and as they were in no way repressed or restrained, they began to spread even as far as Upper India (the PENJÂB). Then, about 1300 A.D., they were once more driven forth homeless, by a Mussulman invasion, which ended in the conquest of Gujerât. This time, however, they did not stray far, but betook themselves to NÂVSÂRI and SÛRAT near the coast, where they came in contact with Europeans, to the great furtherance of their commercial interests. It was undoubtedly this new commercial intercourse which drew them southwards, to the great centre of the western coast, the city of BOMBAY, where we find them as early as about

1650 A.D., just before the transfer of the city and territory from the Portuguese to the English crown. The Presidency of Bombay with its capital has since become the head-quarters of the Parsis, whose numbers in this part of the country and the whole of India amount to something over 85,500.

7. It has always been known in Europe that the Parsis, or GEBERS, ("infidels," as the Mussulmans contemptuously call them), followed a religion of which the most peculiar and striking outer feature was the honor paid to fire; that they had sacred fires kept burning always in chapels, and that when they moved from place to place they carried these fires with them. It was, naturally enough, inferred that Fire was their deity, their god; and the name of "Fire-Worshippers" was universally bestowed on them. Only a scholarly few had a deeper and more correct perception of what was to the mass an absurd superstition, and knew that the Parsis did not *worship* fire as a deity, but admired and honored it as the purest and most perfect *emblem* of the Deity.* They

1. A PARSI GENTLEMAN (MODERN).

---

* The Parsi writer quoted above, in vindicating his brethren from the charge of heathenism, very aptly cites the words of Bishop Meurin, the head of the Roman Catholics of Bombay. "A pure and un-

also knew that the Parsis believe in a number of spiritual beings who take care of the world under the orders and supervision of the Creator, in six spirits more exalted still and partaking in their essence of some of the Divine qualities, also in the existence and power of sainted souls, and that they invoke all these beings in prayer somewhat as the Roman and Oriental churches do angels, archangels, and saints. Lastly, scholars knew that the Parsis professed to follow strictly and undeviatingly the law of Zoroaster, as it was handed down from their ancestors before the conquest, the Persians of the Sassanian period, who were, in their turn, said to have received it from remote antiquity. Now these assertions are strongly confirmed by a great many passages from Greek and Roman writers of various times, whose accounts (fragmentary as they are) of the beliefs and religious practices of the Persians as they knew them in their time, agree remarkably with the beliefs and practices of the modern Parsis. The name of Zoroaster, too, is mentioned by many classical authors, vaguely, it is true, and with many

2. A PARSI LADY (MODERN).

defiled flame is certainly the most sublime natural representation of Him who is in Himself Eternal Light."

contradictions, but always with reverence, as one coupled with much holiness and mystery. It was, therefore, generally understood among the learned: 1st. That the Parsis must possess sacred books of great antiquity, containing and expounding the laws of one of the oldest and most remarkable religions in the world; 2d. That it would be extremely desirable, in the interests of historical and religious research, to gain access to these books, and, if possible, to secure copies of them for the great European libraries.

8. Both these points were partially settled by the happy chance which, in the beginning of the last century, put an English traveller and scholar, GEORGE BOURCHIER, in possession of a manuscript, which he obtained from Parsi priests during a visit to Sûrat. It contained the VENDÎDÂD SADEH, *i. e.*, a compilation of prayers and hymns, in the order in which they are recited at religious services, and was deposited at Oxford. More manuscripts followed, until towards the middle of the century that great university owned a nearly complete collection. But what was the use, when there was no one to read them? The very characters were unknown, and there seemed but little prospect that the puzzle should ever be solved.

9. Fortunately four pages traced from one of the Oxford manuscripts found their way to Paris, and there happened to meet the eye of a young Oriental student, ANQUETIL DUPERRON. Ambitious, eagerminded, and scarcely twenty-two, he saw in this a hint of fate, a great work, worthy of all his energies

and enthusiasm, given into his hand ; in short, that most desirable of boons—an object in life. "I at once resolved to endow my country with this peculiar piece of literature," he says. "I dared to form the design of translating it, and determined to go to the East with that object in view, and learn the ancient Persian language in Gujerát or Kerman." Belonging to a noble family, he could command the influence of high-placed friends, and might, in time, have obtained an appointment at one of the counting-houses of the French East-India Company. But such a roundabout way and its inevitable delays ill-suited with his youthful impatience, and, taking counsel of no one, he committed the reckless step of engaging as a private in the service of the Company, which was sending out a batch of recruits, just to secure an immediate passage. Only when all the arrangements were completed did he inform his elder brother of what he had done, and, unmoved by his dismay and tearful entreaties, marched out with his company one raw November morning of the year 1754.

10. Enterprising and brave to foolhardiness as Anquetil was, from temperament, from national bent, and from the buoyancy which belongs to extreme youth, it is just possible that he might not have embarked in such blind wise on his adventurous errand, had he quite known the number and the nature of the hardships which he was rushing to meet, even though they were greatly mitigated for him by the exertions of his friends, who obtained from the government his discharge from military

service, a small pension, and promise of further assistance even before he left his native soil. The good news reached him at L'Orient, the seaport from which the recruits were to be shipped, and he stepped on board the vessel in February, 1755, a free man. It was well for him that it fell out so; for as we read his account of the voyage and of the share of suffering which fell to him as one of the officers' mess, we ask ourselves with a shudder what would have been his fate had he been counted among the wretched rabble of vagabonds, criminals, and scamps of every description, the scum of prisons and regiments, which made up the Company's soldiery, and were housed, fed, and generally treated accordingly, on a six months' voyage, mostly on tropical seas.

11. Nothing can be more entertaining and instructive, at times more fascinating and thrilling, than Anquetil's own detailed narrative of his long wanderings and manifold adventures. The book is but little read nowadays. We accept the results of a great man's self-devotion, and care little to recall at what cost those results were obtained. Yet there are surely some good lessons to be drawn from the career of men whom we see giving up home, friends, prospects in life, for the sake of knowledge, pursuing this, to the great mass of men, most unsubstantial of goods, at the risk of life and health, grudging neither time nor money, or, far more frequently still, working for it without any money, by sheer personal exertion and perseverance, in the face of appalling privation and hardships, and considering themselves repaid beyond any wealth if they succeed in securing

even but a portion of the knowledge they sought. Such men there have always been; such men there are now, many of them. They work, they succeed, they suffer,—they die, too, more of them than the world knows of, victims of their enthusiasm and self-devotion; witness George Smith,[*] witness the two Lenormants, father and son, Charles and François, and so many others, all smitten in harness by cruel diseases contracted in distant and uncongenial climes, at their noble tasks. Anquetil Duperron was emphatically one of the heroic band. Few suffered as many and varied ills, and if he lived to achieve and enjoy, it was solely owing to an exceptionally vigorous constitution.

12. He was absent seven years. But there was no time lost. When he re-entered Paris, early in 1762, he was barely thirty. The most arduous and adventurous part of his task lay behind him, successfully achieved, and before him—the best years of his manhood, to be devoted to comparatively easy and certainly pleasant work:—that of translating the several books which formed the body of Parsi Scripture, and became generally, though incorrectly, known under the name of ZEND-AVESTA. This translation, accompanied by a detailed narrative of his varied wanderings and experiences, was laid before the public as early as 1771, in three quarto volumes bearing the lengthy but exhaustive title: "ZEND-AVESTA, *the Work of ZOROASTER—Containing the Theological, Physical, and Moral Ideas of that Lawgiver, the Ceremonies of the Religious Worship Es-*

[*] See "Story of Chaldea," pp. 102-105.

tablished by him, and Several Important Traits Bearing on the Ancient History of the Persians." The manuscripts from which he worked had already been deposited in the Royal Library. He had therefore fully redeemed the vow to which he pledged himself seventeen years before on first beholding the puzzling pot-hooks on the Oxford tracing, and now waited anxiously and with natural curiosity to see the impression which his labors would produce on the scholarly world of Europe.

13. Here he was doomed to an unlooked-for and disheartening experience. True, there was here and there a little burst of enthusiasm, but the large majority of scholars held aloof, uncertain and bewildered, while the English scholars, partly moved thereto by personal feeling against the author, who had been guilty of some very ill-tempered and unwarrantable attacks on the University of Oxford, took a decided hostile stand. Their spokesman was WILLIAM JONES, then a very young man, but already distinguished as a linguist and Orientalist, who published in French an anonymous "Letter to Mr. A—— du P——" in the form of a pamphlet. Though so abusive as to be decidedly in bad taste, it was very clever, and the French was so perfect that it was some time before the nationality of the writer was suspected. Jones simply accused the elder scholar of forgery, or else of a credulity passing all reasonable bounds. He objected that the writings, presented to the world as the works of one of the greatest thinkers of all ages, half the time—to use a homely expression,—"didn't make sense,"

and when they did, were insufferably stupid and prosy. "Though the whole college of Gebers were to assert it," he says, "we should never believe that even the least clever of charlatans could have written the nonsense with which your two last volumes are filled. . . . Either Zoroaster was devoid of common-sense, or he did not write the book you attribute to him. If the first, you should have left him to obscurity; if he did not write the book, it was impudent to publish it under his name. You have then either insulted the public by offering them worthless stuff, or cheated them by palming off falsehoods on them, and in both cases you deserve their contempt." On this theme the changes were rung for years with little variety and less good-breeding. "The least reason I shall offer" (for rejecting the authenticity of the book) "is the uncommon stupidity of the work itself," is the verdict of another English scholar.

14. Time and more advanced scholarship have vindicated the memory of Anquetil Duperron. They have long ago assigned to him his true place, established the great and real worth of the work he did, and also its shortcomings. For though it would enter nobody's head nowadays to deny the authenticity of the books he undertook to translate, his rendering of them is so faulty, carried out on such altogether wrong principles, as to be utterly unavailable—the monument at once of a great achievement and a great failure. He had neither the right method nor the right tools. He trusted entirely to his instructors, the Parsi Desturs, or high-priests, and

their word-for-word translations into modern Persian, never dreaming how unreliable their knowledge was. He was aware, indeed, that the mass of the Parsis hear and recite their sacred texts parrot-wise, without understanding or deeming it needful to understand a single word of them, satisfied with scrupulously performing the ceremonies and rites of the worship they were taught. But he was told that on their higher clergy rested the obligation to study the ancient dead languages of their race, so as to hand down from generation to generation the sense and spirit of their religious law as well as its outer forms. How could he suspect that, in carrying the vessel, they had spilt most of the contents, and that their main-stay was a thread of tradition, continuous, indeed, but growing more and more corrupt and unreliable? So he wrote down every word in modern Persian, as his Desturs gave it, then rendered that literally into French, and—to do his opponents justice—half the time it did *not* "make sense."

15. Thus it seemed as though one puzzle had only been exchanged for another, scarcely less hopeless. A great and clear mind was needed to disentangle it and carry on the work which had been dropped from sheer inability to grasp it. Such a mind turned up only sixty years later, in the person of another French Orientalist, EUGÈNE BURNOUF. He thought he saw his way to a more correct understanding of the Parsi sacred books, by means of a more rational and exhaustive method, and although the experiment really lay outside of his special line of studies, he undertook it, more to open the road for others and

"show them how," than with a view to follow it to the end himself. True, he brought to the task a tool which Anquetil had lacked—a perfect knowledge of Sanskrit, the most ancient surviving language of the Aryans of India and the sister tongue of that in which the so called Zoroastrian books were originally written. Curiously enough, this tool, which was the means of establishing Anquetil's claim to honor and recognition, even while exposing his shortcomings, was in a measure supplied by his bitter foe and detractor, Sir William Jones; for it was this great scholar who, being called to India to fill a high official position, first took up the study of the classical language of ancient India himself, and inspired his fellow-workers and subordinates with the same enthusiasm, earning for himself the title of founder of those Sanskrit studies which were to become so principal a branch of the then dawning science of Comparative Philology. The great likeness which was discovered between the ancient languages of the Aryans of India and of Erân suggested to Burnouf that by bringing to bear Sanskrit scholarship on the Eranian texts, the traditional but mostly unintelligent rendering of the Parsi Desturs might be controlled and corrected, and a closer comprehension of their Scriptures attained than they could at all achieve. One chapter was all he worked out according to this plan. But on what scale and with what thoroughness the research was conducted, is shown by the fact that it fills a quarto volume of eight hundred pages.*

* "Commentaire sur le Yaçna," published in 1833-35.

16. All the work that has since been done on this field was carried out along the lines laid down in this first attempt of Burnouf's—a monumental treasury of erudition and ingenuity. But the matter in hand is singularly arduous and obscure, and although patient scholarship has indeed succeeded in restoring the lost religion attributed to Zoroaster in its main features and general spirit, in tracing the various elements which entered into its progressive development, yet many and many are the points still under dispute, the passages—sometimes most important ones—of which we have several conflicting versions, among which even the trained specialist finds it impossible to make a decisive choice. In many ways there is less uncertainty even about cuneiform decipherment. Still much is done every year, and even as matters stand now, we know enough to warrant us in pronouncing the religion so almost miraculously preserved by a handful of followers one of the finest, wisest, loftiest the world has seen. As it was the religion of the race which, in the order of history, takes the lead at the point to which our studies have brought us, we shall pause to gain some knowledge of it, and thus be prepared to follow that race's doings more understandingly and appreciatively.

II.

THE PROPHET OF ERÂN—THE AVESTA.

1. THE religions of the world, apart from their intrinsic differences, may be divided into two great classes: those that have sacred books, and those that have not. The sacred books of a religion embody all its teachings in matters of faith, theology, and conduct. They tell its followers what they should believe, what they should do and avoid doing, how they should pray, worship, conduct themselves on the momentous occasions of human life. All these instructions the faithful are not to take as simply advice for their general guidance, but as absolutely binding, to be believed without discussion, to be obeyed without demurring. When any question arises bearing on religious doctrine in any way, the devout believer ought not to use his own judgment, but to refer to his Sacred Book, or to its privileged interpreters, the priests. This, indeed, is the most commendable and the safer course, as the layman is liable to mistakes from imperfect training and incomplete knowledge; while the priest must perforce understand what he devotes his life to study. A doubt as to the absolute truth of any statement, or as to the necessity or righteousness of

any prescription contained in the Sacred Book is mortal sin, entailing punishment in the next world, and, if expressed in acts of insubordination, here on earth, at the hands of the priests and the government which supports them.

2. Such utter surrender of man's most cherished rights—the right of thought and independent action,—such unreasoning obedience, amounting almost to the abolition of individual will and intellect, could never be demanded or obtained by mere men, either the wisest or the most despotic. Man will obey his fellow-man from choice, and as long as he thinks it to his own advantage to do so, but never admit that such obedience is a paramount and indisputable duty. Every religion, therefore, that has sacred books, claims for them a superhuman origin: they are the Divine Word and the Divine Law, revealed supernaturally, imparted directly by the Deity through the medium of some chosen man or men, who become the prophets, teachers, and lawgivers of their people, but speak not from themselves, but in the name and, as it were, under the dictation of the Deity, with whom they are supposed to have miraculous, face-to-face intercourse. In remote antiquity men were more simple-minded than they are now, and, being devoid of all positive (*i. e.*, scientific) knowledge, found no difficulty in believing wonders. Knowing nothing of the laws of nature, deviations from those laws would not startle them in the same way that they do us, but would strike them at most as extraordinary occurrences, fraught with some portentous significance. They were the more will-

ing to admit the divine origin claimed for the Law offered to them, that the best of every religion, being glimpses of eternal truths, opened by the noblest and wisest thinkers of a race, has always been so far above the average standard of the times as to appear to the mass unattainable by the unassisted efforts of the human mind.*

3. The two great Asiatic divisions of the Aryan stock or race, the Hindus and the Eranians, both followed religions which, their priests taught them, were revealed to the founders directly and personally by the Deity. The Hindus treasured a set of books, which they called "VEDA" (*i. e.*, "Knowledge"), as the repository of the Divine Law, while the Sacred Book of the Eranians has long been known under the name of "ZEND-AVESTA." Neither of these religions is extinct. The former is still professed, in a much altered form, by many millions of the inhabitants of India, while the latter has survived, as we saw, in that handful of descendants of Persian emigrants which forms the Parsi community in India, and the daily dwindling remnant of their brethren in the old country. Between both there are striking resemblances and not less striking differences, as is usually the case between members of one family, be they individuals or nations. But we are, in this volume, directly concerned only with the race which, at the point we have reached, the ever-revolving wheel of history is bringing up to the top, to gather the inheritance of older nations whose greatness is of the past—Assyria, Babylon, and others, lesser in size, power, and influence.

* See "Story of Chaldea," pp. 259, 260.

4. When, on the authority of Anquetil Duperron and his first successors in the field of Eranian research, the title "Zend-Avesta" was universally accepted, and "Zend" given as the name of the language in which the newly found books were written, a misnomer was unconsciously introduced which considerably delayed discoveries and added confusion to an already almost hopelessly obscure subject. In the first place, the title, a compound one, should be "AVESTA-U-ZEND," which may be pretty fairly translated "the Law and Commentary," for "Zend" is not the name of a language at all, but a word, which means "explanation, commentary." In the second place, the books are not written in one uniform language, but in several Eranian dialects of different periods and, probably, different countries. Now that these facts are distinctly understood, it is becoming more and more usual to call the books themselves simply "AVESTA," and the language of the original texts "AVESTAN,"—a name which does not commit to any particular time or country,— while the language in which the Zend or commentary and glosses are written, and which is of far later date, as can easily be proved from inscriptions, has been named "PEHLEVI"—the Persian of the Middle Ages.

5. Pehlevi is a most peculiar language, especially in its written form. Not so much from the difference of the characters, which is not greater than the distance of several centuries would naturally warrant; but at first sight it does not seem to be Persian at all, but rather Semitic. That is, an enor-

mous proportion of the words—nouns, pronouns, verbs, adverbs, prepositions, conjunctions—are Semitic, while the grammar and construction, *i. e.*, the way of using and arranging those words, are Eranian — a proceeding so anomalous as to make it certain that the result could not possibly ever have been the living language of any nation whatever. The solution of the riddle seems scarcely less strange. It is this: that the words which were Semitic to the eye were Eranian in sound; or, to put it more clearly, the reader, in reading to himself or aloud, substituted to each Semitic word its Eranian (or Persian) equivalent. Thus: "king" would be written "*malkâ*" (an old Semitic word), and pronounced "Shâh"; "Malkân malkâ," "King of Kings," became "Shâhân-Shâh"; "*gôsht*" (meat) was substituted in reading to its Semitic equivalent "*bisrâ*," which was the written word. We ourselves do something of the same kind, on a very small scale, when, on meeting, in print or writing, forms like "*i. e.*," "*e. g.*," "*etc.*," which stand for the Latin, "*id est*," "*exempli gratiâ*," "*et cetera*," we fluently read the English words, "that is," "for instance," "and so forth," not to speak of the numeral figures (1, 2, 3, etc.), which every language pronounces in its own way. To indulge in the exercise on such a scale as did the readers and writers of Pehlevi-Persian implies a knowledge of two languages, which is rather surprising, and would alone go far towards proving the indebtedness of the younger race of Central Asia to the ancient cultures of the West. For where and in what way, if not by constant contact with old Semitic nations, like those of Nineveh, of Babylon, of Aram, could the Persians have acquired such familiarity with a language than which none could be more different from the Eranian speech, as to keep writing in that language and translating it into their own as they read?

6. The written Pehlevi language, therefore, is composed of two very distinct elements, which have also been distinguished by different names. That part of it which is written one way and read another has been called HUZVÂRESH, while the purely Persian part goes under the name of PÂZEND. It is clear that it is quite possible for a text to be written entirely in Huzvâresh or entirely in Pâzend, but neither is usually the case. Only it has been remarked that, the older the text, the more Huzvâresh it contains, so that it may be said that the most ancient Sassanian writings are nearly all Huzvâresh, while the latest are almost entirely in Pâzend.

7. From what has been said it is evident that the books which we know under the general name of "Avesta" are composed of parts belonging to very different ages. As the Pehlevi characters differ from the Avestan ones, it is comparatively easy to separate the original text from the Zend, and to assign to the latter its proper time, which is the period of the Sassanian dynasty (226-640 A.D.). Beyond that, every thing is doubt and darkness. It is just the most interesting and important questions to which we have no satisfactory answers. We should like to know: How old is the religion of which the written law has in great part just been recovered? From

which of the countries of Erân did it go forth? Was there really a man of the name of Zarathushtra, who invented and preached it, and when did he live? And *did* he invent it, or only reform it and put it into shape? When were the texts containing the doctrine, the prayer, and the law, written down? All these points have now for years been the subject of researches, which have arrived at conclusions in a great measure conflicting, and which their authors themselves do not attempt to give out as final. It is not for a book like the present, meant essentially for general readers, to enter into the details and merits of special controversies. It can only present, in the briefest and clearest possible form, such results as are certain and such as appear most probable, most likely to be confirmed in the course of further study, as being supported by the greatest amount of intrinsic and circumstantial evidence.

8. Most of the Greek and Roman writers whose works, or fragments of them, have come down to us, speak of Zoroaster as of a wise man of the East and teacher of divine things, and also magic, whose existence it occurred to no one to doubt. True, their testimony, taken separately, would not go for much, as neither of these nations was remarkable for great historical sense or critical discernment,—and besides, they place him at absurdly varying periods, ranging all the way between 6,000 and 500 B.C. But the unanimity of the testimony establishes a strong presumption in favor of the real existence of such a person, at *some* time, as yet not to be determined, although so much can be said with certainty even

now, that both the above extreme dates are equally preposterous, the one for its remoteness, the other for its lateness. More conclusive, however, is the intrinsic testimony we derive from the Avesta itself.

9. There is a small collection of hymns called GÂTHAS (literally "Songs"), written in a peculiar Eranian dialect, either older than the Avestan generally, or belonging to a different part of Erân. They are in verse, and bear the marks of far greater antiquity than any other portion of the book. They evidently present the teachings of a new religion in its earliest and purest stage, and, among sermons, prayers, sayings, loosely strung together in no particular order, contain some of the very few pieces of real poetical beauty which the Avesta can boast. In these "Songs" the prophet stands forth with an unmistakable, living reality. Sometimes he preaches in his own person, expounding to a concourse of hearers the simple and broad principles of his creed; sometimes he cries out to his God, as a persecuted and homeless wanderer among men, with a pathos that strongly recalls some of the Hebrew Psalms: "To what land shall I turn? Whither shall I go? . . . None of the servants pay reverence to me, nor do the wicked rulers of the country. How shall I worship Thee further, O Ahuramazda? I know that I am helpless . . . for I have few men. I implore Thee weeping, O Ahura, who grantest happiness as a friend gives a present to his friend. . . ." At other times he speaks hopefully; for he has found friends: a great king has been moved to believe in the prophet and his mission, his first disciples are among

the royal family and the mighty nobles of the land;
the queen herself is his devoted follower. Then, again,
his disciples seem to be speaking, for he is mentioned
in the third person. But throughout this precious
collection, the grand figure stands out most real,
most human, appealing to the noblest, tenderest
human sympathies, and making you feel sure that
Zarathushtra has once been a living man, and not an
empty name.

10. But when our curiosity prompts us to inquire
for details, for biographical facts, materials fail us
entirely. The Avesta tells us the name of his father
and of his family or clan—SPITÂMA; also those of
his wives, his sons, and his daughter, but beyond
that nothing definite. Still keeping strictly to the
Avestan text, we find that he was born by a great
water, probably a river, in a wooded and mountainous country, and a "mountain of holy communings"
is mentioned—surely a lofty forest retreat, where he
spent a portion of his life—perhaps a large portion
of it,—meditating and lifting his soul higher and
higher, until he felt himself face to face with the
Deity, and came down and went forth to teach his
people, fully believing that he spoke not out of himself, but from what it had been given him to hear,
in answer to his own seeking and questioning of
spirit. For solitude, amidst grand natural surroundings, is a great breeder of thought and visions. Mohammed had been for years a driver of camels and a
leader of caravans, conning the mighty, silent lessons
of the desert and the stars, before he announced
himself a seer and a prophet, and he was forty then.

For years, too, had Moses lived the herdsman's life in the wilds of stony Sinaï before he returned to his people, old in years and in heavenly lore, and told his mission and worked it out. Let us, then, be content with such vague glimpses of the Eranian sage in his human truth, without heeding the flimsy finery of signs and wonders with which the puerile fancy of later ages and the injudicious zeal of followers tricked out the reverend and majestic image.

11. We further know from the Avesta that the king who honored Zarathushtra and believed in him was VÎSHTÂSPA, famous in legendary tradition as one of the early hero-kings of Erân. But it is scarcely admissible that the whole of Erân should have been united under one ruler in pre-historic times. So Vishtâspa will have to be imagined as king of some one Eranian country, almost certainly in the northeastern region, very possibly Bactria, which was early a prosperous and powerful kingdom, the capital of which is called "the beautiful Bakhdhi, with high-lifted banners,"—a designation evidently implying some great distinction, probably a royal residence. Whether Zarathushtra was a born subject of Vishtâspa, or was a native of some other part of Erân and only came thither to preach, is uncertain. Tradition, however, makes him of royal race, and has preserved a long genealogy, which shows him to be descended from one of the very oldest legendary kings. As to the time when king and prophet lived, it is likely that no positive date will ever be reached, and all we can with great probability conjecture, is that it should be placed some-

where beyond 1000 B.C. This date, so easily accessible as to be comparatively modern in Chaldea and Assyria, is so remote as to be virtually pre-historic in a land entirely devoid of monuments, and where we have no grounds for even suppositions as to the time when writing was introduced.

12. This latter fact sufficiently shows how impossible it is to ascertain with any degree of precision at what period the Avesta texts—as well the Gâthas as the later ones—were written down. No manuscripts now extant are really ancient. According to Parsi tradition, there once was a large body of sacred books, all indiscriminately and, beyond doubt, erroneously, attributed to the prophet himself. This so-called Zoroastrian literature is said to have consisted of twenty-one books, written out on twelve thousand cowhides, (parchment), embracing every possible branch of religious discipline, philosophy, and science, but to have been destroyed at the time of the conquest of Persia by the Greeks under Alexander the Great of Macedon, three centuries before Christ. No Greek ever persecuted any religion; but as it is well known that Alexander, in a fit of drunken exaltation after a feast, burned down Persepolis, the capital of the vanquished Persian kings, it is, of course, quite possible that manuscripts may have perished in the conflagration. That an extensive sacred literature did exist at the time is partly confirmed by the testimony of a contemporary Greek writer, (Hermippos), who is recorded to have catalogued the Zoroastrian books, and to have stated the contents of each book. After the great fire we are

told that sacred tradition and law survived only in the memories of the priests for several centuries until, in the Sassanian period, a council of priests was convoked for the express purpose of restoring and committing to writing the ancient texts, and the result is the Avesta text as we now see it, incomplete, fragmentary, confused in the arrangement and order of chapters and even verses. The ancient language had fallen into disuse as early as Alexander's time, wherefore it was found necessary to provide translations and commentaries in the then modern Persian —Pehlevi. It is not to be wondered at that the clergy, seeing, from the disposition of the new reigning house, that their day of power had come, remodelled many of the texts in a way favorable to their own overweening claims, nor could they fail to add or fabricate some to suit their purposes and establish their rule. Persia now became what it never had been—priest-ridden, and an era of fanaticism to the length of persecution was inaugurated by the proclamation of King Shapûr II.: "Now that we have recognized the law of the world here below, they shall not allow the infidelity of any one whatever, and I shall strive that it may be so."

13. It stands to reason that, of a large mass of religious literature entrusted to the memories of that religion's ministers, only such portions will be preserved in tolerable entirety and uncorruptedness as are in daily use for purposes of worship and observance. Such exactly was the case with the Avesta. The portions that have come down to us are collections of prayers and invocations, which the faithful

3. PAGE OF THE AVESTA, FROM THE OLDEST MANUSCRIPT (WRITTEN 1325 A.D.), PRESERVED IN KOPENHAGEN. (ABOUT HALF THE ORIGINAL SIZE.)

are to recite daily, in a certain order,—the service or liturgy proper;—also of hymns of praise to various divine beings whom the modern Parsis regard as subordinate angels or good spirits, which hymns, as well as some short prayers and fragments, are grouped under the title of Lesser Avesta (KHORDEH AVESTA), as being of less vital importance, and to be recited only once a month and on certain occasions. The principal divisions of the Avesta as it has stood since the text was definitively established and sanctioned under the Sassanian king, Shapûr II. (about 325 A.D.), are as follows :

I. The VENDÎDÂD, corrupted from a much longer word which means "the law against the Dévas" (*i. e.*, the Demons). It is, properly, a code of laws and regulations tending towards the establishment of righteousness and the defeat of the Powers of Evil, but includes some interesting mythical legends, traditions, and digressions of various sorts.

II. The VÎSPERED : invocations to all the divine and holy beings, who are honored under the title of "Chiefs of the Good Creation," and invited to assist at the sacrifice that is preparing—very much in the form of a litany.

III. The YASNA, "Sacrifice," *i. e.*, the prayers and text—MANTHRAS—which are to accompany the very minute and complicated performances that compose the sacrifice, in presence of the sacred fire, to which are presented offerings of meat, milk, bread, and fruit, in small quantities, and the juice of a certain plant, the HAÔMA, which is pressed out on the altar itself with many strictly prescribed ceremonies. The

Gâthas are comprised in the Yasna, for no particular reason that one can see, and form twenty-five chapters of it. It also contains forms of confession, invocations, praise, exhortations, etc. These three divisions, Vendidâd, Vispered, Yasna are not recited separately, but intermingled, as suits the progress of the liturgy. When written out in this particular liturgical order they form the VENDÎDÂD-SÂDEH.

IV. The YESHTS, hymns of praise, containing much interesting mythical matter, indeed distinguished altogether by a polytheistic and mythological character entirely foreign to the early stages of Zarathushtra's religion, and clearly showing a far later and greatly corrupted period. These Yeshts, together with a few fragments, short prayers for each day of the month and others, form the Khordeh or Lesser Avesta, perhaps held somewhat less holy than the other three books, as not being in liturgical use at daily worship. It is to be noted that, for the same reasons, very few of the Yeshts have been translated into Pehlevi, so that scholars, in reading and rendering them, have the additional difficulty of being entirely unassisted by tradition.

14. It will be seen from this brief review of its contents, that we would vainly look in the Avesta for the cosmogonical legends which usually form a part of a nation's sacred lore, and which we find in such abundance and richness in the sacred records of the Chaldeo-Assyrians and the Hebrews. Such a blank in our knowledge of so great a race as that of Erân would be an irreparable loss. Fortunately it is

in a great measure filled from sources which, if comparatively modern, are not devoid of authority, since they are beyond a doubt supplied from ancient traditions; these sources are various books composing a voluminous Pehlevi literature, and all belonging to the Sassanian period, but certainly containing much of the material of which the lost books of the old Avestan literature were made up, even though modernized and greatly transformed by ages of oral transmission and altered conditions of culture. Chief and foremost among these late growths of an ancient and much grafted stem is the BUNDEHESH, an invaluable collection of mythical and religious narratives, about the beginning of things, and also the end and regeneration of the world, the order that rules the universe, chapters of a fanciful geography and astronomy clearly betraying the same mythical origin, scraps of national heroic epos, and even philosophical digressions. All these rather heterogeneous elements are worked into a system with a symmetry which detracts from the genuine worth of this compilation by giving it a too obviously artificial character. Where every thing is smoothed and ordered and fashioned to fit, we may be sure that the original material is marred in the handling. Still, if the handling be modern, the material as certainly is old, as is, moreover, abundantly proved by various hints in the Avesta itself, which become intelligible by the light of the Bundehesh. This is why, although this book by its date is far removed from the time which the present volume is meant to cover (nearly a thousand years later than the latest date it will reach), we could not, without referring to it, attempt an intelligent and intelligible sketch of that ancient religion, the moral and philosophical sides of which are mainly represented in the surviving books of the Avesta.

As to the capital question: whether the prophet who preached that religion to Erân was the inventor of it or only a reformer, it is of a bearing too vast, of import too profound, not to claim a separate chapter.

III.

ARYAN MYTHS.

1. IN the first place, no religion is ever invented any more than a language. The many and great varieties of both are accounted for by growth and transformation, in every case where searching investigation is brought to bear on sufficient materials, *i. e.*, where we have knowledge enough to enable us to draw a conclusion capable of test and proof. The result is so invariable and uniform as to warrant an *a priori* conclusion of the same purport, whenever we have to deal with insufficient materials, *i. e.*, we may confidently foretell that, when we do gain more knowledge, the results will necessarily agree with those that have been attained in other similar cases.

2. It follows that man never really invents any thing. At least not in the sense commonly given to the word in our approximate every-day speech. Originally the word, which is a Latin one—*invenio*,—meant simply to " find," or more literally still, " to come upon " something ; a most correct and precise rendering of the thing it stands for, since an " invention " is always, in the beginning, an involuntary act, an illumination of the mind. The inventor ac-

cidentally finds something, stumbles upon an idea, which, if his gifts lie that way, he develops and works out into something serviceable, or beautiful, or wise, and in its final form, new. But he in no case, and in no sense, creates. Man never can produce any thing absolutely new, that never existed at all, in any shape whatever. He compares, arranges, combines, transforms, but he must have something to work upon. To use a homely but very pertinent simile: the spinner, the weaver, the dyer, and the embroiderer produce articles of marvellous variety in quality, texture, color, and design; but they could do nothing had not the raw material been given in the first instance—the flax, or wool, or cotton, or silk.

3. The question with which the preceding chapter closed is virtually answered by what has just been said. Zarathushtra was a reformer. And as one of the chief facts about every new religion is its attitude towards its predecessor, the religion from which it sprang, and which it strives to supplant, the next questions that arise are these: What materials did the master find ready to his hand? What did he retain, what reject, what did he bring of his own? And what were the compelling influences that called for the work? An inquiry of this kind is something like tracing a river to its springs. Even when the visible fountain-head is reached high in the mountain wilds, there is much more to find out; for many are the rivulets that ooze their way through hidden underground passages, that dribble and trickle through spongeous stone and rocky rifts, until they reach the common gathering-point. And it is those unseen

rills and driblets, tinged and flavored by contact with the various substances through which they pass, that determine the purity and wholesomeness of the waters which are to slake the thirst of thousands.

4. We have hitherto been exclusively occupied with the thoughts and deeds of three out of the half dozen leading races of humanity. Of these, one — the Shumiro-Accads of Chaldea — belonged to the yellow, or Turanian, race; the second — the peoples of Canaan — to the much-mixed Hamitic stock; and the third — Babylonians, Assyrians, and Jews — to the Semitic division of the great white family. We saw the moral and intellectual characteristics of each reflected in their religions, while these again reacted on their destinies. The nations of Erân, which in the course of history next claim our attention, belonging as they do to our own division of mankind, the Aryan or Indo-European race, present a subject of study in many ways more congenial, and we feel in far more direct sympathy with their spiritual life, the workings of which, from our kinship of blood and mind, we find it easy to follow and to share. It is, however, scarcely possible, in dealing with them, entirely to separate them from their brethren of India. These two Asiatic branches of the Aryan tree are so closely connected in their beginnings, the sap that courses through both is so evidently the same life-blood, that a study of the one almost necessarily involves a parallel study of the other. We must at all events pause here to attempt a sketch of the conditions of Aryan life, from which both those branches originally drew their being.

5. There was a time when Eranians and Hindus were not yet, but the ancestors of both lived, an undivided nation, in a pleasant country, of which the race retained a dim but grateful remembrance in the shape of tradition, since God himself is made to say in the Avesta: " The first of the good lands and countries I created was the AIRYANA-VAÊJA," *i. e.*, the "Aryan Home " (Vendidâd, I.). How delightful this primeval home of the race was supposed to have been is further shown by this statement, attributed to God in the same passage: " I have made every land dear to its dwellers, even though it had no charms whatever in it; had I not made every land dear to its dwellers, then the whole living world would have invaded the Airyâna-Vaêja." It would of course be vain attempting to locate this region, to which remoteness of time has lent a mythical vagueness; but on the whole it seems most likely that the primeval Âryas dwelt somewhere to the east of the Caspian Sea, in the hilly, wooded, and well watered portions of the high tableland, from which streams of emigrants could freely flow southward and westward. It is very probable that the Indo-Eranians were a large division which, after separating from the main trunk and leaving the primeval Aryan home, the Airyâna-Vaêja, dwelt, for many centuries in another but not very distant region, until their turn came, and they split into the two great branches which were to spread over the lands of India and of Erân.

6. Neither the Indo-Eranians nor their fathers, the primeval Âryas, have left monuments of any

kind from which we might gather indications concerning their mode of life and thought, their conceptions of the world they lived in, and the powers that rule it. But we have a collection of a little over a thousand prayers or hymns, preserved by the Aryan conquerors of India. This collection is the famous RIG-VEDA, one of the Hindus' four sacred books. It is the most ancient of the four; and as such, of the greatest value to us. A goodly portion of the hymns are very old indeed, and take us back to the earliest times of Aryan occupation in the northwestern part of India, named from the river Indus and its principal affluents, "the land of the Seven Rivers," now PENJÂB, a time probably not *very* much anterior to Zoroaster and the Gâthas. As these hymns beyond doubt embody no new ideas, but those which the settlers had brought from their more northern homes, it is not difficult to reconstruct from them the simple creed of the Indo-Eranians, if not of the Âryas themselves, the creed from which two religions were to spring: Hindu Brahmanism and Eranian Mazdeism, religions than which none can differ more widely in scope and character, yet bear more palpable signs of an original common source.

7. At the very earliest stage of their spiritual life at which we can reach them, the Âryas already appear far superior to the Turanians, as represented by those early Shumiro-Accads, who have left such ample records of themselves. This is partly to be ascribed to the difference of time, since Aryan antiquity has nothing to show at all like the prodigious dates—as high as 4000 B.C.—authentically established

for Chaldea, and still more to difference of race. If
the Spiritism or goblin-worship of early Shumir and
Accad have at *some* time necessarily been the religion
of mankind in general, as the crudest, rudimentary
manifestation of the religious instinct inborn in man,
some races took the step to a higher spiritual level
earlier than others, while those purely Turanian
people who remained uninfluenced by foreign cultures have scarcely taken that step even yet.* Our
earliest glimpse of the Âryas shows them to us at
the stage which may be called that of pure nature-
worship, as developed by the particular conditions
of land and clime under which they were placed, and
the life, half pastoral, half agricultural, which they
led. The beneficent Powers of Nature—the bright
Heaven; all-pervading Light; Fire, as manifested in
the lightning, or the flame on the altar and the
hearth; the Sun in all his many aspects; the kindly
motherly Earth; the Winds, the Waters, the life-
giving Thunderstorm;—all these were by them
adored and entreated, as divine beings, gods. The
harmful Powers, far fewer in number, principally
Darkness and Drought, were fiends or demons, to
be abhorred, denounced, and accursed, never propiti-
ated—and herein lay one of the chief differences between Aryan conceptions and those of Turanian and
Canaanitic races. In the ideas of these latter the
Powers that do evil to man are to be conciliated and
inclined to mercy by prayer and sacrifice; in those
of the former they must be fought and vanquished,
a duty which naturally devolves on their adversaries:

* See " Story of Chaldea," Ch. III., " Turanian Chaldea."

it is the natural business of Light to conquer Darkness, of Wind and Storm to gather the clouds driven out of sight by the fiends of Drought, and to pour down rain. Hence the Âryas' simple and manly attitude towards their deities: praise, thanksgiving, and prayers for help, and a religion so plain and transparent that a sketch of it can be given in a very few pages.

8. There are few facts better established than this, —that the oldest known and most exalted Aryan god is Heaven, the luminous, the earth-enclosing. His name in the Sanskrit of the Rig-Veda—which is older than that of any other Sanskrit literature, is DYÂUS, and, at a somewhat later period, VÁRUNA. Both names originally are really common nouns, and mean the same thing. For DYÂUS is the word used in Sanskrit to designate the visible Sky, while VÁRUNA, in a slightly altered form—OURANOS—to this day means "Sky" or "Heaven" in Greek. It is clear that these names carry us back to the primeval Aryan times, the times when those detachments departed which reached Europe in their wanderings. Although the Indo-Eranian religion was frankly polytheistic, yet a certain supremacy seems to have attached to the Sky-god, and he is pre-eminently entitled, in the oldest portions of the Rig, both under the name of DYÂUS and that of VÁRUNA, ASURA— "Lord"; VÁRUNA frequently also receives the epithet of All-Knowing, Omniscient. The sun is his eye; Fire, in its celestial lightning form, is his son, and the visible starry sky is his royal robe. For he is far from being a mere personification of a physical fact.

He is, on the contrary, endowed with the highest moral attributes. He established heaven and earth; he is the giver and keeper of the order and harmony which are the Law of the universe, the Cosmos, and which, transferred from the material to the spiritual and moral world, becomes the Law of Righteousness, deviation from which is sin and the beginning of all wrong and confusion. Hence it is to Váruna that expressions of penitence and prayers for forgiveness are addressed, for he is the punisher; and the sin which he most detests is lying.

9. The name of Váruna is coupled in a great many invocations with that of another bright being, MITRA (*i. e*, "the Friend"), Daylight personified. The association between them is so close, that they present themselves to the mind as an inseparable pair, Váruna-Mitra, or Mitra-Váruna, who drive the same chariot, think the same thoughts. Together they are the keepers of the Cosmic Order and the Law of Righteousness, together they watch the deeds and the hearts of men, equally all-seeing, all-knowing, and the sun is called the eye of Mitra-Váruna as often as of Váruna alone. What more natural than this connection, Heaven and Daylight—Mitra-Váruna—the Luminous Sky? There are indications of Váruna and Mitra having been associated with several luminous deities of rank somewhat inferior to their own (the ÂDITYAS), not only in the Indo-Eranian period, but in the primeval Aryan period, and to have formed with them a company of seven. The sacredness and significance of this number is universal and unspeakably ancient, and it will probably be traced

to primeval humanity before its first separation. One would be inclined to fancy that these seven luminous beings were really only pale reflections of Váruna-Mitra, (they being the first of them), invented for the sake of the sacred number.

10. One of the many Old-Sanskrit names for Lightning, the son of the Asura Váruna, is ATHARVAN, literally " he who has Athar." Sacred tradition has transformed this mythical Atharvan into a high-priest, first bringer of fire to men and institutor of sacrifice in the form of burnt-offering. There is to this day a large class of priests in India—those who have the special charge of the sacred and sacrificial fires,—who are called Atharvans, and tradition makes them lineal descendants of that first mythical high-priest, who on closer inspection resolves himself into the Fire-god, the personified element of Fire, descended from heaven in the shape of lightning, otherwise Athar, the son of Váruna. *Atharî* in Sanskrit means " flame " *atharyu* (" flaming, blazing") is a frequent by-word for AGNI = Fire. ATHAR consequently is one of the oldest Aryan names of Fire; if not *the* oldest, for there is a Greek word which points farther back than the Indo-Eranian period. That word is *athrageni*, the name of a plant, a creeper, the wood of which was used in very ancient times to bring forth fire by friction. Interpreted, it can mean nothing but " *what gives birth to Athar.*" It was obsolete already in the classical Greek times, and the plant has never been identified. As to the sacredness of the element itself, it is as universal and primevally ancient as that of the num-

ber seven. It has always been the object of a peculiarly fervent and, if one may say so, endearing worship, as the friend of man, who sits on his hearth, assists in his tasks, the substitute for the light of day, for the warmth of the sun, the conqueror and disperser of all evil things that lurk in darkness, of phantoms and bad dreams,—lastly as the messenger between the two worlds, whose flames, leaping aloft, carry up to Heaven the prayers and offerings of men.

11. In its original celestial form, as Lightning, Fire, the Son of Heaven, plays a prominent part in the war which the bright Devas, the givers of light, life, and plenty, are forever waging with the demons of Darkness and Drought, and the battle-ground of which is the intermediate region between heaven and earth, the Atmosphere. It is in the poetical descriptions of this warfare that the Aryan race displayed all its gifts of imagery, its exuberant epic genius. The eternal conflict which to us is a series of meteorological phenomena, spiritualized only in rare poetical moods, and always consciously, was to the early Aryas, the most impressionable and imaginative of races, a thrilling drama carried on by living, superhuman beings, mighty for good or for evil. Or rather two distinct dramas, with two different protagonists. The two supreme goods, which give all the others, are Light and Rain. The arch-enemies of mankind are those powers that rob them of these treasures. Now the war with the fiends of Darkness and Night is comparatively a simple affair, which is naturally left entirely to the Sun. Still, the inexhaus-

tible imagination of the Âryas filled it with a variety of incidents replete with gorgeous or delicate poetry, creating that fund of Sun-myths to which fully one half of the stories and poetry of the world are traceable. This, however, is not the place to enter into a study of them, for we are now in search of the sources of Eranian religion and epos, and the Sun-myth somehow never much caught the fancy of that particularly stern and practical race, and so is but feebly reflected in its spiritual life.

12. Far more complicated is the Storm-myth, the story of the struggle for the waters of heaven; far more varied and exciting too, because, through its many stages and incidents to its culmination in the final battle-scene, the thunder-storm, the success often seems doubtful, the advantage frequently remains for a long time with the hostile powers, even though the victory can never be theirs in the end. Numberless are the wiles of the fiends to gain and keep possession of the waters, and desperate their acts of violence and resistance; numberless also the shapes they assume—and no wonder, since they are chiefly the personifications of different kinds of clouds. For there are clouds and clouds, and not all by any means bode or bring rain. If some generously pour down the precious, pure liquid that is life and drink to the parched pining earth, others keep it back, wickedly hide it, swell and spread with the treasure they cover and enclose, and will not give it up, until pierced and torn asunder by the lightning spear of the angry thunder-god. This difference in clouds, which does not strike us except on reflection, su-

perficial as our attention to the outer world has become, could not escape the observation of people who, so to speak, lived on nature's lap, whose simple mode of life fostered the closest, most watchful dependence on her every mood, while the unparalleled vigor and fertility of their poetical fancy not only suggested to them a thousand similes, as striking as varied, but straightway transformed each of these into a person and a story. Let us examine a few of these creations, in which one hardly knows what most to admire—the childlike, *naïve* simplicity, or their unfailing appropriateness. A very few, for the reason expressed above, reserving a thorough exploration of this veritable fairyland of our race's childhood for another volume, to be devoted to ancient India, where it bloomed more luxuriantly than in any other land.

13. It must have been one of the earliest, because the most natural flights of fancy, which compared the light and fleecy clouds to herds of kine lazily moving across space, as across a broad pasture, and pouring down their milk—the rain, to feed the earth and all living things. Somewhat more elaborate and far-fetched, but still perfectly intelligible, is the poetical effort which likens them to graceful women. We thus have the heavenly Water-Maidens, and the divine Waters, wives of the gods, the Asuras, and more especially of the Supreme Asura, Váruna. As such they are the mothers of Lightning, one of whose most sacred names is, very consistently, "Son of the Waters," APÂM NAPÂT. The fiends, therefore, who withhold the rain and bring on the earth

the horrors of drought and famine, are, in mythical speech, stealers of cows or of women. They either spirit them away altogether out of sight, or shut them up in dark mountain caves, or in strongholds —these being standing designations, in Aryan mythology, for the dark, lowering clouds which rise at the end of the sky in the shape of mountain ridges or fortress-walls, with battlements and towers. Then INDRA, the god of the thunderbolt, resplendent in his golden armor, mounts his chariot, drawn by fleet dappled steeds—the racing clouds of the storm, together with his inseparable companion VAYU, the wind that ever moves in the heights of the atmosphere; after them ride the troop of the strong Storm-Winds, and the battle begins. Not long can the mountain or the fortress hold out against their onslaught. After repeated blows from Indra's fiery mace, the rocks, the walls are burst open, the cows are brought forth and pour down their longed-for milk; or, if the other image be adopted, the maidens, the wives are delivered.

14. But there is no end to the suggestiveness of clouds, as whoever has spent idle hours at sea or in the mountains watching them will not need to be told. There is not a child who has not discovered in the sky likenesses, animal shapes, fantastic forms of monsters and giants, landscapes, and cities. To our Aryan ancestors the cloud that gave no rain was the most malignant of fiends; it was to them VRITRA, the "coverer" or "enfolder," and "Killer of Vritra," —VRITRAHAN—is the highest term of praise, the most triumphant title bestowed on the devas who suc-

ceed in piercing his shaggy hide, and letting out the imprisoned waters. This epithet became a special by-word for Indra, as being the demon's most constant adversary, whose own particular weapon, the lightning-spear, alone can end the fray. Another and still more popular cloud-demon is Ahi, "the serpent" who sits on the mountain and defies the devas. It is the dark storm-cloud of many coils, which it slowly winds and unwinds on top of the mountain, clouds banked up against the horizon. It is usually the indefatigable Indra who fights and kills him, and the story is told in a hundred more or less dramatic versions in the Rig-Veda. This same serpent-fiend is one of the most active and ubiquitous, and we find him again and again, in epos and story, in a variety of situations and combinations, where his original nature as cloud- and storm-demon is forgotten.

15. A notable peculiarity of the Aryan conception of nature, earthly and divine, is the extremely dignified attitude apportioned to man in his relations to the higher powers. As in every religion, prayer and sacrifice are required, but in a somewhat different spirit: he does not passively entreat favor, he in a measure also grants it; he is supposed to *help* his bright devas in the good fight against the demons. His songs of praise and thanksgiving encourage them; the sacrificial offerings to which he bids them as guests, and of which they partake as friends partake of a feast in the house of a friend, increase their vigor, just as food increases that of men; above all, the drink-offering, the exhilarating Soma-juice, fills

them with glee, strength, and valor. Nay, they are actually dependent on it for victory, and would be unable to overcome the fiends were they not liberally supplied with the wonderful liquid. It is especially Indra who is said to consume enormous quantities of it, after which his onslaught is irresistible.

16. The Indian SOMA is a plant with soft and flexible stem, which contains a milky juice. This juice, being pressed out and allowed to ferment, gives an intoxicating liquor, the use of which at sacrifices is one of the very earliest customs of the Aryan race. It was poured into the fire, which burned the brighter for the alcohol it contained, and the priests drank it themselves, probably in quantities sufficient to feel the intoxicating effects. Nothing extraordinary so far. But the strange and distinctively Aryan feature of this observance is that the Soma plant and the Soma juice were not only held sacred, but actually worshipped as a divine being, a god ; so that Soma came to be not only one of the devas, but one of the mightiest, most dread, and most beneficent. There is in the effect of stimulants, when used in moderation, an elevating, exhilarating virtue which seems to have struck the discoverers of the plant and its properties as supernatural. The strange light-heartedness, the temporary oblivion of cares and sorrows, the heightened vitality manifested in greater courage, in loosened, eloquent tongue, nay, frequently in poetical, even prophetical, inspiration, made them feel transfigured, as by the presence of a foreign and higher element ; a god, they thought, must have descended and entered into them,—and that god

dwelt in the consecrated plant of sacrifice—the god Soma, the friend alike of gods and men,—for in their crude anthropomorphism they could not but imagine that their devas would be affected in the same manner as themselves, to a proportionately higher degree. So when they bade them to the sacrificial feast, they did not forget to provide their due treat of Soma, and sent them, rejoicing and invigorated, to do battle against Vritra and Ahi and the cow-stealers with their bands of fiends.

17. Great as is the power of prayer which is supposed to *help* the deity, the Âryas went even further: they imagined that in prayer, or rather in the recitation of certain prayers and sacred texts, lay a force that could *compel* the devas' assistance, nay, almost their submission, and defeat the demons by their own inherent virtue. The MANTRA ("Sacred Word," text) thus became a weapon of attack and defence against the demons, a weapon of irresistible might. At a late period of development, this idea of the compelling power of prayer was carried to incredible lengths of absurdity, claiming nothing short of omnipotence for certain peculiarly endowed mortals; but in its origin the notion has nothing impious or unnatural. "Man's prayer," says one of our most eminent mythologists,* " is generally in accordance to nature; he asks for rain in times of drought, —and rain *must* follow on drought; he asks for light in darkness,—and light *must* come after darkness. Seeing that his prayer is invariably heard, he ascribes to it *power* to effect its object." The few other things

* Darmesteter: "Ormazd et Ahriman," page 114, note 1.

that the Âryas prayed and sacrificed for in those primitive times,—a numerous and healthy posterity, increase of cattle, health and long life for themselves, and victory in their wars with the natives of the countries they occupied,—were the very things that could not fail to come to them in the conditions in which their life was passed, and with their superiority of race. So there was nothing to shake, and every thing to confirm, their excessive faith; for man, unenlightened by scientific culture, consequently believing in powers, not laws, is ever prone to admit rather supernatural than natural agencies.

18. From this conception there was but one step—and not a wide one either—to making of the hymn, the Sacred Text (Mantra), a Person, an independent deity, to be individually invoked and adored, as being not only beneficent in a general way, but like Indra, Soma, and other devas, essentially "demon-killing" *vritrahan*. It is to be noted that, in order to insure its full power and effectiveness, the Mantra was to be recited at the proper time, in the proper way, with the proper intonations of voice, all strictly determined by rules; rules—numerous, complicated, and infinitely minute—governing also every step of the sacrifice which usually accompanied the recitation. If these rules be perfectly complied with, the Mantra, the sacrifice will take effect, quite independently of the disposition of mind of the worshipper. If departed from in the smallest particular, prayer and sacrifice both are worse than useless—they most likely will act the wrong way and bring down disaster on the worshipper's head, though his soul may be filled with

the purest and most fervent piety. It is, therefore, safest for the layman not to meddle with these matters at all, but leave them in the hands of the priests, who are qualified by right divine to wield the spiritual power, and will, if meetly remunerated, perform for the layman the necessary ceremonies, instruct him as to his own share in them, and see that he does not come to harm, through ignorance or over-officiousness.

19. It will be seen that so material a conception and use of prayer and sacrifice are more like conjuring, in spirit and object, than anything else. They may be considered as a remnant, slightly transformed, of that grossest and most primitive stage of religious consciousness which every race must start from, and which we saw amply illustrated in the most ancient practices and conjuring-feats of the Shumiro-Accad sorcerer-priests. The old Âryas and Indo-Eranians had by no means shaken themselves free of this primitive materialism. The gods whom they worship often bewilder us by their mixed nature, made up of material and spiritual attributes in such a way as to make it very difficult to know where to draw the line. While at one time Váruna, Mitra, Agni, Soma, are beyond a doubt praised and invoked as the visible, material sky, light, fire, the plant that is brought from the mountains, cut up and pressed, and as the fermented intoxicating beverage; at others they are addressed as the most spiritual beings and invested with the loftiest abstract properties: Váruna becomes the Lord that dwells in or above the sky, whose robe the sky is, the hater of

lies and the punisher of sins; together with Mitra, all-seeing, all-knowing, he is the keeper of the Cosmic Order and the Law of Righteousness; Soma is the Healer, the giver of life and immortality, the god of inspiration and heroism. This second, half material stage in the evolution of religious feeling, is closely matched in ancient Chaldea by the period of those beautiful hymns to the Sun, to Fire, to the Moon, etc., which have been aptly compared with those of the Rig-Veda.*

20. A mythology so rich in dramatic incidents and personages is a very hot-bed for the growth of mythical epos, which every race creates for itself by the simple trick of transferring the various scenes of the atmospheric drama, be it sun-myth or storm-myth, from heaven and cloud-land down to earth, transforming the gods into heroes, the Sun-maidens and Water-maidens into mortal women, the cloud-cattle into herds of real kine, and the demons into wild beasts or monsters, or giants and dragons. Each nation, of course, weaves into this common fund of mythical romance the names and dimly outlined forms of its own ancient heroes, together with such circumstances of its real history as tradition has preserved. Many are the divine champions of the Aryan myth which reappear in such new garb in the epos of India and that of Erân, and consequently must have passed through the Indo-Eranian period. Of these semi-heroic, semi-divine myths, the most important and interesting is that of YAMA.

21. Yama was originally one of the names of the

* See "Story of Chaldea," Chapter III., from p. 170.

setting sun, in the particularly sad and solemn aspect of the departing, dying god, which, however, contained the consoling suggestion of resurrection and immortality.* He was the first to go the way that all must go—"to show the way to many," in the language of the Rig-hymn. He was gradually transformed into the first man—the first who lived, and, consequently, the first who died. Being the first to arrive in "the vasty halls of death," † he becomes master and host there, receiving those who join him in succession, and, by a natural transition, King of the Dead. Then popular fancy goes to work to complete the transformation by picturesque touches of appropriate detail, unconsciously borrowed from the same inexhaustible treasury of myth. So Yama is given two dogs, "brown, broad-snouted, four-eyed," whose business it is to go forth into the world each day, to scent out those whose hour has come, and drive them like sheep to the dread king's presence. Yet King Yama is by no means an image of terror, but rather an auspicious and gracious presence, as he sits with the gods in the highest heaven under the wide-spreading tree—the Cosmic Tree of Life, drinking the Soma that drops from its foliage, and surrounded by the PITRIS—"Fathers"—*i. e.*, the glorified souls of the righteous dead.

22. For the Âryas held their departed relatives in great love and reverence, and did not believe that the mere fact of dying, going from the midst of his

---

* See "Story of Chaldea," pp. 337-339.
† Matthew Arnold, in "Requiescat."

family, severed a man's connection with it. Each individual family honored its own Pitris, assembling at stated times to commemorate their earthly lives, by speaking of them, calling to mind their deeds and good qualities, invoking their protection, and setting out for them offerings of simple food—milk, and honey, and cakes. Families on these occasions partook of a common meal, to which the supposed invisible presence of the Pitris lent a mysterious solemnity. These commemorative festivals were the strongest possible bond between the members of each particular family, and the right to assist in them was strictly limited and determined by custom so sacred, that it became law and the standard for the regulation of the right of succession. The Pitris were supposed to be very powerful to do good or evil to their descendants, but, on the other hand, to depend for their own happiness and comfort on the affectionate remembrance of the living.

23. It stands to reason that the remote ancestors of a group of families connected by blood relationship, i. e., of a clan or tribe, must have been revered by all the branches of the clan ; that festivals on a larger scale must have been kept in their honor, which were the occasions of general meetings of the clans, and kept alive the feeling of kinship and fellowship. Such ancestors frequently became tribal heroes, fit subjects for story and song, which eked out whatever tradition had preserved of their real exploits with mythical traits, the true import of which was soon lost sight of. Such is the origin of most of those demigods, beings mortal yet more than human,

who crowd the borderland between myth and history, whose disembodied spirits were worshipped as tutelary deities, and whose earthly careers, haloed with the glory transferred to them from the divine champions of Sky and Cloud-land, are the materials out of which races weave their National Epos and Heroic Poetry. The Epos of Erân is rich with such mythical heroes, and knows of whole dynasties of them, the reputed ancient kings of the race. But a presentation of them does not lie within the scope of the present work. If some of them confront us and claim our attention, we shall account for them as we go.

IV.

ARYAN MYTHS IN THE AVESTA—THEIR ALLEGORICAL TRANSFORMATION.

1. THE myths of a race—as apart and distinguished from its religion—being reducible to physical phenomena, animated into personal life by poetical and epic treatment,* necessarily convey some indications as to the physical conditions under which that race was placed. Now the influence of India on its population is, on the whole, enervating, both as regards climate and soil. The latter is very rich and produces a great deal in exchange for very little work; the forests, indeed, abound in nourishment— fruits, and berries, and roots—which grows wild, for man or beast, while the rivers are numerous and seldom dry up; the larger ones, like the Indus and Ganges, never. There is therefore, on one hand, little incentive to hard labor, and on the other, the needs of men are few, as regards either shelter, clothing, or food, owing to the climate, which is so hot as to make exertion unwholesome and a spare vegetable diet the only rational one. The Aryan conquerors, as they spread through the land and dwelt in it, suc-

* See "Story of Chaldea," pp. 294, and ff.

cumbed to these influences, lost much of their original hardiness and active vigor, and were gradually transformed into a race of, physically, somewhat effeminate men, of dwindled stature and delicate proportions, in whom leisure and habitual idleness of body developed an extraordinary faculty for spiritual contemplation and an inordinate exuberance of fancy — which two qualities combined give color and tone to their entire mythology, religious and philosophical speculation, and poetry.

4. STEPPE LANDSCAPE IN TURÁN (SEA OF ARAL).

2. Very different were the influences to which that branch of the Aryan family was subjected which wandered into the region west of Central Asia, the different countries of which come under the general name of Erán. Their westward migra-

tion, after taking them through pleasant lands of hills and valleys and streams, of woods and pastures, little differing from their older home, and where they founded prosperous settlements and states—Bactria being the chief of them,—brought them to a region of novel and forbidding aspect, a region of sharp contrasts, nay—contraries, where nature seemed at war with herself, and of which nothing could give a more vivid picture than an admirable page from Max Duncker's "Ancient History," which we will proceed to borrow:

"The centre of Erân was formed of a vast desert; to the north and south stretched far away arid tablelands; the favored districts might almost be called oases. Immediately on the most fertile valleys and slopes bordered endless steppes; blooming plains, densely shaded by groves, were encompassed by sandy wastes. If the mountainous countries of the northeast possessed the stateliest forests, the richest pastures, the snow fell early, the winters were severe. If the vegetation was most luxuriant along the edge of the Caspian Sea, sickness and venomous reptiles dwelt in the marshy lowlands. The people of Erân suffered not only from the heat of summer, but also from the cold of winter; the scorching winds of the desert were not more to be dreaded than the snow-storms of the northern tablelands. Here pastures and cornfields were buried under snow during many weeks; there sand-drifts destroyed culture. Here the camels died of cold and slipped down the icy steeps into precipices; there the winds from the desert choked up the wells and springs. Here was winter, "with the worst of its plagues," "cold for the waters, cold for the earth, cold for the trees" (Vendidâd I., 9-12), there the cattle were tortured by gadflies in the heat; here bears and wolves invaded the herds, there snakes had to be guarded against and the fiercer wild beasts. Life was in this land a fight against heat and against cold, a fight for the preservation of the flocks; and as soon as single tribes had begun to settle in the more favored districts, and to attend to agriculture, it became a fight against the desert and drought. Here the dry soil had to be supplied with water; there the crops had to be protected against the hot winds and sand drifts from the desert. To these hardships and contrasts of nature must be added the contrast between the populations. Most of the native tribes of the central tableland, and many of those who held the surrounding highlands, were debarred by the nature of the country from leading any life but that of nomadic herdsmen. To this day a great portion of the population of Erân consists of nomads. So while the settlers labored lustily, in the sweat of their brow, the others roved about idly with their flocks. There could be no lack of raids into the agricultural districts, of plundering and robbing."*

3. The influences which such conditions of life must perforce have exerted on a naturally gifted and high-spirited race, brave, doughty, and robust, are incalculable. It is entirely owing to them that the Eranians became what we find them at their entrance on the stage of history—a people of most noble presence, of manly beauty of the heroic cast, indomitable fighters, earnest and honest of mind, of a serious and practical turn, far more given to the work of life than to its graces and amenities, who thought agriculture and cattle-raising the highest and holiest of occupations, and art a very secondary matter, in which, indeed, they reached proficiency only at a very late period, and that as imitators. It is evident that their moral and religious sense must have been vastly modified and shaped by the same influences. It was deepened in one particular channel, intensified in one particular direction. The strife which pervaded their existence in the land which they had made their own, became to them the main fact of nature generally, pervading the whole creation. The opposition between Light and Darkness, and, conse-

* "Geschichte des Alterthums," Vol. IV., pp. 105 and ff.

quently, between the powers of Light and Darkness, —the gods and the demons,—is a prominent ground-feature of the primeval Aryan conception of nature, as of every primitive religion in the world. With the Eranians that opposition became the one fundamental law, to the absorption and almost exclusion of the many picturesque mythical details and incidents with which the poetry of other Aryan nations is adorned to overloading. The hard struggle for a life hedged in with dangers, crowded with hardships and difficulties, had weaned them from the idling contemplation, the toying with fancies and images, which is the essence of a myth-making poetry. They drew the great Battle-Myth down to the earth, and embodied it in the contrasts with which their own land teemed, thus preparing the way for the dualism which is the keynote of their national religion.

4. There was no need of inventing new symbols to express this tendency. It was sufficient to emphasize the conflict, which formed the groundwork of the oldest Aryan mythical religion. The ancient Sky-god and his everlasting foe, the Cloud-Serpent— the Obscurer of Light,—became the chief persons in whom all good and all harm were embodied, and gradually drove the other mythical agents into the background. As we trace the ancient myths in what is left us of the Avesta, we are struck with the great development given to the spiritual meaning of them, which, in the sister race of India, is only occasional and subordinate, the physical significance decidedly predominating.

5. Thus we shall have some difficulty at first in

identifying AHURA-MAZDA, the supreme God, the Creator of the world and of the other gods, the master of all, the inspirer and maintainer of holiness and righteousness, such as he appears throughout the Avesta, with the old Aryan sky-gods Dyâus and Váruna. It is only long and attentive study, bringing out little touches scattered through the texts, few and far between, that enables us to trace this grand spiritual conception to its first physical source. And when these touches *are* found, they are such as to place the original identity beyond a doubt. The very name of the one is a combination of titles given to the other. The Sanskrit ASURA becomes, by the law of Eranian pronunciation, AHURA,* with the same sense of "Lord." And of all the by-names given to Váruna, that of "omniscient, all-knowing," was adopted as one of the names of the Deity — MAZDA. Thus "Ahura-Mazda" literally means "the Lord of great knowledge." The material attributes with which he is invested at once betray his origin. In one of those conversations with Zarathushtra, which are the accepted form of revelation throughout the Avesta, he is made to say:

"I maintain that sky there above, shining and seen afar, and encompassing the earth all around. It looks like a palace that stands built of a heavenly substance, firmly established, with ends that lie afar, shining in its body of ruby over the three worlds; *it is like a garment inlaid with stars*, made of a heavenly substance, *that Mazda puts on* . . . and on no side can the eye perceive the end of it.†

* There is the same exchange of letters in Greek and Latin: Greek *hepta* = Latin *septem* (seven); Greek *herpeton* = Latin *serpens*, etc.
† Yesht XIII.

To whom but a sky-god can this magnificent description apply? aside from the star-broidered garment, which also belongs to Váruna. (See p. 40.) The sky is also poetically called his body, and so he is said to be "the one of all whose body is the most perfect," "the finest of body," and homage is paid to his "most beauteous body,"—"we worship his entire body." Still more conclusive is the text in which homage is paid to "the resplendent Sun, *the eye of Ahura-Mazda*"* (See pp. 40, 41). ATAR, Fire (originally the celestial Fire—Lightning; see pp. 40, 42), is invariably spoken of and addressed as "Son of Ahura-Mazda," alone of all the Yazatas or "divine beings," while the Sacred Waters are invoked in a hymn as follows:

"We worship this earth which bears us together with *thy wives*, O Ahura-Mazda! . . ."

"O ye Waters! we worship you, you that are showered down, and you that stand in pools and vats, ye female Ahuras (*Ahurânis* of Ahura), that serve us in helpful ways, well-forded and full-flowing. . . ." (See pp. 45, 46.)

Lastly his name is joined with that of MITHRA, the pure Daylight (of whom more anon), in a manner and with a persistency which makes the couple correspond exactly to the Váruna-Mitra of the Rig-Veda: (See p. 41.) "I announce and complete my sacrifice to the two, to Ahura and to Mithra, the lofty, and the everlasting and the holy" (Yasna I., 11); "I desire to approach Ahura and Mithra with my praise, the lofty, eternal, and the holy two" (Yasna II., 11). And before the battle the worshipper addresses to

* Yasna I., 11.

the divine couple the following poetical invocation :
"May Mithra and Ahura, the high gods, come to us
for help, when the poniard lifts up its voice aloud"
(by clashing with another), "when the nostrils of the
horses quiver, when the strings of the bows whistle
and shoot sharp arrows. . . ." It is most instructive thus convincingly to trace out step by step the
proofs of the material and mythical origin of the
great Eranian God, then to follow the process of
evolution which raised him into the loftiest, purest,
most immaterial abstraction. But we must leave
him awhile before the race's religious consciousness
reaches that highest point, to follow up more traces
or transformations of Aryan myths in the Avesta.
It will be pleasantest to seek the gods in their
luminous homes, and, to find our way thither, we
shall have to look up a bit of celestial geography.

6. Far away in the East, beyond the ridges that
rise in tiers upon tiers, marking the stations of the
race's immemorial migrations, in its descent into the
plains of later Ariana, is the Holy Mountain, the
HARA-BEREZAITI ("Lofty Mountain"), known in the
Pehlevi period and to the Parsis in the corrupted
form of ALBORJ. It rises from the earth, beyond
the sphere of the stars and that of the sun, into the
sphere of Endless Light, Ahura-Mazda's own, where
he dwells in the "shining GARÔ-NMÂNA" ("the Abode
of Song"). This is the Mother of Mountains; although the 2,244 mountains that are on the earth have
grown out of it, and it is "connected with the sky."
Its summit is bathed in eternal glory and is a seat
of everlasting bliss. "There come neither night nor

darkness, no cold wind and no hot wind, no deathful sickness, no uncleanness made by the Daêvas (demons), and the clouds cannot reach up unto the Haraiti-Bareza." It has several notable peaks. That of TAÊRA is the centre of the world and around it the stars, the moon, and the sun revolve. Hence the hymn:

"Up! rise and roll along, thou swift-horsed sun, above Hara-Berezaiti, and produce light for the world, and mayest thou, O man! rise up there" (if thou art to abide in Garô-nmâna)—" along the path made by Mazda, along the way made by the gods, the watery way they opened." ("Watery" because of the clouds.)

"Up! rise up, thou moon . . . rise up above Hara-Berezaiti" (the rest as above).

"Up! rise up, ye stars . . . rise up above Hara-Berezaiti" (the rest as above). (Vendidâd XXI.*)

7. At the foot of the celestial part of the Hara, towards the south, stretches the Sea VOURU-KASHA, which is no other than the old Aryan "heavenly ocean" or cloud-reservoir of the waters which descend on the earth as rain. The same hymn contains an invocation to the Waters, which shows a remarkable comprehension of the continual interchange of moisture between the sky and earth:

"As the Sea Vouru-Kasha is the gathering place of waters, rise up,

* ALBORJ, still further modified into ELBURZ, became the name of an earthly mountain range, that which skirts the southern coast of the Caspian. This is a patent instance of a proceeding familiar to all nations when they reach the stage of transition from myth to reality: that of transferring mythical, heavenly geography to earth—a proceeding which goes hand in hand with the transformation of gods and myths into epic heroes and mythical legend. The Elburz, with its towering peak, MT. DEMAVEND, is shrouded, in the Eranian's eyes, with a mysterious sacredness and awe; it is the scene of various superhuman adventures in the Eranian Epos.

go up the aerial way and go down on the earth; go down on the earth and go up the aerial way. Rise up and roll along!"

This sea is, moreover, everlastingly replenished by the bountiful flow of the celestial spring ARDVI-SÛRA ANÂHITA, which rushes from the peak HUKAIRYA, of the Hara-Berezaiti, and supplies all the rivers of the earth with pure, abundant, and wholesome waters:

"The large river, known afar, that is as large as the whole of the waters that run along the earth; that runs powerfully from the height of Hukairya down to the sea Vouru-Kasha. All the shores of the sea Vouru-Kasha are boiling over, all the middle of it is boiling over, when she runs down there. . . ."

And the waters of this same celestial sea everlastingly feed and protect the Tree of Life and Immortality, the WHITE HAOMA or GAOKERENA, which God himself planted on "high Haraiti" (the same as Hara-Berezaiti), and placed in the centre of Vouru-Kasha together with another divine tree which contains the seeds of all the plants that grow on earth. Of this heavenly and immortal Haoma (Aryan Soma), the Haoma that grows in the mountains of Erân and from which is pressed the golden-colored liquor used at sacrifices is the earthly representative, and from it derives its healing and "death-removing" properties. As for the seeds of the plants, they are carried down to earth by the rain. The summits of Hara-Berezaiti being the abode of the gods, who have their several mansions there, it is but right that there also should be the store-houses of the choicest blessings which the gods bestow on men—the waters and vegetation.

8. Anthropomorphism, in its most direct, rank-

est form, is the very essence of Indo-Eranian and later Hindu speculation, so that, among the Âryas of India, Mythology entirely outgrew and, during a long period of time, almost smothered Religion.* In the sober, earnest-minded sister race, the tendency was all the other way—from anthropomorphism to spiritual abstraction. Therefore Aryan divinities when they turn up in the Avesta, generally retain only a few characteristic features, while the mythical exuberance of incident and description is greatly cut down. Thus we saw the Sun entitled the "swift-horsed." That the Sun has a chariot and horses is an understood thing ever since poetical forms of speech first began to crystallize into myths. Erân retained the standing by-word, without, however, playing on it the infinite variety of changes which we shall find in the Rig-Veda on this one theme. There is only one short, insignificant yesht (hymn) to the "undying, shining, swift-horsed Sun," and all the worshipper finds to say in praise of it is the matter-of-fact remark that its light purifies creation, and that, should it not rise up, the daêvas (demons) would destroy all things and the heavenly Yazatas (good spirits) would find no way of withstanding or repelling them. Again—the Dawn opening the gates of heaven and preceding the Sun on her golden chariot drawn by fleet horses, is an image as old as the first attempts at imaginative poetry and the theme of a hundred stories, for, in her character as the fairest of heavenly maidens, she is the favorite heroine of Aryan nature-myth. The Eranian has preserved only the shortest

* See "Story of Chaldea," pp. 331-334.

and driest mention of her, in a prayer to be recited at break of day, and where she is called "the beautiful Dawn, the shining, of the fleet and glittering horses," and is said to wake men to their work and to give light within the house.

9. Far more accentuated and developed is the mythical individuality of the Eranian Mithra, when separated from his original companion. One of the longest and finest hymns (Yesht X.) is devoted to him. In order to fully comprehend the mythical traits in it, it must be borne in mind that Mithra, like his Aryan namesake, is Light, the pure light of day, which fills the space apart from the splendor of the sun, whence his standing surname "lord of wide pastures" (heavenly space); whence also he is said both to precede the sun at his rising and to follow him after his setting; he is the morning and evening twilight, the dawn and the gloaming:

"The first of the heavenly gods who reaches over the Hara, before the undying, swift-horsed sun; who foremost, in golden array, takes hold of the beautiful summits, and from thence looks with a beneficent eye over the abodes of the Aryans, where the valiant chiefs draw up their many troops in array, where the high mountains, rich in pastures and waters, yield plenty to the cattle; where the deep lakes with salt waters stand; where wide-flowing rivers swell and hurry. . . .

"Who goes over the earth, all her breadth over, after the setting of the sun, touches both ends of this wide, round earth, whose ends lie afar, and surveys every thing that is between the earth and the heavens. . . .

"He who moves along all the Karshvars,* a Yazata unseen, and brings glory. .

* The earth is divided into seven regions or KARSHVARS, of which Erân is the largest and central one.

"For whom the Maker, Ahura-Mazda, has built up a dwelling on the Hara-Berezaiti, the bright mountain around which the many stars revolve, . . . and he surveys the whole of the material world from the Haraiti-Bareza. . . .

"With his arms lifted up towards Immortality" (towards the abode of the Immortals), "Mithra, the lord of wide pastures, drives forward from the shining Garô-nmâna, in a beautiful chariot . . . wrought by the Maker, Ahura-Mazda, inlaid with stars and made of a heavenly substance. . . .

"Four stallions draw that chariot, all of the same white color, living on heavenly food, and undying. The hoofs of their fore-feet are shod with gold; the hoofs of their hind-feet are shod with silver; all are yoked to the same pole, and wear the yoke, and the cross-beams of the yoke are fastened with hooks of metal, beautifully wrought. . . ."

10. Mithra, being in his essence Light, is the natural foe of the daêvas,—*i. e.*, the fiends of Darkness, who flee from before him in fear, or fall under the strokes of his never failing weapons; he is the protector and rescuer of the heavenly cattle which the demons are forever stealing and driving into their robber holds. This most primeval of Aryan myths is reproduced with beautiful entirety in a verse of Mithra's Yesht.

"The cow driven astray invokes him for help, longing for the stables: When will that Bull, Mithra, the lord of wide pastures, bring us back and make us reach the stables? When will he turn us back on the right way from the den of *Druj* (a name for "demon") whither we were driven?"

He is therefore essentially a warrior, the mightiest of warriors, and a patron of warriors, who gives victory in a righteous cause:

"A warrior, with a silver helm, a golden cuirass, who kills with the poniard, strong, valiant; . . the warrior of the white horse, of the sharp, long spear, the quick arrows. . . . Whom Ahura-Mazda has established to maintain and look over all this moving world, . . . who, never sleeping, wakefully guards the creation of Mazda, . . . he who stands up upon the earth as the strongest of all gods, the most valiant, the most energetic, the swiftest of all gods, the most fiend-smiting of all gods."

11. So much for the obviously physical part of the myth. The transition to the spiritual side is wonderfully easy and logical. MITHRA IS LIGHT, AND LIGHT IS ALL-PERVADING; THEREFORE MITHRA IS ALL-SEEING AND ALL-KNOWING; Ahura Mazda gave him a thousand senses and ten thousand eyes to see, he is the undeceivable watcher of men; or else he has ten thousand ears and ten thousand spies. MITHRA IS LIGHT, AND LIGHT IS TRUTH, AND TRUTH IS GOOD. THE DAÊVAS ARE DARKNESS, AND DARKNESS IS LIE, AND LIE IS EVIL. This most simple and primary conception, perhaps the only absolutely universal one, and, in all probability, the very first, because the most obvious, equation between the Visible and Invisible that occurred to thinking man all the world over, at once transfers the struggle, the championship, and the victory from the material into the spiritual world. He who is the Light of Absolute Truth is of his nature the foe and destroyer of Deceit, and Faithlessness, and Wrong, and all the evil brood of Darkness, and, as a practical application, the protector in open warfare of all whose cause is righteous, and, above all, the supreme guardian of covenants and punisher of bad faith. He who eludes or breaks the bonds of a contract is a "deceiver of Mithra,"—but Mithra is "the Undeceivable," his wrath and the curse of all good men is

sure to light on the foolish evil-doer, whom he routs and paralyzes:*

"On whatever side there is one who has lied to Mithra, on that side Mithra stands forth, angry and offended, and his wrath is slow to relent. Those who lie unto Mithra, however swift they may be running, cannot outrun him; riding, cannot outride him; driving, cannot outdrive him. The spear that the foe of Mithra flings darts backward; . . . and even though it be flung well, even though it reach the body, it makes no wound—the wind drives away the spear that the foe of Mithra flings. . . . He takes away the strength from their arms, the swiftness from their feet, the eye-sight from their eyes, the hearing from their ears. . . . He gives herds of oxen and male children to that house wherein he has been satisfied; he breaks to pieces those in which he has been offended. . . . Sad is the abode, unpeopled with children, where dwell men who have lied unto Mithra. . . . The grazing cow goes a sad, straying way, driven along the vales of the Mithra-deceivers; they stand on the road, letting tears run over their chins. . . ."

This is why Mithra is said to be "both good and bad to men, to keep in his hands both peace and trouble for nations." He stands a watchful guardian of the covenant, spoken or unspoken, which rules the relations between friends and kindred, between partners, between husband and wife, master and pupil, father and son, between nations.

"The man without glory, led astray from the right way, thinks thus in his heart: 'That careless Mithra does not see all the evil that is done, nor all the lies that are told.' But I think thus in my heart: 'Should the earthly man hear a hundred times better, he would not hear so well as the heavenly Mithra, who has a thousand senses and sees every one that tells a lie.'"

Nor is the faithful observance of contracts or

---

* Compare "Story of Chaldea." p. 171.

promises confined to fellow-Mazdayasnians ("worshippers of Mazda"). It is expressly said :

> "Break not the contract, neither the one that thou hadst entered into with one of the unfaithful, nor the one that thou hadst entered into with one of thy own faith. For Mithra stands both for the faithful and for the unfaithful."*

12. A spirited picture is that which the great Yesht brings before us, of Mithra going forth in his heavenly chariot, escorted by his helpers and friends, to do battle against the Powers of Evil and their human followers :

> "His chariot is embraced and uplifted by Holiness ; the Law of Mazda opens a way, that he may go easily ; four heavenly steeds, white, shining, seen afar, beneficent, endowed with knowledge, swiftly carry him along the heavenly space. . . . At his right hand drives the good, holy SRAOSHA (Obedience to the Law of Mazda) ; at his left drives the tall and strong RASHNU (Uprightness, Justice) ; on all sides of him . . . the FRAVASHIS of the faithful (the Spirits of the Departed). . . . Behind him drives Âtar (Fire), all in a blaze. . . ."

Before him and close by him run two dread beings—VERETHRAGHNA (Victory), and the "Strong Cursing Thought of the Wise," both described in identical words as wearing the shape of a "sharp-toothed, sharp-jawed boar, that kills at one stroke, pursuing, strong and swift to run, and rushing forward." Mithra is well armed for the fray—

> "Swinging in his hands a club with a hundred knots, a hundred edges, that rushes forward and fells men down ; a club cast out of red brass, . . . the strongest of all weapons, the most victorious of all weapons."

* It is noteworthy that *mithra* at last becomes a common noun, meaning "contract," and used as such in every-day speech.

His chariot, too, is a well-supplied armory: there are a thousand bows with their arrows, vulture-feathered, with golden points; a thousand spears and as many steel hammers; a thousand two-edged swords and as many maces of iron. All these weapons are described as "well-made," and as "going through the heavenly spaces and falling on the skulls of the daêvas." It would seem, from the way it is put, that they fly of their own accord, self-sped, to do havoc on the fiends. Such self-acting divine weapons are very plentiful in the Aryan mythology of India. Well may the worshipper exclaim: "Oh! may we never fall across the rush of Mithra, the lord of wide pastures, in his anger!"

13. This picture of a god riding to battle, with a full description of his armor, his chariot, his band of followers, etc., is a thoroughly Aryan one. Each Aryan god has his own "turn-out," and not one is passed over in the Rig-Veda. The anthropomorphism of the conception is rank. But in the case of the Eranian Mithra, it presents a feature characteristic of the race, and which, in its development, caused a complete revolution. It will have been observed that the followers of Mithra are no mythical persons, *i. e.*, no phenomena of nature turned into persons; but, consistently with the spiritual transformation of the myth, they are abstract ideas, or moral *qualities* personified: Holiness, Uprightness, Obedience to the religious Law; lastly, the "Curse of the Wise." This is not Myth—it is ALLEGORY, and one such instance is sufficient to illustrate the difference between the two notions and

the meaning of the two words. In one of Mithra's band, Myth and Allegory meet, or rather it is shown how easily and smoothly Myth can glide into Allegory. Verethraghna, the genius of Victory, is certainly an allegorical personage, an abstract idea which a capital initial converts into a person; for the word *verethragna* is a common noun which means "victory." But that word itself has a mythical import, being none other than the Eranian transliteration of the "*vritrahán*" ("Vritra-killer") of the Rig-Veda, the title of honor given to various "fiend-smiting" deities, but most frequently to Indra, the champion demon-killer of them all. (See p. 46.) This original meaning must have been quite forgotten before the name changed into a common noun meaning "victory" in general, and became personified once more, no longer mythically, but allegorically.

14. This tendency to close the eyes to the ever-varying play of physical nature and turn them inward, to the contemplation of high moral abstractions, till these seem almost tangible realities, is the indication of a very serious mind and the key to the transformation which the myth-religion of the ancient Aryas underwent at the hands of their sterner Eranian descendants. The most notable instance of such allegorical transformation is that practised on Ahura-Mazda himself. The original identity with the old sky-god once having subsided out of sight, preserved only in a few traditional and unconscious forms of speech, his spiritual nature became the subject of earnest and profound speculation. They sought to express his various attributes by a variety

of names, such as "Perfect Holiness," "Creator," or "Maker of the material world," "Keeper and Maintainer," the Best of Sovereigns," "the Bestower of Health," "All-Weal," "He who does not deceive and is not deceived," etc.; lastly, "the Beneficent Spirit," SPENTA-MAINYU, a name which is used preferably to all others, as fully designating his essence and nature, and opposing him to the Other One, the Spirit of Evil. Certain qualities and properties seemed especially to belong to him, or to be awarded by him, such as (1) good thoughts, (2) perfect holiness, (3) excellent sovereignty, (4) piety, (5) health, (6) immortality; and by dint of being prayed *for*, as Ahura-Mazda's *gifts*, came to be prayed *to*, as his *ministering spirits*, created by him. This, the inevitable anthropomorphic tendency asserting itself, brought about one of the most characteristic institutions of Mazdeism,— the heavenly council of the Bountiful Immortals, the AMESHA-SPENTAS (the AMSHA-SPANDS or archangels of the modern Parsis). They are seven in number, Ahura-Mazda being one of them, though he is said to have created the others. When they are invoked or referred to, it is often quite difficult to distinguish whether their names are used in their literal sense or as persons. The former, however, is most frequently the case in the earliest period, that of the Gâthas, where the allegory is always very transparent. It is only in time that it hardens into solid personifications, when the Amesha-Spentas are not only separate and individual spirits, but have certain clearly defined functions assigned to them in the general guardianship of the world.

15. Before we examine into the nature of the Amesha-Spentas as a body and their relations to their chief and maker, it will be well to review them individually, specifying their original meaning and later development.

1st. Ahura-Mazda, Spenta-Mainyu,—the Beneficent Spirit, uncreated, "creator of all things."

2nd. Vohu-Manô, —the "Good Mind" or "Benevolent Mind" that state of mind which is conducive to peace and good-will toward men generally, and gives the wisdom of moderation, of conciliation. At a later period he became the protector of cattle, cattle-raising being an essentially peaceful and kindly avocation, which, moreover, can prosper only in times of peace.

3rd. Asha-Vahishta,—" Best " or " Perfect Holiness," that conforms in every particular, " in thought, in word, and in deed," to the law of Mazda, especially as regards religious observances; later the protector of Fire, as the embodiment of Purity and Worship, of ritual and priestly functions; in reality the Law itself, the Order which rules the world.

4th. Khshathra-Vairya, — " Excellent Sovereignty," the power which comes from God, and therefore is beneficent, merciful, and the guardian of order and law. Becomes the protector of metals, possibly because royalty has always been in the habit of reserving to itself the wealth drawn from the earth, especially gold and silver.

5th. Spenta-Armaiti, — " Holy Piety," patient and humble simple-mindedness. Also Earth personified, or the Spirit of Earth, and that at a very early period, as early as the Gâthas. The only female Amesha-Spenta, whose sex, name, and attributions are easily explained as a reminiscence of a rather misty Aryan deity, whom we find in the Rig-Veda under the name of ARAMATÎ, and who, like her younger Eranian namesake, personifies both the Earth and the virtue of devotion.

6th and 7th. HAURVATÂT AND AMERETÂT,— "Health and Immortality,"—a divine couple almost never mentioned or invoked separately, and who, by a process at once logical and poetical, remained closely united in the functions assigned to them in the material world,—that of guardians of the waters and the plants on earth. The wholesomeness of pure running water, both in itself and as provoking and fostering vegetation, and its healing properties, naturally commended it to the care of the Genius of Health; while the trees and plants, with their latent and ever-replenished vitality, have always been a meet symbol of immortality. And one must have travelled or lived in lands of drought and barrenness, where the course of the tiniest streamlet is marked by its fringe of verdure or foliage, sometimes no wider than itself, where not a spring or well but is shaded by its palm or plane tree, fully to realize the aptness of the conception which unites the running water and the growing plant into the inseparable couple, "Haurvatât and Ameretât," who are also said to give food its rich and pleasant taste.

16. It is quite evident from several passages that the Amesha-Spentas were originally one with Ahura-Mazda, who, on being asked by Zarathushtra which

of all holy words is the strongest, the most effective, the most fiend-smiting, replies:

"Our Name, O Spitâma Zarathushtra! who are the Amesha-Spentas,—that is the strongest part of the Holy Word, that is the most victorious, that is the most glorious, the most effective, the most fiend-smiting, that is the best-healing. . . ." (Yesht I.)

The most decisive evidence is contained in the following passage:

". . . The luminous ones, . . . who are all seven of one thought, who are all seven of one speech, who are all seven of one deed, . . . *whose father and commander is the same, namely, the Maker, Ahura-Mazda.* Who see one another's souls, thinking of good thoughts, thinking of good words, thinking of good deeds, thinking of Garô-nmâna, and whose ways are shining. Who are the makers and governors, the shapers and overseers, the keepers and preservers of the creations of Ahura-Mazda. . . ." (Yeshts XIII. and XIX.)

The lines in italics have clearly been added when the conception of Mazda's supremacy had reached the height of an almost absolute monotheism, and no Power or Being could be allowed to exist who was not created by him, even though they share the act of creation with him. In the same spirit Ahura-Mazda, in one hymn, is made to present the Immortals to his prophet, singly and by name, thus: "Here is Vohu-manô, my creature, O Zarathushtra! Here is Asha-Vahishta, my creature, O Zarathushtra," etc. (Yesht I.) It is in consequence of the same afterthought that he is made to say of Mithra, originally as much his companion and equal as the Aryan Mitra is of Vâruna: "Verily, *when I created* Mithra, lord of wide pastures, I created him as worthy of sacrifice, as worthy of prayer, as myself,

Ahura-Mazda." Thus again, and consistently with what gradually became the leading idea of Mazdeism, the name of every god, however powerful, however exalted and reverenced, is frequently accompanied, as a reminder, by the epithet "created by Ahura." Therefore it is that all the "created" gods ceased in time to be thus styled, and, together with all beneficent spirits, were gathered under the designation of YAZATAS—the YZEDS, Angels, of the modern Parsis. Mithra, Verethraghna, Sraosha, Âtar, etc., are Yazatas; so are the Sun, the Moon, and all good spirits, whether representing natural forces or abstractions. Their number is unlimited:

"When the light of the sun waxes warmer . . . then up stand the heavenly Yazatas, by hundreds and thousands . . . they pour its glory upon the earth made by the Ahura."

They all dwell in the Endless Light, eternal and uncreated,—"the Garô-nmâna, the abode of Ahura-Mazda, the abode of the Amesha-Spentas, the abode of all the other holy beings."

17. As Ahura surely was himself, once on a time, the original one "Bountiful Immortal," so this title was probably bestowed on other beneficent beings, before the ancient sacredness of the number seven, and, possibly a dim reminiscence of the Aryan Âdityas, of whom Váruna was the chief, (see p. 41) confined it to Ahura and his six doubles. In one passage Âtar is called "the most helpful of the Amesha-Spentas," but it is a solitary, queer survival. His proper titles are, "Son of Ahura-Mazda" and "most great Yazata." As the one who is nearest to man, who sits on his hearth, the kindly bond of family

and state, he is addressed and spoken of with a respectful tenderness, an affectionate familiarity, which is sometimes very pretty in its *naïveté*.

"Âtar, the son of Ahura-Mazda, lifts up his voice to all those for whom he cooks their evening meal and their morning meal. From all those he wishes a good offering. . . . Âtar looks at the hands of all those who pass by: 'What does the friend bring to his friend? What does he who comes and goes bring to him who stays motionless?' And if the passer-by brings him wood holily brought . . . then Âtar, the son of Ahura-Mazda, well pleased with him and not angry, and fed as required, will thus bless him: 'May herds of oxen grow for thee, and increase of sons. . . . mayest thou live on in joy of thy soul all the nights of thy life.' This is the blessing that Âtar speaks unto him who brings him dry wood, well examined by the light of the day, well cleansed with godly intent."

For if to the Âthravans—the officially instituted class of priests—was committed the care of the sacred fires in the public places of worship, each householder's first religious duty was to tend the fire of his own hearth, to trim and clean it, and never suffer it to go out. This was a more arduous task than appears at first sight, as the flame was to be fed not only constantly, but daintily, with small quantities, continually renewed, of driest, finely-cut chips of the best, and in part fragrant, wood, such as sandal, " well examined by the light of the day, and well cleansed," so that no impurity of any kind should pollute the sacred element; besides which a good Mazdayasnian had to get up three times in the night (as the Parsis do now, for that matter) to look after it.

"In the first part of the night, Âtar, the son of Ahura-Mazda, calls the master of the house for help, saying: 'Up! arise, thou master of the house! put on thy girdle and thy clothes, wash thy hands, saw wood, bring it unto me, and let me burn bright with the clean wood, carried by thy well-washed hands. Here comes Aji (the Fiend-Serpent, Darkness), made by the daêvas, who is about to strive against me and wants to put out my life."

And so "in the second," and "in the third part of the night."

18. In the persistent enmity between the demon Aji and Âtar, which endures throughout the Avesta (with the exception of the Gâthas), we easily recognize the struggle between the Aryan Fiend-Serpent Ahi and the Storm-god, as embodied in his principal weapon—the Lightning. In one of the Eranian versions of the conflict, very dramatic in form, the latter even resumes his Vedic name of "Son of the Waters," and is called indiscriminately Âtar, or APĀNM-NAPÂT (see p. 45); it is where the two everlasting adversaries do battle for the light which hides in the sea Vouru-Kasha, the Cloud-Sea. The transformation which this simple myth—one of the oldest—undergoes from the spiritualizing process of Eranian thought is very remarkable: the light, originally meant in a literal sense, becomes a subtle and sacred splendor—the HVARENÔ, or "Glory,"— a peculiar and visible golden sheen, which must be imagined as surrounding the head and shoulders of persons endowed with it, after the manner of the halo around the heads of saints and angels in modern paintings. This "awful Kingly Glory,"—probably a portion or reflection of the eternal, uncreated Endless Light wherein God dwells,—belongs, in the first place, to Ahura-Mazda, to the Amesha-Spentas, and to all the Yazatas, then "to the Aryan

nations, born and unborn," and lastly to every lawful Aryan king as a sign of divine grace, and perhaps, in mythical times, of divine descent. He to whom it "cleaves" is assured of wealth, of power, prosperity, and victory; himself unconquerable, he exterminates his enemies. But the Hvarenô cannot be seized by violence or usurped by aliens; and, if a king endowed with it tells a lie, it straightway passes away from him. Certain Yeshts give instances of both these occurrences, taken from the rich store of the national mythical epos. The most amusing is the story of that "most crafty Turanian ruffian, Frangrasyan," who thrice stripped himself naked and plunged into the sea Vouru-Kasha, "wishing to seize that Glory that belongs to the Aryan nations." But the Glory escaped him every time, until at last he "rushed out of the sea Vouru-Kasha, thinking evil thoughts," and was fain to confess: "I have not been able to conquer the glory that belongs to the Aryan nations, born and unborn, and to the holy Zarathushtra!" A most ingenious, half mythical, half allegorical rendering of unsuccessful Turanian invasions.

19. But the Eranian Storm-god *par excellence* is TISHTRYA, the star Sirius, known also as the Dog-Star. The Eranians very curiously associated rain with certain stars, which are said to contain the "seed of the waters." Over these—and, indeed, it would appear, over all the stars—Tishtrya is set as chief *ratu*:

"We sacrifice unto Tishtrya, the bright and glorious star, who moves in light with the stars that have in them the seed of the waters, whom Ahura-Mazda has established as a lord and overseer above all stars. . . ." (Yesht VIII.)

This star presides over the dog-days, which, in hot climes, are immediately followed by heavy rains. Hence its rising is invoked with passionate longing by the people of a region where the streams are all rain-fed and dry up in the rainless season, while most of them do not flow into other streams, or lakes, but are greedily and profitlessly sucked up by the sand of the desert.

"We sacrifice unto Tishtrya, the bright and glorious star, for whom long flocks, and herds, and men, looking forward for him and deceived in their hope. 'When shall we see him rise up, the bright and glorious star Tishtrya? When will the springs run with waves as thick as a horse's size and still thicker? Or will they never come? . . .'

"We sacrifice unto Tishtrya, the bright and glorious star, for whom long the standing waters, and the running spring-waters, the stream-waters, and the rain-waters. 'When will the bright and glorious Tishtrya rise up for us? When will the springs, with a flow and overflow of waters, thick as a horse's shoulder, run to the beautiful places and fields, and to the pastures, even to the roots of the plants, that they may grow with a powerful growth? . . .'

"We sacrifice unto Tishtrya, the bright and glorious star, whose rising is watched by men who live on the fruits of the year, by the chiefs of deep understanding; by the wild beasts in the mountains, by the tame beasts that run in the plains; they watch him as he comes up to the country, for a bad year or for a good year, thinking in themselves: 'How shall the Aryan countries be fertile?'"

The dog-days are the hottest and driest of the year; it is the time of Tishtrya's great conflict against APAOSHA, the Drought-Fiend, a conflict in which he is several times worsted before he comes off victorious at the last. The god appears in three different shapes—for ten nights in that of a beautiful youth, for ten in that of a golden-horned bull, and for the last ten as a beautiful white horse with golden ears and golden caparison. It is in this shape that he gives the final battle to his demon antagonist, who rushes down to meet him by the Cloud-Sea—Vouru-Kasha,—in the shape of an ugly black horse, with black ears and tail.

"They meet together, hoof against hoof. . . . They fight together for three days and three nights. And then the Daeva Apaosha proves stronger than the bright and glorious Tishtrya ; he overcomes him. And Tishtrya flees from the sea Vouru-Kasha. : . He cries out in woe and distress. . . ." (Yesht VIII.)

He cries out for sacrifices to be offered him, to "bring strength" to him, and, having received them, rushes back to the sea Vouru-Kasha. But it is only at the third encounter that he finally routs the Black Horse.

"He makes the sea boil up and down ; he makes the sea stream this and that way. . . . All the shores are boiling over ; all the middle of it is boiling over. . . . And vapors rise up above the middle of the sea Vouru-Kasha. . . . Then the wind blows the clouds forward, bearing the waters of fertility, so that the friendly showers spread wide over ; they spread helpingly and friendly over the seven Karshvars. ." (Yesht VIII.)

But there is not water enough for all the Aryan countries, and the distribution of it becomes the occasion of another conflict between the warriors of heaven, the FRAVASHIS of the faithful (Departed Spirits, corresponding to the Pitris of the Hindus, see p. 53 54).

"The good, strong, beneficent Fravashis of the faithful ; with helms of brass, with weapons of brass, with armor of brass ; who struggle in the fights for victory in garments of light, arraying the battles and bringing them forwards, to kill thousands of daēvas. . . .

"When the waters come up from the sea Vouru-Kasha, . . . then forwards come the awful Fravashis of the faithful, many and many hundreds, many and many thousands, many and many tens of thousands, seeking water for their own kindred, for their own borough, for their own town, for their own country, and saying thus: 'May our own country have a good store and full joy!'

"They fight in the battles that are fought in their own place and land, each according to the place and house where he dwelt of yore; they look like a gallant warrior, who, girded up and faithful, fights for the hoard he has treasured up.

"And those of them who win, bring waters to their own kindred, to their own borough, to their own town, to their own country, saying thus: 'May my country grow and increase!'"

20. As the Fravashis are also supposed to help their own people in their earthly wars, and to perform all sorts of good offices for the material world in general, it will be seen that prudence no less than affection prompted their living descendants to pay them honor and offer them gifts. Nor are they difficult to propitiate. For they are gentle, and ready to confer benefits; "their friendship is good, and lasts long; they like to stay in the abode where they are not harmed by its dwellers," and they "never do harm first," though "their will is dreadful unto those who vex them." The last few days of the year (10th –20th of March) are specially devoted to them, and at that time

". . . they come and go through the borough . . . they go along there for ten nights, asking thus: 'Who will praise us? Who will offer us a sacrifice? Who will meditate upon us? Who will bless us? Who will receive us with meat and clothes in his hand, and with a prayer worthy of bliss? Of which of us will the name be taken for invocation?' . . . And the man who offers them up a sacrifice, with meat and clothes in his hand, and a prayer worthy of bliss, the awful Fravashis of the faithful, satisfied, unharmed, and unoffended, bless thus: 'May there be in this house flocks of animals and men! May there be a swift horse and a solid chariot! May there be a man who knows how to praise God and rule in his assembly!' . . ."

21. It is not the Fravashis alone who ask thus openly and eagerly for gifts and offerings. We saw the Storm-god Tishtrya crying out for sacrifices to "bring him strength," when sorely pressed by the Drought-Fiend Apaosha. So does Mithra, wishing for strength to perform his appointed work, ever cry out to Ahura-Mazda:

"Who will offer me a sacrifice? . . . If men would worship me with a sacrifice in which I were invoked by my own name, as they worship the other Yazatas, . . . I would come to the faithful at the appointed time of my beautiful immortal life."

Ardvi-Sûra Anâhita, as she drives forward on her chariot, drawn by four white horses, and holding the reins, longs for the worship of men, and thinks in her heart: "Who will praise me? Who will offer me a sacrifice, with libations cleanly prepared and well-strained, together with the Haoma and meat?"

22. The old Aryan conception of the efficacy, the compelling force of sacrifice, asserts itself with great emphasis in the Avesta, where we see not only the famous mythical heroes sacrificing hundreds and thousands of bullocks, horses, and sheep to various deities, principally Haoma, Ardvi-Sûra Anâhita, and Vayu, when asking for some special boon, but the gods offering sacrifices to each other on the heights of the Hara-Berezaiti. Nay, Ahura-Mazda himself

is no exception, and is said to offer a sacrifice to this or that divinity—by him created!—to request his or her assistance in the protection of the material world against the evil powers. This glaring inconsistency can be explained only by the different stages of a religion, in which Ahura-Mazda was a god among other gods before he became the One Supreme God and Creator.

23. Nor has the belief in the conjuring efficacy of prayers and sacred texts—the MANTHRA—at all abated in the Eranian period. The Manthra is again and again spoken of and invoked as a divine person. So are the Gâthas, and also certain prayers which are considered as particularly holy and wonder-working. But the most potent spell of all, the most healing, most fiend-smiting, lies in a prayer known under the Parsi name (corrupt) of HONOVER, called in the Avesta the AHUNA-VAIRYA, a prayer which a devout Parsi even now repeats dozens of times every day on every possible occasion of life. This famous prayer is written in so obscure a language that a final and satisfactory rendering of it has not yet been achieved, though every Avestan scholar has attempted a translation. The discrepancies between these translations are so great and the sense remains so uncertain still, that it is scarcely possible to make a selection between them, and to give them all would be confusing and unprofitable. The most extravagant magic powers are ascribed to this sacred text, which Ahura-Mazda is said to have first uttered "before the creation of heaven, before the making of the waters, and the plants, and the

four-footed kine and the holy biped man, and before the sun," and to have revealed to Zarathushtra, who recited it first to mortal men.

"This word," Ahura-Mazda is made to say, "is the most emphatic of the words which ever have been pronounced, or which are now spoken, or which shall be spoken in future, for the eminence of this utterance is such a thing, that if all the corporal and living world should learn it, and learning it should hold fast by it, they would be redeemed from their mortality!"

The sacred names of Ahura-Mazda, the Amesha-Spentas, and some others, share this power of incantation, as we saw above. (See p. 76.)

24. The process of allegorical transformation which gradually permeated the whole mythic system of Erân, here found a most grateful field. The conjuring spell hurled against the physical fiends representing the evil powers of material nature, were changed into the spiritual weapons of prayer and obedience to the holy Law, used with infallible success against the spiritual fiends,—Anger, Rapine, Sloth, and, above all, the Spirit of Lies,—who dwell in every man's own breast. That is the club, ever uplifted agains the daêvas, which the Yazata Sraosha carries (the personified Obedience to Mazda's Law), he "whose very body is the Law," and who therefore is the most actively militant adversary of the daêvas. It is in this sense that the Ahuna-Vairya is said to smite the fiends "as hard as a stone large as a house." When he hears it recited, the Arch-Fiend himself cowers and writhes and shrinks, and hides in the bowels of the earth.

25. For the Serpent, Ahi, the mythical Aryan

dragon that guards the fastnesses where the stolen cows or maidens are locked away, now called AJI or AJI-DAHÂKA (the "Biting Snake"), touched by the same magic rod of spiritual transformation, henceforth personated moral evil in all its odiousness and ugliness, and began to be called "ANGRA-MAINYU," the "Destructive Sprit," in direct opposition to Spenta-Mainyu, the Beneficent or Life-giving Spirit. By this time system-making had become a habit of the Eranian mind, and as every system, being an artificial construction, requires symmetry, Angra-Mainyu (better known under the corrupt later form, AHRIMAN), from being one of the names of the original Serpent, grew into a separate abstraction, an Arch-fiend, the exact counterpart of Spenta-Mainyu or Ahura-Mazda: the one all Light, Truth, Life, and Good; the other all Darkness, Lie, Death, and Evil. And henceforth the world was divided between them. Both being possessed of creative power, all that was good in it, material or spiritual, was the work of Spenta-Mainyu; all that was evil, of Angra-Mainyu. In this manner those profound but simple-minded thinkers got out of the terrible puzzle of accounting for the existence of evil in the world, for they could not comprehend the necessity of it, and therefore would not admit that it could have been created by the All-good and All-wise Being. The two spirits must have existed from the beginning, independent of each other, and the world and life, as we see them, are nothing but the manifestation of their eternal enmity and conflict. When moral speculation had attained this height the race was ripe for a prophet, to give the gradually evolved new consciousness the form and consistency of a faith, to purify it and separate it from the dross of ancient myth that still clung round it and clogged the spiritual progress of the aspiring but inconsistent popular mind.

26. To carry out the title of this chapter, it should end with a review of such Aryan myths as became the groundwork of the Eranian Heroic Epos, one of the richest in the world, so far as they have found a place in the Avesta. There are many such, but in a very fragmentary condition and too much out of the scope of the present work to be considered. One, however, is given with great completeness, although the different traits and incidents are scattered in many places of the book, and is too important and interesting to be overlooked. It is the myth of YIMA, the first king, the Eranian rendering of the Aryan myth of YAMA, originally the Setting Sun, then the first mortal and King of the Dead (see pp. 52-53). The story, ancient in itself, shows traces of a late rehandling in the way it is told, but must be given as we find it, as it would be spoiled by being picked to pieces.

"O Maker of the material world!" Zarathushtra is made to ask of Ahura-Mazda, "who was the first mortal before myself, with whom thou didst converse, whom thou didst teach the law?" Ahura-Mazda answers: "The fair Yima, the great shepherd"; and proceeds to tell that he offered Yima to be the preacher and bearer of his law to men, but Yima declined, not deeming himself fit. Then Ahura-

Mazda bade him rule his world, and watch over it, and make it thrive. Yima accepted the task, and Ahura-Mazda brought him a golden ring and poniard.* He sacrificed on the sacred height Hukairya to Ardvi-Sûra Anâhita, Haoma, Vayu, asking for various boons which they granted. He became the sovereign lord of countries, and ruled not only over men, but over the daêvas, and Mazda's Kingly Glory (Hvarenô) was around him. That was the Golden Age of the world. In his reign there was neither cold nor heat, neither old age nor death, neither hot wind nor cold wind, and there was great fatness and abundance of flocks in the world created by Mazda. Herds and people were free from death, plants and waters were free from drought; fathers and sons walked about equally perfect in shape, which was that of youths of fifteen years. So were things while Yima ruled, he of the many flocks, and that was during a thousand years. Of these, three hundred years had passed away, and the earth was replenished with flocks and herds, with men and dogs and birds, and red, blazing fires, and there was no more room for flocks, herds, and men. Then Yima, being warned by Ahura-Mazda, pressed the earth with the golden ring and bored it with the poniard, speaking thus: "O Spenta-Armaiti (see p. 75), kindly open asunder and stretch thyself afar, to bear flocks and herds and men." And the earth, at Yima's bidding, grew one third larger than it was before, and there came flocks and herds and men, at his will and wish, as many as he wished. When six hundred years of

* So Darmesteter. DeHarlez renders "a golden plough and an ox-goad."

his sway had passed away, Yima again bade the earth open and stretch, and again when nine hundred years had passed away, and each time the earth grew by one third of its original size. When he had reigned a thousand years, Ahura-Mazda called a great meeting in Airyana-Vaêjâ, and came thither with all the gods; thither also came Yima with the most excellent mortals.

"And Ahura-Mazda spake unto Yima, saying: 'O fair Yima, son of Vivanghat! Upon the material world the fatal winters are going to fall, that shall bring the fierce, foul frost, that shall make snowflakes fall thick and lie deep on the highest tops of mountains. And all the three sorts of beasts shall perish: those that live in the wilderness, and those that live on the tops of the mountains, and those that live in the bosom of the dale under the shelter of stables. Before that winter those fields would bear plenty of grass for cattle; now with floods that stream, with snows that melt, it will seem a happy land in the world, the land wherein footprints even of sheep may be seen. Therefore make thee a *Vara* (an enclosure) . . .'"

Here follow minute instructions: "Thou shalt do so and so," which, being complied with, are repeated word for word with change of tense—past instead of future,—after the manner of ancient epic narrative. We give the narrative as the more lively form:

"And Yima made a Vara . . . to be an abode for men, to be a fold for flocks. There he made waters flow in a bed a *hâthra* long (about a mile); there he settled birds by the everlasting banks that bear never-failing food. There he established dwelling-places. . . . There he brought the seeds of men and women,* of the

---

* To be put in the ground and grow in due time. According to the later Cosmogony of the Bundehesh, the first human couple grew up in the shape of a shrub, then blossomed into human form and separated. So are the different kinds of animals supposed to have come from seed. We saw above that the stars are said to contain the seeds of the waters.

greatest, best, and finest kinds on this earth ; there he brought the seeds of every kind of cattle, of the greatest, best, and finest kinds on this earth ; there he brought the seeds of every kind of tree, of the greatest, best, and finest kinds on this earth ; there he brought the seeds of every kind of fruit, the fullest of food and sweetest of odor. All those seeds he brought, two of every kind, to be kept inexhaustible there, so long as those men shall stay in the Vara. And there was no humpbacked, none bulged forward there ; no impotent, no lunatic, no poverty, no lying, no meanness, no jealousy ; no decayed tooth, no leprous to be confined, nor any of the brands with which Angra-Mainyu stamps the bodies of mortals. . . . Every fortieth year, to every couple two are born, a male and a female. And thus it is for every sort of cattle, and the men in the Vara, which Yima made live the happiest life. . . ."

Some commentators say they live there 150 years, others, that they never die. The latter come nearest to the mythical truth of the story, as there can be no doubt that Yima's Vara originally answered to Yama's seat of bliss, and its inhabitants to the Pitris—the souls of the departed. The Avesta narrative adds, —evidently a late appendage to the old myth,—that a wonderful bird brought the Law of Mazda into the Vara and preached it there. The mythical legends of India know of several such wise and speech-endowed birds.

27. There is another version of the end of Yima's rule, a more human and very tragical one, which has been adopted in the Heroic Epos of Erân. It is also mentioned in the Avesta. There came a day when Yima fell and sinned. He " began to find delight in words of falsehood and untruth." In fact, it is stated plainly, that he told a lie. But what the lie was the Avesta does not inform us. Epic tradition however does. Seeing both men and daêvas subject

to his rule, his heart was lifted up in pride, and he declared himself to be a god. From this moment Mazda's Kingly Glory (the Hvarenô) flew away from him in the shape of a raven — one of the visible forms which Verethraghna, the Genius of Victory, is said to assume. Yima also taught men to kill innocent animals and eat their flesh, which was another grievous wrong. Three times the Glory flew away from him; he lost his sovereignty, wandered about an outcast, and finally perished miserably, being sawed in two, according to the Avesta, by his own brother; according to the heroic legend, by his mortal foe, the wicked usurper ZOHÂK — the Persian corrupt form of "Aji-Dahâk," — the primeval Serpent being, like the other personages of the heavenly drama, brought down to earth and presented in a human incarnation.

28. It is very curious that one detail of the old Aryan myth of Yama should have survived in Erân, in the practical form of a religious ceremony, which is enjoined on the followers of Zoroaster, and strictly observed by them to this day. The reader will remember Yama's dogs, "brown, broad-snouted, four-eyed," who scent out those who are to die and drive them to the presence of the dread king, at the same time guarding them from the dangers and fiends that beset the dark road they travel. (See p. 53). The Avestan Law prescribes that "a yellow dog with four eyes" shall be brought to the side of any person that has just died, and made to look at the corpse, as the look of the four-eyed dog is supposed to drive away the impure demon, (NASU), that strives to enter

it and take possession of the clay tenement, which, from the moment that life leaves it, becomes the property of Angra-Mainyu, in order thence to work contamination and harm on all who approach it. As it may be supposed that some difficulty was found in procuring the animal in question, the law makes the following qualifying concession: "A yellow dog with four eyes, or a white dog with yellow ears." The latter variety being more generally on hand, there is nothing to prevent conscientious Parsis from performing this time-honored ceremony, which they call the SAGDÎD, and of the mythical origin and import of which they are, of course, profoundly ignorant.*

* For the quotations from the Vendîdâd and the Lesser Avesta the translation of Mr. James Darmesteter has been and will be used throughout.

V.

THE GÂTHAS.—THE YASNA OF SEVEN CHAPTERS.

1. MAZDAYASNIANS and DAÊVAYASNIANS,—
"Worshippers of God and worshippers of the
Fiends"; such is the division of mankind according
to the Zoroastrian faith. There can be no middle
way. Whoever is not with Mazda is against him.
Whoever does not enlist to fight the good fight with
Spenta-Mainyu, the Spirit who is all Life, necessarily swells the ranks of Angra-Mainyu, the Spirit who
is all Death. The material world is divided between
them, and its various phenomena are but the visible
manifestation of the war they wage against each
other. That war has its parallel in the spiritual
world. There the battle-ground is in every man's
own breast, and the stake is every man's own soul.
But not without the man's consent can the stake be
won by either; it is with him to choose. And as he
chooses and abides by his choice, so will it fare with
him when his day of combat is done, and he either
crosses the Bridge of the Gatherer,* and passes into
the abode of God that dwells in Endless Light, or

---

* The Bridge CHINVAT, which is thrown across space from one of
the highest peaks of the Hara-Berezaiti to the Garô-nmâna, for the
soul to pass after death. This is the last ordeal, which none but the
godly successfully pass through.

misses his footing, and is dragged down into the "abode of Lie," which is Endless Darkness.

2. Towards this loftiest and purest, while also simplest, of all the doctrines that the ancient world has taught, tended the evolution of the primeval Aryan Dualism of Nature, as it was effected in the Iranian spiritual consciousness, moulded and directed by the peculiar conditions of Iranian life. That this evolution did not waste itself in vague and profitless repinings and speculations, like the streams of Erân in the barren sands, but culminated in a positive faith, fruitful in works, like cloud-fed springs that are gathered to a head and flow forth, a mighty and life-giving river, into the haunts of men—this is due to the genius and preaching of Zarathushtra. He laid before his people their own thoughts in all the pure transparency of crystal waters cleared from muddiness and unwholesome admixtures in the filter of his own transcendant and searching mind. He guided their groping hands, and made them grasp the truth for which they were blindly reaching. Such is the mission of every true prophet. Had the people not been ripe for his teaching, he could not have secured a hearing, or made himself understood; the people, on the other hand, could never have worked out unaided the ideal to which they were vaguely and only half-consciously drawn. They listened and understood, and were won, because, to use the expression of a great writer,* they

---

* Voltaire. He says of the hero of one of his stories, that he reflected profoundly on a certain idea, " of which he seemed to have the seed in himself."

had in themselves the seed of the thoughts which the prophet expounded to them.

3. Even if we lack data to determine the time of Zarathushtra's life and work, there is sufficient intrinsic evidence in the Gâthas, which were most probably taken down partly from the prophet's own words and partly from those of some of his immediate disciples, to show that he lived at a period which must be considered an early one in the history of his race. In their slow advance to the West, the Eranians were continually harassed by fleetly mounted Scythian hordes (Turân), and encountered scattered tribes of the same hostile race all along the broad and irregular track of their migration. These savage nomads, ubiquitous with their small, untiring steppe-horses and their unerring lassoes, were the standing terror of the Eranian settlers, whose pastures and farms were not for one moment secure from their raids. In the national Heroic Epos, which is the Battle-Myth of the Skies transferred to earth, the Eranian hero-kings answer to the Aryan gods, whose names they ofttimes bear, and their Turanian adversaries—lawless invaders, iniquitous usurpers and tyrants,—to the Aryan demons.* And in the time of the allegorical transformation of myths, which already approaches the historical period, we see Violence, Lawlessness, and Rapine,

* Compare Yima, son of Vivanghat — Yama, son of Vivasvat. Also, Thraetaôna, son of Athwya — Trita, son of Aptya; in the Epos Thraetaôna becomes the famous Persian hero-king FERIDÛN, who vanquishes the wicked usurper Zohâk — Aji-Dahâka, and chains him under Mt. Demavend in the Elburz.

the characteristic features of the Turanian nomads and raiders, embodied in the person of AÊSHMA-DAÊVA, the first and worst of daêvas after the Arch-Fiend himself, as Sraosha, the personified Obedience to Mazda's holy Law, is the first of the Yazatas. The prayer, "Deliver us from Aêshma," therefore has a twofold purport: "Deliver us from the raids of the Turanians, the foes of the honest herdsman and tiller of the land," and also, "Deliver us from the temptation of ourselves committing violence and robbery."

4. That the Turanians were accounted Daêva-yasnians, worshippers of Fiends, is self-evident. But not they alone. Scarcely less hated of Zarathushtra and his followers are such communities of their own Aryan race as resisted the progressive movement towards spiritual and enlightened monotheism, and persisted in sacrificing to the gods of the old Aryan nature-worship. There were doubtless many such, and it is certainly to them, their leader, and their priests, that Zarathushtra alludes when he speaks of the evil teachers that corrupt the people's mind, of the persecutions which made him and his followers homeless wanderers (see p. 24). Nor can the prophet be said to advise his own disciples to deal with these unbelievers exactly in a spirit of charity. Not only are they bitterly, wrathfully denounced throughout the Gâthas, but their extermination is demanded in no equivocal terms: he who hurls from power or from life " the evil ruler who opposes" the progress of Righteousness in his province, will treasure up "a store of sacred wisdom"; any one who brings

harm on the settlements of the prophet's followers, let his evil deeds recoil on himself, let his prosperity be blighted, let him perish and "no help come to him to keep him back from misery. And let this happen as I speak, Lord!" On the other hand none, not even Turanian tribes, if they will be converted, are excluded from the community of the pious. An important and authentic precept for this triumph of religious brotherhood over race-feeling is established by the following explicit statement ·

"When from among the tribes and kith of the Turanians those shall arise who further on the settlements of Piety with energy and zeal, with these shall Ahura dwell together through his Good-Mind (*vohu-manô*) [which will abide in them], and to them for joyful grace deliver his commands." (Yasna XLVI, 12. L. H. Mills' translation.)

5. There can be little doubt that the feelings of hatred and contempt with which Zarathushtra inspired his followers against those of the old Aryan religion were amply reciprocated by the latter, not only by such as still lived or roamed side by side with them in the cultivated regions or the wilds of Erân, but also by those who had already descended into India. This supplies us with the most natural explanation of some facts which would otherwise be difficult to account for: the use by the Zarathushtrian Eranians of the word *daêva* with the meaning of "demon, fiend," while Sanskrit *deva* continued in the sister nation of India to denote the gods of Light, the bright and beneficent Powers, as it had done in the joint Indo-Eranian period, and probably in the primeval Aryan times,—together with the corres-

ponding use by the Aryan Hindus in the same evil sense of the Sanskrit *Asura* (= Eranian *Ahura*). This latter fact derives its significancy from the circumstance that the older Aryan Hindus gave to the word the same meaning as the Eranians, that of "Lord," "divine," and used it as the loftiest title of several of the deities, especially of their Sky-gods, the primeval Dyáus and his successor Váruna, to whom a certain notion of supremacy or overlordship seems to have attached from the earliest times. *Asura* is used in this wholly reverential sense in the greatest part of the Rig-Veda, but the change has taken place already in the later hymns of the collection, where the Asuras appear as the fiends and devils—Powers of Evil—they remain throughout the later literature of India, religious and profane. Now, these hymns were gathered in their present form and order, according to the latest and most moderate calculations, between 1500 and 1000 B.C. This gives us an indirect but not unimportant hint as to the probable time of Zarathushtra and his reform.

6. Nothing can be more impressive or majestic than the purely fanciful scene in which the prophet and his mission are introduced to the world. It is a sort of Prologue in Heaven, enacted by the denizens of the spirit-world. GEUSH-URVAN (literally "Soul of the Steer"), the guardian spirit or "Chief" (*ratu*) of animal creation, and especially domestic cattle, raises up his voice to heaven and complains of the ill-treatment and sufferings which he and his kind endure at the hands of men, while it had been foretold him that they would be benefited by the insti-

tution of agriculture. Asha (Righteousness and Order, personified as one of the Amesha-Spentas) replies that, though no really benevolent man will be hard on his cattle, yet people in general don't always know in what manner they should behave to their inferiors, and adds: "Mazda knows best the deeds of daêvas and men, both those that have been and those that are to be. He, the Lord (Ahura), has to decide; as he wills, so shall it be." Mazda then speaks, and his decision brings scant comfort to the Guardian of the Flocks, for he informs him that there is no special protector for cattle, since they have been created for the use of the tiller and herdsman, whom, by his own—Mazda's—and Asha's ordinance, they are to supply with meat and drink, by giving him their milk and their flesh. Geush-Urvan, in despair, then asks: "Hast thou no one among men who would take kindly care of us?" Whereupon Mazda answers—and here lies the gist of the poetical apologue:—" I know on earth only one man who has heard our decrees—Zarathushtra Spitâma. He will announce from memory my and Asha's teachings, when I endow him with sweetness of speech." Then the Spirit of the Flocks moaned aloud: "Woe is me! and is the powerless word of an unwarlike man all I am to look to, when I wished for the protection of a mighty hero? When will he ever come, he who is to lend my cattle efficient help? . . . But I know that thou, O Mazda, knowest best. Where else should be justice, benevolence, and power! . . . And thus the Spirit of the Flocks departs, more disappointed than consoled, nor knows that the Word is far mightier than the sword.*

7. After this preamble, we are prepared to see the prophet enter on his mission. There is no thread of narrative to inform us of the course of events, but the text speaks for itself, and as we read the famous Chapter XXX. of Yasna, we have no difficulty in imagining the preacher addressing an assembled multitude of men—people and nobles—in the presence, as can be inferred from one passage, of the king, who had believed in him, probably KAVA VÎSHTÂSPA. As this discourse is to Mazdeism, in its first and pure stage, what the Sermon of the Mount is to our own religion, we shall give it almost uncurtailed.†

"1. Now shall I proclaim unto you, O ye all that here approach me, what the wise should lay to their hearts; the songs of praise and the sacrificial rites which pious men pay the Lord (Ahura), and the sacred truths and ordinances (Asha), that what was secret until now may appear in the light.

"2. Hear with your ears that which is best, and test it with a clear understanding, before each man decides for himself between the two teachings. . . .

"3. The two Spirits, the Twins, skilfully created, in the beginning, Good and Evil, in thought, in speech, in deed. And, between these two, the wise have made the right choice; not so the senseless.

"4. And when these two spirits had agreed to institute the springing up and the passing away of all things [to create Life and Death], and to decree that in the end the lot of the followers of Lie (*drujvan*, *i. e.*, holders of the false gods and religion) should be the worst life, and that of the followers of Truth (*ashavan*, of the true religion) should be the happiest mental state,—

* Freely given from the translation of Bartholomae, in " Arische Forschungen," III.

† From Bartholomae's translation in " Arische Forschungen," II.

"5. Then of these two Spirits the lying one elected to do evil, while the holiest Spirit (*Spenta-Mainyu*), he who is clothed with the solid heavens as with a robe, elected the Right (*asha*), and with him all those who wish to do right in the eyes of Ahura-Mazda.

"6. And to his side came with Khshathra, Vohu-manô and Asha, and Âramaiti the eternal, who made the earth her body. In these mayest thou have a share, that thou mayest outdo all others in wealth.*

"7. The daêvas also made not the right choice (between good and evil), for, as they were debating, folly overcame them, so that they chose the Worst Mind (*ako-manô*, opposed to *vohu-manô*). And they assembled in the house of violence (*a*ẽ*shma*) to destroy the life of man;" (*i.e.*, they joined with the enemies of the Zarathustrians, the plunderers and destroyers of their settlements, farms, and cattle.)

"8. But when the vengeance comes for their deeds of violence, then, O Ahura-Mazda, surely the sovereignty will be given by thy Good Mind to those who will have helped Truth (*asha*) to overcome Lie (*druj*).

"9. Therefore will we belong to those who are in time to lead this life on to perfection. Grant us then, O Mazda, and ye gods, your assistance, and thou also, O Asha, that every man may be enlightened whose understanding, as yet, judges falsely.

"10. For then the blow of destruction shall fall on the liar, while those who keep the good teaching will assemble unhindered in the beauteous abode of Vohu-manô, Mazda, and Asha.

"11. If, O men, you lay to your hearts these ordinances which Mazda instituted, and the good and the evil, and the long torments which await the followers of falsehood, (*drujvan*), and the bliss that must come to the holders of the true faith, (*ashavan*), it will go well with you."

8. We have here the essence of Mazdeism in its sublime simplicity, its absolute purity, as it shaped itself in the mind of the founder. All further devel-

---

* This last sentence would seem to be addressed to the king. The benediction, in plain words, amounts to this: "Mayest thou be endowed with the sovereign power, the peace of mind, and the piety that go hand in hand with the true religion, and thus deserve a share in the dominion of the earth, and outdo all other kings in wealth."

opments as given in the rest of the Gâthas may well be said to be but commentary. The Dualism here announced is absolute: the two Spirits are twins, not hostile in the beginning, nor separated, and together create the world, material and spiritual, visible and invisible; the result is of necessity a mixture of opposites, for we can know a thing only by its contrary: how should we know light, warmth, health, but from their contrast with darkness, cold, sickness? Life, then, *must* be balanced by Death; Truth by Falsehood; in other words, Good by Evil. So far there is no right or wrong, only necessity. But now comes the choice. *Now* the twin spirits, having each taken his part, become the " Spirit which is all Life" and the "Spirit which is all Death" (life and death being considered the supreme expressions of Good and Evil), to be foes for evermore; and now begins the warfare in which nothing is indifferent or purposeless, but every move tells for one or the other, and in which all mankind, without exception, "each man for himself," must freely choose his side, fight on it, and abide the consequences. It is noteworthy that even the daêvas, the uncompromisingly abhorred fiends and demons of later Mazdeism, are not presented by the prophet as evil originally and in themselves, but only *from the evil choice they make* when, as free agents, the choice is before them as before the two Supreme Twins. So absolute is his belief in the free-will and responsibility of every being, whether of the spirit world or the material world.

9. Little could be added to the great Declaration

of Faith known as "Chapter XXX. of Yasna," in point of doctrine, by ransacking the rest of the Gâthic poems. A profound conviction of his heaven-sent mission ("I am thy chosen one from the beginning; all others I consider as my opponents") — outpourings of personal feelings in the days of persecution and distress, appeals for help and enlightenment often worded with great pathos and tenderness —("To thee I cry: Behold, O Lord, and grant me assistance, as a friend grants it to a dear friend!")— such is the strain that runs through all these ancient hymns, lending them a thoroughly human, living interest. One of them (chapter XLIV.) especially breathes the purest poetical feeling, and keeps on a lofty level rarely maintained for so long a stretch in these often crude literary efforts. The questionings, the doubts, the longings of the prophet's spirit are put in the form of a series of questions addressed by him to his heavenly "friend" and teacher. Some bear upon points of doctrine, some on the issue of a coming struggle:

"This I will ask; tell it me right, O Lord (Ahura)—will the good deeds of men be rewarded already before the best life comes? . . ." (The "best life"—future life, for the good.)

"This I will ask thee; tell it me right, O Lord—are those things which I will proclaim really so? Will the righteous acquire holiness by their good deeds? Wilt thou award them the kingdom (of heaven—Khshathra) through the good mind? (*vohu-manô*) . . . How will my soul attain to bliss? . . . Will piety (*ârmaiti*) come to those, O Mazda, to whom thy faith is declared? . . .

"This I will ask thee; tell it me right, O Lord—who of those to whom I am speaking here is a friend of Truth (*asha*), who of Falsehood (*druj*)? On which side stand the wicked? And are *they* not wicked, the unbelievers, who make thy benefits vain? (by attacking and robbing the followers of Ahura-Mazda) . .

"How shall I turn from us the Spirit of Lie? (*druj*) . . . How shall I procure the triumph of Righteousness (*asha*) over the Spirit of Lie (*druj*) so that it may, according to the promise of thy teaching, inflict on the unbelieving a fell defeat, and deal unto them death and destruction?

"This I will ask of thee; tell it me right, O Lord—canst thou indeed protect me when the two hosts meet? . . To which of the two wilt thou give the victory? . . . ."

Some of the questions are a poetical form of homage to the Creator of all things, whose glory they indirectly proclaim:

"This I will ask thee; tell it me right, O Lord:—Who sustains the earth here below, and the space above, that they do not fall? Who made the waters and the plants? Who to the winds has yoked the storm-clouds, the two fleetest of things? . . . Who skilfully created light and darkness? Who sleep and wakefulness? Who the noontide and the night, and the dawns that call the wise to their work?

". . . Who created the blessed Ârmaiti and Khshathra?* Who made the son to be the image of the father?—I will proclaim, O Mazda, that thou, O Beneficent Spirit! (Spenta-Mainyu), art the Maker of all things."

10. These specimens of the Gâthic hymns are sufficient to show, besides the doctrine, the characteristic drift and the tone of Zarathushtra's own teaching: a great directness of speech, a studied avoidance of even the familiar language of poetical imagery, as tending to perpetuate that spirit of mythical redundancy which it was the object of his reform to eradicate. Nor are passages wanting where he denounces in direct terms the false and evil teachers, doubtless the priests of the nature-deities of India and the unbelieving Eranian tribes.

* "Earth and Heaven" in this place. See Bartholomae, "Arische Forschungen," II., p. 163.

Most noticeable is the fact that the prophet scarcely ever lapses even into the religious allegory which supplanted the Aryan mythology in the later development of Mazdeism, peopling the unseen world with a theological hierarchy of Archangels, Angels, and Saints (Amesha-Spentas, Yazatas, and Fravashis) in the place of the ancient nature-deities. The Fravashis do not occur at all in the Gâthas, nor the Amesha-Spentas as a body of spiritual persons. We see "good mind," "righteousness," "piety" ("*vohu-manô*," "*asha*," "*ârmaiti*"), used as common abstract names, in their direct and proper meaning, not as names of allegorical persons, even in a remarkable passage where all six are mentioned as the gifts of Ahura-Mazda. Thus "obedience to the Law of Mazda" (*sraosha*), the cardinal virtue of the Mazdayasnian, is spoken of only as such, and not yet allegorized into the Chief of the Yazatas, the champion "fiend-smiter," a sort of Eranian Saint Michael. Nor, on the other hand, is "Aêshma," the later leader of all the demon-host,—Aêshma-Daêva, the special opponent of Sraosha, the leader of the Yazatas,—mentioned in any sense but the direct one of "violence" or "spirit of violence." There is no faintest trace of superstition or idolatrous worship in the reverence paid to "Ahura-Mazda's Fire," the symbol and rallying sacrament of a pure faith; sacrifices and "meat-offerings" are spoken of, but there is no insisting on a tiresomely minute ceremonial; no mention of either Mithra or Haoma; the heathenish rites connected with the use of the intoxicating drink of the same name are not encouraged;

indeed, there is one passage (Yasna, XLVIII., 10) which is interpreted as expressing abhorrence of those rites, and classing them with the sacrifices to the daêvas, "the seed of Evil," as an act of impiety.

"When, O Mazda! shall the men of perfect mind come? And when shall they drive from hence *this polluted drunken joy* whereby the Karpans (hostile priests) with angry zeal would crush us, and by whose inspiration the tyrants of the provinces hold their evil rule!"

And though the prophet repeatedly speaks of the "open Chinvat Bridge" (Bridge of the Gatherer), which the soul of the righteous cross with ease on their passage into Ahura's own abode of bliss, the Garô-nmâna, while the wicked fall from it "into the abode of Lie forever," he abstains from imaginative descriptions that might too easily slide back into mythology and polytheism. In short, to use the words of an eminent scholar, the latest translator of the Gâthas * : "In the Gâthas all is sober and real ; .... the Karpans, etc., are no mythical monsters ; no dragon threatens the settlements, and no fabulous beings defend them. Zarathushtra, Djamaspa, Frashaostra † ... are as real, and are alluded to with a simplicity as unconscious as any characters in history. Except inspiration, there are no miracles. All the action is made up of the exertions and passions of living and suffering men. . . ."

11. "With the 'Yasna of Seven Chapters,'" re-

* L. H. Mills, in vol. XXXI. of "The Sacred Books of the East."

† Two great nobles and chiefs of Vishtâspa's following, ardent and powerful supporters of Zarathushtra, whose daughter one of them married.

marks the same scholar, "which ranks next in antiquity to the Gâthas, we already pass into an atmosphere distinct from them. The dialect still lingers, but the spirit is changed." The fact is that all history shows how impossible it is for any religion or doctrine to maintain itself on the level of absolute loftiness and purity on which it was placed by the founder or reformer. *He* is one man in a nation, above and ahead of his time, his race, nay, mankind in general ; so are, in a lesser, degree, his immediate followers, his first disciples. But the mass of those who learn from him and them—the herd—is composed of average minds, which, after the first enthusiasm has cooled and the novelty has worn off, feel but ill at ease on an altitude that makes too great demands on their spiritual powers. Then there are the old habits, which, as the strain is irksomely felt, reassert themselves with all the sacredness of early nay, ancestral, association, all the sweetness of familiarity. Then begins the work of adaptation ; the new religion is half unconsciously fitted to the old ; there is a gradual revival of ancient ideas, ancient poetry, ancient forms and usages—and scarce a lifetime has elapsed after the reformer has passed away, when his work is changed beyond recognition, and the doctrine and practice of those who still call themselves his followers, have become a medley of what he taught and the very things against which he rose in protest. Still, *on the whole*, there is real progress: the new spirit remains, the standard has been raised, and a new step taken towards the ideal— a step which can never be retraced.

12. Of this process of adaptation the collection of prayers in Gâthic dialect, set apart in the body of the Yasna-liturgy under the name of "Yasna of Seven Chapters," offers a striking illustration, though it is of course impossible to surmise how long an interval separates them from those older Gâthas which may be said to embody the Zoroastrian Revelation. Set forms of invocation and a regular working ritual, presupposing a strictly organized class of priests, have gathered round the substance which alone engrossed the prophet; his abstract speculations have become greatly materialized, and the allegorical forms of speech in which he but sparingly indulged have crystallized into personifications solid enough to start a new myth-development. The attributes of the Deity and the qualities it vouchsafes to its pure-minded followers—Good Mind, Righteousness, Piety, etc.—have become the fully organized body of the Amesha-Spentas; Fire has become the object of a special worship somewhat idolatrous in form; and—surest sign of future decadence—the mythical taint begins to crop up in the worship and sacrifice expressly paid to natural objects: "we sacrifice to the hills that run with torrents, and the lakes that brim with waters, . . . to both earth and heaven and to the stormy wind that Mazda made, and to the peak of high Haraiti, and to the land and all things good." We have here the whole Aryan nature-pantheon in subdued form; indeed so strongly does the old mythical habit of speech reassert itself, that the Waters are called "the Wives of Ahura" and "female Ahuras" (see p. 62). The Fravashis,

not once mentioned in the original Gâthas, are here invoked and "worshipped" together with Ahura-Mazda himself and the Bountiful Immortals, although their number is restricted to those " of the Saints, of holy men and holy women" (followers and propagators of the new religion). Lastly Haoma reappears, " Haoma golden-flowered that grows on the heights, Haoma that restores us . . . that driveth death afar." We shall see, however, that the rites of this, one of the most primeval Aryan deities, were not restored in the coarse form which Zarathushtra seems to have particularly denounced (see p. 108).

13. The Yasna has preserved to us an important document—the profession of faith which was required from each Mazdayasnian convert, the true Avestan Creed. Although too long to be reproduced here entire, some of the principal verses will prove of interest:

"1. I curse the daêvas. I confess myself a worshipper of Mazda, a follower of Zarathushtra, a foe to the daêvas, a believer in Ahura, a praiser of the Amesha-Spentas. . . .

"2. I believe in the good, holy Ârmaiti, may she abide with me. I forswear henceforth all robbing and stealing of cattle and the plundering and destruction of villages belonging to worshippers of Mazda.

"3. To householders I promise that they may roam at will and abide unmolested wherever upon the earth they may be dwelling with their herds. Humbly with uplifted hands to Asha I swear this. Nor will I hereafter bring plunder or destruction on the Mazdayasnian villages, not even to avenge life and limb. . . .

"8. I confess myself a worshipper of Mazda, a follower of Zarathushtra, professing and confessing the same. I profess good thoughts, good words, good deeds.

"9. I profess the Mazdayasnian religion which, while girded with armor, resorts not to weapons, and the righteous marriage among kindred; which religion, as established by Ahura and Zarathushtra, is the highest, best, and most excellent among those that are and that are to be. . . . This is the profession of the Mazdayasnian religion."*

14. The last verse contains an allusion to a singular custom, sanctioned, if not originated, by Mazdeism, and which has drawn much censure on its followers: the custom of intermarriage between kindred, even so near as brothers and sisters. It is not only permitted, but absolutely enjoined and invested with a peculiar sanctity. This notion possibly had its source in the necessity of drawing the family ties, the clanship, as closely as possible, in self-defence, and also of fostering matrimonial alliances within the circle—narrow at first—of the faithful. Anyhow, the defenders of this to us abominable custom claim that, if mankind be descended from one couple, the first marriage *must* have been one between brother and sister. Besides, it should be remembered that it was not regarded with uniform horror by remote antiquity, and was in general use as late as among the Egyptians, that most intellectual and certainly not immoral people. The probabilities are that it was a very ancient Eranian custom, confirmed by the new religion on practical grounds.

* Translation of Mr. A. V. W. Jackson, of Columbia College, New York.

VI.

MIGRATIONS AND FOREIGN INFLUENCES—THE VENDÎDÂD—HEATHEN REVIVAL—THE KHORDEH-AVESTA.

1. If with the "Yasna of Seven Chapters" we already pass into an atmosphere distinct from that of the Gâthas (see p. 108), the Vendîdâd takes us into another world. The most cursory perusal of the book shows us that the religion carried westward by its Eranian bearers has wandered far from its cradle, and has assimilated many foreign elements in its wanderings. The Vendîdâd, the only book of Avestan law preserved entire out of the mass of Avestan literature, is devoted to only one subject, but that a most important one: the means of maintaining the ideal Mazdayasnian purity and of fighting and defeating the daêvas. It is the extreme minuteness and puerility of most of the observances prescribed, together with the importance given to mere points of material detail, which produce so startling a contrast between this later development of Mazdeism and the pure abstraction of Zarathushtra's own teaching. Still the spirit of that teaching is there in its essential features; and the regulations contain much that is excellent and wise under all

the rubbish of priestly discipline. Moreover, we must bear in mind that Mazdeism in this particular form was not by any means adopted by *all* the followers of Zarathushtra, and, indeed, seems to have been at first confined to the northern Eranians, especially the Medes, and to have become generally enforced only at the revival of the national religion under the Sassanian kings.

2. Three fundamental principles underlie this priestly legislation, and make it at once intelligible, even in its extravagances: (1) There is only one thoroughly noble and honorable calling, and that is agriculture and cattle-raising, for as much land as is reclaimed and made productive or used for pasture, just so much is wrested from Angra-Mainyu and his daêvas. (2) The entire creation is divided into "the good" and "the bad." Ahura-Mazda made all useful creatures; foremost and holiest among these are cattle, the guardian dog and the vigilant cock. It is a duty to tend them and a sin to neglect them. Angra-Mainyu made all the noxious creatures. It is a duty to destroy them on all occasions. They are classed under the generic name of KHRAFSTRAS, and we are surprised to see the most harmless insects, and animals like the frog, the lizard, included in the doom of destruction together with wolves, serpents, flies, and ants. Heretics and wicked men also sometimes come under this denomination. (3) The elements—air, water, earth, and fire—are pure and holy, and must not be defiled by the contact of anything impure. The priest, therefore, while officiating before the fire, wears a cloth before his mouth, that

5. PARSI IN PRAYING COSTUME.

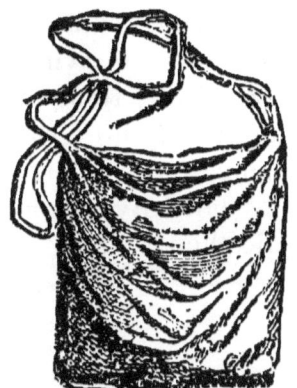

6. "PAITIDÂNA" (PENÔM) —CLOTH WORN BY THE PARSIS BEFORE THEIR MOUTHS IN PRESENCE OF THE SACRED FIRE.

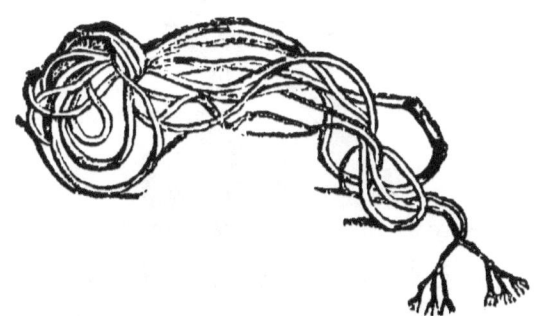

7. "KOSTI" SACRED GIRDLE WORN BY PARSIS WHILE PRAYING OR DURING ANY SACRED CEREMONY.

his breath may not sully the supremely holy element. Such a cloth is worn to this day by every Parsi while tending the sacred fire of his own home-altar, or even saying his prayers.

3. Every thing in the Vendidâd, as well as in the later purely liturgical portions of the Yasna, and the litany known as the "Vispered" (see p. 30), betrays the authority of a long-established and all-powerful priesthood. This would be obvious enough, even

8. "ÂTESH-GÂH" OR "FIRE-ALTAR" OF MODERN PARSIS.

without the evidence of a passage (*Fargard—i. e.*, "chapter"—IX.) where Zarathushtra is made to complain to Ahura-Mazda of the harm that is done by any person—layman or heretic—who, "not knowing the rites of purification according to the law of Mazda," presumes to perform the ceremony for any of the faithful who have incurred uncleanness. Ahura-Mazda expressly states that "sickness and death, and the working of the fiend, are stronger than they were before" in consequence of such sacrilegious interference, and, on being asked " What is the penalty that he shall pay?" gives the following directions :

"The worshippers of Mazda shall bind him ; they shall bind his hands first ; then they shall strip him of his clothes, they shall flay him alive, they shall cut off his head, and they shall give over his

9. "ÁTESH-GÁH" OR "FIRE-ALTAR"; SEEN BY ANQUETIL DUPERRON AT SÚRAT.

corpse unto the greediest of the corpse-eating creatures made by Ahura-Mazda, unto the ravens,* with these words : 'The man here has repented of all his evil thoughts, words, and deeds. If he has committed any other evil deed, it is remitted by his repentance . . for ever and for ever.'" †

* Although there is no worse pollution than touching a corpse, these birds are "made by Ahura-Mazda," *i. e.*, pure, because they are necessary to remove the pollution from the face of the earth.

† The punishment atones for all offences, and the soul goes to Paradise free from taint or guilt.

4. The Âthravan—Fire-priest—is indeed a majestic figure, as he stands forth, in flowing white robe, the lower part of his face veiled, beside the *âtesh-gâh*, or "fire-altar," a metal vessel placed on a low stone platform and filled with ashes, on top of which burns the fire of dry, fragrant chips, continually trimmed and replenished. In one hand he holds the *Khrafstraghna* (the "khrafstra-killer," an instrument of unknown form for killing snakes, frogs, ants, etc.), in the other the *Baresma*, a bundle of twigs, uneven in number—five, seven, or nine—probably divining-rods, without which the priest never appeared in public.* Near the âtesh-gâh stands a stone table, set forth with the sacred utensils for the performance of the daily Haoma-sacrifice, which, though ignored and probably abolished by the prophet, has resumed its place of honor in the religious practice of this essentially Aryan people. It should be mentioned, however, that the sacrificial drink was prepared from another plant than the Hindu Soma,—one that grows in Erân, and the juice of which is far less intoxicating, nor is it subjected to a process of fermentation. Besides, only a small quantity was drunk by one of the officiating priests, after the liquor had been consecrated by being raised before the sacred flame, "shown to the fire."† The mystic rite is thus shorn of its coarsest and most ob-

* Originally the twigs for the *Baresma* were to be cut, with certain ceremonies, from either a tamarind or a pomegranate tree, or any tree that had no thorns. The modern Parsis have, very prosaically, substituted flexible rods of brass wire.

† This is the identical Haoma-sacrifice of the modern Parsis, as witnessed and described by Dr. Martin Haug.

TONGS TO TRIM SACRED FIRE.

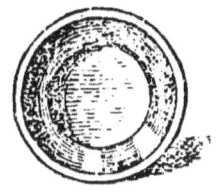

SAUCERS FOR MILK AND FRUIT OFFERINGS ("MYAZDA").

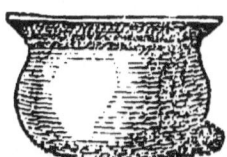
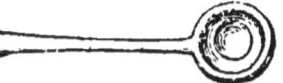

LADLE FOR ABLUTIONS AND PURIFICATIONS.

CUP FOR HOLY WATER ("ZAOTHRA.")

HAOMA-KNIFE.

HAOMA-MORTAR AND PESTLE.   HAOMA-STRAINER.

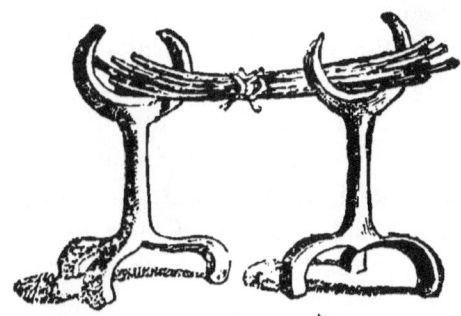

"BARESMA" (BARSOM) WITH STAND.

10. SACRIFICIAL IMPLEMENTS USED IN PARSI WORSHIP.

noxious feature, the intoxication in which it too often ended in India, and becomes purely symbolical. Such, too, is the character of the other offerings, consisting of a few bits of meat (to which the modern Parsis have substituted a little milk in a cup), some small cakes, and some fruit, all of which, moreover (representing the various kinds of human food), are not consumed in the fire of the altar, but only held up before it, presented, so to speak, as a symbolical offering and for consecration. The Yasna and Vispered continually invoke and glorify these parts of the daily sacrifice; the HAOMA, the MYAZDA (offering of meat or milk, cake and fruit), and the ZAOTHRA (holy water), together with the BARESMA (bundle of sacred twigs), and the sacrificial vessels—mortar and pestle, strainer, cups, etc.—are exalted as the most fiend-smiting of weapons. "The sacred mortar, the sacred cup, the Haoma, the Words taught by Mazda (manthras), these are my weapons, my best weapons!" Zarathushtra is made to say (Vendidâd, XIX.). Nay, in a poetical introduction to the long and elaborate hymn to Haoma (Yasna, IX.), the heavenly Haoma, "the Holy One who driveth death afar," appears to Zarathushtra, incarnate, in human form, clothed with a body of marvellous beauty, at the sacred hour of sunrise, while the prophet is "tending the sacred fire and chanting the Gâthas." Whereupon a dialogue ensues, in which Haoma bids Zarathushtra "Pray to me, O Spitâma, and prepare me for the taste" (*i. e.*, press and strain the juice of the plant Haoma), and tells him of the heroes who, " the first of men, prepared him for the incarnate world," and obtained as a reward glorious and renowned sons. The first of these was Vivanghat, father of the great Yima (see pp. 89 93), the king of the golden age; and the last Purushaspa, the father of Zarathushtra himself, who, having heard the wondrous revelation, speaks: " Praise to Haoma ! Good is Haoma, well-endowed, healing, beautiful in form. . . . golden-hued, and with bending sprouts. . . ." This long narrative is one of the few passages in the Avesta which are brimful of ancient mythic lore.

5. " Which is the first place where the Earth feels most happy?" asks Zarathushtra of Ahura-Mazda, who replies (Vendidâd, III.): " It is the place whereon one of the faithful steps forward with the holy wood in his hand, the baresma, the holy meat, the holy mortar, fulfilling the law with love. . . ." The description of the other places where the Earth feels most happy presents the complete Eranian ideal of a prosperous and holy life.

"It is where one of the faithful erects a house with cattle, wife, and children, and where the cattle go on thriving ; the dog, the wife, the child, the fire are thriving, and every blessing of life . . . where one of the faithful cultivates most corn, grass, and fruit ; where he waters ground that is dry, or dries ground that is too wet . . . where there is most increase of flocks and herds . . . and where they yield most manure."

It is the perfection of a farm.

" He who would till the earth "—it is still Ahura who speaks—
" with the left arm and the right, with the right arm and the left, unto him will she bring forth plenty, like a loving bride unto her beloved. . . . Unto him thus says the Earth : 'O thou man who do-t till me with the left arm and the right, with the right arm and the left ' here shall I ever go on bearing, bringing forth all manner of food, bringing forth profusion of corn.'

"He who does not till the earth, O Spitâma Zarathushtra! with the left arm and the right, with the right arm and the left, unto him thus says the Earth: 'O thou man! . . . ever shalt thou stand at the door of the stranger, among those who beg for bread; ever shalt thou wait there for the refuse that is brought unto thee, brought by those who have profusion of wealth.'"

6. "HE WHO SOWS CORN SOWS HOLINESS" (Vendidâd, III., 31). Where there is plenty and prosperity there is no room for wickedness—no room for envy, violence, rapine, and all evil passions; besides, honest toil leaves no time for evil thoughts, evil words, and evil deeds. This great truth is thus expressed in quaint, truly Avestan phrase:

"When barley is coming forth, the daêvas start up; when the corn is growing rank, then faint the daêvas' hearts; when the corn is being ground, the daêvas groan; when wheat is coming forth, the daêvas are destroyed. In that house they can no longer stay; from that house they are beaten away, wherein wheat is thus coming forth. It is as though red-hot iron were turned about in their throats, when there is plenty of corn."

Therefore, to "sow corn" is more meritorious than "a hundred acts of adoration, a thousand oblations, ten thousand sacrifices."

7. But, sowing corn—and holiness—and routing the daêvas by the toil of "the left arm and the right, the right arm and the left," requires bodily strength and endurance. So this most practical and rational of religious laws proceeds, with admirable consistency, to enjoin proper care of that necessary servant—the body:

"Then let the priest teach his people this holy saying: 'No one who does not eat has strength to do works of holiness, strength to do works of husbandry. . . . By eating every material creature lives, by not eating it dies away.'"

Not only are practices of abstinence and asceticism—the so-called " mortification of the flesh "—not praised or encouraged, but—and herein Avestan Mazdeism differs from almost every other religion—they are condemned, denounced as a foolish and wicked error, that strengthens the hands of the Arch Enemy.

"Verily I say unto thee, O Spitâma Zarathushtra! the man who has a wife is far above him who begets no sons; he who keeps a house is far above him who has none; he who has children is far above the childless man*; he who has riches is far above him who has none. And, of two men, he who fills himself with meat is filled with the good spirit much more than he who does not do so. . . . It is this man who can strive against the onsets of the Death-fiend †; that can strive against the winter-fiend, with thinnest garments on; that can strive against the wicked tyrant and smite him on the head; that can strive against the ungodly *Ashemaogha* (heretic, false teacher), who does not eat." ‡ (Vendidâd, IV.)

8. Symmetry, that inevitable characteristic of a system of universal dualism, pervades the Vendidâd

---

* Herodotus tells us that in his time prizes were given in Persia by the king to those who had most children; while sacred texts of the Pehlevi period expressly declare that " he who has no child, the bridge of paradise shall be barred to him."

† Astô-Vidhôtu," the bone-divider," who has a noose round every man's neck, and is the immediate cause of death. So that we are told (Vendidâd, V.) that water and fire kill no man; the holy elements could not do the work of Angra-Mainyu. No, it is Astô-Vidhôtu who " ties the noose," then " the flood takes the man up, or down, or throws him ashore "; or the fire burns up the body previously killed by the fiend.

‡ This thrust, if the passage be comparatively ancient (B.C.), may be pointed against the Hindu Brahmen, or Buddhists, both great adepts at ascetic practices. If belonging to Sassanian Mazdeism, it would be directed against the Manichaeans, a Persian sect, which enjoined fasting and abstinence of every sort.

in form and substance. Every set of definitions, of queries and answers, is exactly matched by its corresponding opposite set. So, after ascertaining from Ahura-Mazda what are the places where the Earth feels most happy, Zarathushtra proceeds to inquire what are the places where she feels sorest grief, and receives, among others, the following replies: ". . . It is the place wherein most corpses of dogs and men lie buried. . . . It is the place whereon stand most of those DAKHMAS, whereon corpses of men are deposited. . . ."

The Dakhma—also called by the modern Parsis "the Tower of Silence"—is the burying-place, or rather, the cemetery, for the name of "burial" would ill become the singular and, to us, revolting way in which the Mazdayasnians of Northern Erân disposed of their dead, religiously followed therein by their Parsi descendants. This brings us to the contemplation of the most extraordinary refinement of logical consistency ever achieved by human brains.

9. Given the two absolute premises: 1st, that the elements are pure and holy and must not be defiled; 2d, that the essence of all impurity is death, as the work of the Angra-Mainyu, "the Spirit who is all death," and who takes undisputed possession of the human body the moment that the breath of life, the gift of Ahura-Mazda, has left it,—the question, "What is to be done with the dead?" becomes an exceedingly complicated and difficult one. The presence of a corpse pollutes the air; to bury it in the earth or sink it into the water were equally sacrilegious; to burn it in the fire, after the manner of

the Hindus and so many Indo-European nations, would be the height of impiety, an inexpiable crime, involving no end of calamities to the whole country. Only one way is open: to let the bodies of the dead be devoured by wild animals or birds. Such, indeed, is the law: the corpses shall be taken to a distance from human dwellings and holy things, if possible into the wilderness, where no men or cattle pass, and be exposed "on the highest summits, where they know there are always corpse-eating dogs and corpse-eating birds," and there be fastened by the feet and by the hair with weights of brass, stone, or lead, lest the dogs and birds carry portions of the flesh or bones to the water and to the trees and thus defile them. The worshippers of Mazda are enjoined, "if they can afford it, to erect a building for the purpose of exposing the dead, of stone and mortar, out of the reach of the dog, the wolf, the fox, and wherein rain-water cannot stay*; if they cannot afford it, they shall lay down the dead man on the ground, on his carpet and his pillow, clothed with the light of heaven (*i. e.*, naked), and beholding the sun."

10. Such is the origin of the Dakhmas or Towers of Silence. We give the description of one of these unique cemeteries in the words of the dis-

* This last clause, like many other minute prescriptions, is founded on the very correct conclusion that it is moisture which retains and carries pollution—infection,—and must be considered as a sanitary provision. A corpse of a year's standing and dried up does not pollute; even the site of a Dakhma is pure once more, when the bones are reduced to dust; for it is said: "The dry mingles not with the dry."

tinguished Parsi writer who has been quoted once already*:

"A circular platform about 300 feet in circumference, entirely paved with large stone slabs and divided into three rows of exposed receptacles, called *pavis*, for the bodies of the dead. As there are the same number of *pavis* in each concentric row, they diminish in size from the outer to the inner ring, so that by the side of the wall is used for the bodies of males, the next for those of females, and the third for those of children. These receptacles, or *pavis*, are separated from each other by ridges which are about one inch in height, and channels are cut into the *pavis* for the purpose of conveying all the liquid matter flowing from the corpses and rain-water into a *bhandar*, or deep hollow in the form of a pit, the bottom of which is paved with stone slabs. This pit forms the centre of the tower. When the corpse has been completely stripped of its flesh by the vultures, *which is generally accomplished within an hour at the outside*, and when the bones of the denuded skeleton are perfectly dried up by the powerful heat of a tropical sun and other atmospheric influences, they are thrown into the pit, where they crumble into dust—the rich and poor meeting together after death in one common level of equality. Four drains are constructed. . . . They commence from the wall of the *bhandar* and pass beyond the outside of the tower down into four wells, sunk into the ground at equal distances. At the mouth of each drain charcoal and sand are placed for purifying the fluid before it enters the ground, thus observing one of the tenets of the Zoroastrian religion that 'the mother earth shall not be defiled.' The wells have a permeable bottom, which is covered with sand to a height of five or seven feet. These Dakhmas, or Towers of Silence, are built upon one plan, but their size may and does vary.† . . .

"When the Parsis begin to build a Dakhma, . . . they fix nails in the ground and enclose it by a thread, indicating thereby

---

* Dosabhai Framji Karaka, "History of the Parsis," vol. I., pp. 200 and ff.

† Dimensions of the Dakhma at Navsari: interior diameter, 62 feet; outer diameter (from the outside of the wall), 70 feet; diameter of the "*bhandar*," 20 feet; maximum height of the tower, 16 feet; height of granite platform, 8 feet.

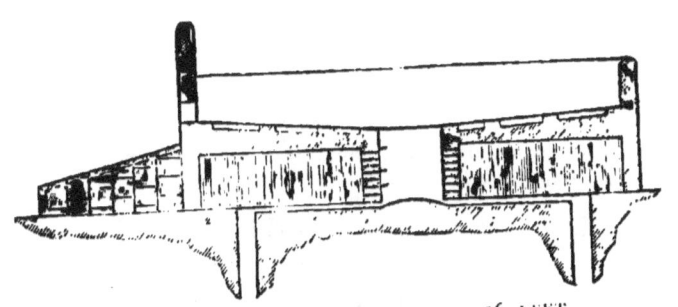

SECTION. TOTAL HEIGHT ABOUT 16 FEET.

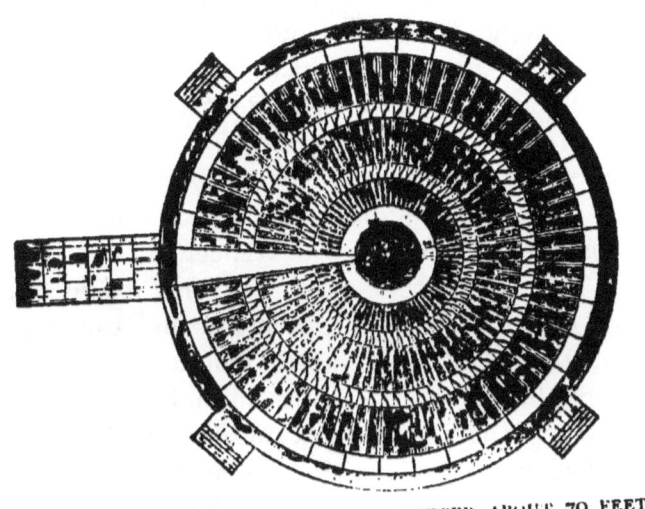

VIEW OF THE INTERIOR. OUTER DIAMETER ABOUT 70 FEET.

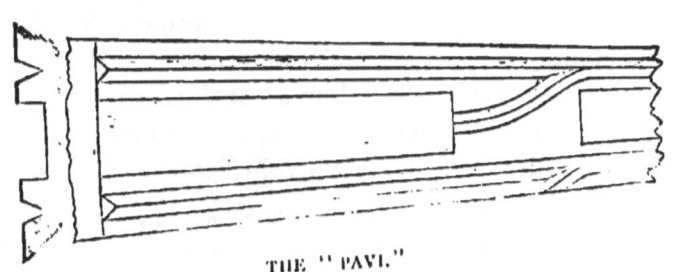

THE "PAVI."

1.—A "DAKHMA," OR "TOWER OF SILENCE."

that only that particular portion of the ground shall be set apart for the dead. . . . Iron nails are used.* . . . The structure is separated from the adjoining ground by digging a trench all round it, about one foot deep and wide."

It is evident from the tone of this passage that the author entirely approves of this peculiar treatment of the dead. Certain it is that the Parsis contemplate it without repulsion for themselves, and claim that it is at all events the most perfect solution of the sanitary question—which it undoubtedly is, especially in hot, yet moist, tropical climes. As a solemn reminder of the equality of all men before the laws of nature, and an efficient preventive to the vanities of funeral pomp and posthumous distinctions, the custom is also entitled to respect.

11. The attempt to carry out the exaggerated notion of the purity of the elements and the impurity of death with the most rigorous consistency, involves the priestly lawgivers in endless contradictions, places them in the most puzzling predicaments. They become conscious that so many occasions of pollution arise which are wholly beyond their control, that existence threatens to become impossible, unless they draw the line somewhere on this side of what may be termed the reduction *ad absurdum* of their doctrines. This they do in the form of an extra revelation, contained in a special chapter of the Vendîdâd (Fargard V.), wherein Zarathushtra is made

---

* Thus also the stretcher on which the dead are carried must be of iron. Metal is supposed to retain infection less than any other substance. According to the laws of purification a tainted vessel of metal can be cleansed, while one of wood cannot, but remains unclean forever and ever.

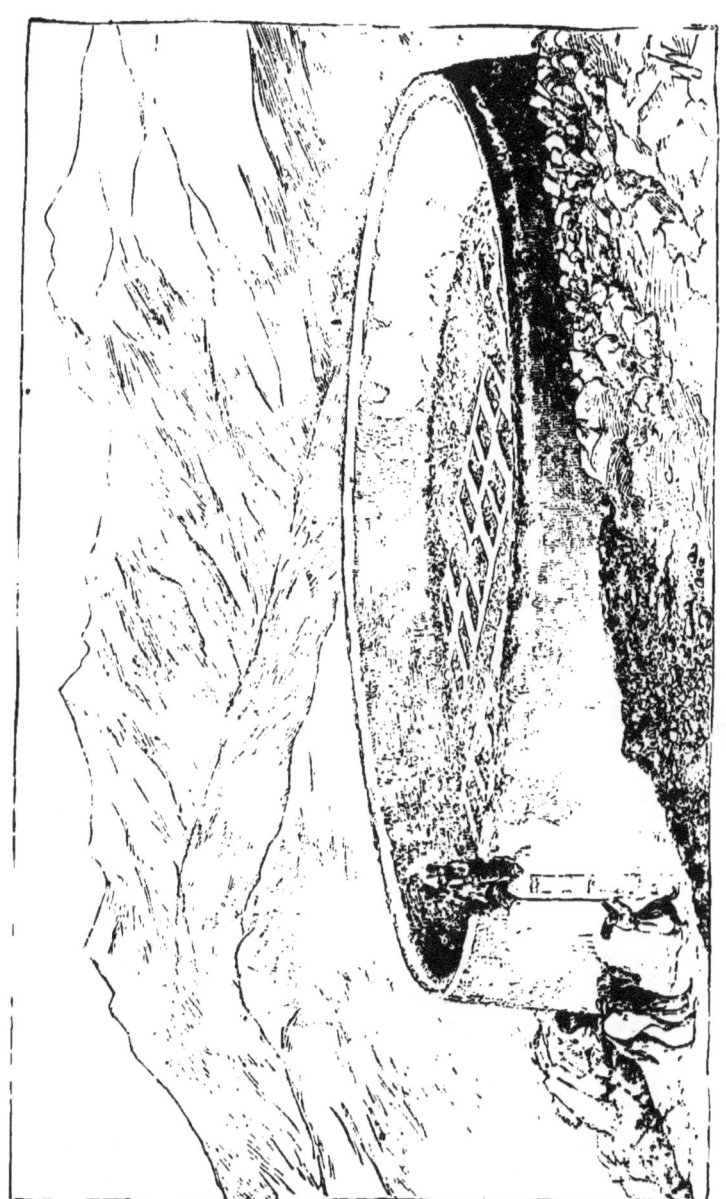

12.—ANCIENT "DAKHMA," NEAR TEHERÁN, IN PERSIA.

to propound nice and puzzling points, in the form of hypothetical cases, for Ahura-Mazda to solve. We give the first part of this curious dialogue whole, as a specimen:

"There dies a man in the depths of the vale: a bird takes flight from the top of the mountain down into the depths of the vale, and it eats up the corpse of the dead man there; then up it flies from the depths of the vale to the top of the mountain, it flies to some one of the trees there, of the hard-wooded or the soft-wooded, and upon that tree it vomits, it deposits dung, it drops pieces of the corpse.

"Now, lo! here is a man coming up from the depths of the vale to the top of the mountain; he comes to the tree whereon the bird is sitting, from that tree he wants to have wood for the fire. He fells the tree, he hews the tree, he splits it into logs, and then he lights it on the fire, the son of Ahura-Mazda. What is the penalty that he shall pay?"

Ahura-Mazda answered: "There is no sin upon a man for any dead matter that has been brought by dogs, birds, by wolves, by winds, or by flies.

"For, were there sin upon a man for any dead matter that might have been brought by dogs, by birds, by wolves, by winds, or by flies, how soon this material world of mine would have in it only *Peshô-tanus*" (*i. e.*, people guilty of death), "shut out from the way of holiness, whose souls will cry and wail!" (After death, being driven away from paradise.)

In like manner the agriculturist is not to be held responsible for any dead matter that any animal may have brought into the stream that waters his field. Zarathushtra next takes Ahura-Mazda himself to task for apparent violation of his own laws:

"O Maker of the material world, thou Holy One! Is it true that thou, Ahura-Mazda, sendest the waters from the sea Vouru-Kasha down with the wind and with the clouds, and makest them flow down to the corpses? That thou, Ahura-Mazda, makest them flow down to the Dakhmas, to the unclean remains, to the bones? And that thou, Ahura-Mazda, makest them flow back unseen? . . ."

To which Ahura-Mazda answers: "It is even so as thou hast said, O righteous Zarathushtra!" but explains that, when the rain-water, thus polluted, returns unseen to whence it came (by evaporation), it is first cleansed in a special heavenly reservoir, called the sea PÛITIKA, from which it runs back into the sea Vouru-Kasha as pure as ever, and as fit to water the roots of the sacred trees that grow there (the Gaokerena and the tree of All-Seeds, see p. 65), and to rain down again upon the earth, to bring food to men and cattle.

12. The same inevitable inconsistency shows itself in the feeling about the Dakhmas. Although the existence of these constructions is a matter of absolute necessity, we saw above that the sites on which they are erected are numbered among those places "where the earth feels sorest grief." Nay, they are denounced, on unimpeachable hygienic grounds, as the trysting places of all the fiends—"where the troops of daêvas rush together, to kill their fifties and their hundreds, their thousands and their tens of thousands. . . . Thus the fiends revel on there as long as the stench is rooted in the Dakhmas. Thus from the Dakhmas arise the infection of diseases, fevers, humors. . . . There death has most power on man from the hour when the sun is down." And, although the building of Dakhmas has at all times been considered a meritorious act of piety, we are told that the man who gladdens the earth with greatest joy is, first, "he who digs out of it most corpses of dogs and men," and, second, "he who pulls down most of those Dakhmas on which corpses of men are deposited."

"Urge every one in the material world, O Spitâma Zarathushtra!" Ahura-Mazda is made to say, "to pull down Dakhmas. He who should pull down thereof, even so much as the size of his own body, his sins in thought, word, and deed are atoned for. Not for his soul shall the two spirits wage war with one another, and when he enters the blissful world, the stars, the moon, and the sun shall rejoice in him, and I, Ahura-Mazda, shall rejoice in him, saying: 'Hail, O man! thou who hast just passed from the decaying world into the undecaying one!'" (Vendidâd, VII.)

13. And yet—such is the tyranny of circumstances—not only must the earth endure the pollution of Dakhmas, and men go on building them, but there may arise even worse complications, which have to be met in some way. There is no desecration, no calamity equal to the presence or vicinity of a corpse; but men die at all seasons, and what is to be done in winter—those terribly severe winters of Central Asia—when the Dakhma, built at a more or less considerable distance from the villages, cannot be reached? Zarathushtra places the case before Ahura-Mazda, (Vendidâd, Fargards V. and VIII.):

"O maker of the material world, thou Holy One! If in the house of a Mazdayasnian a dog or a man happens to die, and it is raining or snowing, or blowing, or the darkness is coming on, when flocks and men lose their way, what shall the Mazdayasnians do?"

Ahura-Mazda's instruction is, to choose the most sequestered and driest spot near the house, at least thirty paces from the water, the fire, and the inhabited parts of the dwelling, and there temporarily to place the body in a grave dug half a foot in the ground if it be frozen hard, or half the height of a man if it be soft, covering the grave with dust of bricks, stones, dry earth:—

"And they shall let the lifeless body lie there until the birds begin to fly, the plants to grow, the floods to flow, and the wind to dry up the waters off the earth. . . . Then the worshippers of Mazda shall make a breach in the wall of the house, and they shall call for two men, strong and skilful; and those having stripped their clothes off, shall take the body to the building of clay, stones, and mortar, where they know there are always corpse-eating dogs and corpse-eating birds."

In another place, (Fargard V.) Ahura-Mazda directs that in every borough there shall be raised, in the prevision of such an emergency, "three small houses for the dead," large enough that a man standing erect in such a house should not strike his skull, nor, should he stretch out his hands and feet, strike the walls with them.

14. Proportionate to the merit of relieving the Earth from the pollution which is "sorest grief" to her, is the sin of wilfully inflicting such grief on her by burying the corpse of a dog or of a man; and as any sin or guilt is removed by the former act, so no punishment, not even death in this world, can atone for the latter, if the offender does not repent and disinter the corpse before the end of two years: "For that deed there is nothing that can pay . . . nothing than can cleanse from it; it is a trespass for which there is no atonement for ever and for ever"; which means that the offender's soul must go to hell and stay there until the general resurrection. Provided always that he is a professer of Mazdeism and has been taught the law, for contrariwise he does not know that he is committing a sin, and cannot in justice be held responsible for it.

15. This principle, sound as it is in itself, culmi-

nates in strange anomalies, when applied with the tenacious but one-sided logic of the race: thus it is only the corpses of Mazdayasnians and animals belonging to the good creation of Ahura which defile the elements and endanger the living. The corpse of a Khrafstra is harmless: "as its life was incarnate death, the spring of life that was in it is dried up with its last breath; it killed while alive, it can do so no more when dead—it becomes clean by dying." The same is said of an Ashemaogha or heretic. (Vendidâd, V.)

16. Very nearly one half of the Vendidâd is filled with prescriptions about purification and atonement for every kind of uncleanness, involuntary or unavoidably incurred. Sickness of every kind is looked upon in the light of possession, and the sick, accordingly, are treated more like criminals than suffering brethren: sequestered in rooms built for the purpose, away from the fire, from the light of the sun, nourished sparingly, as the food they took would strengthen the fiend who has taken up his abode in them, scarcely permitted to touch water even to drink, for fear of defiling the pure element, unapproached by the inmates save in case of absolute necessity and with humiliating precautions, —such as having the food passed to them in ladles with very long handles,—and covered with coarse clothes thriftily kept on purpose for such occasions.

17. Thriftiness, indeed, is enjoined on the faithful as a matter of salvation:

"Ahura-Mazda does not allow us to waste any thing of value that we may have, not even so much as a small silver coin's weight of thread, not even so much as a maid lets fall in spinning. Whosoever throws any clothing on a dead body" (because it would be wasted, as nothing could cleanse them of the pollution of such contact), "even so much as a maid lets fall in spinning, is not a pious man whilst alive, nor shall he, when dead, have a place in the happy realm. He shall go away into the world of fiends, into that dark world, made of darkness, the offspring of darkness."

The modern Parsis, indeed, do clothe their dead, but the shroud must be made of old, worn-out material, the older the better, only well washed.

18. But the most horrible and dangerous of fiends is the fiend of corruption and contagion, personified in the DRUJ NASU, who takes possession of the body at the very instant that the breath leaves it, "rushing upon it from the regions of the north,* in the shape of a raging fly, . . . the foulest of Khrafstras," and thence, as from a citadel, deals "infection, pollution, and uncleanness" on all around, even to the tenth row of those near the corpse, and further still, for each man imparts the uncleanness to his neighbor, only it grows weaker with each remove from the centre of infection,—the corpse. It has been very plausibly remarked that "in the fly which is attracted by the smell of dead flesh they saw the fiend which takes possession of the corpse in the name of Angra-Mainyu." (Justi, "Geschichte der Perser.") It is to exorcise the Nasu that the *sagdid* ceremony is performed (see pp. 93-94), and those same "four-eyed or yellow-eared dogs" must be made to pass several times along the way by which

---

* Hell lies in the North, where its entrance is in the mountains of the daêvas, Mount AREZÛRA.

the corpse has been taken to the Dakhma before men or flocks are allowed to tread the same way. As for those who have been compelled to touch a corpse, (whether of a dog or a man, the dog being an eminently sacred animal), they have to undergo a thorough process of purification, by means of repeated ablutions. As the "good waters" reach this or that part of the body, the Druj Nasu is supposed to leave that part and rush to the next nearest, until from spot to spot, beginning with the forepart of the skull, the left toe is reached, from which the Nasu at length flies off " to the regions of the north" in her proper shape as a hideous fly. The enumeration of these different spots of the human body, together with the repetition of the formula of expulsion, all in the usual dialogue form, continues through several pages, and strikes one, it must be confessed, as the most ludicrous and puerile piece of absurdity. It is in reading such passages as this that one understands the objections raised by Anquetil Duperron's enemies (see pp. 12-13). The purifications prescribed and regulated in the Avesta, and still observed by the Parsis, are very peculiar and exceedingly disgusting. Their essential feature is the ablution with *gômêz*, the urine of cows or steers, a liquid equally held sacred and cleansing by the Brahmanic Hindus. The person to be purified washes his or her entire body with *gômêz*, then rubs it dry with handfuls of earth or dust, and lastly washes it again, this time with water. The performance is repeated several times. The great purification takes nine nights (the *Barashnûm*). Of course these ceremonies are performed and directed by priests, and we saw above (p. 116) how jealously, even fiercely, the clergy guarded the privilege. *Gômês* is used to purify houses, clothes, drinking vessels, just as we use a disinfectant; the lips of new-born children are moistened with it, and the mothers are made to swallow a considerable quantity mixed with ashes before they are allowed to touch water.

19. Never is the corpse-fiend so dangerous as when it finds one of the faithful alone, unprotected by the presence and prayers of another Mazdayasnian. Therefore a man who would carry a corpse alone were irretrievably lost; the Nasu would rush upon him, and enter into him, and make him unclean for ever and for ever; he would become, so to speak, a Nasu incarnate, and must be set apart from all human intercourse. The directions concerning the treatment of a "carrier-alone" are the following: an enclosure shall be erected on a dry and barren spot, at a distance from the fire, the water, and all holy things; there the "carrier-alone" shall be established and shall be supplied with the coarsest food and the most worn-out clothes, and there he shall live until he attains an advanced old age, when he shall be put to death in the same manner as the unlicensed purifier (see p. 117), his death atoning for his offence both in this world and the next. The words used in both passages are identical.

20. Although diseases are looked upon in the Avesta as forms of demoniac possession, yet we find a short chapter of the Vendidâd on physicians, their modes of treatment, and the fees they are entitled

to. As might be expected, the precedence is given to the treatment by spells, the reciting of sacred texts—manthras:

"If several healers offer themselves together, namely one who heals with the knife, one who heals with herbs, and one who heals with the holy word, it is this one who will best drive away sickness from the body of the faithful."

A late commentator, with the sceptic shrewdness born of more fastidious times, remarks: "It may be that he will not relieve, but he will not harm"; so advises to give the conjuring doctor a trial by all means. As to the surgeons—the "healers with the knife"—they do not seem to have enjoyed unlimited confidence, as they were allowed to practise subject to a sort of examination which does credit to the shrewdness of that eminently practical people, the Eranians: they were to try their skill first on aliens, followers of false religions, who were abandoned to the tender mercies of the graduating students much as condemned criminals were sometimes used in the Middle Ages for experiments *in animâ vili*:

"On worshippers of the daêvas shall he first prove himself. . . . If he treat with the knife a worshipper of the daêvas and he die," —and a second and a third—" he is unfit to practise the art of healing for ever and for ever. . . . If he shall ever attend any worshipper of Mazda . . . and wound him with the knife, he shall pay for it the same penalty as is paid for wilful murder."

"If he treat with the knife a worshipper of the daêvas and he recover,"—and a second and a third—" then he is fit to practise the art of healing for ever and for ever. He may henceforth at his will attend worshippers of Mazda . . and heal them with the knife."

At all events this is a notable improvement on the

treatments in use in ancient Chaldea and later Babylon.*

The fees are all valued in kind : oxen, asses, mares, camels, sheep,—and graded according to the rank and wealth of the patient, so that while "he shall heal the lord of a province (a king) for the value of a chariot and four," "he shall heal a sheep for the value of a meal of meat,"—for the duties of a physician were not separated from those of a veterinary surgeon. The only fee required of a priest was "a holy blessing."

21. Not the least peculiar feature of the Vendidâd legislation is the exceeding honor paid to the dog. We have repeatedly seen the dog associated with man, as equally sacred, possessing equal rights to respect, in such phrases as : "The corpse of a dog or a man"; "the murder of a dog or a man." But that is not enough; we find several chapters devoted to the treatment of the animal in health or sickness, and the explanation of this extreme solicitude is placed in the mouth of Ahura-Mazda himself:

"The dog, O Spitâma Zarathushtra ! I, Ahura-Mazda have made self-clothed and self-shod, watchful, wakeful, and sharp-toothed, born to take his food from man and to watch over man's goods. I have made the dog strong of body against the evil-doer and watchful over your goods, when he is of sound mind. And whosoever shall awake at his voice, neither shall the thief nor the wolf steal any thing from his house without being warned ; the wolf shall be smitten and torn to pieces ; he is driven away, he flees away. . . .

". . . If those two dogs of mine, the shepherd's dog and the house-dog pass by the house of any of my faithful people, let them never be kept away from it. For no house could subsist on the earth

* See " Story of Chaldea," p 163.

made by Ahura, but for those two dogs of mine, the shepherd's dog and the house-dog."

It is because of his dependence on man and his disinterested service,—"watching goods none of which he receives"—that the dog should be tended and fed with "milk and fat with meat," and giving bad food to a dog is accounted as great a sin as serving bad food to a guest; nay, it is a sin of the first magnitude to give a dog too hard bones or too hot food, so that the bones stick in his teeth or throat and the food burns his mouth or his tongue. And "if a man shall smite a house-dog or a shepherd's dog so that it gives up the ghost and the soul parts from the body," not only will that man be severely punished for the deed, but his soul shall not in the other world be defended from the howling and pursuing daévas by the dogs that guard the Chinvat Bridge. If there is in a house a scentless dog or a mad dog, "they shall attend to heal him in the same manner as they would do one of the faithful," and if they fail, they shall put a wooden collar round his neck and tie him to a post, lest he come to harm and the owners of the house be held responsible for his death or wound. In like manner a dog-mother must be looked after exactly as a woman; she and her litter must be supported by the man on whose property the whelps were born, until they are capable of self-defence and self-subsistence, and if he fails in this, he shall pay the penalty as for wilful murder. "Young dogs," it is explained, "ought to be supported for six months; children for seven years." Lastly—

"If a man shall smite a shepherd's dog or a house-dog so that it becomes unfit for work, if he shall cut off its ear or its paw, and thereupon a thief or a wolf break in and carry away sheep from the fold or goods from the house without the dog giving any warning, the man shall pay for the lost goods, and he shall pay for the wounds of the dog as for wilful wounding."

The stray dog—who has no home or master—is ranked somewhat below those canine aristocrats, the shepherd's dog and the house-dog; still he is entitled to respect as he is more especially used for the *Sagaíd;* he is compared to a holy man of the wandering class, a sort of "begging friar," remarks Darmesteter. The same author informs us that "the young dog enters the community of the faithful at the age of four months, when he can smite the Nasu."

22. Other animals are mentioned in the same chapters as varieties of dogs, but the passages are fanciful and obscure. Of greater interest are those that refer to the merits of the cock, the bird of Sraosha, the router of daêvas, the messenger who calls men to the performance of their religious duties:

". . . the bird named PARÓDARSH. . . . that lifts up his voice against the mighty Dawn : 'Arise, O men ! . . . Lo ! here is *Búshyansta*,* the long-handed, coming upon you, who lulls to sleep again the whole living world, as soon as it has awoke : 'Sleep, she says, sleep on, O man ! the time has not yet come. . . .'

". . . And then bedfellows address one another : 'Rise up, here is the cock calling me up.' Whichever of the two first gets up, shall first enter paradise, whichever of the two shall first, with well-washed hands, bring clean wood unto the Fire, the son of Ahura-Mazda . . .

". . . And whosoever will kindly and piously present one of the faithful with a pair of these my Paródarsh birds, male and fe-

* A female fiend, personifying sloth, immoderate sleep.

male, it is as though he had given a house with a hundred columns. . . . And whosoever shall give my Paródarsh bird his fill of meat, I, Ahura-Mazda, need not interrogate him any longer; he shall directly go to paradise."

23. The merest perusal of the Vendidâd suffices to show the threefold alteration which Mazdeism had undergone from the lofty simplicity of the Gâthic period: 1st, an excessive development in the direction of dogmatism and discipline; 2d, the revival of certain old heathen associations and tendencies; 3d, the adoption of certain foreign elements. The latter fact is easily accounted for, if we remember that the race of which the Avesta is the memorial did not work out its spiritual life as a compact, permanently settled nation, but while still in a nomadic, fluctuating, migrating condition. This is abundantly shown by such passages as, for instance, that which prescribes (Vendidâd, VIII.) what should be done with the corpse of a dog or a man, if there is no Dakhma within reasonable distance:

"*If they find it easier to remove the dead than to remove the house*, they shall take out the dead, they shall let the house stand, and shall perfume it with sweet-smelling plants.

"*If they find it easier to remove the house than to remove the dead, they shall take away the house*, they shall let the dead lie on the spot, and shall perfume the house with sweet-smelling plants."

What can such a movable "house" be but a hut of branches or a tent, the nomad's temporary shelter?

24. Now we know not only what, in a general way, the direction of the Eranian migration was— from east to west,—but we also know about what time they began to reach the term of that migration,

13. VIEW IN ÁDERBEIDJÁN

the eastern spurs and valleys of the Zagros region, and the still more rugged highlands between the Caspian Sea and the great lakes of Urartu—Urumieh and Van—the district now known as ÂDERBEIDJÂN, corrupted from the classic ATROPATÊNE, itself a transformation of an older Eranian name meaning "Dominion of Fire." We have monumental proof that the Eranian branch then already known as MEDES (MADAI) were dislodging the tribes among the eastern ridges of Zagros, and were themselves attacked by the Assyrian arms as far back as the ninth century B.C. under Ramân-Nirari III.,* and were probably mentioned already under that king's grandfather, the great Shalmaneser II. We are further led to suppose that portions at least of the advancing Medes must have passed through or near the territories of various savage and semi-barbarous people in the vicinity of the Caspian Sea, the region known to later, classical antiquity as HYRCANIA. All this knowledge enables us to do more than guess at the origin of certain observances prescribed and certain conceptions inculcated in the Vendidâd, and flowing from no Aryan sources assuredly: the use of the Baresma, the treatment of the dead, the treatment of diseases by conjuring-spells, the exaggerated reverence paid to the elements, the belief in numberless hosts of fiends always on the watch to pounce on men and draw them to perdition. Now all these customs and conceptions, foreign to the Aryan spiritual bent, are in perfect accordance with what we know of the Turanian religious system;

* See "Story of Assyria," p. 194.

14. VIEW IN ÁDERBÍDJÁN. (MODERN CITY OF MARAGHA.)

some of them indeed are extremely familiar to us from the texts and spells of Shumir and Accad,— ancient Chaldea,* and the presumption is very strong that the populations of the Zagros and Caspian regions which the Medes, in the course of some three hundred years, dislodged or reduced under their rule, belonged in great part to the division of mankind which the Eranians sweepingly designated as "Turân" (the Yellow Race),† in opposition to themselves.

25. There is nothing unnatural in the fact that the Aryan conquerors should have been influenced by the people amongst whom they came ; indeed the contrary would have been rather remarkable, since they were comparatively few in number, and it was no more than sound policy to conciliate the new subjects, whom a military rule unsoftened and unaided by moral influence would surely have been insufficient to keep under control. For the conquerors to impose on them their own religion was the first and most necessary step towards asserting that moral influence, but it was a step which could not be achieved without

* See "Story of Chaldea." Chapter III.

† This presumption would now be considered an established fact but for the violent opposition it has met from the Assyriologist and Semitist, Mr. Halévy, who strenuously denies the Turanian element in the tribes conquered by the Medes and even in ancient Shumiro-Accad itself. For a long time Mr. Halévy stood entirely alone ; he was, however, joined by the late S. Guyard, and another French scholar, Mr. Pognon, now supports his views. Still this minority, however eminent, will scarcely prevail in the end. Besides, the views held by the two opposing camps are not, in some cases, as irreconcilable as they seem at first sight—at least as respects the Median conquests.

numerous concessions to the local, already long established, religions. No new religion, however superior, ever supplants an older one without such concessions; in making them, it grows familiar with the lower standard, and—such is the innate propensity of things to deterioration—inevitably becomes tainted with the very beliefs and practices which it is its loftier mission to abolish. Thus we saw the rudimentary goblin-worship of Shumir and Accad with all its train of degrading superstitions (conjuring, divining, spell-casting, etc.) incorporated into the far higher and nobler religious system of Semitic Babylonia.* Moreover, the Eranians were notoriously fond of novelty and prompt to imitate.

26. This question of Turanian influences traceable in the Avesta, a question so important for the comprehension of what we might call the geological stratification of the religion that grew out of the Gâthic revelation, has been made the object of exhaustive research by Mgr. C. de Harlez, the French translator of the Avesta.† We can do no better than follow his conclusions, point by point, as far as the peculiar character of a popular work will allow.

1st. "The incantations, of which the Vendidâd supplies a few specimens, assuredly have their origin in Shumir and Turanian Media. Such long and monotonous enumerations as the following recall the Accadian formulas: 'To thee, O Sickness, I say avaunt! to thee, O Death, I say avaunt! to thee, O Pain, I say avaunt! to thee, O Fever, I say avaunt! to thee, O Disease, I say avaunt!

---

* See "Story of Chaldea," pp. 235-237.

† "Les Origines du Zoroastrisme." See also the same writer's monumental "Introduction" to his translation of the Avesta.

". . . I drive away sickness, I drive away death, I drive away pain and fever, I drive away the disease, rottenness, and infection which Angra-Mainyu has created by his witchcraft against the bodies of mortals. . . .'" (Vendidâd, XX.)*

"The multitude of daêvas in the Avestan world, the belief in their unremitting action, in their continual attacks, in the necessity of incantations and conjuration to defeat them, the superstitions such as that about the parings of nails being turned into weapons for the daêvas,† —all this dark and gruesome side of Zoroastrism is certainly the product of Chaldean and Turanian habits of thought. . . . To the Chaldeans disease was the work of the fiends; magic words were the surest cure. Just so the Avesta tells us that the best physician is he who heals with the holy word (manthra). . . ."

2d. The Baresma is probably due to the same influences. All Turanian peoples have used divining rods, and the peculiar direction to the priest to hold the bunch of twigs extended before him during divine service points to the notion that it keeps the evil spirits from his person and from the altar. This would also explain why the Median priests, the MAGI, were never seen in public without the Baresma. Here another question suggests itself in connection with the outer forms of the Mesopotamian religions, about which so little is known from lack of documents. There is, on Assyrian sculptures, a very peculiar object, which frequently recurs in scenes of worship and sacrifice, where it appears deposited on

---

* For this and all that follows, compare "Story of Chaldea," Ch. IV., "Turanian Chaldea."

† Every Mazdayasnian is directed to bury the parings of his nails in a hole dug on purpose in the earth, reciting certain prayers at the same time. If he neglects this precaution, "the nails shall be in the hands of the daêvas so many spears, knives, bows, falcon-winged arrows, and lingstones." The combings of hair and the hair that is cut or shaved off are to be buried in like manner. (Vendidâd, XVII.)

the altar. The use of it, or the nature, has never yet been explained. But on close inspection it looks extremely like a bundle of twigs, uneven in number, tied together with a ribbon. Is it not rather likely that it may represent the sacred divining rods and be the original of the Avestan Baresma? It were a question certainly well worth investigating.

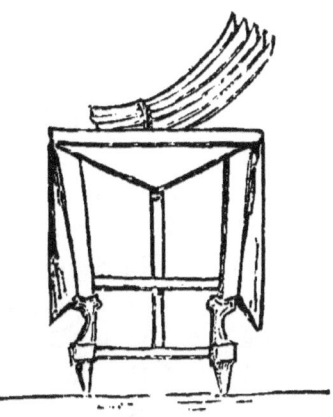

15. ASSYRIAN ALTAR (COMPARE ILL. 10, "BARESMA WITH STAND").

3d. "The belief in the Druj Nasu, or corpse-fiend, in the irremediable pollution caused by corpses and all that follows therefrom concerning the funeral rites and purifications, the setting out of the dead to be devoured by wolves and vultures—these conceptions and customs belong neither to the Âryas, nor to the Chaldeans, nor to the Accadians. They must have originated in a mountainous country, very little civilized, and under the inspiration of a Turanian people. The Greeks expressly tell us where they were in force. . . . They have ascertained that only the Bactrians and Caspians followed them, the former partially, the latter entirely."

The later name of this region, Hyrcania, has become a byword for savage fierceness, and it was undoubtedly a portion of the vast extent known as "Turân."

Mgr. de Harlez further points out that the Nasu closely corresponds to those evil spirits of Shumir and Accad from whose persecution men are never safe,—who fall as rain from the sky,—who spring from the earth,—who creep in at the door like serpents,—who steal the child from the father's knee,—who withhold from the wife the blessing of children.* Besides, the Nasu-Druj is not alone; here, as in Turanian Chaldea, their name is Legion. Chapter XI. of the Vendidâd, which is entirely composed of incantations and exorcisms to repel the evil influence from the house, the fire, the earth, the tree, the cow, the faithful man and woman, etc., gives a long list of fiends whose names have not yet been identified or explained. Here, as there, too, the North is the fateful region; in the north lies Mount Arezûra, the meeting-place of the daêvas, with its gate of hell opening from the west.

27. The excessive reverence shown to Fire and expressed in observances so strict and ritualistic as to have gained for the Zoroastrians the name of "Fire-worshippers" from superficial observers, also appears to have been a later development. The word ÂTHRAVAN ("Keeper of the Fire"), which designates the priest throughout the later Avesta, does not occur once in the Gâthas. The priest is there designated by a descriptive periphrase—such as "Master of Wisdom," "Messenger of the Law." Now the worship of the elements is a well-known

* See "Story of Chaldea," pp. 155, 156.

16. RUIN OF ÂTESH-GÂH AT FIRÛZABAD.

Turanian feature, and as regards specially that of Fire, it is quite likely that the Eranians already found it in full force in the region bordering on the Caspian Sea from the west. That maze of mountains and valleys, uniting the foot of the Caucasian range and the head of the Zagros, abounds in underground springs and reservoirs of naphtha—a perfectly inexhaustible wealth of fuel, which a very little labor could bring to the surface by means of pipes, and utilize for entertaining quenchless fires. Thus the institution of sacred fires is absolutely suggested by the nature of the country, and is accordingly intimately associated with that country even in its name—Atropatêne = Âderbeidjân—to our own day. (See p. 144.) Some few so-called "Gebers" or "Fire-worshippers" still linger among the mountains of Âderbeidjân and Upper Kurdistân, attracted by the flame which still glimmers on the top of some of the ancient Fire-towers, the gigantic Âtesh-gâhs or Fire-altars constructed in the times of their fathers' glory;—unique and most impressive constructions, now mostly in ruins. The sacred flame, kindled in the pure mountain air, high above all defiling contact, drew its nourishment by a pipe that passed straight up through the centre of the building, directly from the invisible store below. Truly, few forms of worship appeal more to our imagination and our sense of reverent awe than the homage paid to this purest of symbols on the stainless mountain tops, by white-robed Âthravans, raising their voice in song amid the silence of a wild and undesecrated nature.

28. More traces of Turanian influence might cas-

17. RESTORATION OF THE PRECEDING.

ily be adduced, but they are too indistinct and subtle to allow of discussion in a merely popular work. There is one, however, too peculiar and striking to be passed over; it is the strange transformation undergone by the Fravashis, or glorified spirits of the departed, who, as we can establish clearly, and without straining a point, originally answer to the Pitris of the Veda (see pp. 83, ff.). That of the host of "the good, strong, beneficent Fravashis of the faithful," those of the first and sainted champions of the true faith should be honored with a special reverence, is right and natural, and there is nothing startling in the long litany (over twenty pages) which recalls them all by name, repeating the same form of invocation, beginning with "the Fravashi of the holy Zarathushtra, who first thought what is good, who first spoke what is good, who first did what is good. . . . who first knew and first taught,"—and ending with this beautiful proclamation of universal brotherhood: "We worship the Fravashis of the holy men in the Aryan countries, . . of the holy women in the Aryan countries, . . . of the holy men, of the holy women in the Turanian countries, . . . of the holy men, the holy women in all countries." From these unsubstantial spirits to the host of heavenly warriors, "with helms of brass, with weapons of brass, with armor of brass, who struggle in the fights for victory in garments of light, arraying the battles and bringing them forwards, to kill thousands of daēvas," who help their own people in their wars, who fight for the waters to be distributed to their clans, the transition, by a bold touch of anthromorphism, is easy, the proceeding familiar and thoroughly Aryan. But when, in the same hymn (Yesht XIII.), we find a long string of invocations to the Fravashis of the living, of those to be born, nay, of animals and inanimate objects, when, indeed, Ahura-Mazda and the Amesha-Spentas are said to have their own respective Fravashis, we are no longer in an Aryan world. Here are some of the passages :

"Of all those ancient Fravashis, we worship the Fravashi of Ahura-Mazda, who is the greatest, the best, the fairest, etc. . . . We worship the good, strong, beneficent Fravashis of the Amesha-Spentas, the bright ones, etc. . . . We worship the souls ; those of the tame animals ; those of the wild animals ; those of the animals that live in the waters ; those of the animals that live under the ground ; those of the flying ones ; those of the running ones ; those of the grazing ones ; we worship their Fravashis.* . . . We worship the good, strong, beneficent, Fravashis . . . of the most rejoicing Fire, . . . of the holy, strong Sraosha, who is the incarnate Word, a mighty-speared and lordly god, . . . that of Mithra, the lord of wide pastures ; that of the Holy Word (Manthra-Spenta) ; that of the sky ; that of the waters ; that of the earth ; that of the plants ; that of the Bull ; . . . We sacrifice unto the Fravashis of those that have been ; of those that will be ; all the Fravashis of all nations, and most friendly to those of the friendly nations."

"The most powerful amongst the Fravashis of the faithful, O Spitâma ! are those of the men of the primitive law, or those of the Saviours not yet born, who are to restore the world.† Of the others, the Fravashis of the living are more powerful than those of the dead."

We see here in the Avesta the beginning of a de-

* The soul is to be imagined as distinct from the Fravashi.
† In the fulness of time three prophets, or "Saviours," miraculously born from Zarathushtra are to appear on earth, to prepare the world for final regeneration.

velopment which is worked out far more thoroughly in the Bundehesh and other Pehlevi books of the Sassanian period, and which would be inexplicable but for the affinity which the student of Chaldean antiquity cannot but instantly detect between these spiritual doubles and those which the primitive faith of the Shumiro-Accads ascribed to every individual, whether human or divine, and to every material object or phenomenon.* The influence is unmistakable, though there is far from Turanian goblin-worship to the nobler form which the same conception assumed when received and reproduced by the more refined Aryan intellect. In their last development the transformed Fravashis came to be, as one might say, the pre-existing prototypes created in heaven of all that is ever to be born or have visible shape on earth,—the abstract form, to be at some time incarnated in a body. The most intelligible and exhaustive definition of this class of beings is that given by Dr. E. W. West, perhaps the greatest living Pehlevi scholar: ". . . A preparatory creation of embryonic and immaterial existences, the prototypes—*fravashis*—spiritual counterparts or guardian angels of the spiritual and material creatures afterwards produced." †

29. We lastly come to the affinities, between Avestan and Hebrew conceptions, which are many and striking. The almost identity of the Angra-

---

* See, in "Story of Chaldea," the explanation of the expression "the son of his god," pp. 176 ff., and Turanian spirit-worship in the same chapter, pp. 151 ff.
† In a note to Chapter I. of the Bundehesh.

Mainyu of Mazdeism with the Biblical Satan, as well as the close approach of Ahura-Mazda in sublimity and supremacy to Jehovah himself, (not Yahveh, the tribal god of the early Hebrews, but Yahveh, the One God and Lord of the great prophets), has long been acknowledged by the greatest scholars; some of whom * are much inclined to attribute the similarity to direct Hebrew influences. All that can be said here on this very far-reaching subject is that we have historical evidence of the possibility of contact and intercourse between the Eranian and Semitic minds at least as early as the eighth century B.C.; since we know that Sargon of Assyria, when he carried Israel away into captivity after the fall of Samaria, sent a number of Jews to "the cities of the Medes." † Also, the scene of the dramatic story told in the Book of Tobit, as occurring in the reign of King Sennacherib, is placed in "Ecbatane, a city of Media," and in "Rages of Media" (Rhagae), where we are shown Jewish families residing permanently, keeping their law, and transacting the varied business of life. The fiend Asmodeus, with whom young Tobias wrestled for his wife, is no other than the Eranian Aêshma-Daêva, very slightly disguised by foreign pronunciation. So if the Jews borrowed from the Medes, the reverse is by no means improbable. Only we must remember that Ahura-Mazda stands forth in all his great-

* Foremost among these, indeed too absolutely and sweepingly—Friedrich Spiegel ; also, within much more reasonable bounds—Mgr. de Harlez.
† See "Story of Assyria," pp. 245, 249.

ness, as the One God, Omniscient Lord, the Creator, in the primeval Zoroastrian revelation, as embodied in the Gâthas, consequently anticipates by several hundred years the possibility of Hebrew contact and influences. To these, therefore, Mazdeism may have owed some later developments, some finishing touches, but in no case its original and fundamental conceptions.

30. It may have been noticed that in this necessarily condensed, but not therefore incomplete, sketch of the Avestan legislation (as much of it as has reached us) no mention has been made of any penal regulations, or code of punishments. The fact is that, although the Vendîdâd does contain such a code, it is the most incomprehensible part of the whole book; its provisions, *if* they have been rightly interpreted, being so wildly extravagant as almost to warrant the severest strictures of Duperron's enemies. The penalty always consists of a certain number of stripes, applied first with one instrument and, in equal number, with another. The names of these instruments—the *Aspahê-ashtra* and the *Sraoshô-Charana**—become very familiar after perusing certain portions of the Vendîdâd, where they occur at every other line; but no one has ever yet found out what they really were, or looked like. Furthermore, scholars are not yet agreed as to whether the stripes —so many with the one, as many with the other —were to be *received* by the culprit, or *given* by him, *i. e.*, given to unclean animals or insects— khrafstras—in which case "so many blows or stripes"

* *Ch* pronounced as in "Church."

would mean "so many khrafstras killed," the act of penance being turned to the profit of the "good creation" by so much damage done to the "bad creation." De Harlez, Spiegel, Justi, hold this latter view, while most other Avestan scholars—Anquetil, Haug, Darmesteter, and several more—advocate the other. As long as we have to do with a reasonable gradation of punishment, such as from five stripes to ten, fifteen, thirty, fifty, seventy, ninety, up to two hundred, there do not seem to be any objections on the plea of humanity or possibility; but when it comes to a thousand stripes, and in one case *ten thousand* (for the killing of a particularly sacred animal, called "water-dog," but not yet perfectly identified), feeling and reason equally revolt and prompt us to look for some other interpretation. One is that corporal punishment, though extensively used even now among the Parsis, as throughout the East, was very early commuted to the payment of fines, according to a corresponding, strictly graded scale. "The Pehlevi Commentary," we are told,[*] "expressly distinguishes three sorts of atonement: the atonement by money, the atonement by the *Sraosho-Charana*, and the atonement by cleansing." And further—"In later Parsism, every sin (and every good deed) has its value in money fixed, and may thus be weighed in the scales of Rashnu" (the Angel of Justice). It has been calculated that a stripe is equal to about fifty cents of our money.

31. Altogether this is certainly one of the most puzzling and unedifying portions of the Avesta, es-

[*] Darmesteter, "Introduction to the Zend-Avesta," p. xcix.

pecially when we consider what seems to our modern and uninitiated eyes the preposterous disproportion between offence and punishment. We can understand the infliction of from five all the way to two hundred stripes for assault and battery, manslaughter, and premeditated homicide, according to the injury suffered, from "drawing blood" to "a broken bone," or "giving up the ghost," and think the punishment just, and even moderate; we can understand a maximum of two hundred stripes for any act that defiles sacred things, such as tilling land wherein a corpse has been buried within the year, performing a sacrifice in a house where a man has just died, throwing on the ground a bone of a corpse, etc., because such pollution was believed to affect the whole community, and to give power to the Evil Ones; but when we find the same punishment—two hundred stripes—awarded for giving bad food to a shepherd's dog, we "feel uncomfortable," as Darmesteter says; and when it comes to five hundred stripes for killing a puppy-dog, six hundred for killing a stray dog, seven hundred for a house-dog, eight hundred for a shepherd's dog, one thousand for a hedge-hog, and ten thousand for the mysterious "water-dog" (otter?), we give it up, and are fain to confess our incapability of identifying ourselves with all the workings of our far-away ancestors' minds.*

* A young Avestan scholar, Mr. A. V. Williams-Jackson (of Columbia College, New York), thus sums up the proper attitude towards all such special questions: "The query as to the 10,000 stripes I do not feel at all certain in answering. I had always held the view that the practice denoted in the *Sraoshô-Charana* was much the same as has survived in the horrors of the modern Persian bastinado, and that

32. When, in a preceding chapter (Ch. IV.), we attempted to trace out the mythical elements contained in the Avesta and to connect them with the nature-myths of a primeval Aryan religion, the illustrations were drawn almost entirely from the Yeshts, or hymns, which, with a few fragmentary collections, form the so-called KHORDEH-AVESTA ("Lesser Avesta"). It is therefore unnecessary here to dwell on this portion of the book further than to point out how that, being undoubtedly a late growth, yet unmistakably polytheistic in tendency, it bears witness to that heathen revival, that reaction against the pure spiritualism of the Gâthic revelation of which we saw the first indications in the "Yasna of Seven Chapters" (see pp. 108, ff.), and more decided signs in the Vendîdâd. No matter that the former gods are now called Yazatas, spirits, and are said to be not only subject to Ahura-Mazda, but created by him,[*] the tendency *is* there and the saving clause is

---

the extraordinary figures 10,000, etc., were little more than Oriental playing with numbers . . . while, on the other hand, the regular series, 5, 30, 50, 90, 100, 200 might be literally taken. . . . The idea is nearly what is expressed by Darmesteter in the 'Introduction,' . . . particularly what he says about the money payments. Yet in spite of that, I now see objections . . . hence uncertainty. It is hard at best, in the present condition of Avesta subjects, to have decided views. It is more liberal to avoid as yet being dogmatic in this field. . . . Where progress is being made each day, we may think thus and thus *now*, but in a month may learn the errors of our views, and must abandon them. . . . This is the right ground to hold, is n't it?"—(From a private letter).

[*] "We sacrifice to Verethraghna, made by Ahura. ."
'We sacrifice to the awful Hvarenô, made by Mazda. . . ."
"We sacrifice unto the powerful Drvâspa (same as Geush-Urvan,

introduced merely as a salve to conscience. As Mgr. de Harlez says in his masterly summing up*:

"Zoroastrism at first attempted a far more radical reform, of which the Gâthas give us the measure; but the reaction of the national spirit restored the worship of the ancient genii to its former splendor, and revived early traditions. Later Mazdeism found nothing better than to force the genii into the heavenly hierarchy, proclaiming them to be creatures of Mazda, and the Eranian heroes into the dualistic order of things, re-handling the stories about them as needful. . . .

"Three grades are distinguishable in this evolution. Eranian religion passed from polytheism to dualism . . . then rose towards monotheism, to fall back again into spirit-worship. Zoroastrism proper belongs to the first or second phase—rather to the second, the movement towards monotheism."

33. It is to be expected that every conception, even the most inherent and deeply rooted in the Eranian spiritual consciousness, must be affected by these successive evolutions before it reaches its final form. Such is the case with the belief in a future life, an existence after death, which is to bring the reward or punishment earned by every soul during its earthly career. This belief is as old as any with which we can credit the Eranian mind. It is continually expressed in the Gâthas, but, quite in accordance with the spiritual character of that stage of religious thought, it does not assume there any material features, even though the Chinvat Bridge is re-

see p. 100), made by Mazda and holy, who keeps the flocks in health. . ." "When I created Mithra, the lord of wide pastures . . ." says Ahura. And again: "I have created that star Tishtrya. . . ."

* See De Harlez, "Les Origines du Zoroastrisme," pp. 317-319.

peatedly mentioned*; the nature of the bliss or suffering which awaits the departed spirit is left vaguely undefined, and sometimes almost seems to be conceived rather as a state of mind than an actual existence with sensations and feelings.† Not so in the Vendidâd. The ancient dreamlike speculation has already materialized into the very beautiful and poetical vision which later Mazdeism presents to the faithful, with clear and well-established details, as the revealed picture of the trial and judgment that every soul is to encounter. Nor are heathen features wanting: the mythical dogs that guard the bridge and escort and defend the righteous spirit, the celestial mountain, the god Mithra. Every detail of the thoroughly worked out vision is real and thrilling in the extreme. It is partly given in the Vendidâd (Ch. XIX.) in the consecrated form of a direct revelation to the prophet, and what is wanting there is completed in

* " And when they approach there where the Chinvat Bridge is, in the Lie's abode (Hell), forever shall their habitation be." (Yasna, XLVI., 11.) —" The righteous man's conscience will truly crush the wicked man's, while his soul rages fiercely on the open Chinvat Bridge. . . ." (Yasna, LI., 13.)

† " The truth is that the mental heaven and hell with which we are now familiar as the only future states recognized by intelligent people, and thoughts, which, in spite of their familiarity, can never lose their importance, are not only used and expressed in the Gâthas, but expressed there, so far as we are aware, *for the first time*. While mankind were delivered up to the childish terrors of a future replete with horrors visited upon them from without, the early Eranian sage announced the eternal truth that the rewards of Heaven and the punishments of Hell can only be *from within*." (L. H. Mills, Introduction to his translation of the Gâthas.")

one of the last Yeshts (XXII.), so that, by combining the two, we obtain a beautifully complete narrative, if such a word may be applied to a vision of the future.

"Zarathushtra asked Ahura-Mazda: 'O thou all-knowing Ahura-Mazda! Should I urge upon the godly man and upon the godly woman, should I urge upon the wicked daêva-worshipper who lives in sin, that they have once to leave behind them the earth made by Ahura, that they have to leave the waters that run, the corn that grows, and all the rest of their wealth?' Ahura-Mazda answered: 'Thou shouldst, O holy Zarathushtra.'

"'O Maker of the material world, thou Holy One! where are the rewards given . . . that, in their life in the material world, they have won for their souls?'

"Ahura Mazda answered: 'When the man is dead, when his time is over, then the hellish, evil-doing daêvas assail him, and when the third night is gone, when the dawn appears and brightens up, and makes Mithra, the god with beautiful weapons, reach the all happy mountains, and the sun is rising—then the fiend named Vîzaresha carries off in bonds the souls of the wicked daêva-worshippers who live in sin.* The soul enters the way made by Time and open both to the wicked and the righteous.'" (Vendîdâd, XIX.)

During three nights the soul is said (Yesht XXII.) to have its seat near the head of the body it has just quitted. If the deceased was a righteous man, "his soul in those nights tastes as much of pleasure as the whole of the living world can taste." During these three nights the relatives offer prayers and sacrifices to Sraosha, Rashnu, and Vayu.

* Commentary: "Every one has a noose cast around his neck; when a man dies, if he has been a righteous man, the noose falls from his neck; if a wicked, they drag him with that noose down into hell." The good and evil spirits struggle on the bridge for the possession of the soul.

At the end of the third night, when the dawn appears, it seems to the soul of the faithful one as if it were brought amidst plants and scents; it seems as if a wind were blowing from the region of the south,* a sweet-scented wind, sweeter scented than any other wind in the world. And it seems to the soul of the faithful one as though he were inhaling that wind with his nostrils, and he thinks: "Whence does that wind blow, the sweetest-scented wind I ever inhaled?" (Yesht XXII.)

"Then (at the head of the Chinvat Bridge, the holy bridge made by Mazda) comes the well-shapen, strong, and tall-formed maid . . ." (Vend., XIX.) "fair, white-armed, beautiful of body, of the size of a maid in her fifteenth year, as fair as the fairest things in the world . . ." (Yesht XXII.) "with the dogs at her sides. . . ." (Vend., XIX.) "And the soul of the faithful one addresses her, asking : 'What maid art thou, who art the fairest maid I have ever seen?' And she answers him : 'O thou youth of good thought, good words, and good deeds, of good religion, I am thy own conscience. . . ." (Yesht XXII.)

"She makes the soul of the righteous one go up above the Hara-Berezaiti ; above the Chinvat Bridge she places it in the presence of the heavenly gods themselves. Up rises Vohu-manô from his golden seat ; Vohu-manô exclaims : 'How hast thou come to us, thou holy one, from that decaying world into this undecaying one?' Gladly pass the souls of the righteous to the golden seat of Ahura-Mazda, to the golden seat of the Amesha-Spentas, to the Garô-nmâna, the abode of Ahura-Mazda, the abode of the Amesha-Spentas, the abode of all the other holy beings." (Vend., XIX.)

In the Yesht it is one of the faithful that had departed before him who welcomes the righteous soul,

* The south is the auspicious direction, since Mount Arezûra, the fiends' mountain, containing the entrance to hell, is in the north. The daêvas always come "from the region of the north ' and retire thither when baffled and driven away.

and asks: "How didst thou come from the abodes full of cattle and full of the wishes and enjoyments of love? From the material world into the world of the spirit? From the decaying world into the undecaying one?" But Ahura-Mazda, interposing like a courteous host, who will not have a weary guest disturbed, says: "Ask him not, who has just gone the dreary way, full of fear and distress, where the body and the soul part from one another. Let him eat of the food brought to him. . . ."

34. After enjoying the exquisite poetry and imagery of this description, it is somewhat of an anti-climax, though quite in accordance with the rules of a system of perfectly balanced dualism, to read the whole over again, word for word, only reversed, for the wicked soul. It tastes as much suffering during the three first nights "as the whole living world can taste," a foul-scented wind meets it from the region of the north, it is confronted by the man's evil conscience in the shape of a hideous hag, and so on to the end. We may be very sure that the beautiful creation is the spontaneous one, and that the ugly *pendant* has been added in the days of symmetry and dogmatic rehandling of older materials.

35. We have now arrived at the end of what may at first sight appear in the light of a long digression. In reality it is not so. If Carlyle's saying be true, that "the main fact about a man is his religion," it is truest when extended to nations. For nations are more apt than individuals to *act* up to their religion. A nation sets up its religion as a stand-

ard embodying its loftiest and holiest ideals, worked out collectively and unconsciously by its members, and summed up by some great teacher and leader. By those ideals, by that standard, a nation should be judged, its historical mission and influence appraised, not by the fallings-off and shortcomings of individuals,—just as an individual's intrinsic worth can be fairly estimated only by noting the high-water mark his spiritual consciousness reaches in moments of insight and uplifting, not by the shallows and lowlands in which existence drags on, more from necessity—or at least feebleness of purpose—than choice, nor by the leaps and convulsive starts occasioned by moments of passion and general disturbance. Nor should a religion be judged by the amount of ancient mythic dross clinging to it, or its puerilities of superadded theological dogmatism and priestly discipline, but from the amount of pure spiritual food it contains, also the practical help it gives towards righteous and happy living.

There are two short Avestan texts, which would alone suffice to atone for all the dross contained in the book, and establish a moral elevation that can hardly be overrated for the people who could think and feel thus. The first is a verse towards the close of the great hymn to the Fravashis, (Yesht XIII.): " We worship the souls of the holy men and women, born at any time or in any place, whose consciences struggle, or will struggle, or have struggled for the good." The other text is a prayer (in the Lesser Avesta) which, for conciseness, comprehensiveness, and depth of thought, has never been surpassed:

"Give us knowledge, sagacity; quickness of tongue; holiness of soul; a good memory; and then the understanding that goeth on growing, *and that understanding, which cometh not through learning.*" Judged by all these tests and standards, the Eranian race and their religion hold a very high standing indeed; and a thorough comprehension of the latter will be of no little help in duly estimating the former's triumphant progress through the ancient world, which we now prepare to follow, taking up the thread of historical narrative where we last dropped it—at the Fall of Nineveh and the Assyrian Empire.

VII.

THE LAST DAYS OF JUDAH.

1. WHILE Asshur, the dying giant, lay in the throes of dissolution, the last ebb of animation feebly surging in Nineveh, the still throbbing heart,—a stir, as of returning life, passed over the remoter provinces as the pressure of the iron hand that held them down relaxed in death. Of the number was Syria. Once more the procession of familiar names passes before us: Hamath and Judah and Damascus, Moab and Ammon and Edom, spectres of former greatness, roused into a brief spell of energy by a draught of that "wine of fury," which the last of Jerusalem's prophets was bid to cause all the nations to drink that they might "reel to and fro and be mad," one with another (Jeremiah, XXV.). Egypt too, with wounds scarce healed, and tottering still, but undaunted and aggressive as ever, appears once more, for the last time, in Asia, on the scene which she had swept triumphant through so many centuries, but was now to abandon, stricken and crestfallen, like an actor hissed off the stage.

2. Psammetik, the deliverer of Egypt,* had been

---

* See "Story of Assyria," p. 395.

succeeded in 610 by his son, NECHO II., who immediately set to work to carry out his father's policy with regard to Syria. True, Psammetik's long years of warfare had not brought him farther than the Philistine cities,* but he had been interrupted by the downpouring of the Scythian and Cimmerian hordes and the necessity of retreating into his own equally open country to be in readiness for an invasion. That obstacle was now removed; interference from Assyria was the last thing to be feared, and a warm welcome from the Syrian princes, judging from precedents, could be counted upon. Necho's plan probably was to assure himself of their allegiance, and, his rear securely covered by a breastwork of tribute-paying friends, to proceed to the Euphrates, to the main business of the campaign—the actual conquest of Assyria itself. There is no reason why this plan should not have been successful, but that others were beforehand with the Egyptian.

3. Moreover, the princes may not have been so ready to welcome him. Now that their colossal foe lay at the last gasp, their dreams must have been of total emancipation, not of exchanging one foreign rule for another, even though probably a milder one. That such was their feeling, and that Necho's progress was not a peaceful one, we may conclude from the fact that it took him four years to get to the Euphrates, and from the hostile attitude of one of them, Josiah, King of Judah, recorded

---

* See "Story of Assyria," pp. 418, 423.

at length in the Bible books, (Second Kings, Second Chronicles, and Jeremiah).

4. Since the unexpected deliverance from Sennacherib's host in 701,* Judah had, on the whole, with the exception of Manasseh's short-lived rebellion,† and the descent of the Scythians, enjoyed a pretty quiet time. The now reigning king, Josiah, Manasseh's grandson, had come to the throne in 638, a child only eight years old. Early moulded to the double influence of the priests and the prophets, he grew up into a religious reformer, whose holy zeal restored the worship of Yahveh in more than ancient purity and splendor. At the approach of the Egyptian army he roused himself from his peaceful and pious occupations to oppose the invader—an imprudent step, since his material means were unequal to it, and taken, it would appear, against the advice of his wisest councillors. A battle was fought in the valley of Megiddo. Here where, a thousand years before, the great Dhutmes III. had broken the Canaanite league,‡ fortune again prospered the Egyptian arms; Necho's victory was complete, and Josiah himself fell on the field. His son and successor JEHOAHAZ, who came to humble himself at the victor's feet in his camp by the Orontes, found no favor in the Pharaoh's eyes, but was by him deposed and carried captive into Egypt, and there was great mourning for him : "Weep ye not

Battle of Megiddo; Defeat of Josiah by Necho. 609 B.C.

---
* See "Story of Assyria," pp. 305-311.
† See "Story of Assyria," pp. 341, 342.
‡ See "Story of Assyria," p. 27.

for the dead, neither bemoan him; but weep sore for him that goeth away, for he shall return no more, nor see his native country" (Jeremiah, XXII., 10).

5. Having appointed another of Josiah's sons, JEHOIAKIM, to reign in Judah, and taken much gold and silver out of the land, Necho followed in Dhutmes' steps, and pursued his way to the Euphrates, probably conquering the countries as he went. In 605 he reached the great river; but here he was confronted by a foe for whom he was little prepared. Things had gone faster than he had expected, and differently: Nineveh had fallen the year before under the united efforts of the Medes under Kyaxares and the Babylonians under Nabopolassar.* It was therefore not the worn-out old lion of Asshur whom the Pharaoh encountered, but the strong and victorious lion of Babel, with threatening fangs and ominous growl. The Babylonian army, commanded not by Nabopolassar, who was old and infirm, but by his young son, Nebuchadrezzar, already a renowned warrior and accomplished general, met the Egyptian force near Karkhemish, and completely routed it. How Necho returned to the Nile after this disaster, and how long it took him, we have no hint,—he is heard of no more.

<small>Battle of Karkhemish; Defeat of Necho by Nebuchadrezzar.—605 B.C.</small>

6. The victory of Karkhemish would have been followed up more vigorously and immediately, had not Nebuchadrezzar, soon after he started in pursuit of the routed Pharaoh, been hastily summoned to Babylon. His father, Nabopolassar, had died after

* See "Story of Assyria," pp. 427, 428.

a short illness, and though a competent regent was appointed by the priesthood, the presence of the new king was urgently required, and affairs at home for a time took the precedence over foreign wars. It was a new and vast inheritance which Nebuchadrezzar was called upon to receive and organize. For at the division of spoils which followed on the destruction of Nineveh, the ancient empire of Asshur had been pretty equitably divided between the two principal champions—the kings of Media and Babylon. The former, true to the tendency of his people, which had always been drawn on in a westerly direction, retained the long-disputed Zagros region, the land that might be called Assyria proper, down to the alluvial line, and such power or claims as Assyria possessed over the entire mountain-land of Naïri, from the Caspian Sea to the Mediterranean, from the highlands of Urartu to those of Masios and Amanos—or, in other words, all that lay east and north of the Tigris. This, joined to the Medes' vast dominions in their native Erân, made up the new and, for a short while, powerful Median Empire. The Babylonian Empire was formed of the rest of Mesopotamia, with Chaldea proper, down to the Gulf, and all that lay westward of the Euphrates to the sea. This empire, if inferior in extent to the other, was superior in so far that it was more homogeneous, including countries of one race, one culture, and almost one language—the Semitic. It will be seen that both these empires, in transferring to themselves the possessions and claims of Assyria, burdened themselves with its wars, especially the southern empire, which could not possibly forego the sovereignty over the lands of Syria, as it was a matter of vital importance to Babylon, both from a military and commercial point of view, to hold control over the two great caravan routes—the one across the desert to the Phœnician cities of the sea-shore, and the other, from these cities, through Damascus and Karkhemish, to Asia Minor. As for Elam, it seems, at this time, to have been already occupied in part by an advanced detachment of a new nation—the PERSIANS, Aryan Eranians like the Medes—to whom they were subject. This detachment was commanded by a branch of the royal family of Persia; but not for fifty years yet were they to come forward in any way. Through all this time we never hear of Elam. It is more than probable that it was tributary to Media, and did not court notoriety.

7. We are not told to whom Judah and the other Syrian princes paid tribute during the five years that elapsed between the battle of Karkhemish and the surely not unexpected coming of Nebuchadrezzar. One thing must have been clear to them: that the question for them could only be between two masters. Nor would that question be left in doubt long, as it was not likely that the king of Babylon would suffer the rivalry of Egypt one moment longer than he should be kept busy at home. So that his coming in 600 B.C. was more like that of a sovereign returning to claim his own than the invasion of a conqueror. Jehoiakim of Judah, wisely hastened to tender his submission, and Nebuchadrezzar seems to have spent the next three years in Syria, in desultory

warfare, graphically described by a contemporary—
the prophet Habakkuk:

"Lo, I raise up the Chaldeans, that bitter and hasty nation, which march through the breadth of the earth, to possess dwellings that are not theirs. They are terrible and dreadful. . . . Their horses are swifter than leopards, and are more fierce than the evening wolves. . . . They fly as an eagle that hasteth to devour. They come, all of them, for violence; their faces are set eagerly as the east wind, and they gather captives as the sand. Yea, he scoffeth at kings, and princes are a derision unto him · he derideth every stronghold. . . . He shall sweep by as a wind; . . . even he whose might is his god. . . . He taketh men with the angle, he catcheth them in his net, and gathereth them in his drag; therefore he rejoices and is glad. . . ."

8. The leading spirit in Jerusalem at this time was the prophet Jeremiah. Like Isaiah, but with infinitely greater violence, he opposed and denounced all plans of resistance. He was profoundly convinced that Judah's only chance of safety lay in abject submission and discouraged, nay, cursed in the name of the Lord, all attempts which could only bring destruction on the city, death and ruin on the people. His preaching was considered unpatriotic and was far from popular. Besides, the accusations and invectives which he never ceased to hurl at the wealthy and powerful, not sparing the king himself, reproving their evil ways, made him bitter enemies in the ruling classes. So the policy which he advocated, though it had prevailed under the pressure of imminent danger, was soon abandoned. The same pitiable old farce with the tragic ending was enacted once again: forlorn hopes centred on promises from Egypt, revolt, then disappointment, as the " broken

reed" failed to give support,—and retribution, swift and terrible.

9. Three years after his submission Jehoiakim appeared in arms and refused the tribute. Nebuchadrezzar, who had other matters on his hands just then, sent against Judah bands of Chaldeans, Moabites, Ammonites, and other loyal Syrian nations, and only when he had driven out the Pharaoh so thoroughly that he "came not again any more out of his lands," and "when he had taken, from the river Euphrates to the Brook of Egypt, all that pertained to the king of Egypt," did he join the besiegers before Jerusalem. Jehoiakim meantime had died. From a passage in Jeremiah it would appear that there had been a revulsion of popular feeling against him, which had vented itself in indignities perpetrated on his body. "They shall not lament for him," says the prophet; . . . "he shall be buried with the burial of an ass, drawn and cast forth beyond the gates of Jerusalem." Nor had the prophet any but words of wrath for Jehoiakim's son and successor, JEHOIACHIN (also called JECONIAH): "As I live, saith the Lord, though Jeconiah were the signet upon my right hand, yet would I pluck thee thence; and I will give thee into the hand of them of whom thou art afraid. . . ." The poor youth (only eighteen years old) did not attempt further resistance. but went out to Nebuchadrezzar's camp and gave himself up, with his mother, his princes, and his servants. Jerusalem was not destroyed yet this time, but its population was thinned of 10,000 cap-

First taking of Jerusalem by Nebuchadrezzar.— 597 B.C.

tives, chosen among the "mighty men of valor," including a thousand craftsmen and smiths, "all of them strong and apt for war." The prophet Ezekiel was one of this first batch of captives, who were taken to Babylon together with the king and his house. Nebuchadrezzar made an uncle of Jeconiah, ZEDEKIAH, a son of Jehoiakim, king in Judah, entered into a covenant with him, and made him swear the oath of allegiance.

10. Four years now passed peacefully enough, but it was a peace fraught with fears, forebodings, and dissensions. The spirit of Judah was not broken yet, and popular feeling was all for revolt. Jeremiah's persistent warnings scarcely sufficed to hold it in check, all the more that they were counteracted by other prophets, who foretold that the yoke of Babylon should be broken and the captives should return after a short interval, some said within two years. At times Jeremiah was actually forbidden to speak in public. But the consciousness of his mission was strong within him and banished fear. Bitterly he complains of the persecutions to which he was subjected, curses the day that he was born, "the man who brought tidings to his father, saying— A man-child is born, making him very glad," but speak he must, even though his life be the forfeit: "I am become a laughing-stock all the day, every man mocketh me; . . . the word of the Lord is made a reproach unto me, and a derision all the day. And if I say—I will not make mention of him, nor speak, then there is in mine heart as it were a burning fire shut up in my bones, and I am weary

with forbearing, and I cannot contain...." When, in the fourth year of Zedekiah's reign, messengers came from the kings of Moab, Ammon, and Edom, and from those of Tyre and Sidon, to propose a renewal of the usual combination, the prophet opposed their errand with even more than his usual vigor and explicitness. He "gave them a charge unto their masters," saying:

"Thus saith the Lord of Hosts, the God of Israel: ... I have given all these lands into the hands of Nebuchadrezzar the king of Babylon, my servant. ... And it shall come to pass that the nation and the kingdom which will not serve the same Nebuchadrezzar, that will not put their neck under the yoke of the king of Babylon, that nation will I punish with the sword and with the famine and with the pestilence. ... And hearken not unto the words of the prophets that speak unto you, saying—Ye shall not serve the king of Babylon, for they prophesy a lie unto you. I have not sent them. ... Bring your necks unto the yoke of the king of Babylon, and serve him and his people, and live. ..."

And when, about this very time, Zedekiah went to Babylon, it was probably by the advice of the cautious prophet, and to clear himself from any suspicion of complicity in a conspiracy which could not be unknown to the king.

11. Not content with preaching in Jerusalem, Jeremiah sent written words to the captives in Babylon, exhorting them to bear their lot in patience and to make the best of it; to "build houses and dwell in them," to plant gardens and eat the fruit of them, to marry and multiply and "not be diminished." "And," he added, "seek the peace of the city and pray unto the Lord for it, for in the peace thereof shall ye have peace." And yet was the prophet's

soul filled with wrath against the conquerors, and he took comfort in the prevision that their turn would come, expatiating on the future ruin of Chaldea with vindictive delight, as the fit retribution for the woes brought on Judah. The last chapters of Jeremiah, written after the final catastrophe had been enacted, breathe this spirit of revengeful exultation throughout, and are full of dire predictions, in the usual lofty strain of prophetic poetry,—passages the substance of which can be summed up in the following extract:

"Israel is a scattered sheep; the lions have driven him away; first the king of Assyria hath devoured him; and last this Nebuchadrezzar king of Babylon hath broken his bones. . . . Behold, I will punish the king of Babylon and his land as I have punished the king of Assyria. . . ."

And even while preaching resignation and cheerful endurance under the hardships of captivity, even while prevailing on the unwilling king to go to Babylon on his humiliating errand, Jeremiah managed to convey to his captive brethren the assurances of coming retribution. He "wrote in a book all the evil that should come upon Babylon," and gave the book to one of the royal officers, bidding him read out "all these words" when he should have arrived at Babylon, then bind a stone to it and cast it into the midst of the Euphrates, saying, as he did so: "Thus shall Babylon sink and not rise again."

12. Thus, at his own imminent peril, the prophet succeeded in putting off the evil hour for a few years more. But when, in 589, the grandson of

Necho II.,* Hophra, (the Greeks call him Apries), succeeded to the throne of Egypt and immediately showed signs of meditating a Syrian campaign, the temptation was too strong for the war party in Jerusalem; Zedekiah, perhaps rather unwillingly, but unable to withstand the pressure of popular feeling, openly rebelled. It was not long before Nebuchadrezzar was reported to be on the march. More than ever Jeremiah inveighed against this recklessness, upbraiding the king moreover for his breach of faith, and no messages or enquiries could draw from him any but the one obnoxious advice, "submit." "Thus saith the Lord: I myself will fight against you with an outstretched hand and a strong arm. Behold, I set before you the way of life and the way of death. He that abideth in this city shall die, by the sword, and by the famine and by the pestilence. But he that goeth out and falleth away to the Chaldeans, he shall live."

13. Egypt, as usual, was not ready in time. Before her army had crossed the frontier, Nebuchadrezzar already stood under the walls of Jerusalem. The Pharaoh, however, now made up for lost time by rushing onward with such energy and swiftness as to claim the Chaldeans' immediate attention, so that they raised the siege of Jerusalem in order to hasten southwards with undivided forces. Great was the joy in the doomed city, but Jeremiah sternly chid all hope, saying to those who were sent from

* Necho had died in 594 and been succeeded by his son Psammetik II, who did not come out of Egypt at all during his short reign.

the king to enquire of him: "Behold Pharaoh's army, which is come forth to help you, shall return to Egypt, to their own land. And the Chaldeans shall come again and fight against this city; and they shall take it, and burn it with fire." And to a secret message from the king, asking: "Is there any word from the Lord?" he replied: "There is: thou shalt be delivered into the hands of the king of Babylon." In vain his life was threatened almost daily; in vain he was lowered by cords into a noisome dungeon filled with mire, by order of the princes of the city, who said: "This man weakeneth the hands of the men of war that remain in this city, and the hands of all the people, speaking such words as these: for he seeketh not the welfare of the people, but the hurt." When secretly rescued by the command of the king, and brought into his presence, he steadfastly repeated the same message in the same words. At last the king, unable to protect him otherwise, bade him remain in the palace, and there he stayed in the court of the guard, until Jerusalem was taken, when Nebuchadrezzar ordered him to be treated with honor and set at liberty.

14. For it came to pass according to the prophet's words. The host of Egypt was struck down at one blow and Nebuchadrezzar returned with all his army and besieged Jerusalem, establishing his own headquarters, however, at some distance, at Riblah on the Orontes, in the land of Hamath, whence he could not only overlook the operations against Judah, but keep an eye on all the lands of Syria and the cities

Destruction of Jerusalem by Nebuchadrezzar. — 686 B.C.

of the sea-coast. The siege lasted nearly a year and a half and the horrors of it pass description. According to the account given by Jeremiah, (in the Lamentations), hunger was the worst.

"The priests and the elders," he writes, "gave up the ghost in the city, while they sought them meat to refresh their souls. . . . The young children and the sucklings swoon in the streets of the city; they say to their mothers, Where is corn and wine? When they swoon as the wounded, . . and their soul is poured out into their mothers' bosom. . . . Her nobles were purer than snow, they were whiter than milk. . . . Their visage is blacker than a coal; . . . their skin cleaveth to their bones; it is withered, it is become like a stick. They that be slain with the sword are better than those that be slain with hunger. . . . The hands of the pitiful women have sodden their own children; they were their meat in the destruction of the people."

At last a breach was made in the wall, and the Chaldeans gained possession of one of the gates. The king and his men of war then made a bold sally and attempted to cut their way through the besiegers. They had actually broken through the lines, out into the open country, but were pursued, overtaken, and scattered. As to king Zedekiah, he was taken before the king of Babylon, to Riblah, where he suffered the most barbarous treatment. His sons were slain in his presence, after which his eyes were put out and he was carried in chains to Babylon, there to end his days in prison. The walls of Jerusalem were broken down; the temple and the royal palace built by Solomon were burned entirely, as well as the houses of the wealthy inhabitants, and all their treasures and works of art were carried away; those that were cumbrous by reason of their size, like the pillars of brass and the brazen sea, were broken in pieces. All the people of Jerusalem were carried into captivity, with the exception of the very poorest, who were left behind to be vine-dressers and husbandmen.

15. We have already seen that the Hebrew prophets, although deeply versed in the politics of their times, and foretelling with unerring insight the ruin which, in the course of history, was inevitably to overtake the various states, great and small, which formed their political world, were sometimes misled, by their eager impatience to see the wrongs they were powerless to avert avenged on their rivals and enemies by a higher power, into appointing too early a date for their destruction.* Ezekiel especially repeatedly falls into this error. Thus the defeat inflicted on the Pharaoh Hophra did not result in the Chaldean invasion and total destruction which he depicts in his otherwise magnificent dirge over Egypt. (Ezekiel, ch. XXXII. and other passages.) No less premature is his eloquent prophecy of the fall of Tyre (ch. XXVI.-XXVIII.), which Nebuchadrezzar proceeded to blockade as soon as he had done with Judah. The Jews suspected the proud queen of the seas of being at heart rather pleased than grieved at the disaster which struck them from the roll of nations, and their captive prophet accordingly denounces her and calls down destruction on her head :

"Because that Tyre hath said against Jerusalem, Aha ! she is broken that was the gate of the peoples ; I shall be replenished now

* See " Story of Assyria," p. 429.

that she is laid waste ; therefore thus saith the Lord God: Behold, I am against thee, O Tyre, and will cause many nations to come up against thee, as the sea causeth his waves to come up. And they shall destroy the walls of Tyre, and break down her towers. I will also scrape her dust from her, and make her a bare rock. . . . For behold, I will bring upon Tyre Nebuchadrezzar king of Babylon, king of kings, from 'the north, with horses, and with chariots, and with horsemen. . . ." (Ch. XXVI., 2-14.)

That the Phœnician capital suffered severely is most probable, since the siege is said to have lasted nigh on thirteen years. On the other hand, the very fact that it could last so long and not end in conquest even then, shows that the blockade could not have been very close. How should it, when the sea remained open? It seems to have ended in a capitulation, the people of Tyre acknowledging the king of Babylon's overlordship and accepting a new king from his hands, in place of the "rebel" who was deposed.

<small>Siege of Tyre by Nebuchadrezzar.—585-573 B.C.</small>

16. The prophet Ezekiel, seeing his prediction, for the time being, only half fulfilled, takes a peculiar view of the event. He appears to have considered the sack of Tyre as a reward due to the king of Babylon for the work he did as instrument of the Lord's vengeance against Judah, and speaks in a one of disappointment of his being deprived of it:

"Nebuchadroezar, king of Babylon, caused his army to serve a great service against Tyre ; every head was made bald, and every shoulder was peeled* ; yet had he no wages, nor his army, from Tyre."

Then the prophet promises the conquest of Egypt as a compensation :

<small>* By the long friction of the helmet and the shield-strap.</small>

"Therefore, thus saith the Lord God: Behold, I will give the land of Egypt unto Nebuchadrezzar king of Babylon, and he shall carry off her multitude, and take her spoil, and take her prey; and it shall be the wages for his army. I have given him the land of Egypt as his recompense for which he served, because they wrought for me."

But Nebuchadrezzar never invaded Egypt. Though a good general, he was not a conqueror after the pattern of the Assyrian kings. He was a statesman as well, inclined by preference to works of peace, and gave the most unslackening attention to the establishment of his home-rule at Babylon on broad and solid bases—an object which could be best achieved by a continuous personal residence in his own native state, Chaldea, and its capital—Babylon. War, therefore, was always with him a matter of necessity, not of choice, and he strove to ensure general peace even by acting as peacemaker between his neighbors.

VIII.

LYDIA AND ASIA MINOR—THE BALANCE OF POWER IN THE EAST.

1. A GLANCE at the map shows that the doom of Judah and the other Syrian states was inevitable. Their position made it a necessity for whoever ruled in Mesopotamia to take and to hold them. They really were part and parcel of the Assyrian inheritance, and when the founders of a Chaldean monarchy at Babylon entered into that inheritance, it was but natural that they should reach out for the seashore and keep a heavy master's hand on all that lay between. The case was different with such countries as were separated by natural barriers from what may be called the Semitic and Canaanitic region—such as lay in and beyond the highlands of Taurus and Naïri, *i.e.*, in Asia Minor and the mountain land between the Black and Caspian seas.

2. Of these countries some had been only partly subject to Assyria, like the kingdom of Van and the other principalities of Urartu on one hand, Cilicia and Cappadocia on the other, while some had never been subject to it at all, but only endangered by its nearness; these were the countries of that advanced part of Asia Minor, of which the course of the river

Halys (the modern Kizil-Irmâk), according to Herodotus' just remark, almost makes an island. For, it is very certain that the Assyrians never saw the Ægean Sea—(that part of the Mediterranean which flows amidst the Greek islands and along the Ionian shores)—any more than the Black Sea. And if Lydia, at a moment of sore distress, exchanged her independence against Assyrian protection, the submission was only temporary and almost immediately repented of.*

3. We saw that soon after that passing triumph, Asshurbanipal became too much engrossed with vital struggles nearer home—against Chaldean Babylon and Elam and the advancing Medes—to repress the risings of his outlying subjects and vassals. Much less were his feeble successors able to attend to anything but their most immediate interests, and while the Scythian invasion was acting on the tottering empire as an earthquake on an already ruinous building, changes were taking place in and beyond its northern boundaries, which it is impossible to trace in those unrecorded years, but which we find accomplished when the darkness is lifted and some degree of order restored. Thus we hear no more of Urartu. It is certain that, in the course of the seventh century B.C., the Hittite Alarodians were supplanted by that Thraco-Phrygian branch of the Aryan race, which is represented in the enumeration of the Japhetic family given in Chapter X. of Genesis, as Tôgarmah, son of Gômer,† and has been familiar under the name of Armenians ever since

* See "Story of Assyria," pp. 378-382.   † *Ibid.*, pp. 367, 368.

the Greek writers introduced them to the world by that name.

4. Lydia, from its greater remoteness, was still in more favorable conditions, and, being governed by a wise and enterprising royal house, made the best use of her opportunities, enlarging her territory at the expense of her neighbors. This dynasty was that of the MERMNADÆ, the founder of which, Gugu (Gyges), we saw calling in Assyrian help against the Cimmerians, and who fell in the struggle. The Mermnadæ were a native Lydian family who had been raised to the throne by a revolution. Gyges murdered KANDAULES, the last king of the preceding dynasty, which had ruled the country through several hundred years, and probably married the murdered man's widow, to create for himself a claim, not neglecting, however, the support of some troops from the adjoining land of CARIA. The story of this revolution is told in several ways, one more unbelievable than the other. The favorite version, and also the least improbable in itself, though there is absolutely no real authority for it, is given by Herodotus. He tells us, in his usual discursive but always charmingly entertaining way, how Gyges was Kandaules' bosom friend, and how the king, being violently in love with his own wife, and thinking her beauty peerless among women, was so anxious to convince his friend that his praise of her was no exaggeration, that he insisted on placing him behind the door of her apartment, so that he should see her through the chink when she disrobed at night. In vain Gyges protested against being forced

into an action which, if discovered, must bring on him the queen's deadly vengeance. " For," adds the narrator, "among the Lydians, and indeed among the Barbarians (*i.e.*, the Orientals), it is reckoned a deep disgrace, even for a man, to be seen unclothed." Gyges had to comply, and as he was gliding out at a moment when the queen's back was turned, she just caught sight of him, but had the presence of mind to make no sign. The next morning, however, she sent for the unwilling culprit and placed before him the alternative, either to die on the spot, or to kill the husband who had so beyond pardon affronted her, then to marry her and reign. After some hesitation and entreaties to spare his foolish and unfortunate friend, he chose life and crown for himself. The deed was done that very night, and the new king proclaimed the next day.*

5. Herodotus adds that the people at first flew to arms, to avenge their king, but the matter was referred for arbitration to the oracle of the Greek Sungod Apollo, in his own shrine at Delphi. The oracle was given in the usurper's favor, only adding that vengeance should come in the fifth generation —"a prophecy," says the historian, "of which neither the Lydians nor their princes took any account until it was fulfilled." Of all the more or less fabulous incidents which Greek historical gossip has reported in connection with this revolution and change

* Herodotus, Book I., Ch. 8-14.—A very popular tradition gives Gyges an invisible-making ring, which he uses on the occasion, but is a little too quick in turning on his finger, so the queen sees him. The miraculous finding of the ring on a dead giant's finger in a cave is also reported.

of dynasty, this last statement is the one which there is least reason to doubt. For Lydia, like most of the adjacent countries of Asia Minor, was at this time already deeply permeated with Greek influences and culture; indeed their population was much mixed with Greek, or, at any rate, Aryan elements.

6. There are few regions of which the early history is so inaccessible as this of Western Asia Minor. Literary sources we have none, save Greek histories and legends written down so late as to be much posterior even to the period at which we have now arrived. Monuments have been discovered not a few, but of a peculiar nature, and offering a deplorable want of variety. They are, firstly those rock, sculptures, with inscriptions in a hitherto undeciphered language, which have been mentioned in a preceding volume*; secondly, a large number of tombs. Of these, some—like the tombs of the kings of Lydia—are constructed in the primeval form of high mounds or "barrows," containing a good-sized sepulchral chamber in solid masonry. The rest—and such are found in bewildering numbers in Lycia—are hewn in live rocks. These tombs are real works of art, and unlike any others in the world, being elaborate imitations of the dwellings of the living, which, as we can see from these reproductions, were of wood, of well-joined timberwork. The tomb usually represents the front of a house—porch, pillars, door, windows, roof-gable—closely copying the joining, even the dovetailing of the timber and the protruding

* See "Story of Assyria," pp. 362-366.

AT MYRA. *Face page* 190.

ends of the beams that run through the building; the copy is perfect in every detail; thus where a closed door is represented, not only are the panels indicated, but frequently the nails also that studded the original; even the knocker. (See ill. 19.) One door, or, if large, part of one, is left open, to serve as

19. LYCIAN ROCK-TOMB AT TELMESSUS.

entrance into the grave-chamber behind, which, from the height at which these excavations are hewn in the quite, or nearly, perpendicular rocks, can have been reached only by means of ladders, except where steps have been cut for the purpose. There is no doubt but that the entrance was closed with a well-fitting slab or block, but the rapacity of generations of plunderers and conquerors was sure to be attracted by these retreats of the dead, which might well be supposed to contain valuables of various kinds, and in no case have the modern explorers found the rock-

20. LYCIAN ROCK-TOMB AT TELMESSUS.
(The block has been detached at some time, and slid down to the foot of the mountain.)

chambers occupied by their silent tenants. These rock-hewn house fronts vary much in elaborateness, ranging from plain timberwork (see ill. 19 and 20) to highly ornamented porches, the architectural character and figure decorations of which betray a late and thoroughly Greek period of art. (See ill. 21 and 22.) It is easy to see that these differences cover a span of many centuries; nor can one help surmising that each particular rock-tomb may have been a conscious imitation of the deceased's own dwelling. This original variety of sepulchral monuments found imitators not only among the Greeks, but among the Persians. (See further on, Chap. XIII.) Some of these monuments stand isolated, presenting copies of entire wooden houses, not façades only (see ill. 18, left side), or assuming the form of towers. Such is the famous tower-shaped monument at Xanthus, in Lycia; it rises above the graves, which, though rock-hewn, have been cleared by cutting away and removing the blocks immediately surrounding them; and the four sides are covered with sculptures referring to the fate of the soul after death. The winged death-goddesses, the Harpies, carry the soul away in the shape of a new-born child, and above the opening of the grave-chamber we see the sacred cow, the emblem of life-giving nature, a grateful and consoling reminder. (See ill. 23.) Some few of the isolated tombs represent a sarcophagus (the model being, like the houses, evidently of wood.) The sculptured lid shows four handles, in the shape of lion heads. (See ill. 24.)*

* It seems scarcely credible that a certain style of building should endure in the same locality through thousands of years; yet that such is the case in Lycia, is proved by ill. 25, 26, and 27, representing rural and excessively rude constructions, but of a character unmistakably identical with that of the dwellings reproduced in the earlier rock-tombs.

21. FAÇADE OF LYCIAN ROCK-TOMB AT MYRA.
(Late, Greek period.)

22. ROCK-TOMB AT MYRA.

(Figures outside the house sculptured in the rock; those inside the porch painted al fresco.)

7. Interesting and important as these sepulchral monuments are, they do not supply us with what we seek. We find no clue to help us date the most archaic of them, as these are not generally furnished with inscriptions. Many of the late ones, indeed, make up for it by presenting us with a double set, what has been called "bilingual inscriptions," *i.e.*, inscriptions in two languages—the native, and Greek. From these we see that the alphabets used for the two languages have much resemblance. The same remark applies to such Phrygian inscriptions as have been discovered. The languages of this group of nations, *i.e.*, such scraps as the few inscriptions have preserved, although they can be deciphered with but little difficulty, owing to the familiar alphabet, have not been reconstructed to any satisfactory extent, mainly from scantiness of material. Even these slender resources, however, establish the existence of at least two different groups among the languages of ancient Asia Minor in historical times: those of Phrygia, Mysia, and others in the west and the northwest are found to incline towards a very ancient Aryan philological type, the PELASGIC, from which the Greek language is descended, while there is great uncertainty about those of Lycia and the neighboring Caria.*

8. It is evidently impossible, from such slight and scattered data, to gather materials for any thing that could be called history, yet perhaps not quite im-

---

* Professr A. H. Sayce, in one of his latest works, positively declares that the Lycian language "is not Aryan,' in spite of all the attempts that have been made to show the contrary."

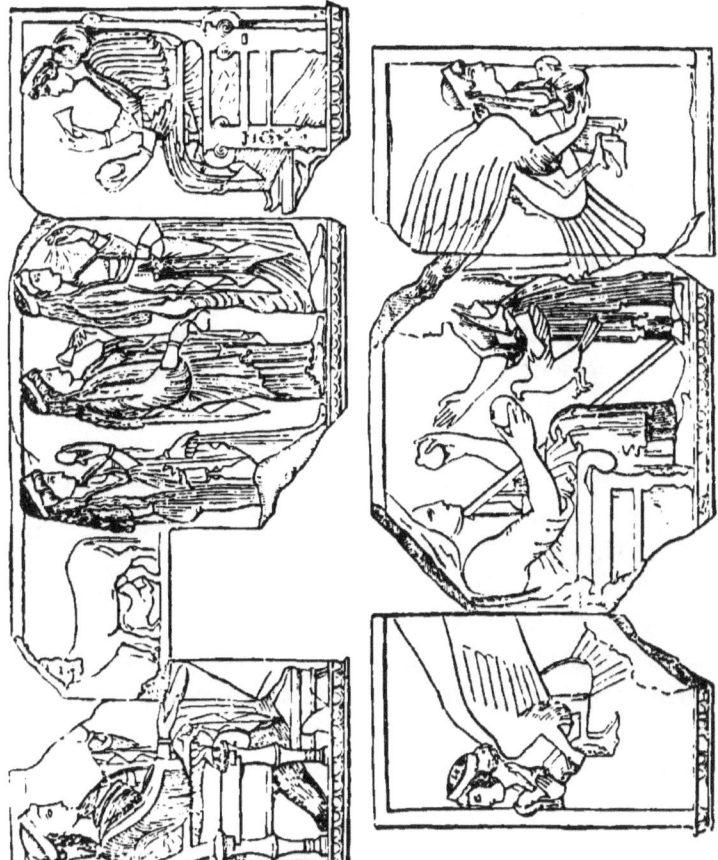

RELIEFS ON THE SO-CALLED "HARPY-TOWER," AT XANTHOS, IN LYCIA.

practicable to reconstruct, in very broad outlines, the periods of formation through which Asia Minor must have passed before it stands out in the full light of history, with its division into numerous more or less independent states, its mixed population, its complicated combination of religions and cultures as different as the races which originated them. The oldest traditions, repeated by the writers of classical antiquity, represent all Western Asia—of which Asia Minor is undoubtedly a part—as having been occupied, in immemorial time, during a number of centuries, by Turanians; a report which modern science sees little reason to dispute.* The immense chasm between this remote, misty past and the dawn of recorded historical times, though still greatly mixed with myth, we can partly bridge over, owing to Professor Sayce's Hittite discoveries. He has shown, by a comparative study of the peculiar rock-sculptures at Boghaz-Keui in Cappadocia, at Ibriz in Cilicia, at Karabel, near Smyrna, and in many more places of Asia Minor, with their inscriptions in characters identical with those found at Hamath,† that this powerful and gifted Hamitic race, the Hittites, at one time covered and ruled the whole of the region between the Black and Mediterranean seas, as far east as the Halys, and probably somewhat beyond, leaving their traces not only in those sculptures, but in several sanctuaries of their religion, devoted to the worship of the nature-goddess common to them and their Canaanitic and Semitic brethren, and whose

---

* See "Story of Chaldea," Chapter II., especially pp. 136–139.
† See "Story of Assyria," ill. 5, p. 36.

24. SEPULCHRAL MONUMENT AT XANTHOS (MARBLE).

25. MODERN CONSTRUCTIONS IN LYCIA.

temples, with their crowds of ministering women, gave rise to the Greek legend of the Amazons.* The fabled empire of these much-famed warrior-women —the head-quarters, so to speak, of the legend—was placed on the banks of the THERMODON, at no very great distance from the present ruins of Boghaz-Keui, and we know that the goddess, here named MÂ, had one of her principal temples served by no less than 6,000 women, in that same neighborhood, at KO-MANA in Cappadocia, a province which in very olden

26. GRANARY IN MODERN LYCIA.

times stretched farther towards the Black Sea than at a later, classical period. The Amazons were said to have founded cities. Wherever this is the case, we may be sure that ancient Hittite sanctuaries existed. Ephesus, Smyrna, Kymê, and several other places along the Ionian coast come under this head.†

9. It is probable that the Hittite rule and culture reached their widest westward expansion soon after

* See " Story of Assyria," pp. 30, 35, 205, 206, and 360-367.
† See A. H. Sayce's " Ancient Empires of the East," p. 130.

the fifteenth century B.C., and maintained their supremacy until about the year 1000 B.C., at least in Asia Minor, as in Syria—"The Land of Khatti" of the inscriptions,—they had already begun to recede before the aggressive advance of Assyria, and the pressure of Semitic elements generally. But even in Asia Minor the great Thraco-Phrygian migration had overspread the forgotten Turanian subsoil and Hittite cultivated ground with an Indo-European top-layer,* and apart from this movement, during the century ranging from somewhere in the tenth—*i.e.*,

27. GRANARY IN MODERN LYCIA.

soon after 1000 B.C.—to the middle of the ninth or later, Asia Minor was subjected to a continuous flow of Indo-European influences from a far more congenial and civilizing quarter—the continent and islands of Southern Greece and Peloponnesus.

10. An important revolution was then slowly, but by no means peacefully, changing the face of the rather motley assemblage of small states, republics, and free cities which was a couple of hundred years later to glory in the common name of HELLAS. The

* See "Story of Assyria," pp. 360 and 367-369.

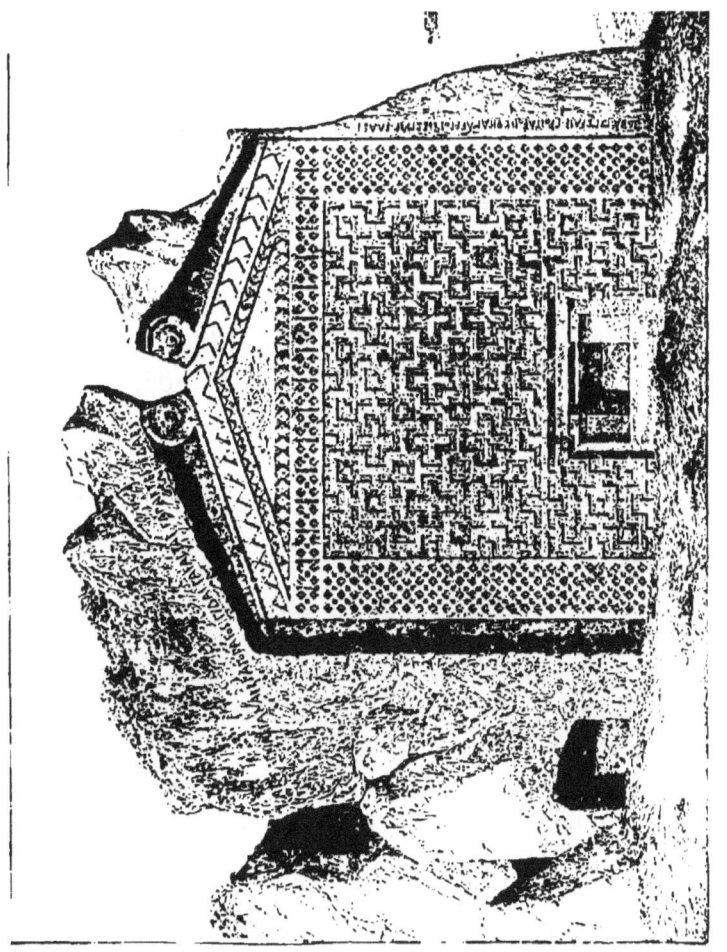

28. ROCK-TOMB OF A KING OF THE NAME OF MIDAS, IN PHRYGIA

people, whose differences and hostilities were to be merged in the proud and all-embracing nationality of the HELLENES (whom we have learned from the Romans to designate, less correctly, as GREEKS), were as yet broken up into a variety of tribes, all highly gifted, and all descended from the old stock of the PELASGI. Two of these, the ACHÆANS and the IONIANS, were in possession of the Peloponnesus and of a considerable strip of sea-coast north of the Isthmus of Corinth, including the peninsula of Attica. A third tribe, the DORIANS, had, for times untold, dwelt in the higher belt of Epirus and Thessaly, mountain-lands where they developed the stern and rugged temper, the love of war, and contempt of trade and crafts so generally characteristic of highlanders. Some time about 1000 B.C., there was a great stir among them. Moved by awakening ambition of conquest and power, perhaps also crowded by their increasing numbers in their numerous but narrow valleys, they began to descend southward, into the milder, more beautiful land by the sea. Where they passed, they appropriated the soil, enslaving its former owners, who were now expected to work it for the conquerors; in cities they established an iron rule, and wherever they met resistance, they waged war, even to extermination. It took this movement, known in history as "The Descent of the Dorians," about a hundred years to reach the Corinthian Isthmus, that short and narrow causeway which alone prevents Peloponnesus from being an island, torn from the Greek mainland, as Sicily is from that of Italy. They poured into the

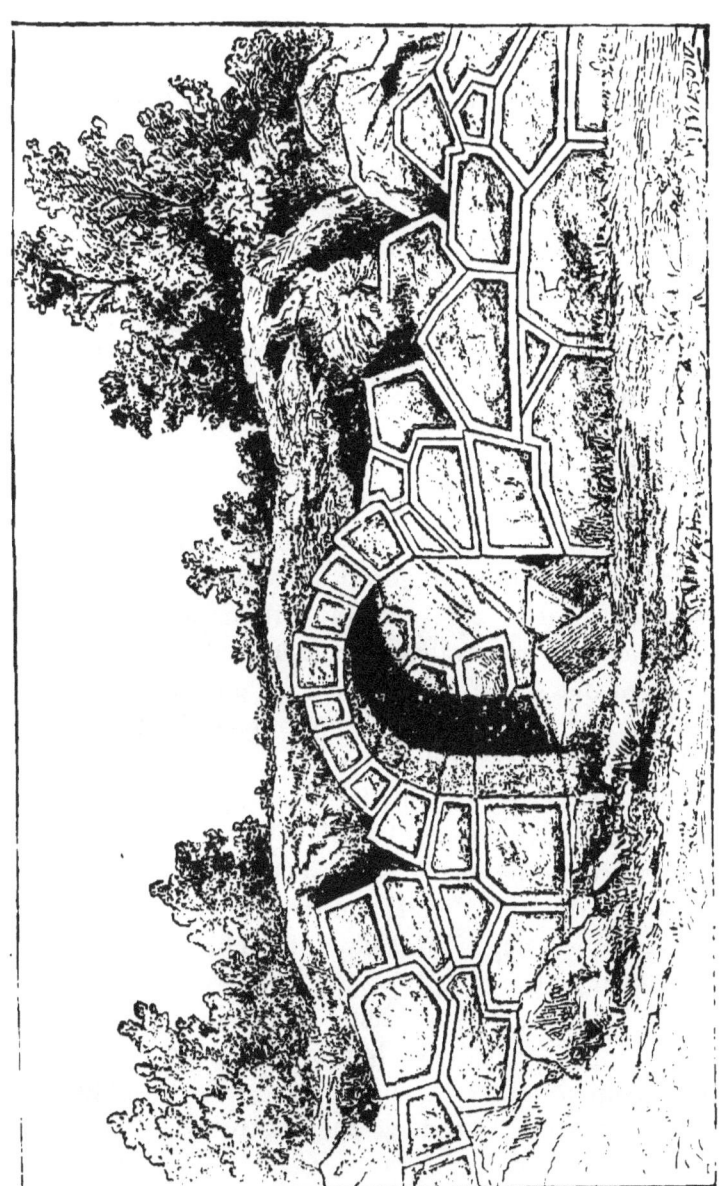

29 CITY WALL OF CNIDUS.
(Early Greek wall masonry.)

peninsula through this entrance, and also in ships,
across the long and narrow gulf, and there their ad-
vent produced the effect of a heavy body falling into
a vessel filled with liquid: there is a splash, a spurt,
and the liquid overflows on all sides. There was no
getting rid of the Dorians, for they were no common invaders. Their genius for war made them
proceed after a uniform and systematic fashion that
crushed resistance, while, being equally possessed of
the qualities that organize governments and ensure
the duration of states, their watchfulness and energy
baffled conspiracies and made popular risings hopeless. The ancient Achæan commonwealths and
more recent Ionian confederations of free cities had
but one alternative before them: submission or self-
banishment. Thousands of people, led by noble
families of oldest and most firmly established standing, chose the latter—and the age of colonies began.
Greek ships bore away detachment after detachment
of exiles, of all stations in life and all pursuits, and
landed them at innumerable points along the shores
of the surrounding seas: at various parts of Sicily
and Southern Italy, on the coasts of Illyria and
Epirus on one side, of Macedon and Thracia on the
other, as far as the mouth of the Bosporus, nay, the
inside of the Black Sea itself. Many such detachments stopped on this or that of the many islands
which seemed scattered broadcast over the blue
waters on purpose to receive them. And wherever a
handful of sad-faced emigrants raised their huts and
tents, bearing with them out of the old life nothing
but a few family relics, a little of their native earth,

and a spark of the sacred fire, kindled at the old cityhearth,—there, in an amazingly short time, blossomed and prospered first a settlement, then a thriving city, the colonies becoming so many stations of Greek commerce and Greek culture. So that after a while it became customary for Greek cities to send out colonies without any mournful occasion, simply to extend their influence and increase their own prosperity, by opening out new channels of trade and enterprise in distant and only partially explored countries. Many, indeed, were founded by the Dorians themselves.

11. Of all these outposts of Hellenic culture, none rose so rapidly or prospered so luxuriously as the colonies, founded chiefly by fugitive Ionians, along the shores of Asia Minor, to which they gave their name. The movement, an immediate consequence of the Dorian conquests, began soon after 1000 B.C., and continued through more than two centuries. The emigrants selected the sites of their settlements with admirable skill, mostly at the mouth of rivers— the HERMOS, the KAYSTER, the MÆANDER—at the foot of sheltering mountains, on commanding promontories, on points that invited commerce, yet ensured defence and seclusion if necessary, by no means a secondary consideration, since the new-comers did not plant their tents in waste and unclaimed lands, but in the midst of populous and already civilized countries, where they could not expect to obtain a firm footing without encountering resistance on the part of the native people. Both the Lydians and Carians were nations renowned in war, and were not

likely to allow strangers to have possession, unopposed, of their choicest territories, their sea-coast, and the mouths of their rivers. Yet we have no positive knowledge of the wars which must of necessity have accompanied the establishment of the Greek settlers. Nor do they appear to have been as long and fierce as might be expected, for when real history begins, it shows us the Greek cities clustered in well organized confederacies, individually flourishing, mutually protected, and apparently unmolested by the surrounding population, with which they seem to have, to a great extent, mingled by intermarriage and social intercourse. Even religion does not appear to have formed any impassable barrier between them. At SMYRNA, KYMÊ, MYRINA, EPHESUS, the Greeks found sanctuaries of the ancient Hittite nature-goddess, with the,

30. STATUE OF THE ARTEMIS OF EPHESUS.
(For the *Kerubim* winged bull's heads within the disk, compare "Story of Chaldea," p. 164.)

to them so novel, Amazonian worship, and unhesitatingly adopted the deity, merely changing her name to the familiar one of their own ARTEMIS.* The Oriental origin of the conception embodied in the goddess is sufficiently shown by the uncouth but transparent symbolism of her statue in her great temple at Ephesus, foreign to all Greek principles of beauty in art (see ill. 30), yet so expressive of what it is meant to convey: the idea of nature as the source of all life and nourishment. The sun-god of the Asiatics, too, in his different aspects, the Greeks easily identified with their own youthful and radiant god APOLLO, or their toiling, travelling semi-human solar hero, HERAKLÊS, himself an inheritance of Phœnicia and Chaldea, a revised edition of the Syrian Melkarth and the Babylonian Izdubar.† The Lydian name of the sun-god was SANDÔN, and he had a highly revered national sanctuary near the place where the Greeks built MILETUS, the queen of Ionian cities. This sanctuary was served by a native hereditary priesthood of the family known as the BRANCHIDÆ. When the Greeks came, they at once adopted the sanctuary, which became as famous as that of the Ephesian Artemis, under the name of temple of "Didymæan Apollo," and was left in the charge of its high-born guardians. Nor were the people of Asia Minor at all unwilling to acknowledge the spiritual kinship on their own side; and so it came to pass that, being moreover attracted by the surpassing loveliness of Greek culture and myth, they fell into the

* See above, p. 208, and "Story of Assyria," pp. 365, 366.
† See "Story of Assyria," p. 99; and "Story of Chaldea," Ch. VII.

habit of sending presents to the most renowned centres of Greek worship, and consulting the Greek gods through their oracles—*i. e.*, through those of their ministers who were considered to possess the gift of divine inspiration and to deliver the messages of the god or interpret the signs sent by him. The temple and oracle of Apollo at DELPHI was the most widely famed and revered, and became a favorite resort of the "Barbarians," whose lavish offerings greatly enriched its treasure-houses. This is why we may consider the report of Gyges referring his claim to the Lydian throne to the arbitration of the Delphic Apollo as the least doubtful of the statements made concerning the revolution which transferred the royal power to the dynasty of the Mermnadæ. Herodotus specifies the gifts sent by Gyges to the Delphic shrine, in gratitude for the verdict which confirmed his title; they consisted in a large quantity of silver and "a vast number of vessels of gold." Gyges, according to the same historian, "was the first of the barbarians whom we know to have sent offerings to Delphi," with the exception of a certain king of Phrygia who, even before his time, sent thither and dedicated to the god the royal throne whereon he was accustomed to sit and to administer justice—"an object," Herodotus adds, "well worth looking at."

12. In point of material civilization, the Lydians were probably far ahead of the new-comers, at the early period of Greek emigration. They were possessed of great skill in various industrial arts, especially those of dyeing wool and weaving; and Lydian

31. RUINS OF THE TEMPLE OF THE DIDYMÆAN APOLLO, NEAR MILETUS.

carpets and rugs enjoyed a reputation which we see surviving even to our own day, after so many ages and vicissitudes, in the great demand for Smyrna rugs. The influence, then, must have been mutual, more spiritual on the Greek side and more material on that of the Lydians. The country, moreover, abounded in precious metals, and that led to an invention which opened a new era to social and international intercourse and made a revolution in the commercial ways of the world: the invention of coining money. It is most probably to Gyges, the first of the Mermnadæ, that the credit of this invention is due, so simple in its principles, yet so portentous in its results.

13. Even so late as this, the seventh century B.C., a vast proportion of the active trade between nations was still carried on on the primitive basis of barter, *i. e.*, exchange of one commodity for another, of raw materials for manufactured products, of art luxuries for the necessaries of life, or other luxuries, etc. This must have necessarily been the case especially in the commercial transactions between civilized nations and savages or semi-civilized peoples, to whom direct exchange was the only intelligible and safe financial operation. But in the transactions between merchants of the same nation or of different equally civilized nations, the need of some less cumbrous means of doing business had long been felt,—and supplied. It consisted in substituting *purchase* for *barter*, *i. e.*, exchanging merchandises, not against other merchandise, but against something of equal value, convenient in shape and volume, which at any

32. FRAGMENT OF ORNAMENT FOUND AT THE TEMPLE OF THE DIDYMÆAN APOLLO.

moment could be in its turn exchanged for whatever wares the owner needed. Of course the intrinsic value of such a medium of exchange must be a universally acknowledged one, determined by general agreement. It has from times immemorial been found expedient to invest with such standard value the so-called precious metals, gold and silver. Once the positive value of a given weight of the metal had been settled, it only remained to divide masses of it into a great many smaller pieces, each weighing a certain fraction of the standard weight, and consequently representing a certain, well-defined fraction of the standard unit value. Henceforth the merchant who sold a rug, or a dagger, or a vessel of fine glass, was not forced to take in payment a number of live sheep, or of sheepskins, or of measures of grain, or a wagon-load of hay,—or any other ponderous and cumbersome wares that his customer might happen to have on hand; nor need a farmer, disposing of his surplus stock or grain, take in exchange for it articles that, perhaps, were not at all what he wanted. A bar, or a certain number of rings of gold or silver did the business much better and could be put away and kept till needed for a purchase. The facility thus offered for transfer of bulky property—such as land, houses, etc.,—was immense; and how early it was made use of, we see from that curious statement in Genesis (Ch. XXIII.) which shows us Abraham, a contemporary of the Elamite Khudur-Lagamar,[*] paying his Hittite hosts, for the field he requested of their courtesy, 400 shekels of silver, "such as are current with the merchants."

[*] See "Story of Chaldea," pp. 222–224.

14. Gold and silver, used in this manner—with a well-defined unit-weight of standard value divided into corresponding fractional weights—evidently answered the purpose of money in commercial transactions. Can, then, those bars, ingots, and rings be called "money"? They might—but for *one* thing: *they are not warranted*. Who is to assure the seller who receives them in payment, of the fulness of the weight and the purity of the metal? No one. Accordingly we see that Abraham *weighs out* the 400 shekels which he pays for the field. After this manner—by weighing—were all payments made, and the quality of the metal was tested by means of a touchstone. And it remained with the seller to accept or reject the bars or rings, according as he thought the weight full or short, the quality pure or inferior. Now *we* do not weigh the coins we pay and receive, nor are we allowed to reject them. We take them *on trust*. We are bound so to take them, because they are *warranted* of good weight and standard purity, by our governments, who, in token thereof, stamp each coin with a certain device and legend which private persons are forbidden to use. Guarantee and trust—this is the mutual contract between ruler and ruled which at once converts a mere merchandise into money or state currency. There was just this one step to take, and it seems strange that the Phœnicians, those matchless traders, should have missed it. Nor can we well account for the fact that so momentous an improvement should have been made in Lydia rather than anywhere else, except by the large quantities of precious metals which this

country yielded, almost for the trouble of picking them up. Not only were easily accessible veins of precious ore worked in the principal Lydian mountain ridges, TMOLOS and SIPYLOS, but the sands of the river PACTOLOS, which flowed through the capital, Sardis, carried along a bountiful per-

33. EARLY AND LATER LYDIAN COINS.

centage of a peculiar kind of pale gold, largely mixed with silver, obtainable by the easy process of washing. This mixture, in which the proportion of silver ranges from twenty to over forty per cent., is known under the special name of ELECTRON, whether natural, as found in Lydia, or imitated artificially, as it has been at various times. Of this electron, which was considered inferior in value to gold, but superior to silver, the first Lydian coins were made. Numbers of them, and also of pure gold and silver coins, have been found within a circuit of thirty miles round Sardis, and very rude they were, showing only the square punch mark. Only after a series of gradual improvements, we see the well-drawn device of royal Lydia—a lion's head, or a lion and bull—make its appearance, under Gyges' fourth descendant, the celebrated Kroisos. The invention, however, has remained associated with the name of the former, and late Greek authors speak of ancient coins which they call "gold pieces of Gyges." Thus it is that of the half-dozen great inventions which, each in turn, can be said to have changed the face of the world—the alphabet, coining, printing, gunpowder, the use of steam and electricity—we owe two to remote antiquity and to Oriental nations. *

15. When the dynasty of the Mermnadæ came to the throne in the person of Gyges, the change made itself felt at once in the greater energy, ambition, and sounder statesmanship which were exerted, both in foreign and domestic affairs. A steady policy of territorial aggrandizement was inaugurated by the annexation of Mysia. The blunder that had been made by former kings, in suffering the Greek settle-

* Several writers, both ancient and modern, claim the invention of coining for the Greeks and attribute it to a Greek tyrant, PHEIDON OF ARGOS, who seems to have been a contemporary of Gyges. The probabilities are that Pheidon was the first to appreciate the new invention and to introduce it into his own country.

ments to extend their chain of many links all along
the sea-coast, was to be retrieved, and Gyges began a
systematical attack against the Greek cities, com-
mencing with those nearest to him, with the firm intent
of making them subject to Lydia, that the country
might repossess itself of the mouths of its own rivers
and the harbors of its own sea-coast. But the cities
had become populous and strong, and valiantly held
their own. Moreover, the operations were unexpectedly interrupted by that Cimmerian invasion of which
we know the fatal issue for the Lydian king.*

16. His son ARDYS, however, and his grandson
SADYATTÊS, when freed from the inroads of the
obnoxious freebooters, resumed the thoroughly national war against the Greek cities. Some they took,
others repulsed them, and Miletus especially, which
had defied Gyges, was still as unconquered as ever
half a century later, under Sadyattês, actually sending out colonies, and generally living its busy, prosperous life under the very eyes of the besieging
Lydians. Then Sadyattês, not to weary his soldiers'
strength and patience, invented a new and most ingenious mode of warfare, which is best described in
Herodotus' own entertaining narrative:

"When the harvest was ripe on the ground, he marched his army
into Milesia to the sound of pipes and harps and flutes. The
buildings that were scattered over the country he neither pulled
down nor burnt, nor did he even bear away the doors, but left them
standing as they were. He cut down, however, and utterly destroyed all the trees and all the corn throughout the land and then
returned to his own dominions. It was idle for his army to sit down
before the place, as the Milesians were masters of the sea. The reason

* See "Story of Assyria," I p. 378-381.

that he did not demolish their buildings was, that the inhabitants might be tempted to use them as homesteads from which to go forth and till and sow their lands, and so each time he invaded their country he might find something to plunder. In this way he carried on the war for eleven years, in the course of which he inflicted on them two terrible blows."

17. Of these eleven years, six only fall to the reign of Sadyattès; the other five belong to that of his son ALYATTÈS. This was the greatest of the Lydian kings. Under him the dynasty of the Mermnadæ, which was to end so tragically already in the next generation, reached its culminating point of glory. The Lydian monarchy had gradually absorbed all the surrounding countries of Asia Minor as far as the river Halys, which now marked its eastern boundary. There, however, it was confronted by the newly formed Median monarchy, which had reached the same line moving towards it from the opposite direction. There can be no doubt that each potentate was anxious to cross the slight dividing line and therefore looked grimly and threateningly on the other, and that the only question was: Which of the two would find a plausible pretence for aggression? Chance gave this advantage to Kyaxares of Media. A body of Scythian soldiers, probably a picked guard composed of survivors of the massacre which delivered the Medes from their troublesome guests,—who had been some time in Kyaxares' service, left him secretly, being discontented with something or other, and, crossing the Halys, sought the protection of Alyattès. Kyaxares demanded that the deserters should be sent back to him, and, on the Lydian's refusal to do so, declared war.

18. Alyattes was ready for him, having some time before closed the conflict against the Greek cities, in a manner, on the whole, satisfactory to himself: the smaller cities had submitted to Lydian supremacy and agreed to pay tribute, but with the proud and unconquerable Miletus he had been fain to make peace and to enter into a treaty of friendship and alliance. He was therefore free to give his whole attention to a war from which perhaps he was not averse in the beginning, but which soon grew into a vital conflict. It is probable that he found in the young and aspiring power of the Medes a more formidable foe than he had counted upon. Still Lydia stood her ground most bravely, and the success of the war kept evenly balanced between the two adversaries through five whole years; but the final victory was about to incline towards Kyaxares, and he would surely have annexed at one stroke the whole of Asia Minor, but for the timely interference of neighbors, who saw great danger to themselves in the sudden aggrandizement of their rising rival. An unlooked for accident gave them the best possible opportunity. A great battle was fought, which would probably have been decisive, when the sun suddenly was obscured, and such darkness set in that the day was turned into night. An eclipse of the sun was even then no very terrible thing, and the Greeks claim that this particular one had been predicted by one of their wise men, THALES OF MILETUS. But the Medes, on one side, were very much behind their time in knowledge of all sorts, and so, for that mat-

Battle of the Eclipse. 585 B.C.
Death of Kyaxares. 584 B.C.

ter, was the bulk of the Lydian army. So there was a general panic, and both armies refused to continue an engagement begun under such disastrous auspices. Here was a chance for peace-makers to be heard. Nebuchadrezzar of Babylon and SYENNESIS, King of Cilicia, a country that had recovered its independence by the fall of Assyria, and maintained it, like Lycia, against all comers, undertook the task of reconciliation. They seem to have spoken to willing ears, and arranged a marriage which was to cement the friendship between the two kings who had learned, at all events, to respect each other, and to prefer an alliance to further hostilities. ARYÉNIS, the daughter of Alyattés, was given in marriage to ASTYAGES, eldest son of Kyaxares and heir presumptive to the Median Empire. As Kyaxares' daughter, AMYTIS or AMUHIA, was already queen of Babylon,* these three great powers—Media, Babylon, and Lydia, now formed a triple alliance, which could not but carry all before it, and against whom any small principality had little chance indeed. Western Asia was now pretty evenly divided between them, for what might be wanting to Lydia in mere extent of territory, was amply made up for by the extreme fertility of her dominions, her flourishing trade and boundless natural resources, as well as by her dense population and the exhaustless wealth of her cities, among which she now numbered most of the Greek colonies. Thus a real balance of powers was established in the East—the first known instance of that jealous policy which has now for so

* See 'Story of Assyria," p. 428.

long been the leading principle of European statesmen.

19. The date of the Battle of the Eclipse has been the subject of unending discussion, because, unfortunately, there have been several eclipses about that time, within some thirty years, and it was found very difficult to determine which was the one predicted by Thales. Scholars, however, influenced by various historical and chronological considerations, at present generally incline to give it the latest possible date—which would be 585, as Kyaxares died in 584.

1. WHERE possessions and power are nicely balanced by common consent, the natural consequence is mutual watchfulness and suspiciousness. An association is formed, the members of which agree to be content with what they have and not to seek aggrandizement at one another's expense. But even as they make the agreement, each knows perfectly well—judging from his own inclination—that they will all keep to it just as long as they will think proper or until a tempting opportunity offers, and not one moment longer. For this opportunity each of the associates watches with a double eagerness: not to miss it himself and to prevent any of the others availing himself of it. Moreover, as a balance of power is more frequently organized for the unavowed purpose of restraining the excessive growth of some alarmingly vigorous and enterprising neighbor than simply on general principles, there is usually a sense of danger impending from some particular quarter, which quarter naturally becomes the object of more jealous supervision and suspicion. Usually, too, all the watching and fencing serves but little in the end, for where strength is, it will be put forth and prevail by

a necessity as unfailing as the law of nature which makes the greater weight draw down the scale. And if there is a lesson which history teaches more glaringly than another, it is that races and nations have their turns, and that when a race's "turn" has come, all the opposition in the world could no more hinder it from taking it and running its appointed course, than the same race could be kept alive by all possible propping and supporting once its day was done and its possibilities exhausted.

2. It was the Eranians' turn now in Western Asia. The race was in its prime of vigor, adventurous recklessness, and youthful curiosity to see and take more lands, and more still. Fresh from its long migrations, which could not be said to be ended even yet, their forward push was irresistible and could be restrained only temporarily. No one felt this better than Nebuchadrezzar of Babylon, the far-seeing, the wary, who, with a wisdom born of age,—the age of his race rather than his own,—forswore the delights of conquest for its own sake, drew the line at invasion, and centred all his care on the consolidation of the empire which he never doubted but he would transmit to a long line of descendants, *if* only he could guard it from Media, of whose eventual advance he felt so sure that he spent his life preparing against it. Kyaxares was dead, the great organizer and conqueror, who, though by no means the first Median king, was considered by posterity the founder of the monarchy. His son and successor, whom the Greeks have called ASTYAGES,—we find his name given as ISHTUVÊGU on cuneiform monu-

ments,—was Nebuchadrezzar's brother-in-law and not formidable in himself, being as inferior to Kyaxares, as great men's sons usually are to their fathers; yet the Babylonian never relaxed in his vigilance. Ever alive to the danger from the north, he sought to avert it by works of fortification on a gigantic scale, and skilfully combined them with works of public utility and adornment.

3. He first of all undertook to fortify Sippar, the most northern of Babylonian cities, exposed to become a dangerous centre of operation in an invader's hand, and did so in a way which at the same time furthered commerce and agriculture. With this view he not only had the half-choked-up canals of ancient kings cleaned out and their sluices and dams repaired and put into working order, but created a new system of canals: four he cut across land, to unite the Tigris and Euphrates, each wide and deep enough to carry merchant ships, and branching into a network of smaller canals and ditches for irrigating the fields. In order fully to control the increased mass of waters which he thus obtained, he had a huge basin or reservoir dug out near Sippar, on the left bank of the Euphrates, some thirty-five miles in circumference and as many feet deep,* provided, of course, with an elaborate and complete set of hydraulic works, to fill or empty it as needed. To complete the subjection of the mighty river, the course of its bed was slightly altered, being made to wind in a sinuous line by means of excavations made

* These are the figures given by Herodotus; they are more moderate and seem more probable than some given by later writers.

at some distance from one another. This broke the force of the current, which is very great in the high-water season, and not only made navigation up the stream easier, but gave fuller control of the river, when a great part of its waters had to be diverted into the basin of Sippar in times of inundation. Thus, by the same act which remedied the evils of spring floods, a provision of water was laid up for distribution in times of drought. So admirably were these various forces calculated and balanced, and so perfectly did they work together, that when Nebuchadrezzar built his celebrated bridge across the Euphrates in Babylon, he could empty the bed of the river, so as to allow his workmen to construct the mighty buttressed piers of quarry stones clamped with iron and soldered with molten lead, and to line the banks with masonry of the best kiln-burned brick.

4. It is evident that these waterworks—the four canals and the reservoir at Sippar—were at the same time part of a very efficient system of defence against possible invasions from the north. Not only did they present obstacles which it would take time to overcome, but in a case of desperate emergency whole regions could be flooded and thus made inaccessible or untenable. But even this did not seem a sufficient safeguard to the king's anxious foresight. The boundary so slightly marked by the alluvial line * had never been much respected, and he determined to strengthen it by the more tangible addition of a wall, which he built across the valley, from river

* See "Story of Assyria," p. 1.

to river, somewhat below that line, but above that formed by the canals and the now well fortified city of Sippar. A wall—childish as the contrivance may appear in our time of scientific warfare—was no mean defence, if sufficiently strong and properly manned, before the days of artillery; and several centuries later we see the Romans, the finest strategists of antiquity, build walls across the narrow part of Britain as a defence against the inroads of the northern tribes. This of Nebuchadrezzar's was built entirely of burned brick held together by asphalt cement; and Xenophon, who saw some portions of it standing still and calls it the "Median Wall," values its height at a hundred feet, its thickness at twenty.

5. In all Nebuchadrezzar's inscriptions that have been found—and we have a great many—he especially glories in his constructions. He seems to have repaired almost every great temple in the land and built not a few new ones. From the detailed account he gives of the condition in which he found the "Temple of the Seven Spheres" at Borsip and of the work he did there, it is evident that he considers the completion and adornment of this his patron's Ziggurat and shrine (temple of Nebo) as one of his best claims to fame and the favor of the gods.* But what he did at Babylon not only surpasses all his other works, but eclipses those of all former kings, even those of Sargon at Dur-Sharrukin, not so much in splendor as in the vastness and originality of his conceptions,—an originality due probably to that

* See "Story of Chaldea," p. 72, pp. 280–283, and p. 293.

besetting idea of coupling adornment with military requirements, which consistently underlies most of the public works he undertook. In this, however, he appears to have followed a line traced out first by his father. Of some of his greatest constructions,—such as the new palace, the great city walls, and the embankments of the Euphrates,—he especially mentions that they were begun by Nabopolassar, but left unfinished at his death. Babylon, sacked once by Sennacherib, then rebuilt by Esarhaddon, had gone through a conflagration when besieged and taken by Asshurbanipal, and must have been in a sad condition when the Chaldean usurper made it once more the seat of empire. Hence, perhaps, the thought of reconstructing it in such a manner as would make it a capital not only in size and magnificence, but in strength: it was to be at once the queen of cities and the most impregnable of fortresses.

6. The last time that Babylon had been taken it had been reduced by famine.* This was the first contingency to be guarded against. For this purpose the city was to be protected by a double enclosure of mighty walls, the inner one skirting its outlines narrowly, while the outer was moved to such a distance as to enfold a large portion of the land, which was to be cultivated so that the capital could raise enough grain and fodder for its own consumption. This vast space also would serve to shelter the population of the surrounding villages in case of an invasion. It has not been possible to trace the line of this outer wall, which received the name of NIMIT-

See "Story of Assyria," p. 396.

ti-Bel, nor consequently to determine how many square miles it protected, and the reports of ancient writers are somewhat conflicting, as none of them, of course, took exact scientific measurements after the manner of our modern surveyors. Herodotus gives the circumference as somewhat over fifty English miles. A large figure certainly. But it has been observed that it scarcely surpasses that yielded by the circumvallation of Paris; and besides the arable and pasture land, it must have embraced suburbs, not impossibly Borsip itself, which was also well fortified at the same time. This is the highest estimate. The lowest (and later) gives forty miles. The Nimitti-Bel rampart was protected on the outside by a wide and deep moat, which at the same time had supplied the material for the wall. In mentioning it Herodotus stops to give a very faithful and vivid account of the local mode of construction, now so familiar to us, but which, when described to him, seems to have considerably astonished him:

"And here I may not omit to tell the use to which the mould dug out of the great moat was turned, nor the manner wherein the wall was wrought. As fast as they dug the moat, the soil which they got from the cutting was made into bricks, and when a sufficient number were completed, they baked the bricks in kilns. Then they set to building and began with bricking the borders of the moat, after which they proceeded to construct the wall itself, using throughout for their cement hot bitumen, and interposing a layer of wattled reeds at every thirtieth course of the bricks."

The reports about the height and thickness of this celebrated wall vary still more considerably. Herodotus says it was 350 feet high * (apparently includ-

* Calculation of Mr. J. Oppert ("Athenæum Français," 1850, p. 370).

ing the height of the towers, which were built at regular intervals on the top of it), with a thickness of 75 feet. Now no effort of imagination, even with the knowledge that the walls of Babylon were numbered among the "Seven Wonders of the World," can well make us realize a city wall, nigh on fifty miles long, surpassing in height the extreme height of St. Paul's of London.* The estimates of various later writers range all the way between that exorbitant figure and that of 75 feet,—very possibly too moderate. For the fact remains undisputed that the Nimitti-Bel rampart was stupendous both in height and in thickness; that towers were built on the top of it, on the edges, two facing each other, and that there remained room between for a four-horsed chariot to turn. And the contemporary Hebrew prophet, Jeremiah, speaks of Babylon as "mounting up to heaven," of "the broad walls of Babylon" and her "high gates." Of these there were a hundred in the circuit of the wall, according to Herodotus, "and they were all of brass, with brazen lintels and side-posts." †

7. This outer wall Herodotus calls "the main defence of the city." The second or inner wall, named IMGUR-BEL, he described as being "of less thickness than the first, but very little inferior to it in strength." Then there were the walls which enclosed the two royal palaces, the old one on the right bank of the

---

* See Geo. Rawlinson's "Herodotus" (third edition, 1875), vol. I., p. 299, note 9.

† Probably cased with worked brass, like the gate of Balawat. See "Story of Assyria," p. 190 and ill. No. 34.

Euphrates, and the new one on the left,—and made of each a respectable fortress; for it was part of the plan of reconstruction that the city should be extended across the river, to gain a firmer seat and full control of this all-important thoroughfare; and an entire new quarter was built on the left bank around the new and magnificent palace. And as it was desirable, both for convenience and defence, that the two sides should be united by permanent means of communication, Nebuchadrezzar built the great bridge mentioned above (p. 226), but so that it could be kept open or shut off at will, as a further safeguard against surprises. This was effected by means of platforms made of beams and planks, which were laid from pier to pier in the daytime, and removed for the night. Of course one solitary bridge could not suffice for the traffic of a population which cannot have been under half a million, and the river was gay with hundreds of boats and barges darting with their load of passengers from bank to bank, or gliding down the current, or working against it. There were many landing-places, but no quays or broad paved walks bordered with handsome buildings, such as in our ideas appear as the necessary accompaniment of a beautiful river in a great city. The Euphrates flowed along imprisoned between a double wall, of burnt brick like the others, which followed its course on either bank and close to the edge from end to end of the city. Only where the streets abutted on the river—and these were disposed at regular intervals, in straight lines and at right angles— there were low gates to allow pedestrians to descend to the landing-places. The general effect must have been peculiar and rather gloomy.

8. The site of Nebuchadrezzar's own palace—the "new palace"—has been fully identified; it is the mound known as the KASR, one of the first explored, and which drew travellers' attention by its exceptionally handsome, neatly moulded and stamped

34. BRICK OF NEBUCHADREZZAR.
(One foot square; thickness, 3 inches.)

bricks, as well as by the cement which joined them, and which is considered the finest in the world, not excepting the best that England produces in our day. What best served the purpose of identification was the accumulation in the rubbish of countless fragments of painted and glazed tiles, showing portions of figures, human and animal; here a lion's paw, there a horse's hoof, there again a bit of curly beard or filleted hair. As we are told by ancient writers that the outer walls of the palace were adorned with hunting scenes in many colors, the inference was not difficult to draw. Some of these fragments are large enough to show the number near the top and part of the inscription—white, on blue ground. The Jewish historian, JOSEPHUS, who lived in the first century A.D., has a short memorandum to the effect that "the palace was built in fifteen days," a statement which appeared so palpable an exaggeration that not much attention was ever paid to it. What, then, was the amazement of the decipherers when on a cylinder of Nebuchadrezzar, now in London, they read these words: "*In fifteen days I completed the splendid work.*" Even supposing all the materials to have been brought together, all the art work to have been done beforehand, and only placed and put together in this space of time, what a command of human labor does not such a statement represent!

9. The most characteristic of Babylonian mounds, from its well-defined flat-topped outline, is also the only one that has retained the old name, and is still known as BABIL.* For a long time it was supposed to be the Ziggurat of the celebrated temple of Bel-Marduk, although oriented, contrary to custom, with its *sides* to the cardinal points, not with its angles.†
But the researches undertaken by Mr. H. Rassam a few years ago (1883–84), with such rich and varied results, have somewhat shaken that belief: he thinks

* See "Story of Chaldea," Ill. 4.   † *Ibid.*, pp. 234 ff

that the constructions entombed in this mound were of a very different nature. Sloping towards the river and on two sides, while the back presented a perpendicular wall, probably not much lower than that of the city, this mass of solid brick masonry, according to him, represents one of the few truly poetical creations of the age; poetical alike in its nature and in the circumstances which gave rise to it—the famous Hanging Gardens.* It is said that Nebuchadrezzar's Median queen, Amytis,† pined for the mountains of her native land, with their cool shades and verdant bowers, in the wearisome flatness and prostrating sultriness of the Chaldean lowlands; whereupon her royal lord, with a chivalrous gallantry that would have done honor to a far later time, ordered the construction of an artificial hill, disposed in terraces, which, being covered with a layer of earth, were planted with the handsomest trees, amidst which, on the topmost terrace, a villa-like residence was erected for the queen, where she could enjoy, not only purer air and pleasant shades, but a vast and beautiful prospect. If this pretty legend be true—and why should we deny ourselves the pleasure of believing it, since there is nothing to disprove it?—the woman so loved might well feel compensated even for the loss of her native scenery in the Zagros wilds, for which, of course, her terraced bower, some 500 feet square, could be but a poor substitute.

*See Kaulen, "Assyrien und Babylonien," p. 76.
† A daughter of the great Kyaxares. See "Story of Assyria," p. 428.

35. HANGING GARDENS OF BABYLON.
(Attempt at reconstruction.)

235

10. Yet, poor as it may have been when compared to nature's own mountain architecture, as a piece of human art it was a marvel which the Greeks thought worthy of a place among their "Seven Wonders," along with the walls of Babylon, the temple of Bel, that of Artemis at Ephesus, and a few other monuments. The terraces are described by Greek and Roman writers to have been borne on arched vaults supported by pillars, all of well cemented bricks. On the topmost terrace was the pump-house, with the hydraulic machinery for raising the water through pipes from the Euphrates, or rather, from canals which brought the water within easy reach, and so that the contrivance should not be noticed from the outside. Mr. Rassam found some of the pipes, cut through limestone, and having cleared one of the rubbish that choked it, actually came upon water which still partly filled it. It is said that the earth was carted up in loads and spread out on a layer of plates of lead, for the protection of the masonry from the destructive action of the moisture which had to be kept up around the roots of the trees. The terraces were four in number, the pillars sixty feet apart, and twenty-two feet in circumference; as could be verified from the remains. On the whole, this *Paradeisos*, as the Greeks called it, disposed somewhat on the principle of the Ziggurat, was not an innovation, and we have seen in a preceding volume that similar constructions—terraces upon arches, bearing groves or gardens and forming artificially watered slopes—have been portrayed long before Nebuchadrezzar on Assyrian wall-sculptures, the

36. MOUNTAIN SCENERY IN MEDIA.
(In the Zagros, now Kurdistan.)

type of both Ziggurat and hanging gardens having been carried north in remote antiquity from Chaldea where, beyond doubt, it originated, and was closely connected with the religious traditions of the Holy Mountain and Sacred Tree.*

11. If the mound of Babil has been correctly identified as the site of the hanging gardens, that of the great temple of Bel-Marduk will have, until further discoveries, to remain doubtful. Both temple and Ziggurat, the latter with a chapel on the top stage, are thus described by Herodotus:

"The sacred precinct was a square enclosure two *stadia* (1200 feet) each way, with gates of solid brass, which was also remaining in my time. In the middle of the precinct there was a tower of solid masonry, a *stadion* (600 feet) in length and breadth, upon which was raised a second tower, and on that a third, and so on up to eight. The ascent to the top is on the outside, by a path which winds round all the towers.† When one is about half-way up, one finds a resting-place and seats, where persons are wont to sit some time on their way to the summit. On the topmost tower there is a spacious temple, and inside the temple stands a couch of unusual size, richly adorned, with a golden table by its side. . . . They declare—but I for my part do not credit it—that the god comes down in person into this chamber, and sleeps on the couch. . . . In the same precinct there is another temple, in which is a sitting figure of Zeus" (*i. e.*, Bel-Marduk), "all of gold. Before the figure stands a large golden table; and the throne whereupon it sits, and the base on which the throne is placed, are likewise of gold. . . . Outside the temple are two altars, one of solid gold, on which it is lawful to offer only sucklings; the other a common altar, but of great size, on which the full-grown animals are sacrificed. It is also on this great altar that the Chaldeans burn the frankincense, which is offered every year at the festival of the god. . . ."

* See "Story of Chaldea," pp. 274-280, and ill. 68.
† See "Story of Chaldea," ill. 70, "Ziggurat Restored."

Four hundred years later the great temple was only a memory. "In the middle of the city," the historian, Diodorus of Sicily, reports,* "used to stand the sanctuary of Bel. As different writers have said different things about it, and the building itself has broken down with age, nothing certain can be found out concerning it. On one thing, however, all agree: that it was of stupendous height, and that the Chaldeans used to take astronomical observations from the top of it, as the height of the structure made it convenient for them to observe the rising and setting of the stars." Alexander of Macedon, who lived only one hundred years after Herodotus, already found the temple a ruin. We are told that he intended to repair and rebuild it, but could not spare the time and the labor on the work, as the removal of the rubbish would alone have employed 10,000 men during two months. And besides, the young conqueror died before he could accomplish even so much. It was thus that all these costly and stupendous, but unwieldy and perishable structures collapsed and literally crumbled to dust and rubbish the moment they were left to themselves, even when the work of destruction was not accomplished or helped by the hand of man—as was too often the case in these countries, exposed as they were to continual invasions and change of masters. The wonder is that Herodotus should have found Babylon still so much the city that Nebuchadrezzar left it, for, in the hundred years that separated him from that

* Herodotus died about 425 B.C., and Diodorus was a contemporary of Julius Cæsar and of Augustus.

monarch, the great capital had been taken thrice by force of arms, once after a long siege.

12. It is curious that the works which we know to have been carried out by Nebuchadrezzar should have been credited by the Greeks of almost the next generation not to him, but to two queens, one of them entirely fabulous, even mythical, and the other, if not exactly unreal, still more or less apocryphal. The legend of Semiramis (see "Story of Assyria," p. 198) ascribes to her the building of Babylon generally, the construction of the hanging gardens, the great walls, the temple of Bel, and the bridge. Herodotus, on the other hand (Book I., 184-186), claims the latter, as well as the basin at Sippar, and the turning of the Euphrates, for a certain queen, NITOKRIS, of whom contemporary records know nothing whatever. This perversion of history is the more to be wondered at, that there certainly was intercourse between Babylon and Greece at the time, since we know of Greek volunteers serving in Nebuchadrezzar's army, and among these of at least one illustrious name—a brother of the poet Alkman.

13. The pride which Nebuchadrezzar took in the city wellnigh created by him, has become proverbial from the celebrated passage in which the prophet Daniel presents the lifelike picture of the king walking upon the terraces of his palace, surveying the unspeakably gorgeous prospect around him and at his feet, and exclaiming: "Is not this great Babylon, which I have built for the royal dwelling-place, by the might of my power, and for the glory of my majesty?" How well these words, reported by the

Hebrew eye-witness, accord with the tenor of certain passages in the great king's inscriptions. ". . . For the astonishment of men I built this house ; awe of the power of my majesty encompasses its walls. . . . The temples of the great gods I made brilliant as the sun, shining as the day. . . . In Babylon alone I raised the seat of my dominion, in no other city." This excessive pride in his works is betrayed in all his inscriptions, which, on the other hand, are strangely silent about his wars and victories, and we would not know that he had reduced many Arabian peoples to submission but for some vague passages in the book of Jeremiah. It is obvious, however, that the main feature of this great monarch's reign is his admirable home-rule. When to his vast system of fortifications and irrigation in the north we add the improvement and regulation of the drainage of the Chaldean marshes by the mouth of the rivers, the foundation of a commercial city with harbor— TEREDON or TIRIDOTIS—at that of the Euphrates, and of a colony, GERRHA, on the Arabian coast of the gulf, we shall see that he did as much for trade as for agriculture, national defence, and the adornment of his cities, opening a most convenient thoroughfare by water, for the transport of wares from Arabia and India all the way up the Euphrates to Karkhemish. The restoration of the Chaldean monarchy in more than its ancient glory—that dream of national revival and greatness which the princes of Kaldu had pursued, openly or in secret, through more than three centuries,[*] for which Merodach-

---

[*] See "Story of Assyria," pp. 170-174.

Baladan and his heroic house of Bit-Yakin had plotted and fought, suffered and died,* had at length become a reality. And if the glory was fleeting, the empire short-lived, it was because one man, however great his genius and power, cannot stay or turn the current of historical law. Nebuchadrezzar and his people belonged to a race whose day of leadership was done, and when he died, things resumed their course on the incline down which they were drawn by natural gravitation.

14. Babylon, like the great cities of Assyria, has survived only in the ruins of her principal public or royal buildings. Of her streets, squares, private dwellings, we vainly seek a trace. We only know from Herodotus that the streets all ran in straight lines, not only those parallel to the rivers, but also the "cross streets which lead down to the waterside," where they ended in the low gate already mentioned (see p. 231). The same traveller describes the houses as being mostly three or four stories high. It is probable that our curiosity on many points will never be satisfied, and until quite lately we knew scarcely more of the Babylonians' private life than of that of their northern neighbors. In fact, for a long time we had to be content with scraps of information from Greek sources, like the following, also from Herodotus:

"The dress of the Babylonians is a linen tunic reaching to the feet, and above it another tunic made of wool, besides which they have a short white cloak thrown around them, and shoes of a peculiar

* See "Story of Assyria," reigns of Tiglath Pileser II. and the Sargonides.

fashion. . . . They have long hair, wear turbans, and anoint their whole body with perfumes. Every one carries a seal, and a walking-stick, carved at the top into the form of an apple, a rose, a lily, an eagle, for it is not their habit to use a stick without an ornament."

This description, superficial as it is, and bearing on the merely outer traits which would naturally strike a foreigner, contains two details which guarantee its faithfulness, being amply corroborated by modern discoveries; in the seals which every one carries, we recognize the familiar seal-cylinders, the general use of which accounts for the enormous number of specimens which has been found, amounting to several thousands, scattered in various collections, public and private, that of the British Museum alone counting over six hundred. As to the ornamental knobs of the walking-sticks, such articles are often found in the ruins, and are thought to have served for the very purpose mentioned by Herodotus. He also notes some of the more remarkable customs of those which would be sure to strike a traveller or be pointed out to him, even without his knowing a word of the language. Such is the custom of laying people in the street when they were very ill, for the passers-by to advise them on their case*; also that of holding a matrimonial auction once a year,—a sort of fair, at which, marriageable girls being collected in one place, the men assembled to inspect them, forming a circle around them.† Then a herald or public crier called their

* For the meaning and origin of this custom see "Story of Chaldea," p. 103.

† Herodotus says "all the marriageable girls," and makes the cus-

names and offered them for sale, one by one, to the highest bidder. The most beautiful came first, as they, of course, fetched the highest prices. When all the pretty girls were disposed of, the plain ones had their turn, but for them the proceeding was reversed, marriage portions being offered with them. The herald began with the most homely one, asking who would take her with the smallest dowry. She was knocked down to the man who contented himself with the lowest sum. The marriage-portions were furnished out of the money paid for the beautiful damsels, and thus "the fairer maidens portioned out the uglier," remarks Herodotus, who thinks the whole arrangement a wise and admirable one.

15. It is but lately that our materials for a knowledge of Babylonian life, manners, and customs have received an important and unlooked for addition. In a field of research where so much is due to chance, and where every great success is a piece of luck and a surprise, not the least of these was the discovery of the secret archive of a family which has been called THE BANKING HOUSE OF EGIBI. Already in 1874 some Arab diggers disinterred from a large mound known under the name of DJUMDJUMA several well-preserved terra-cotta jars, packed full of small tab-

---

tom universal. It was most certainly not so, as proved by the vast number of documents on private life, of which an account follows further on. Still, as later writers mention it, it may have existed as a local survival from barbarous antiquity, piously preserved by some of those worshippers of "the good old times," who are a standing feature of all ages and countries.

lets covered with writing. They had learned by
this time the value of such "finds," and carried the
jars to a dealer in Baghdad, from whom George
Smith bought them for the British Museum, though
far from suspecting what treasure he had stumbled
on. The tablets were about three thousand in number, varying in size from one square inch to twelve.
It was found on examination that they were documents recording all sorts of commercial and pecuniary
transactions, and bearing the names of the contracting parties and of witnesses. Among these names,
either as principal or witness—more often the former,—always figured the name of some son, or grandson, or descendant of a certain ÊGIBI, evidently the
founder of a firm possessed of immense wealth and
influence, and which, through many generations,
indeed several centuries, transacted money affairs
of every sort and magnitude, from the loan of a few
manehs to that of many talents, from witnessing a
private will or a contract of sale or partnership
between modest citizens of Babylon or some neighboring city, to the collecting of taxes from whole
provinces farmed to the house by the government.
As these documents, which come under the class
known as "contract tablets," are carefully dated,
giving the day and month, and the year of the
reigning king, it has been found possible to make
out a genealogical table of the firm,[*] the head of
which, it appears, generally took his sons into partnership in his own lifetime. This table shows that

[*] See paper by Mr. S. Chad Boscawen, "Transactions of the Society of Biblical Archæology, vol. VI., 1878.

the founder, Êgibi, "was probably at the head of the house in the reign of Sennacherib, about 685 B.C." Professor Friedrich Delitzsch has quite lately come to the conclusion that the name ÊGIBI is the equivalent to the Hebrew YAKUB (Jacob),* from which fact he infers that the great banker must have been a Jew, probably of those carried into captivity by Sargon out of Samaria.† He remarks, that many of the tablets bear unmistakably Jewish names, and thinks they will yet shed many a light on the life and doings of the Hebrew exiles in Babylon and other Chaldean cities. If this philological point is established, it would be curious to note at how early a date the blessing uttered on the race in Deuteronomy (xxviii., 12): "Thou shalt lend unto many nations and thou shalt not borrow," began to take effect.

16. However that may be, the firm of "Êgibi and Sons" had reached its climax of wealth and power under Nebuchadrezzar, a century after its foundation, having weathered the storms of the two sieges, under Sennacherib and Asshurbanipal, as they were to pass unscathed through several more similar political crises, protected by their exceptional position, which made them too useful, indeed too necessary, to be injured. "All the financial business of the court," Professor Fr. Delitzsch tells us, "was entrusted to this firm through several centuries. They collected the taxes with which land, and the crops of corn, dates,

---

* See article "Gefangenschaft," in the Calwer Bibel-Lexikon; also, *Zeitschrift für Keilschriftforschung* for 1885, pp. 168, 169.

† See "Story of Assyria," p. 247.

etc., were burdened, also the dues for the use of the public roads and the irrigation canals, etc., etc. Thus, these insignificant-looking little cakes of clay unrol before us a vivid picture of Babylon's national life; we see people of all classes, from the highest court-officer to the lowest peasant and slave, crowd the courts of this treasure-house to transact their business." At first (in 1878), it was thought that the palmy days of the firm extended only to the reign of the Persian king, DAREIOS HYSTASPIS, and the genealogical table (see p. 245) went no further than a certain MARDUK-NAZIR-PAL, who appears in the first year of that king, and continues to act until his thirty-fifth year. But Professor Delitzsch informs us (in 1882), that Mr. H. Rassam added several hundred tablets to the batch first purchased, and that, among these, there are some dated from the reign of *King Alik-sa-an-dir*, i. e., Alexander the Great. This would give these Babylonian Rothschilds a known and provable duration of very nearly four centuries.

17. If there should ever arise among Assyriologists a scholar gifted with imaginative power and literary talent,—like Georg Ebers, the pride of Egyptology, —such a scholar will find ample material for historical romances of real value in the materials extracted from the jar-safes of the House Égibi. Many an epoch not half so remote in time cannot produce one quarter so much documentary evidence. The Égibi tablets, with their dry records of transactions in all branches of social life and mutual relations, present a very complete skeleton, which it would be

a delightful and not over-difficult task to clothe with the flesh and blood of poetically created living persons. The greatest difficulty at present would be the number of unintelligible words. It stands to reason that the language of every-day life and business transactions must be very different from that of historical annals, as represented by the royal wall-inscriptions and cylinders. These monotonous and stiff productions continually repeat not only the same words, but whole sentences and set forms of speech. Large portions of them are very much like blank forms in which the names only have to be filled in. In short, the public documents are written in an official and conventional style, while the private tablets represent what might be called idiomatic literature ; and we all know how much easier it is to learn the book-language than every-day speech of even a modern people, with all the facilities and assistance we command, let alone a dead one.

18. It has been objected that to give the firm of Égibi & Sons the title of " banking-house " is misleading, since the bulk of their tablets shows them to have done the business of money-lenders and perhaps notaries public. Yet it is certain that the bank deposits, with their natural accompaniment, drafts, and cheques, were in use much before the invention of coining. Fr. Lenormant quotes such a document (of the reign of Nabonidus, the last king of Babylon),—a real banker's draft—by which a person living at Ur gives to another an order on a person living at Erech.* To another such draft or cheque

* "La Monnaie dans l'Antiquité," vol. I., p. 117.

of the reign of Nebuchadrezzar, the sender (at Kutha) and the payer (at Borsip) are named, but not the payee: it is a cheque " to bearer."* That such documents were negotiable, like our own letters of exchange or cheques, *i. e.*, could be indorsed and exchanged for their value in gold or silver (discounted), and that in very ancient times, is shown by a bilingual text (Accadian and Assyrian), which says: " His mandate—not paid, but yet to be sent—he exchanged against silver."† These are real banking-operations, the invention of which has always been attributed to the Jewish financiers of the Middle Ages, and which it is quite startling to see in familiar operation among their ancestors or kindred over twenty centuries before them.

"And yet," remarks Lenormant,‡ "if we stop to consider the peculiar conditions under which the commerce of the Assyrians and Babylonians was carried on, we shall be able to account for this at first sight strange fact ; we shall understand the causes which led these nations to invent the draft or exchange system so much earlier than others. Their trade, from the geographical position of their countries, was necessarily carried on by land, by means of caravans which had to traverse, in all directions, deserts infested by nomadic robbers. In such conditions, one of the merchant's first cares was to find a way to avoid the transporting of money in cash to distant points. Every thing made it desirable to find such a way : the cumbersome nature of metallic values, the number of beasts of burden required to carry great quantities of it, as well as the unsafe roads. Therefore, as soon as there was a creditor at one end of a caravan line and a debtor at the other, the idea of the draft-system must have dawned on the mind of the creditor. This is so natural that a renewal of the same conditions gave rise to the same results, after a

---

* " La Monnaie dans l'Antiquité," vol. I., p. 120.
† *Ib.*, p. 119. ‡ *Ib.*, pp. 121, 122.

long oblivion, in the Middle Ages, when the Jews and the Italian merchants, hampered by the difficulties of transporting coined money and beset by innumerable risks, re-invented the letter of exchange, but in the more perfect form which has prevailed down to our own times."

There is no reason to suppose that the firm Egibi & Sons did not transact business of this order, and they would therefore be, strictly speaking, entitled to the name of "banking-house," even though their principal business was lending money, which they did on a large scale—like modern banks, which by no means confine their operations to the exchange and transfer of values.

19. It is certain that the documents recording the sales—of slaves, cattle, horses, houses, furniture, land, etc.—are the most numerous, together with those recording loans—obligations we would call them—at shorter or longer dates, with the interest computed in money, or in grain,* sometimes even in days of work, and often with the provision of penalties, should the payment not be made on time, such as that, if not paid on a certain day, the debt shall be increased one third. There are usually several witnesses: the scribe put down the name of those who could not write and they made a mark in the soft clay with their nails. In many cases the loan was made on security given by a third party, or on mortgage of property, under which head the borrower frequently included his children, nay his own person. We are told that, if tabulated, these

* This was a convenient arrangement to both sides, as many of the government taxes were paid in grain.

tablets might give the average price of every article sold in Babylon, or even hired; for it was not uncommon for people to rent out their slaves, and there seem to have been speculators who made it a regular trade to train and hire out slaves, by contract, in which case a sum of money is usually agreed on to be paid to the owner should the slave be lost, killed, or injured. Sometimes a condition of the transaction is that the hirer shall teach the slave a trade. Slaves were frequently marked—probably branded—for identification, with their master's name, on the wrist, the arm, the shoulder. This facilitated another transaction, which must have been very convenient for people in temporarily straitened circumstances—the conditional sale of slaves, with the provision that whenever the original owner claimed the slave sold on this understanding, that slave should be returned to him or her, the purchase-money being refunded. If children had been born meanwhile, the purchaser could keep them if he chose, on paying a small sum for them. All these transactions could equally well be performed through a third person, by power of attorney. In wealthy establishments this power was usually given to the head-slave or steward. If a freeman, it behooved the agent to be very careful, as ignorance or neglect of nice points of legal form were just as apt to get people into trouble then as nowadays. Thus we have a contract by which a certain Ibâ, son of Silla, buys some property on behalf and by authority of a man and his wife; Bunanitu is the name of the latter. Had the scribe omitted the clause, "by the authority of . . . ," and had the employer afterwards chosen to deny or repudiate the purchase, Ibâ, son of Silla, would have been compelled to keep and pay for it himself, the law being explicit on the subject: "If a man has contracted for a field and house in the name of another, but has not received a letter of authority concerning it, or has not shown a duplicate of the tablet, the man who wrote the tablet and contract in his name shall lose that house and field."

20. Not that we can boast the recovery of a complete code of Babylonian law. It is even very doubtful whether such a code existed at all. The lawyers and judges looked for guidance to some very ancient documents, now known as "tablets of precedents." These tablets, several of which have been found and deciphered, seem to have formed a continuous series, and are bilingual, the text being in the old Accadian language, accompanied by an Assyrian translation. These texts or sentences are said to be not exactly laws, but to "give precepts or rules for the conduct of man in his various occupations."[*] Had we the entire collection, we should probably find that these "rules and precepts," the accumulated fruits of perhaps centuries of experience and observation, embraced the whole range of human life, in its private, social, and public capacities. As it is, we find there much valuable material. One tablet gives instruction for the agriculturist, "when and how he is to

[*] See the paper of Mr. George Bertin, " Accadian Precepts for the Conduct of Man in Private Life," in "Trans. of the Soc. of Bible Archæology," vol. VIII., 1884.

prepare and sow his fields, build his house and barn, what are his relations towards his landlord in such and such a circumstance." The most important is the tablet which instructs a man as to his private life and his duties towards his relatives. Beginning with simple rules, it ends with what might almost be called criminal laws.

21. After mentioning (§ 1) what time a child shall be declared a freeman, *i. e.*, of age, and describing (§ 2) the ceremony which accompanies the declaration, §§ 3 and 4 speak of the first act of the child when he became a man, which consisted in paying tribute, double the usual sum; §§ 5 and 6 state that "the child is henceforth answerable for his actions and will bear the consequences of his sins." The paragraph on the nursing and education of the child are hopelessly injured; one line, however, stands out clear and significant: "*He* (the father) *makes him* (the child) *learn inscriptions.*" Then comes another line: "*He makes him take a wife.*" This was the "chief wife," who seems to have been chosen and asked from her parents by the father, as a last act of parental authority. This union was indissoluble, as can be inferred from the lines: "*Henceforth, the husband cannot remove her who possesses his heart.*" The bride, who was to remain the head of the household for life, was to be a free-born maiden, and brought a dowry, which, on the death of the husband, returned to her and to her children, or, if there were no children, to her parents, *i. e.*, the source whence it originally came.

22. Then follows the second part of the tablet,

containing a rudimentary attempt at a penal legislation.

1st. A son is forbidden to deny his duty to his father, under penalty of being reduced to servitude and sold as a slave: "*When a son to his father 'my father thou art not' has said, the nails he shall cut him,** . . . *for money he shall sell him.*"

2d. For the same offence against his mother, a son, besides being enslaved and expelled from the house, is exposed in the middle of the town (probably pilloried).

3d. If a husband ill-treats his wife so that she denies him, he is to be thrown into the river,— whether to die, or only undergo an ordeal, a punishment, is not specified: "*When a wife, her husband having done wrong to her, 'my husband not thou art' has said, in the river they place him.*"

4th. "*When a husband 'my wife not thou art' has said,* (*i. e.*, refuses her her rights), *half a manch of silver he weighs.*"

This clause probably answers to our provision of "alimony to be paid by the husband to his deserted or injured wife. There are also penalties against the father and the mother who deny their son.

Lastly, if a man ill-uses a slave whom he has hired from another, so that the slave dies, or if the slave runs away, breaks down from exhaustion or

---

* "Long nails," remarks Mr. George Bertin, who, it should be remembered, is responsible for the translation, "seem therefore to have been the mark of freedom, as long hair and beard were among the Semites. The slaves and people of low condition are always represented on the bas reliefs as shaved."

illness, that man "weighs" half a measure of corn to the master of the slave, for every day, as a compensation.*

23. It is rather startling to find that these undoubtedly very ancient texts or "precedents"—a veritable "custom-law"—(*loi coutumière*) secure to women a position not only honorable and influential, but almost entirely independent. The laws of property and inheritance are always a fair test of the position which the women occupy in a commonwealth. Now we have seen above (see p. 253) that a woman's dowry by no means became her husband's property. That law was completed by the following still more liberal clause: if a widow wished to marry again,—(" *set her face to go down to another house*")— she took with her not only her own dowry, but all the property which her first husband had left her. At her death, her dowry was to be divided between the children of both marriages. Here the tablet is broken off, and we lose the conclusion of the regulation—though it is supposed that, to be logically consistent, it enacted that the first husband's property should go to his children alone. One of the most interesting documents is a will in due and legal form, witnessed and attested, by which a man pro-

It should be noted here on high Assyriological authority that the translations from the document mentioned in § 22 must be taken very guardedly, especially in the peculiar details, and as by no means final. "The text is defective and the translation necessarily so. The interpretation of this tablet is still so obscure that one could not well say too little about it in a history of Babylonia."—(Dr. D. G. Lyon, in a private letter.) This applies particularly to the special provisions, the general sense being tolerably well established.

vides for his wife: he leaves certain property to be held in trust for her by his three children. She is to have the use of it during her life, and, when she dies, it reverts to the children.

24. A large number of the Égibi tablets, as well as of the older contract tablets, show us women not only concerned as principals in every kind of commercial and legal transactions,—in which the husband frequently appears merely as witness, or even as his wife's agent,—but personally pleading for their rights before the royal judges, and gaining their suit too. Thus Bunanitu—the same woman whom we saw giving a power of attorney, jointly with her husband, for the purchase of some property in Borsip—reappears as a widow, when she enters a civil suit against her brother-in-law, who wished to despoil her and her daughter of their inheritance, by laying claim to that very house and land. She proved that the purchase was made with her dowry, to which her husband added a sum which he borrowed, and that, on her request, and to secure her interests "for future days," he gave her a document witnessing that he had traded with her dowry, and that the purchase was their joint act. "He sealed his tablet and wrote upon it the curse of the great gods . . . I have brought it before you. Make a decision." The judges "heard their words," discussed the tablets, and decided in favor of the widow. The matter is related at far greater length in the original document, and is followed by a general settling up of all the family affairs. It is very entertaining to see the same persons turn up again and again, now

as principals, now as agents, now as witnesses. Thus the money which Bunanitu's husband added to her dowry is said to have been borrowed from a certain Iddina-Marduk son of Bashâ, whose name we find as witness on the bill of sale (see p. 251), while still another tablet gives us his own marriage contract. This shows that the house Êgibi, like modern firms, had its well-established circle of permanent clients, and there is no doubt that by carefully studying and sifting their archives, it would be possible to trace the fortunes and mutual relations of various families through several generations. This fascinating task will devolve on the future novelist of Assyriology, and spare him, to a great extent, even the trouble of inventing a plot for his story. He will also find numbers of expressive and peculiar idiomatic forms of speech, to add a picturesque local color to his narrative—such as when two men entering into partnership and bringing each so much to begin operations with, call the capital thus formed "*mother of business.*"

25. Another class of documents, which will be to our novelist a rich and choice feast, is the daily increasing collection of private letters, of which quite a number have been deciphered of late. Scant room limits us to but one specimen. It is a request for assistance, addressed by an aged father to an absent son:

[*Obverse.*] "(Letter) from Iddina-âha(?) (to) Kêmut his son.

"(Bel) and Nebo peace and life for my son may they bespeak. He, my son, knows that there is no corn in the house. 2 or 3 *gur* of corn by the hands of some one whom thou knowest may my son

S

cause to be brought. There is none. By the hands of the boatman whom thou indicatedst, send"
[*Reverse.*] ". . . unto me. Send the gift. Cause it to go forth to thy father. This day Bel and Nebo for the preservation of my son's life grant Rêmat after the peace of Rêmat her son asks." (=Thy mother asks after thy health.) *

26. We have seen above (pp. 251-2) that among a father's first duties to his child was numbered that of sending him to school—"making him learn inscriptions." That this was no empty talk is amply proved by a large class of tablets—perhaps the most amusing of all—which have been found to be nothing more nor less than reading-books and children's copy-books, with school exercises, consisting in short sentences and lists of signs, written out a great many times, for practice, through all the stages of bad spelling and worse calligraphy. A great many such tablets are bilingual, and Professor A. H. Sayce had the good fortune of lighting on one sufficiently well preserved to be intelligible through several consecutive lines. It proves to be a simple nursery tale, which he translates, as far as the text goes, under the attractive title, "STORY OF THE FOUNDLING," as follows :

" The child who had neither father nor mother, who knew not his father or mother,—Into the fishpond(?) he came, into the street he went ;—From the mouth of the dogs one took him, from the mouth of the ravens one led him away ;—Before the soothsayer one took him from their mouth.—The soles of his feet with the soothsayer's seal underneath him were marked.—To the nurse he was

* The original tablet is in the private collection of the Misses Bruce, of New York, together with the manuscript translation by Mr. Theo. G. Pinches—both as yet unpublished.

given ; To the nurse for three years his grain, his food, his shirt, and his clothing were assured.—So for a time his rearing went on for him.—He that reared him rejoiced.(?)—His stomach with the milk of man he filled and made him his own son. . . ."

Here the tablet breaks off. But the fragment is quite sufficient to show to what kind of literature the document belongs, especially by the light of Professor Sayce's remarks, which we cannot do better than copy for our readers. He classes this text as "an Accadian reading-book, intended to teach the elements of the extinct Accadian language of primitive Chaldea to Babylonian boys of a later day"; then goes on :

"Easy passages in Accadian have been selected for the purpose and provided with Assyrian translations, while the text is interspersed with exercises upon the principal words occurring in it. Thus the phrase 'he made him his own son," is followed by examples of the various ways in which the words composing it could be combined with other parts of speech or replaced by corresponding expressions—' his son '—' his sonship '—' for his sonship '—' for his son he reckoned him '—' in the register of sonship he inscribed him,' * etc. Like the lesson-books of our own nurseries, the old Babylonian lesson-book also chose such stories as were likely to interest children, and the author wisely took his passage from the folk-lore and fairy tales of the boys' nursery rather than from the advanced literature of grown men. . ." †

In the same manner our children first learn the dead languages of their own race, Latin and Greek

---

* Adoption seems to have been common in Babylonia, especially in families where there were no sons. In the document quoted o· pp. 255-6 Bunanitu tells the judges that she bore her husband only one daughter, and that he formally adopted a stranger—"took him to sonship and wrote a tablet of his sonship."

† See A. H. Sayce's paper "Babylonian Folk-Lore," in the *Folk-Lore Journal*, vol. I., January, 1883, pp. 1 ff.

in collections of fables and anecdotes or short stories.

27. These are not the only school-exercises that have survived, and the method of impressing things on the mind by writing them out does not appear to have been limited to children. Mr. H. Rassam has brought home many fragments containing lawtexts from the "tablets of precedents," copied out carefully three times, evidently by law-students, for purposes of memorizing. As for the class of documents known as "contract-tablets," they do not by any means cease with the Babylonian Empire. Stray specimens bring down the use of them to an astonishingly late period—as late as the first centuries after Christ,—if we are to trust one which is dated from the reign of a Persian king who reigned about 100 A.D.,—showing that the use of cuneiform writing died out very gradually and prevailed much longer than had at first been supposed.

X

MEDIA AND THE RISE OF PERSIA.

1. HAD the throne of Media, during Nebuchadrezzar's long reign, been occupied by Kyaxares, or a monarch of the same ambitious and active stamp, it is very probable that the Babylonian would have had occasion, in his lifetime, to test the efficiency of those bulwarks and defences which his foresight so busily devised. For relationship, especially the artificial connection by marriage, has not much weight in politics, and if the founder of the Median Empire had seen an opening toward "rounding it off" (as the modern phrase goes), at the expense of either or both his neighbors, it is not likely that consideration for either his daughter or daughter-in-law would have stopped him. But he died quite early in Nebuchadrezzar's reign (584), and his son and successor, Astyages (the "Ishtuvêgu" of cuneiform records. See p. 221), was a man of self-indulgent habit, indolent and pleasure-loving, the very model of the spendthrift heir, bent merely on enjoying the greatness he has not helped to build, until, by his carelessness, he loses it. His accession, therefore, was a very good thing for his brother-in-law of Babylon and his father-in-law Alyattes, of Sardis, who, with the help of his son

Kroisos (Cræsus), went on consolidating and enlarging the dominion of Lydia, and settling old-standing accounts with the Greek cities of the sea-shore.

2. Nor was the change that had come over the nation less great. The Medes were no longer the rough warriors, inured to hardships, careless of wealth, of which they had not learned the value, who "did not regard silver, and as for gold, took no delight in it" (Isaiah xiii., 17). The booty of Nineveh and the other Assyrian cities had taught them the uses of luxury, and the court of Agbatana was not outdone in splendor by either Babylon or Sardis. The palace of Median royalty, too, was fully equal in magnificence to those of the older capitals; it is even possible that it outshone them in mere barbaric gorgeousness, such as the lavish use of gold and silver, though there is great reason to believe that it remained far behind in point of artistic decoration. For the Aryan conquerors had no art of their own, and had not yet had time to learn that of their neighbors, nor, perhaps, to find out that art was in itself desirable and worth learning—a notion originally foreign to the rather stern and practical Eranian mind. But, as national dignity demands that royalty should be housed in seemly splendor, an effect of great magnificence and imposing majesty was produced by other means.

3. For, if they had not made a study of art, especially that of decoration, the Medes had brought with them a manner of building which was to be fruitful of artistic results, and inaugurate a style of architecture entirely different from that with which we have

become so familiar in the lands of the Tigris and Euphrates. In the abundantly wooded mountains and valleys of Eastern Êrân the building material indicated by nature is timber. The nomad's movable tent or hut is imitated in wood, enlarged, and becomes the cabin of logs or boards, with porch and gallery resting on roughly hewn trunks of trees. This, again, in constructions destined for public purposes, expands into the hall with aisles of columns supporting the roof, and with wide pillared porch. The transition is easy to the combination of public and private apartments which forms the royal dwelling or palace. By devising the plan on a grander scale, by the choice of hard and handsome woods, of tall and stately trees, and by great finish of workmanship, it was possible to produce a building of real beauty, preserving the original and characteristic feature—a profusion of columns, to be distributed in every possible combination of aisles, porches, porticos surrounding the inner courts, etc. Exactly such a construction was the palace at Agbatana. The forests of the Zagros supplied fine timber as bountifully as those of Bactria, and the Medes could preserve their own traditional style of building without falling into the absurdity of the Assyrians, who went on heaping mountains of bricks, after the manner of flat and marshy Chaldea, when they had quarries of fine stone at hand all around them.

4. The ancient Greek writers describe the palace of the Median kings (possibly begun by Deïokes, and enlarged by Kyaxares), as occupying an area of fully two thirds of a mile, at the foot of Mt. ORONTES

(modern ELVEND); it was built entirely of costly cedar and cypress, but the wood was nowhere visible, as not only the columns and beams, but the ceilings and walls, were overlaid with gold or silver plating, while the roof was made of silver tiles. Herodotus is filled with admiration at the effect produced by the walls which enclosed the palace, "rising in circles, one within the other. The plan of the place is that each of the walls should out-top the one beyond it by the battlements. The nature of the ground, which is a gentle slope, favors this arrangement in some degree, but it was mainly effected by art. The number of the circles is seven, the royal palace and the treasuries standing within the last. . . . Of the outer wall, the battlements are white; of the next, black; of the third, scarlet; of the fourth, blue; of the fifth, orange; all these are covered with paint. The last two have their battlements coated respectively with silver and gold." The city was built outside the circuit of the walls. The only drawback to this picturesque and well-defended situation was the want of water. There was none nearer than the other side of Mt. Orontes, several miles from the city, where a small lake fed a mountain stream. That stream was turned from its course and brought by a tunnel, fifteen feet in width, which was cut through the base of the mountain for the purpose. This is the work which Median legend, followed by the Greeks, attributed to the fabulous Queen Semiramis.* It is very probable that it was planned and carried out by Kyaxares.

* See "Story of Assyria," p. 108.

5. The general effect, as beheld from a distance, especially from the low level of the plain, must have been marvellously quaint and impressive. The graded height of the seven concentric walls and the combination of colors at once recall the great Ziggurat of Nebo, at Borsip,* and naturally suggest that the general idea may have been borrowed from there. This may well be, and, if so, we may be sure that the significance and sacredness of the number seven in the Eranian religion prompted the imitation. Besides, the legend of the original Holy Mountain, of which the Chaldean Ziggurat was a reminder,† was common to both races, and Duncker no doubt comes very near the truth when he explains the peculiar construction and decoration of the Median palace in the following words: "As Ahura-Mazda sat on his golden throne in the sphere of pure Light on the summit of golden Hukairya, so the earthly ruler was to dwell in his palace at Agbatana, in golden apartments, enclosed within a golden wall. The Avesta shows us Mithra in golden helmet and silver cuirass; the wheels of his chariot are of gold; his milk-white steeds' forefeet are shod with gold, their hindfeet with silver. So it was meet that the royal roof and battlements should gleam in silver and in gold." Nor can the account be rejected as improbable on the plea of extravagance. The booty from Assyria could surely cover the outlay, and that without materially draining the treasury. We are expressly told that when Alexander of Macedon

---

* See "Story of Chaldea," pp. 280-283.
† See "Story of Chaldea," pp. 274-276.

conquered Asia, he carried away most of the silver tiles off the roof; yet seventy-five years later another conqueror still found at Agbatana booty to the amount of about five million dollars, in gold and silver-plating and silver roof-tiles. Yet the bulk of the gold and silver, to the value of eight and a half millions dollars, had been removed by the Persian king before Alexander came. We must remember that the accumulation of wealth in Nineveh and Kalah must have far exceeded our powers of calculation, and that one of the very last acts of Assyrian power was the wholesale cleaning out of the treasure-houses of the kings of Elam, at Shushan, "where no other enemy had ever put his hand"* through all the twenty centuries of that kingdom's prosperity.

6. Whether Agbatana was surrounded, like Babylon, by an outer wall of defence, we do not know. There was no such wall at the time of Herodotus, or he would have mentioned it. Still, as Agbatana had been taken in the interval, it is quite possible there may have been a wall and it was demolished by the victors. This question and many others may be cleared up some day when serious diggings are undertaken at Hamadân. Unfortunately, nothing of much importance has yet been done, and of the few fragmentary relics that have been found, it is impossible to say whether they belong to this period or a later one. The same uncertainty confronts us at every turn when we attempt to enquire for details concerning the Median nation, its institutions, and its life. Perhaps no other empire of like extent and

* See "Story of Assyria," p. 399.

power has left so few traces of its existence, so few handles for history to take hold of. This is certainly owing to the lack of durable monuments. Not an inscription has reached us; not one undoubtedly genuine specimen of art or craft; nothing but legends of epical character, and those not in native form or garb, but transmitted through Greek writers, who got them in fragments, through the channel of ignorant, unreliable interpreters, and proceeded to impart them as history. Of the real value of such history, we have a sample in the accounts of Semiramis. But, though modern research has very well established what is *not* true in the old Greek stories, it has hitherto failed in procuring much positive information concerning the Medes.

7. A few facts, however, we may hold for certain. One of the principal is that the Medes used to call themselves Âryas, and were generally known under that name to their neighbors and subjects; another, that the population of the empire was mixed. Herodotus knows by name of six so-called "tribes," and these names it has been found possible to trace from the Greek corruption to the original Eranian forms. They tell their own story. One means "natives," another "nomads," a third "dwellers in tents," a fourth "owners of the soil," and only one is expressly designated as "Aryan people" ("*Arizantos*," in Persian "*Aryiazantu*"). Such a distinction strongly implies that the others were not Aryans, and admirably tallies with the theory of the gradual advance of the Aryan Medes and their occupation of Ellip and the other portions of the Zagros

highlands, where they became a ruling class, a military aristocracy, which held the "natives," the "owners of the soil" (of different, mostly Turanian, race), in subjection. The seven-fold belt of defence, with which the foreign royalty enclosed itself, may have been at first a necessary precaution against possible risings. In the course of time, as the distinction grew less marked, and the enmity of the races became merged in a common national feeling, the conquerors' name was adopted by the rest of the population, and they all called themselves "Medes" together. As to the "nomads" and the "tent-dwellers" (shepherds), this designation probably covers a large proportion of still fluctuating population in the steppes of Central and Western Erân, composed mainly of Eranian elements; for the Median Empire at this period of its greatest extension covered an area reaching from the Halys and Araxes on one side, across a vast tract of desert and mountain wilds on the other, some say, as far as the Indus itself. But its eastern boundaries were never very well defined. It seems certain, however, that most countries composing Eastern Erân—Hyrcania, Parthia, Bactria, and several more which figure on ancient maps, were subject and paid tribute to Media; some of them probably were ruled by Median governors.

8. The sixth Median tribe on Herodotus' list bears the name of MAGI. That these were the priests, forming a separate body, there is no shadow of a doubt. It is the name—and the only one—under which the Eranian priesthood has been known to foreign nations. Yet, as we have seen, it is not

the name that is given them in the Avesta, where the priests, ever since they form a body or class, are uniformly designated as "Âthravans." There is a contradiction here, which is further enhanced by the fact that the Magi, although undoubtedly the guardians of Avestan law and worship, indulged in practices foreign to that law, nay, directly opposed to it, principally that of conjuring and divining, which has become inseparably associated with that priestly class, in the universally accepted words "magic," "magician." Herodotus tells us that the Magi presided at sacrifices, where they chanted hymns, and that they delighted in killing with their own hands ants, snakes, flying and creeping things, in fact, all sorts of animals except dogs. This is quite in accordance with the Avestan law. Much later writers report that the Magi worshipped and sacrificed to the Evil Power, and one of them expressly relates that they press in a mortar the herb called *Omomi* (Haoma), invoking the Power of Evil and Darkness, then mix the juice with the blood of a sacrificed wolf, and pour the drink-offering on a spot on which the sun never shines.* Such practices, judged by the light of the Avesta, are nothing less than impious, and could not possibly have been originated by the Eranian Âthravan of early Mazdeism. But they are by no means incompatible with the spirit of Turanian or so-called Shamanistic religions, like that of pre-Semitic Chaldea, several of which incline to pay the rites of worship rather to the Powers of Darkness than those of Light. The Shamans or sorcerer-

* Plutarch: "Is and Osiris."

priests of many Turanian tribes of our own day, from Lapland through Siberia and Central Asia, are the representatives of the still surviving hideous superstition.* Indeed, there still exists, among the Kurds who live in Assyria, in the Sinjar hills, where Layard visited and studied them, as far as they would permit, a very curious sect which, together with many old-Christian and Mussulman features, presents a survival of what was probably the religion of pre-Aryan Media. They are called the YEZIDIS, or "Devil-worshippers." They believe in God, but do not show him any observance, while they show servile reverence to the Devil, who has a temple among them, and to whose symbol, the serpent, they pay public honor. For, they say with a kind of perverse logic, God, being good of his nature, can do nothing but good to men, and there is no necessity of asking him to do so; the Devil, on the contrary, being bad, is inclined to do harm, unless kept in a good humor by constant entreaty and propitiation. Traces of similar conceptions still linger among various mountain tribes of Armenia and Kurdistân (ancient Zagros).

9. After all that has been said, we shall not be far from the truth if we assume the Magi to have been originally the native priesthood of the vast mountainous region subsequently occupied by the Medes and known as Western Erân. With the arrival of the Aryan conquerors, who brought their own lofty, pure, recently reformed religion, began the process of mutual concessions and assimilation which marked the third stage of the Avestan evolution,

* See "Story of Chaldea," p. 180.

and to which we referred the foreign and mostly
Turanian practices that make up so great a portion
of the Vendidâd (see pp. 142-156). The fusion of
the two religions was followed by that of the two
priesthoods, and the Âthravans were merged in the
Magi, the sixth Median tribe on the list of Herodotus. How the fusion was effected, and why the
name "Magi" absorbed and was substituted for the
older one, will probably never be found out. Indeed,
that very name has been and still is the subject of
discussion among the leading scholars. Many connect it with the Accadian *imga* (priest), Semitic *mag*,
which enters into the familiar title of *Rab-mag*.*
Others will not hear of this Chaldean connection,
and assert a purely Aryan origin of the word, accounting for it by the Vedic word *maghâ*, "great,"
perhaps "holy." Whether traces of an original conflict and hostility should be detected in certain passages of the Avesta, and the pre-Aryan priesthood
should be understood under the "false Âthravans"
denounced in those passages, as some would have it,
is too doubtful a question to be here discussed. We
must be content with the certainty that, in historical
times, the Magi were the national priestly class of
Media or Western Erân, the keepers and propagators
of the Avestan law as represented by the Vendidâd,
keeping in view the important fact that the observances which they so severely enforced, such as the
exposure of the dead, were not by any means adopted
by all the Eranian nations. It was only in the ulti-
mate development reached by Zoroastrian Magism

* See "Story of Chaldea," p. 255.

under the Sassanides, that the religious law of ancient Media was proclaimed the only orthodox one, and made obligatory for the whole of Erân (see p. 28).

10. The Magi of this period appear as a powerful separate body, possessing large territories with cities of their own, the centre of which is Rhagæ, in olden times the chief city of Media after Agbatana. In these territories they seem to exercise something like actual independent sovereignty, and Rhagæ is the seat of their chief and head. As they claim to form a clan, descended directly from Zarathushtra, this their high-priest, a sort of Zoroastrian pope, invested with both spiritual and temporal power, bears the title of ZARATHUSTRÔTEMA, or "Chief Zarathushtra," literally "Most Zarathushtra" (of all Zarathushtras). We see from this that the name was sometimes used as a title. It is used in this manner in a fragment of catechism which we find at the end of a chapter of Zend (commentary) on the Ahunavairya (Yasna, XIX.) and which clearly defines this state of things. The four classes and the five chiefs having been mentioned, an examination begins, by question and answer, of which the following is an extract:

"*Q.* What classes of men?
"*A.* The priest, the warrior, the tiller of the ground, and the artisan. . . .
"*Q.* What are the chiefs?
"*A.* They are the house-chief, the village-chief, and the tribe-chief, the chief of the province (king), and the Zarathushtra as the fifth. That is in those provinces which are outside the Zarathushtrian domain. Ragha, the Zarathushtrian city, has only four chiefs.
"*Q.* How are these chiefs constituted?

"*A.* They are the house-chief, the village-chief, the tribe-chief, and the Zarathushtra as the fourth."

Evidently there is no king in Rhagæ, and his place is occupied by the high-priest, who, let it be noted, is ranked above the kings in the hierarchy of the other provinces. We cannot say at what time the priestly class achieved so high a position, but there may have been something of the kind in the time of Herodotus, which would justify him in making of the Magi a separate tribe. Certain it is that the religion of Zoroaster, as it was rehandled by the Magi, spread westwards as far as the Median domination reached; for, centuries after its fall, Greek writers find fire-chapels and Magi officiating therein, with *paitidâna* and *baresma*, chanting sacred songs from a book, in Lydia and Cappadocia. How far that domination extended in the east, it were difficult to say. Some think that it stretched from the Indus to the Halys, and only failed to reach the Ionian sea-coast because it was unexpectedly cut off by a kindred and hitherto vassal nation, the PERSIANS.

11. We have no means of ascertaining at what time or in what manner took place the migration of this Eranian people, or when they reached the rugged but well-conditioned country by the Persian Gulf to which they gave their name, PERSIS, and which corresponds pretty accurately to the province still known under the same, but slightly altered, name of FARS or FARSISTÂN. It will probably always remain a matter of uncertainty whether they came from the northeast across the desert by a

route of their own, as a separate body and independently of the main current of Eranian migration more directly making for the west; or whether they formed part of that current, and only after reaching the upper highlands of the Zagros (Âderbeidjân and Kurdistân), branched off on a further tramp, and, following the direction of the valleys imbedded between the seven-fold ridges of the Zagros, settled in that continuation of it which rounds off to skirt the sweep of the Gulf, and sends out decreasing spurs to meet those that may be called the outposts of the great SULEIMAN range. What speaks most in favor of the latter supposition is that ever since the name of the Medes—(Madaï, Mataï, Amadaï)—makes its appearance in the royal annals of Assyria, i. e., as early as Shalmaneser II., another name almost invariably accompanies it, or at least occurs on the same inscription,—that of the land and people of BARSUA or PARSUA, which have been located with almost certainty just beyond the principalities of Urartu (Armenia), somewhere in Âderbeidjân. There is nothing unlikely in the hypothesis of the Parsuas having first occupied the Zagros highlands jointly with the Medes, then separated and founded a new and more independent principality of their own. At all events they call themselves Âryas, as did the Medes; and one of their mightiest kings, Dareios I., in his great rock-inscription (of which more fully hereafter), glories in being "a Persian, son of a Persian, an Ârya, of Aryan seed." If the identity of the Barsuas or Parsuas of the Assyrian inscriptions with the later Persians be accepted, it may further be admitted as not entirely unlikely that religious differences may have had something to do with the separation, for we shall see that the Persians retained the Zoroastrian revelation in a far purer and more unalloyed form than their kindred, the Medes.

12. By its conditions of soil and climate, Persia proper—as Persis may be called—was eminently apt to produce a race of a high moral and physical standard. Notwithstanding its almost tropical latitude, the elevation of its ground gives it the advantages of moderate zones, as shown by the vegetation of the country, which, together with sycamores, cypresses, myrtles, the fig-tree, the date-palm, the lemon, orange, and pomegranate, embraces trees and fruits common to far more northern regions, such as the oak, the poplar, willow, acacia, even the juniper, pears, apples, plums, nuts, and various berries. The peach with its varieties is indigenous to the country of which it bears the name in several languages. The valleys, too, produce different kinds of grain and vegetables—wheat, barley, millet, beans, etc. Such wealth of field and orchard is sufficient to ensure the well-being of a nation, but, requiring assiduous cultivation, does not expose it to lapse into idleness, while the climate in the uplands, moderate in summer, severe in winter, with several months of snow and frost, and great variations of temperature within the twenty-four hours, is wholesome and bracing, and certainly does not encourage effeminacy. The want of water, the great plague of the level parts of Erân, which begins to be felt at once in the plains into which the mountains of Persis slope down, to

the east and north, does not affect the uplands, which abound in mountain springs, although there is no room for long and wide rivers, the five ridges which stretch across the country being broken only by narrow and precipitous passes. The wooded pastures on the mountain sides and the rich meadows in the valleys were a very paradise for cattle, so that the Eranian settlers had every encouragement to follow the two pursuits recommended to them as essentially worthy and holy—farming and cattle-rais-

37. PERSIAN AND MEDIAN FOOT-SOLDIERS.

ing. The Greeks ascribed much of the endurance and warlike qualities for which they respected the Persians to the fact of their living so much out-of-doors and being trained to watchfulness by their occupation of guarding flocks and herds by day and by night. Riding, also, was in much favor among them, and hunting of every kind was their favorite exercise and pastime, for their mountains swarmed with pheasants, partridge, grouse, and other small game, while the open country teemed with lions, bears, antelope, wild asses, etc., and invited to all the royal sports of the Assyrians. It naturally follows that the Persians were accomplished bowmen. Indeed Herodotus, in a celebrated passage, expressly says that "their sons were carefully instructed from their fifth to their twentieth year in three things alone—to ride, to draw the bow, and to speak the truth." Of course this description applies only to the class of warriors or nobles—as the agriculturists and the priests would have many more things to learn; but it gives one the idea of a simple and manly training, wholly in accordance with the principles of the purest Mazdeism. The national garb, too, was hardy and simple: a short coat and trousers, both of dressed leather, with a plain belt, the whole calculated to favor the greatest freedom and ease of motion. But when they came in contact with the luxurious and effeminate Medes, the Persians, being naturally imitative to excess, soon began to adopt, together with more refined and courtly manners, the long-flowing, wide-sleeved robe, wrapped round the body and gathered up on one side in graceful folds, which was known to the Greeks as "the Median robe," being characteristic of and probably invented by that nation. It is clear that the costliness of this garment could be increased to any amount by the fineness of the material and of the dye (Tyrian purple for instance), and by the addition of embroidery and ornament.

13. The population of Persia proper was not more unmixed than that of Media. The native inhabitants were, as usual, not extirpated by the new-comers, but reduced to subjection. This is

how it comes about that, of the ten or twelve tribes into which Greek historians divide the Persian nation, only three are named—the PASARGADÆ, the MARAPHIANS, and the MASPII—as "the principal ones, on which all the others are dependent." (Herodotus, I., 125.) These are clearly the Eranian conquerors, the ruling class, the aristocracy. Of "the others," four are expressly said to be nomads, and were surely not Aryan at all, while the rest may have been of mixed race. Of the nomad tribes the only one which we can identify with any degree of certainty, is that of the MARDIANS, who lived in the western highlands of Persis, and were probably a branch of or identical with the better known AMARDIANS. These latter were a people probably of a mixed race, akin to the Elamites and Kasshi, and occupied the mountain region now known as BAKHTIYARI MOUNTAINS. Their language appears to have been quite, or very nearly, that spoken in Elam, the SUSIANA of the Greeks, and to have belonged to the agglutinative type (Turanian or Ouralo-Altaïc *), consequently to have been closely related to the ancient language of Shumir and Accad.† It is most probably this region which is repeatedly mentioned in the Assyrian royal annals under the name of ANZAN, ANSHAN, and sometimes ASSAN and ANDUAN. It was a part or a dependence of the kingdom of Elam, figuring at

---

* The Turanian race is frequently called "Ouralo-Altaïc," from the fact that the valleys of the Oural and Altaïc ranges have always been the chief nests and strongholds of its tribes.

† See "Story of Chaldea," pp. 145 ff.

times among its allies, and at others included in the title of the kings of Elam.

14. The beginnings of Persia as a nation were not different from those of Media, or, indeed, any other nation. The process is always the same. It is the gathering of the separate and in a great measure independent clans or tribes under the leadership of one more numerous, more powerful, more gifted than the others. That such a movement can be effected only through the agency and authority of one master-spirit stands to reason, and the successful chieftain naturally becomes the king of the state he has created. Such was the origin of the Persian hereditary monarchy, the founder of which is known, from testimony too public and solemn to be disputed, to have been HAKHAMANISH (more familiar under the Greek form of the name as AKHÆMENES), a prince of the clan of the Pasargadæ, which was always held to be the noblest of the three ruling tribes. (See p. 278.) He must have been a contemporary of Asshurbanipal, and was succeeded by a long line of kings, famous under the name of AKHÆMENIDÆ or Akhæmenian dynasty, the last scion of which lost his crown and life in the struggle with the young Greek conqueror, Alexander of Macedon (331 B.C.). The tribal city of the clan, also called Pasargadæ, became the royal capital of the united nation. It was regarded with great reverence ever after as the cradle of the monarchy, and when that monarchy extended into the mightiest empire that the world had yet seen, and its kings had the choice of four great capitals for their residence, the

sacredness attached to their modest ancestral city was so great that each succeeding king came there to be inaugurated. It was like the French kings going to Reims, or the Scotch kings to Scone, for their coronation. The place where Pasargadæ stood is now called MURGHÂB, and there are some ruins there, the oldest in Persia.

15. The Persians were by nature a conquering people; and although not strong enough at this early stage of their national life to undertake distant expeditions, they found close at hand an opportunity for an easy acquisition too tempting to be neglected. Elam was utterly destroyed; its people carried away and scattered, its princes slain or dragged into bondage, its cities and temples sacked and turned into dens for beasts to lie in, its trees burned, and its wells dried up.* Not a condition this, in which a country could defend its very heart against an invader, much less its outlying provinces. The land of Anshan was open to its Persian neighbors; and it must have been at this time that TEÏSPES, (CHISHPAÏSH), the son of Akhæmenes, occupied it, and assumed the title of "Great King, King of Anshan, or "of the city of Anshan." After his death, the royal house of the Akhæmenians split itself into two lines: one of his sons, KYROS I. (KURUSH) succeeded him in Anshan, while another, ARIARAMNES (ARIYÂRÂMANA), reigned in Persia. These were followed respectively by *their* sons, KAMBYSES I., in Anshan, and ARSAMES (ARSHÂMA), in Persia. It is extremely probable that Kyros and Ariaramnes were

* See "Story of Assyria," pp. 399-401.

among the allies or vassal princes who helped Kyaxares to overwhelm Assyria. There is no doubt, at all events, that Persia stood towards Media in the position of a subject and tributary country, since the beginning of its greatness dates from its revolt against the Median rule under Kyros II. and the overthrow of the Median Empire by that King.

16. None of the histories we inherit from antiquity, either entire or in fragments, nor, consequently, of the modern histories compiled from those materials, gives us the facts crowded into the last few paragraphs. No one had the remotest idea of Kyros having been any thing but a king of Persia, or of the Akhæmenians having reigned in a double line, and the very name of Anshan was unknown. Two sets of monuments accidentally discovered at various times and in various places revealed these facts, which, standing forth in the uncompromising simplicity and stubbornness of contemporary evidence, overthrew the familiar structure raised out of the stories—half fabulous as they now turn out to be—which the Greek writers took on trust from Median and Persian sources, epical ballads, most of them, not untainted with myth. Of these monuments some are Persian and three are Babylonian cylinders recording some of the acts of Nabonidus, the last king of Babylon, and the capture of that city by Kyros, who on both cylinders is called and calls himself " King of Anshan," *not* of Persia. It is well-established that Kyros, at the time of the conquest of Babylon, was already king of Persia; but that country was rather distant and probably little known

to the Chaldeans, whereas the Land and City of Anshan were very near and had long been familiar to them, as doubtless also the new reigning family that had established itself there. As to his lineage, this is how he sets it forth in his proclamation, on mounting the throne of Babylon:

"I am KYROS (KURUSH), the great king, the powerful king, the king of Tintir*), king of Shumir and Accad, king of the four regions; son of KAMBYSES (KAMBUJIYA) the great king, KING OF THE CITY OF ANSHAN, grandson of Kyros, the great king, king of the city of Anshan, great-grandson of TEĪSPES (THESPISH) the great king, king of the city of Anshan."

17. Very different in size from these tiny Babylonian monuments are the Persian ones, and, like the cylinders, somewhat posterior to the time our history has reached, indeed still later, since we owe them to Persian kings, successors of Kyros. The most important one for the point now under examination is the famous ROCK OF BEHISTÛN or BISUTÛN, or rather the inscription engraved on that rock by Dareios, second successor of Kyros, and after him the greatest of the Akhæmenians. The rock, noticed from very ancient times on account of its isolated position and peculiar shape, rises nearly perpendicular to a height of 1700 feet, the most striking feature of the road from Hamadân (ancient Agbatana) to Baghdad, and near the modern town of KIRMANSHÂH. On the straightest and smoothest face of the rock Dareios determined to perpetuate, by means of sculpture and writing, the great deeds of his reign. The monument was to be absolutely

---

* Tintir,—the most ancient name of Babylon, in the Accadian, or pre-Semitic period; see "Story of Chaldea," p. 216.

38. ROCK OF BEHISTUN.

indestructible, and, first of all, inaccessible to the sacrilegious hand of invader or domestic foe. This was so well secured by the height at which the work was executed—over 300 feet from the base,—that it could be scarcely got at for the purpose of studying or copying it. Indeed, the French scholars, Messrs. Flandin and Coste, after many attempts, gave up the task, which it was the glory of Sir Henry—then Major—Rawlinson, with the help of field-glasses successfully to achieve, at the cost of three years' labor (1844-1847)—infinite hardships and dangers, and an outlay of over five thousand dollars. How the artists and engravers originally ever got to the place, is a question which the steepness of the ascent makes very puzzling, unless there were some practicable paths which were cut away subsequently; and even then they could not have worked without ladders and scaffoldings. Besides, the rock had to undergo an elaborate preliminary preparation. Not only was the surface smoothed down almost to a state of polish, but wherever the stone showed crevices or dints, it was closely plastered with a kind of cement, matching and fitting it so exactly as to be hardly distinguishable. The result of all this foresight and painstaking, we have before us in the shape of a very remarkable piece of historical sculpture, surrounded by numerous columns of inscription, making in all over one thousand lines of cuneiform writing. The long narrative is repeated three times in the different languages, so as to be intelligible to all the three races which the new empire had united under its rule: in Persian, in Assyrian, and in the language of Anshan, which was probably that of all Elam,—or Susiana,

39. SCULPTURES AND INSCRIPTIONS ON THE ROCK OF BEHISTÛN.

as the country began to be called from its capital Shushan or Susa,—and possibly of the un-Aryan population of the entire Zagros region. For this language has been shown to belong neither to the Aryan nor to the Semitic, but to the Turanian or agglutinative type. It used at first to be called "Proto-Median," *i. e.*, "earliest Median," but now it is proposed to call it "Scythic," *i. e.*, Turanian, or "Amardian," in compliment to the nation who is thought to have inhabited Anshan. This immense monument of human pride, labor, and patience was attributed by the Greeks, like every thing out of the common in these parts of Asia, and in a distorted form, to the mythical queen Semiramis.*

18. The Persian kings, succeeding, as they did, long lines of Assyrian and Babylonian monarchs, appropriated their literary style, which henceforth became the set and invariable form of Oriental public speaking and writing. This style we accordingly recognize in the trilingual Behistûn inscription, with perhaps just a shade less of stiffness. Like Kyros, like every long-descended prince, Dareios (DARAYAVUSH is the Persian form), begins by establishing his genealogy:

"I am Dareios the great king, the king of kings, the king of Persia, the king of nations, the son of Hystaspes, the grandson of Arsames, the Akhæmenian.

"Says Dareios the king: My father was Hystaspes (Vishtâspa); of Hystaspes the father was Arsames (Arshâma); of Arsames the father was Ariaramnes (Ariyârâmana); of Ariaramnes the father was Teïspes (Chishpâish); of Teïspes the father was Akhæmenes (Hakhâmanish).

"Says Dareios the king: On that account we are called Akhæmenians. From ancient times we have descended; from ancient times our family have been kings.

* See "Story of Assyria," p. 198.

"Says Dareios the king: There are eight of my race who have been kings before me; I am the ninth. *In a double line we have been kings.*"

The Behistûn inscription was known and deciphered long before the discovery of the cylinders of Nabonidus and Kyros. Therefore the last words of the above passage (printed in italics), were found so extremely puzzling, that the decipherers entertained great doubts about it, and intimated by the sign (?) that they considered the translation uncertain and provisional. By comparing the whole passage, however, with the corresponding one from Kyros' proclamation, given above (p. 282), we shall at once see how beautifully the two complete each other: each of the kings traces his separate line upwards, till both unite in their common ancestor, Teïspes, the conqueror or annexer of Anshan. Evidently he divided his kingdom between his two sons, Kyros I. and Ariaramnes, at his death, and the Akhæmenian house continued to reign " in two lines,"—one in Anshan, and one in Persia proper. And in numbering those of the race who were kings before him, Dareios clearly includes those of the Anshan line. This gives the following genealogical scheme:

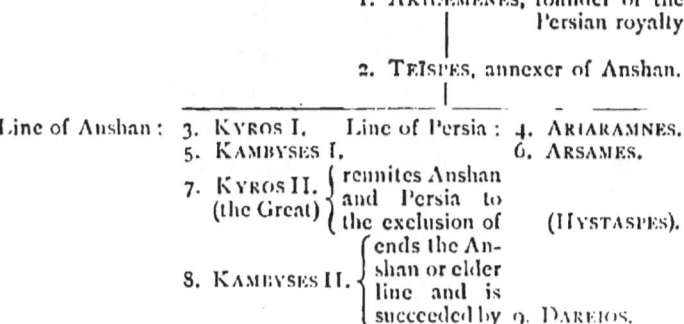

1. AKHÆMENES, founder of the Persian royalty
2. TEÏSPES, annexer of Anshan.

Line of Anshan:	3. KYROS I.	Line of Persia:	4. ARIARAMNES.
	5. KAMBYSES I.		6. ARSAMES.
	7. KYROS II. (the Great) {reunites Anshan and Persia to the exclusion of		(HYSTASPES).
	8. KAMBYSES II. {ends the Anshan or elder line and is succeeded by	9. DAREIOS.	

Had Hystaspes reigned, Dareios would have been *the tenth*. But he expressly states that *eight* of his race reigned before him, and he is the ninth. On the other hand, Hystaspes is never given the title of king in the numerous inscriptions recording the genealogy of Dareios and his descendants on the walls of their palaces at the royal city of Persepolis. These two indications converge to the conclusion that Kyros, before he overthrew the Median Empire and started on his career of conquest, established himself as king of both Anshan and the ancestral country—Persia, to the exclusion of Hystaspes, who would seem to have submitted with a good grace, since history shows him an honored and trusted kinsman and councillor at the court of Kyros and governor of an important province, Hyrcania. When the elder line became extinct in the person of Kambyses, the son of Kyros the Great, the nearest and natural claimant was Hystaspes, the representative of the younger line, but he appears to have been a singularly unambitious person, for we again find him passed by, this time in favor of his son Dareios, who reigns long and gloriously, while he is content to command some of that son's armies.

We have been forced to anticipate considerably in order to establish our authorities for a narrative conflicting in many points with the course of events universally accepted until very lately. We will now resume it at the next authentic move—the fall of the Median Empire.

XI.

"KURUSH THE KING, THE AKHEMENIAN."

1. Of the three cylinders mentioned on p. 281, and the one brought over by Mr. H. Rassam, which surpasses both the others in importance as an historical document, contains the annals of the reign of Nabonidus, last king of Babylon, and the capture of Babylon by Kyros. In the second column we read as follows:

Fall of the Median Empire, 549 B.C.

". . . Against Kurash (Kyros), king of Anshan, came Ish. . . . Ishtuvegu's (Astyages') army revolted against him, captured him and delivered him over to Kurash. Kurash (marched) into the land of Agamtunu (Agbatana), the royal city. He took silver, gold, furniture, valuables; from Agamtunu he carried off all and brought to Anshan the treasure and goods which he had captured."

Further on Kyros is once named "King of Persia." This cylinder was written in the reign of Kyros as king of Babylon. Another, known more especially as "the Nabonidus Cylinder," and somewhat earlier in date, alludes more briefly to the same event.*

". . . He (the god Marduk) caused Kurash, king of Anshan, his young servant, to go with his little army. He overthrew the widespread *Sabmanda* (" barbarians," a name here given to the Medes), " he captured Ishtuvegu, king of Sabmanda, and took his treasure to his own land."

* This is the famous cylinder which helped to establish the date of the first Sargon of Agadé. See " Story of Chaldea," p. 213.

2. All this thoroughly confirms one portion of the narrative as it stands in Herodotus. According to him, Kyros, having spent part of his youth at the court of Astyages, had formed a party for himself among the Medes, headed by a certain HARPAGOS (a great lord, and kinsman of the king), with whom he corresponded, and by whose advice he was guided when he incited the Persians to open revolt. This he is said to have done by appealing to their national pride and saying to them, in substance: "Follow my bidding and be free. For myself, I feel that I am destined by Providence to undertake your liberation; and you, I am sure, are no whit inferior to the Medes in any thing, least of all in bravery." It is not at all unlikely that he increased the ardor of his comparatively penurious countrymen by holding out to them the prospect of securing wealth and the delights of luxury. "The Persians," continues Herodotus, "who had long been impatient of the Median dominion, now that they had found a leader, were delighted to shake off the yoke." Astyages immediately sent out an army against the rebels, but as it was commanded by Harpagos, the result can be guessed: "When the two armies met and engaged, only a few of the Medes who were not in the secret fought; others deserted openly to the Persians; while the greater number counterfeited fear and fled." Kyros thereupon marched to Agbatana; the old king came out to meet him with a hastily summoned body of citizens, both young and old, but was utterly defeated and taken prisoner. "Thus, after a reign of thirty-five years, Astyages lost his crown,

and the Medes were brought under the rule of the Persians." He was not beloved, and was accused of having caused the disaster by his cruel and tyrannical ways. Still Kyros, who was by nature magnanimous and mild, did his royal captive no injury, but kept him at his court until his death, honorably treated and amply provided for.* This revolution took place in 549 B.C. The Median Empire, counting from the fall of Nineveh, had lasted fifty-seven years.

3. So far the narrative of Herodotus is proved by contemporary monuments to be correct; but only in portions and in substance. The details are historically as worthless as the Greek stories about Semiramis, and evidently derived from the same source—Median and Persian epic ballads, largely mixed with myth. This narrative, too widely known to be ignored, must be briefly touched upon, even at the risk of spoiling by condensation one of the most entertaining and best-told stories in the world. The only touch of reality about it is the statement that Astyages had no son, which, however, immediately branches off into folk-lore. First of all the king has a dream, which the Magi interpret as meaning that the son of his daughter MANDANÊ would rule the whole of Asia, whereupon he marries her away from his court to a Persian named Kambyses, a private man, "of good family, indeed, but of a quiet temper, whom he looked on as much inferior to a Mede of even middle condition." In consequence of another dream, he sends for Mandanê, so as to have her and

* See Herodotus, Book I., 123-130.

her child in his power, and when that child, the little Kyros, is born, the king immediately orders his kinsman and trusty servant Harpagos to carry him to his home and slay him. Harpagos has not the heart to do the cruel thing himself, but makes over the babe to one of the royal herdsmen, whose range of pastureland lay among mountains infested with wild beasts, with the order to expose him " in the wildest part of the hills, where he should be sure to die speedily." The herdsman's wife, whose own babe had just died, persuaded her husband to exchange the two, and three days later the dead child, arrayed in all the other's costly attire, is shown to the men sent by Harpagos, while the royal infant is brought up by the herdsman's wife, whose name is SPAKA (which means " bitch, female dog "), as her own and under an assumed name.

4. When he reached his tenth year Kyros made himself conspicuous by his masterful ways among his comrades, with whom he used to play at being their king, making them obey him in real earnest and punishing severely any act of insubordination. This led to complaints from the parents of the other boys, some of whom were of noble birth and resented the supposed little plebeian's insolence, and the matter ended by being brought before the king, who had Kyros and his playfellows summoned to his presence. Something in the demeanor of the boy, his free and haughty manner of answering questions and accusations, a certain family likeness, too, roused Astyages' suspicions, and the herdsman was easily frightened into confession. Astyages, who

had taken a liking to his grandson, was sincerely glad that he should turn up alive, and sent him home to Persia, to his father and mother, having first taken the advice of the Magi, who were of opinion that, the boy having been king in play, the dreams had been literally fulfilled, and there was no further danger. But not therefore was Harpagos forgiven for his breach of trust. Cruel and revengeful as he was, Astyages dissembled his anger under a great show of friendliness, and bade his kinsman send his son to the palace as attendant to the newly found prince, and to come to supper that evening himself. The meat placed before Harpagos was the flesh of his own child, whose hands and feet and head were presented to him in a basket after he had eaten. He made no sign, but from that moment secretly worked against the king, alienating from him the great Median nobles and preparing the general falling off in favor of Kyros, with whom he communicated as soon as the boy was old enough. From this point the narrative, as given above, is in the main correct, though not free from fanciful embellishments.

5. So Herodotus knows nothing of Kyros' royal parentage on the father's side. This at once suggests Median informants. It would be soothing to the vanity of the conquered people, even after they had long accepted the new ruler and lived prosperous under him and his descendants, to connect him with their own royal house, thus creating an hereditary claim for him on their own side, and taking the bitterest sting from conquest—submission to a stranger

and foreigner,—and at the same time looking down on *his* father as being "much inferior to a Mede of even middle condition!" But the inconsistencies which grow out of this perversion of facts are very glaring. This objection, for one, is unanswerable: if Kyros was Astyages' natural heir, as this story makes him out to be, why should the old king be incensed at the prospect of his accession to power, to the extent of seeking his life? Is it not unnatural to madness for him to cut off his own line, contrary to the instinct common to all mankind, let alone sovereigns, who are always so ambitious to found or continue dynasties, that they are much more likely to supply the want of heirs by adoption, or even fraud, than to destroy those given them by nature? As to the story of Kyros' exposure, providential escape, and obscure bringing up, it is an old, old bit of Aryan folk-lore,* which has been told various times of almost every national hero. Of course every nation that repeats it stamps it with some national peculiarity. In its application to Kyros, we detect the Eranian touch in the name of the woman, Spaka. The *real* story was that the child was saved and suckled by a dog, Ahura-Mazda's own sacred animal (see pp. 139-141), to intimate miraculous preservation, divine protection. Indeed Herodotus in one place tells us as much. But the Greeks, who had not the remotest comprehension of their own myths, let alone other people's, were

---

* Not confined to the Aryan race, however, but turning up also in the treasury of Semitic tradition. Compare the legends of the first Sargon of Agadê ("Story of Chaldea," pp. 205, 206), and of Moses.

shocked by the absurdity of the statement, and explained it away in the manner we have seen. *

6. There were several other versions of the story of Kyros' youth. They have been retailed by various Greek writers, without any attempt at criticism, and do not appear much more reliable than that selected by Herodotus, except only that the miraculous element is wanting.† They all agree in making him a resident at the Median court during his boyhood and early youth, and one makes him a Mardian (or Amardian), thus unconsciously coming near the truth as concerning his connection with Anshan (see p. 280), of which, however, not one of these compilers knows any thing, any more than of his supposed relationship to Astyages. One of these versions gives an exceedingly probable account of his proceedings after his victory. Astyages, this informant tells us, had one daughter, Amytis (not Mandanê), and she was married to a noble Mede of the name of Spitâma, who thus found himself heir to the throne. This dangerous claimant Kyros put to death when he had made himself master of Agbatana and the royal family, but spared his two sons and treated the princess with every respect, then took her to wife, thus transferring her claim to himself.

---

* This is the passage in "Herodotus": "So it happened that his parents, catching the name" (his nurse's), "and wishing to persuade the Persians that there was a special providence in his preservation, spread the report that Kyros, when he was exposed, was suckled by a bitch. This was the sole origin of the rumor." It was the reverse that was really the case.

† "I know three ways in which the story of Kyros is told, all differing from my own narrative."—Herodotus, I., 95.

As to the old king, he honored him as a father, and made him Satrap (governor) of Hyrcania. There is a tradition that the king of Armenia, TIGRANES I., a monarch with whom began a long and famous line, aided Kyros in his revolt, although his own sister had lately become second wife to Astyages. Armenian historians add that the perfidious old Mede had invited his new brother-in-law to visit him, with the intent of murdering him, but that Tigranes was warned in time by his sister. It is further reported that it was on this occasion Tigranes, who always remained Kyros' devoted friend and ally, adopted the Zoroastrian religion and introduced it into Armenia. This report must be taken for what it may be worth, as there is no evidence that could be called proof, to confirm it. It may have been owing to the Armenian alliance that Kyros within the next two years extended his rule westward as far as the Halys —*i. e.*, to the farthest boundary of the Median Empire on the western side. He does not seem to have encountered much resistance in this quarter, as Herodotus merely remarks: "The Cappadocians submitted to Kyros, after having been subject to the Medes." There is a tradition to the effect that the king of Cappadocia was married to a sister of Kambyses, the father of Kyros; but it may have been an invention, to give a plausible and creditable color to his submission.

7. We do not know how much time and labor Kyros expended on the countries of Eastern Erân that made up so important a portion of the Median inheritance which he claimed and systematically

gathered under his rule. It is probable that their reduction and the necessity of keeping them in a state of submission provided him with occupation for the rest of his life, and that at intervals between the acts of the great undertakings in the West, to which his ambition chiefly inclined him, he may have personally headed an expedition into the East and North-east. It would be as vain as unprofitable to try and follow the fortunes of all the obscure nations —Bactrians, Sogdians, Chorasmians, Hyrcanians, Saki (*i. e.*, Scythians, Aryan and Turanian,) etc., who are little more than names in the history of the world. In his treatment of them, as in all other respects, Kyros showed himself superior to all the conquerors the world had yet seen. He is said to have left it to the peoples he subdued to fix the figure and nature of the tribute they were able and willing to pay.

8. His just and mild rule soon reconciled the Medes to the change of masters, and he made special efforts to secure their devotion. He never forgot, indeed, that his first favor and duty was owing to his own people, the Persians, and made it understood at once that they were to be the first in the new empire, by exempting them from tribute and selecting his generals and Satraps (governors) from their number, besides having his choicest troops composed of Persians. His chief wife, his queen, was herself an Akhæmenian ; her name, as given by the Greeks, was KASSANDANÊ; she is frequently spoken of as a woman of great mental power and real influence. Kyros was deeply attached to her, and when

she died, caused "a great mourning" to be made for her throughout the empire. But the second place was ungrudgingly allotted to the Medes. After the first excitement of war and victory, they were never treated as a conquered nation, but as a brother-people. In war and in peace, in the army and the council, in attendance on the royal person, they always come next to the Persians; indeed we find Medians entrusted with important military commands scarcely ten years after the fall of the Median Empire. Unity of race and, to a great extent, of language and religion must have largely contributed to this result, which, however, might not have been as easily achieved under a monarch less temperate and judicious than Kyros proved himself throughout. If he really did marry the daughter of Astyages, the connection must have helped to smooth matters, though the Median princess never could claim precedence over the Persian one, the two queens faithfully representing in their relative position that of their respective countries. Still the fusion was so complete as to become invisible to the eyes of foreigners, who speak of "the Medes and Persians" jointly, as of one people, not infrequently using one name for the other.

9. It has been asked: What was the capital of the Persian Empire? and it is a question not easy to answer. In reality, there were several, according as the kings resided in the royal city of this or that of the countries which composed the empire. Kyros, indeed, true to his nation and ancestry, apparently conferred this dignity on his

40. GATE-PILLAR OF KYROS' PALACE AT PASARGADÆ, WITH INSCRIPTION: "I AM KURUSH, THE KING, THE AKHÆMENIAN."

own clan-city PASARGADÆ. He built a palace there, and a treasury, and his body rested there in death. A great sacredness attached to the place in consequence, and every Akhæmenian king went there for his inauguration. But it did not possess the conditions that go to make a thriving, populous centre, and became neglected as a residence. It is now represented by a knot of ruins, not very striking or numerous, in the valley of MURGHÂB, watered by the PULWAR, a scant and insignificant stream, formerly named after the great king himself, KYROS; it is uninteresting and short-lived, as most watercourses of this arid region, and after receiving a single tributary, ends in a salt lake. A few truncated columns, and many more bases without columns, a few gate-pillars, and a platform with a casing of very fine stone masonry, are all that remains of these constructions. Interesting as they are, they are eclipsed by two relics which appeal more powerfully to the fancy of the beholder: one is a square, isolated, and very massive stone pillar, bearing a bas-relief representing a human figure with four unfolded wings and a most peculiar head-dress (see ill. 41). That this strange figure is meant for Kyros is placed beyond doubt by the inscription which we read at some height above its head. But there is some reasonable doubt as to whether it was intended for the living king, or rather for an ideal representation of his glorified Fravashi after death. The other relic is the great king's tomb, or rather grave-chamber, which stands well preserved, but open and empty, on its base of seven retreating stages or high steps, all of solid

41. BAS-RELIEF REPRESENTING KYROS, OR POSSIBLY HIS GLORIFIED FRAVASHI, WITH TRILINGUAL INSCRIPTION ABOVE: "I AM KURUSH, THE KING, THE AKHÆMENIAN," (Pasargadæ.)

blocks of white marble, surrounded by fragments of what evidently was once a colonnade. The monument was found intact by Alexander of Macedon, who visited it. His historians describe it as "a house upon a pedestal," with a door so narrow (it is moreover only four feet high) that a man could scarcely squeeze through. The gilt sarcophagus, we are told,

42. TOMB OF KYROS AT PASARGADÆ.
(Entire height, 36 feet; height of chamber or chapel, 7 feet; area, 7 by 10½ feet; thickness of walls, 5 feet.)

stood by a couch with feet of massive gold, covered with purple-dyed draperies, and the walls were hung with Babylonian tapestries. Suits of clothes were also found, of costly material and workmanship. There was, besides, a table on which were deposited various precious relics—Persian weapons, some jewels, the king's own bow, shield, and sword. The inscription was brief and simple: "O man! I am Kurush, the son of Kambujiya, who founded the greatness of Persia, and ruled Asia. Grudge me not this monument." Inside the inclosure was a small house, occupied by some Magi, who received an ample daily allowance of provisions, and whose duty it was to guard the place and keep it in order. The office had been first instituted by Kambyses, the son of Kyros, and was hereditary. When Alexander returned to Pasargadæ from his unsuccessful expedition to India, he found the noble shrine desecrated and plundered, the sarcophagus gone, and could do nothing but give orders to repair the monument, and restore it, at least outwardly, to a decent and seemly condition.

10. The ruins of Pasargadæ are the most ancient monuments we have of Persian art, and the merest glance at them suffices to show that it was, from first to last, and in its very essence, imitative, with the single exception of the Aryan principle of building, consisting in the profuse use of columns. As the Persians, fortunately, used stone, their monuments have survived, while nothing is left of the Median constructions, which were of wood. These monuments show traces of the influence of every country they have known or conquered. Had we no other specimen of Persian sculpture than that bas-relief (ill. 41), we should be justified in declaring it to be imitated from Assyrian models; even the close-fitting fringed robe betrays the originals from which the Persian artist copied. As to the head-dress, it is one frequently seen on the brow of Egyptian divinities and royalties, while the massive pillar itself

is a clumsy imitation of an Assyrian stele. That the Tomb of Kyros (ill. 42) reproduces, on a small scale and in different material, the Assyro-Babylonian Ziggurat is too obvious to need demonstration, while the chapel is distinctly Greek in design, and what little remains of Kyros' own constructions, shows that he employed Greek artists from the colonies on the sea-shore: the column-bases are exactly like those found in the ruins of some Ionian temples, and the masonry of the great platform recalls early Greek wall-masonry (see ill. 29). We shall soon become acquainted with far more numerous, imposing, and elaborate monuments of Persian art, but shall find nothing, even in its most beautiful productions, to reverse the verdict of lack of originality which was pronounced on that art as soon as it was discovered.

11. But, to return to the political world of Western Asia, which we left unheeded for years to follow the rising star of Persia. With Kyros still on the eastern side of the Halys, the balance of power, established after the Battle of the Eclipse (see pp. 220-222), was as yet unbroken, no changes having taken place in the territorial conditions of the potentates who concluded that memorable agreement. The greatest of the three states in point of extent had merely changed hands and name: it was the Median Empire no longer, but the Persian, that was all. In 546 B.C. every thing was apparently undisturbed, yet every thing trembled in the balance. For the men were no longer the same. The petty, indolent, tyrannous Mede had been forced to yield

43. SUPPOSED TOMB OF KAMBYSES I. AT PASARGADÆ.
(Possibly an Âtesh-Gâh, or Fire-Chapel.)

his place to one who was a hero and a genius, while in Babylon the change was reversed: the great Nebuchadrezzar's sceptre had passed into feeble and incapable hands, discord and civil troubles filled the land he had ruled so wisely and strongly, and opened the way for the invasion against which he had accumulated so many defences. The fate of Babylon was so inevitable that her dreaded neighbor could leave her for the last while he attended to more pressing business. Lydia's turn was to come first.

12. Alyattes' long reign (fifty-eight years), ended, with his life, in or about 560 B.C. He was by far the wisest and greatest of the Mermnadæ,—indeed, so far as we know, of all the Lydian kings. By successive conquests and annexations, he left Lydia the most extensive and powerful state of Asia Minor, with a numerous and well-ordered army, especially formidable from its trained and splendidly mounted cavalry, and a treasury overflowing with wealth of every description. He well deserved the affection and reverence of his people, who erected to his memory, at public cost, the gigantic sepulchral mound or barrow, a full half mile in circumference, which is even now a conspicuous feature of the plain by the Hermos, near the ruins of Sardis.* Herodotus calls it "a structure of enormous size, only inferior to the monuments of Egypt and Babylon." He was succeeded by his son (some say grandson †), KROISOS,

---

* Excavations have repeatedly been made in the mound and have led to the discovery of the sepulchral chamber (eleven feet long by eight broad and seven high), all lined with polished white marble, but empty, cleaned out at an unknown time by unknown plunderers, for the sake of the many precious things it doubtless contained.

† See Dr. Victor Floigl's "Cyrus und Herodot.," pp. 132-138.

a brilliant and magnificent prince, of good parts, of an amiable and humane disposition, whose unheard-of prosperity and sudden fall have made him a favorite theme with Greek moralists. His greatest fault seems to have been an exceeding self-complacency and an inordinate pride in the immense wealth which have made his name a by-word for all times.

13. Kroisos was the first openly to resent the elevation of Kyros, who was to him nothing more than an usurper. His motive in so doing was a mixed one, as very well indicated by Herodotus: "He learnt that Kyros had destroyed the empire of Astyages, and that the Persians were becoming daily more powerful. This led him to consider with himself whether it were possible to check the growing power of that people. . . ." Furthermore, "he coveted the land of Cappadocia, which he wished to add to his own dominions"; and lastly he felt called upon to avenge the wrongs of his kinsman. He felt very sure of victory, still he did not undervalue the foe on whom he meditated an attack, and cast about him for allies. The most natural ones were Babylon, who was threatened by the same danger as himself, and Egypt, who owed Lydia a good turn for the aid received from Gyges at the time of her own war of independence,* although the dynasty whose establishment was helped by that assistance had lately been overthrown by a revolution. An upstart usurper, a mere army officer, of the name of AAHMES, supported by the soldiers whom he commanded, had dethroned Hophra (569 B.C.), and

* See "Story of Assyria," p. 380.

soon after put him to death. (The Greeks mispronounced his name AMASIS, which form is the generally accepted one.) Nor did Kroisos content himself with human means to insure his success. He sent to the most famous Greek oracles to inquire what would be the result if he crossed the Halys and attacked the Persians. The replies were encouraging, especially that of the Delphic oracle. In the joy of his heart, Kroisos overwhelmed Apollo's temple with his gifts—not unmindful, very probably, of the god's favorable reply to the suit of his forefather Gyges, but heedless of the ugly qualifying clause, and little thinking, at all events, that *he* was the fifth descendant appointed for the expiation of the ancestral crime (see p. 189). The oracles had added "a recommendation to look and see who were the most powerful of the Greeks, and to make alliance with them." This was patriotic advice, and the object of it—to bring Greece forward and open to her an influence in the affairs of the great political world of the day—an altogether praiseworthy one. The Spartans were, at the time, unquestionably the most powerful among the Greek nations, so Kroisos sent to them messengers "with gifts in their hands," who informed them of the god's bidding, and declared in the king's name: "Knowing that you hold the first rank in Greece, I desire to become your friend in all true faith and honesty." The Spartans, who were, moreover, grateful to Kroisos for some substantial favors formerly received of him, "were full of joy at the coming of the messengers, and at once took the oaths of friendship and alliance."

14. The enumeration of Kroisos' gifts to the Delphic Apollo is too astounding to be passed over. And as they existed in the temple treasuries and could be seen by visitors in the time of Herodotus, he cannot be taxed with exaggeration. This is the passage:

"Kroisos, having resolved to propitiate the Delphic god with a magnificent sacrifice, offered up three thousand of every kind of sacrificial beast, and besides made a huge pile and placed upon it couches coated with silver and with gold, and golden goblets and robes and vests of purple; all of which he burnt in the hope of thereby making himself more secure of the favor of the god. Further he issued his orders to all the people of the land to offer a sacrifice according to their means. When the sacrifice was ended, the king melted down a vast quantity of gold * and ran it into ingots, making them six palms long, three palms broad, and one palm in thickness. The number of ingots was one hundred and seventeen, four being of refined gold, the others of pale gold [probably *electron*, see p. 216]. . . . He also caused a statue of a lion [the royal emblem of Lydia, see ill. 33], to be made in refined gold, the weight of which was ten talents. . . . On the completion of these works, Kroisos sent them away to Delphi, and with them two bowls [*craters*], of an enormous size, one of gold, the other of silver, which used to stand, the latter upon the right, the former upon the left as one entered the temple. . . . The silver one holds six hundred *amphorae* [over 5000 gallons]. . . . He sent also four silver casks . . . and two lustral vases [for holy water]. . . . Besides these various offerings, Kroisos sent to Delphi many others of less account, among the rest a number of round silver vases. Also he dedicated a female figure in gold, three cubits high, . . . and further he presented the necklace and the girdles of his wife."

15. There was nothing now to delay Kroisos in the execution of his cleverly laid plans. If we are to

* This gold must be understood to have been melted down in the flames of the sacrificial pyre, by way of consecration. On the custom of burning large quantities of precious things in sacrifice, see "Story of Assyria," p. 122.

believe Herodotus, warning voices were heard amidst his own councillors, bidding him consider that the Persians were poor, and if he conquered them he would reap no advantages from his victory, while his own stake was so tremendous that if he lost, nothing would be left him to live for, so that, far from attacking the Persians, he should be thankful to the gods, that they had not put it into the heads of the Persians to invade Lydia. That, however, is just what the Persians would inevitably have done, had not Kroisos been beforehand with them, and he would have earned great praise had he been successful. He had every reason to hope, being well provided with treasure, men, arms, and allies, and leaving no secret enemies or doubtful friends in his rear. For at the very last moment, Kyros had sent heralds to the Ionian cities, with an invitation to revolt from the Lydian king, and they had refused to do so. But as men's judgments go by the event, the blame of the disaster which befel Lydia was laid entirely on Kroisos, whom historians have found fault with, among other things, for over-hastiness in leading his troops across the Halys; yet it has always been considered good tactics, once hostilities are opened, to carry the war into the enemy's territory, and Kyros was on the march.

16. The first battle was fought in Cappadocia. "The combat," Herodotus reports, " was hot and bloody . . . nor had victory declared in favor of either party, when night came down upon the battle-field. Thus both armies fought valiantly." This result, though far from unfavorable, seems to

have dashed the exuberant spirits of the Lydian, whose chief mistake was overweening confidence, and to have thrown him into a confusion and vacillation of which his adversary was too great a general not to take advantage. The tardiness of the allies did the rest, and Kroisos, owing to the precision and rapidity of the Persian's movements, was actually left alone to fight out a war for which he had thought he could not provide enough assistants. The end came very quickly; an outline of the event can best be gathered (in short passages) from Herodotus' leisurely narrative :

"Kroisos laid the blame of his ill success on the number of his troops, which fell very short of the enemy; and as on the next day Kyros did not repeat the attack, he set off on his return to Sardis, intending to collect his allies and renew the contest in the spring. He meant to call on the Egyptians to send him aid . . . he intended also to summon to his assistance the Babylonians . . . and further he meant to send word to Sparta. . . . Having got together these forces in addition to his own, he would, as soon as the winter was past and springtime come, march once more against the Persians. With these intentions Kroisos, immediately on his return, despatched heralds to his various allies, with a request that they would join him at Sardis in the course of the fifth month from the time of the departure of his messengers. He then disbanded the army, consisting of mercenary troops . . . never imagining that Kyros, after a battle in which victory had been so evenly balanced, would venture to march upon Sardis. . . .

"Kyros, however, when Kroisos broke up so suddenly from his quarters after the battle, conceiving that he had marched away with the intention of disbanding his army, considered a little, and soon saw that it was advisable for him to advance upon Sardis in all haste, before the Lydians could get their forces together a second time. Having thus determined, he lost no time in carrying out his plan. He marched forward with such speed, that he was himself the first to announce his coming to the Lydian king. That monarch, placed in the utmost difficulty by the turn of events which had gone so entirely against all his calculations, nevertheless led out the Lydians to battle. In all Asia there was not at that time a braver or more warlike people. Their manner of fighting was on horseback; they carried long lances, and were clever in the management of their steeds.

"The two armies met in the plain before Sardis. It is a vast flat bare of trees, watered by a number of streams, which all flow into one larger than the rest, called the Hermos. ... The combat was long, but at last, after a great slaughter on both sides, the Lydians turned and fled. They were driven within their walls, and the Persians laid siege to Sardis.*

"Thus the siege began. Meanwhile, Kroisos, thinking that the place would hold out no inconsiderable time, sent off fresh heralds to his allies from the beleaguered city ... to say that he was already besieged, and to beseech them to come to his aid with all possible speed. Among his other allies Kroisos did not omit to send to Lacedæmon.† It chanced that the Spartans were themselves just at this time engaged in a quarrel ... when the herald arrived from Sardis to entreat them to come to the assistance of the besieged king; yet notwithstanding they instantly set to work to afford him help. They had completed their preparations, and the ships were just ready to start, when a second message informed them that the place had already fallen, and that Kroisos was a prisoner. Deeply grieved at his misfortune, the Spartans ceased their efforts."

17. Thus the dynasty of the Mermnadæ was overthrown, and Lydia ceased to be a kingdom—all at one blow. The fall was as rapid and irretrievable as that of Assyria, but aroused very different feelings in the lookers on. Neither Lydia as a country

* This is the battle which Kyros is said to have won by the cunning device of placing the camels in front of his troops, in order to rout the Lydian cavalry—seeing that horses have a natural detestation of the sight and especially the smell of camels, which is overcome only by habit and training.

† Lacedæmon—another name for Sparta.

nor her rulers personally were regarded with hatred. The Mermnadae had been mild masters and generous friends, open to all the influences of a refined and genial culture, delighting in intercourse with wise and accomplished foreigners. The catastrophe which cut them off with a suddenness comparable only to descending lightning, and strongly suggestive of divine judgment, was witnessed by neighbors and subjects with silent awe and feelings made up in about equal parts of sympathy with the sufferers and apprehension for themselves,—an awe which was heightened by the grand closing scene of the tragedy, which the Greeks utterly misunderstood, and consequently misrepresented in their reports.

18. This is how Herodotus, Diodorus, and others relate it, with but slight variations. Kyros, they say, determined to make an example of his prisoner, and ordered Kroisos to be burned alive with fourteen young Lydians. One author even describes the procession: how the women preceded and followed the king and the fourteen boys, as they were led along in chains, with loud lamentation and tearing of clothes; how the richest ladies of Sardis sent their slaves with gifts of costly robes and ornaments of every kind, to be laid on the pyre and burned with the victims. The wood had actually been set on fire, when Kyros relented, moved by some words uttered by Kroisos, and ordered the flames to be put out. But they had gained too much ground already, and all efforts to quench them were unavailing. Then Kroisos offered up a prayer to Apollo, who sent a violent shower, which extinguished the

fire. And thus was Kroisos saved, and lived henceforth, more friend than prisoner, at the Persian court. Now this account bristles with incongruities and contradictions. In the first place such a proceeding is utterly inconsistent with the Persian hero's humane and magnanimous temper, and, besides, we had just before been told that he had given order, before the city was taken, to spare the king in battle. As for the torture and slaughter of fourteen innocent boys, it is a cruelty which he cannot for a moment have contemplated. Then, again, as a Zoroastrian, Kyros could not possibly commit such an outrage on the most sacred element of fire, even admitting that the Zoroastrian religion, as professed by the Persians, was free from the exaggerated fire-worship introduced by Median Magism. But if a fallen foe, a great king, *elected* to die rather than bear the ignominy of defeat and bondage, and chose to do so in a sacrificial ceremony sanctioned by the sacred traditions of his country, it was not the victor's place to prevent him; his very respect would forbid interference, while his presence at the solemn act would be meant as a mark of courtesy and admiration. This then is the now generally accepted explanation of a statement which has long puzzled and, one may almost say, scandalized every student of ancient history. Such royal sacrifices—in the king's own person or that of his first-born son—were familiar to Oriental religions and of not infrequent occurrence; still less unusual was the sacrifice of youths or children as expiatory offerings. Every thing points to this explanation as the only correct

one—even the account of the quantity of precious
things laid on the pyre.* If Kroisos prayed aloud,
he certainly prayed that the sun-god might accept the self-offered victim and show mercy to
his people. When a heavy shower interrupted
the self-immolation in the very act of consumma-
tion, it was most natural to interpret it as a sign
that the god rejected the sacrifice. Nor is it unreasonable to believe that the humane and sensible
Kyros took occasion from it to urge his deeply
bowed captive to give up his desperate intent,
assuring him of treatment befitting a noble foe and
a king, or that Kroisos, finding out what manner of
man this was that had conquered him, yielded his
will to him and consented to live, henceforth his
captive no longer, but his friend.† Kyros, who did
not do generous things by halves, gave him a city in
the neighborhood of Agbatana, the income from
which was to provide for his wants, and became so
much attached to the gentle and wise quondam king,
that he seldom dispensed with his company even in
his most distant expeditions, always asked and often
followed his advice, and before his death is said
to have commended his son Kambyses to his kind
and watchful care, knowing how much the rash and
headstrong youth needed a counsellor and modera-
tor. The grandson of Kroisos, an infant at the time
of the disaster, lived to a great old age, and is men-

* See above, p. 309, the account of Kroisos' great sacrifice in
honor of the Delphic Apollo, and " Story of Assyria," pp. 120-139.
† See Duncker, vol. IV., pp. 330-332; also Ed. Meyer, " Geschichte des Alterthums," vol. I., p. 604.

tioned as an aged grandee under one of the late Akhæmenians.

19. Kyros was planning great things; not only was his presence required in the far East, where the Bactrians and some nomadic tribes were showing themselves unmanageable, but he contemplated a personal expedition against Babylon, and even an Egyptian campaign—for the Pharaoh's interference in the favor of Lydia was not to be forgotten or condoned even though it had been only an intention to which circumstances denied fulfilment. Kyros was therefore impatient to depart from Sardis, and left the subjugation of the Greek cities of the sea-shore to one of his generals, his old friend Harpagos, that being a necessary sequence of the conquest of Lydia. But before he left, he was confronted by some Lacedæmonian envoys, who addressed him with great boldness, forbidding him, in the name of their people, to molest any Greek city in any way, since they would not suffer it. Great must have been the astonishment of the mighty conqueror at this, to him, inconceivable presumption, when the envoy's words were conveyed to him by the interpreter. It must have been in simple amazement that he asked some Greek bystanders who these Lacedæmonians were, and what was their number, that they dared to send him such a notice? "If I live," he is then said to have replied, "the Spartans shall have troubles enough of their own to talk of, without concerning themselves about the Ionians." Such was the first tiny cloud of the great thunderstorm that was to burst over Hellas fifty years later. The Greek cities, meanwhile, submitted with-

out very much resistance. Within three years they
were successively brought under the yoke, with the
exception of Miletus, who made special terms and
retained her independence. Kyros did not make
any exorbitant demands on his new subjects' purse
or allegiance. But he placed each city under a chief,
chosen among its own nobles, whom he made responsible for her conduct and the payment of the
tribute; in fact, a tyrant, who governed with almost
royal authority, but was himself under the constant
supervision and authority of the Persian Satrap,[*] residing at Sardis. Whatever it became under later
kings, the Persian rule under the first Akhæmenians
was moderate and mindful of the various peoples'
welfare. Lycia and Cilicia, after some demurring,
followed suit. Nor had Kyros during his lifetime to
contend with rebellion in this part of his dominions,
though he never visited it again, with the exception
of a single rising in Sardis, immediately after his
departure; a rising which was easily quelled, and,
being treated with wise leniency, was not repeated.
Indeed, so thoroughly did the Lydians become
reconciled to the new order of things, that they
gave themselves up entirely to the arts and industries of peace, which formerly had shared their attention with the manlier games of ambition and
war, and soon became notoriously the most luxurious,
pleasure-loving, and effeminate of Asiatic nations.
Their influence in this direction on their conquerors
was very great, and by no means wholesome.

[*] *Satrap*, old Persian *Khshatrapá*, "defender of the empire" or
"of royalty."

20. The turn of Babylon was coming at last. Indeed a first and unsuccessful attempt (probably because premature and ill-managed), was made in this same year 546 B.C., or the next, from Elam. Here arises the question: *when* was the whole of Elam conquered and annexed by the Persian king? It must have been no long or difficult task, and, in the absence of all information on the subject, it is suggested, with great probability, that it may have been accomplished immediately after the overthrow of Lydia and before the first attack on Babylon. For Herodotus tells us that Kyros returned to Agbatana with the bulk of his army straight from Sardis, and the nearest way to Accad lay undoubtedly through Elam. In whatever manner he may have occupied the capital, Shushan (henceforth better known as Susa), he was delighted with its situation, and turned it into a thoroughly Persian city and his own favorite royal residence, in preference to his own city of Pasargadae, which, from its insignificance, remoteness, isolation, and unfavorable geographical conditions, was little fit to be the capital of a great empire, embracing a vast variety of countries and nations, while Susa, contrasting favorably with the clan-city of the Akhæmenians in every one of these particulars, seemed made for the purpose. Henceforth Susa may be considered as the principal capital of the Persian Empire, and its river, the CHOASPES, a branch of the Eulæus (Ulaï), had the honor of supplying the kings with the only drinking-water they would use. Kyros first instituted this custom, which was religiously kept up by his successors.

"Wherever the great king travels," Herodotus reports, "he is attended by a number of four-wheeled cars drawn by mules, in which the Choaspes water, ready boiled for use, and stored in flagons of silver, is moved with him from place to place." * Later Akhæmenian kings built there palaces, the gorgeousness of which is brought home to us by the numerous and magnificently preserved specimens and fragments discovered by Mr. Dieulafoy, within the last three years.† There, like the Assyrian kings in Nineveh, they stored most of the wealth furnished them by tribute and conquests, and such was the accumulation in the treasure-house of Susa, that Alexander of Macedon, when he took possession of it (331 B.C.), found in it, besides immense sums of money, 50,000 talents of silver in ore and ingots (equal in value to about 38 millions of dollars); also 5,000 quintals of finest purple dye,—a quintal being equal to about one hundred pounds, and the value estimated at 125 dollars per pound.

21. The affairs of Babylon between the death of Nebuchadrezzar (561 B.C.) and the first Persian invasion (546 B.C.) can be disposed of in a very few lines. His son AVIL-MARDUK (the EVIL-MERODACH of the Bible,) is said to have governed in a reckless and headstrong manner. Some Egibi-tablets are dated from his short reign, and the only other mention of him we find is the grateful report

---

* It is amusing to find so early an instance of this hygienic precaution—the boiling of water,—which we are wont to consider as so very modern.

† See Appendix to this chapter.

of the Bible historian of the favor he showed to the king of Judah, Jeconiah, whom, after a captivity of thirty-six years, he "took out of prison":

"And he spake kindly to him and set his throne above the thrones of the kings that were with him in Babylon. And he changed his prison garments, and did eat bread before him continually all the days of his life. And there was an allowance given him of the king, every day a portion, all the days of his life." (Second Kings, XXV., 27-30.)

Avil-Marduk was assassinated, after a reign of only two years (559 B.C.), by his brother-in-law, NERGAL-SHAR-UZZUR, known through the Greeks as NERI-GLISSAR, who succeeded him and reigned four years, peacefully enough it would seem, completing some works left unfinished by Nebuchadrezzar, such as the walls along the Euphrates, and repairing temples. His son, LABASHI-MARDUK,* was but a boy, but is said to have shown a thoroughly perverse disposition, and perished, after only nine months, in a palace conspiracy. His assassins placed on the throne a certain NABU-NÂHID, better known as NABONIDUS (555 B.C.) He was the son of the Rab-mag (probably high-priest, or chief of the priesthood), of Babylon, and it is uncertain whether he was connected with the royal family. But his mother was Nitokris, that same queen to whom Herodotus erroneously attributes so many of Nebuchadrezzar's works. (See p. 240.) From a mention of this princess in one of Kyros' cylinders, we are justified to assume that she was a woman of remarkable parts, and wielded an unusual power and influence in

* The name is mutilated by the Greek writers in all sorts of ways: Labassoarakhos, Laborasoarchod, etc.

state affairs. It is surmised by some scholars that she may have been a daughter of Nebuchadrezzar, which would indeed account both for her character and the position she held, as also for the fact that her son reigned for so many years unopposed and unmolested. As it is highly probable that there still were some public works to finish, and that the queen-mother may have taken an active interest in them, we may find in this circumstance the most natural explanation of Herodotus' mistake.

22. There can be little doubt that Nabonidus owed his elevation in a great measure to the priesthood, to which he, by birth, belonged. His zeal in building and especially repairing temples surpasses that of his most pious predecessors, and seems to have been accompanied by a sort of antiquarian taste, which prompted him to search for the cylinders of the original founders, so as to establish the age of each sanctuary. To this remarkable peculiarity we owe some of our most precious discoveries, and in fact a new departure in the chronology of Ancient Chaldea.* Unfortunately for himself, however, Nabonidus appears to have devoted most of his care and to have shown a marked preference to the older temples of the land, whereupon the priesthood of the capital itself, the guardians of the more special patrons of later Babylon, Bel-Marduk and Nebo, took offence on behalf of these deities and considered their own dignity slighted and their interests neglected by one who, in their opinion, should have

* See the discovery of Nabonidus' cylinders at Sippar and Larsam, "Story of Chaldea," pp. 213, 218, 219.

been their devoted champion. If this feeling was openly expressed, it is clear that Nabonidus took no pains to conciliate this dangerous class. In the great cylinder which contains the annals of his reign, we are struck with the sullenly spiteful persistence with which the priestly scribe repeats, at each new year: "Nebo came not to Babel, Bel came not forth . . ." *i. e.* the customary processions were omitted. Kyros was a great hero and statesman, still it is more than doubtful whether he would have had quite such easy work with Babylon had not treachery done most of it for him. It was probably in reliance on his secret intelligences in the capital that he hurried his first attempt, of which the great cylinder gives an account : " In the ninth year (546 B.C.), Nabu-nâhid the king was in Tevâ*; the king's son, officers, and army were in Accad." The king's eldest son BEL-SHAR-UZZUR (the BELSHAZZAR of the Bible) is here meant, whom his father had associated with himself in the government, much in the same way that Esarhaddon shared the royal power with his son Asshurbanipal. We have a small cylinder, found in the temple of the Moon-god at Ur (Mugheir), with a very fervent prayer addressed to that god on behalf of himself and his son by Nabonidus: " As for me, Nabu-nâhid, king of Babel, in the fulness of thy great divinity, grant me length of life, to remote days, and for Belshazzar, my first-born son, the desire of my heart. Reverence for thy

---

* Tevâ is thought to be a separate quarter of Babylon,—perhaps the new quarter built by Nebuchadrezzar, on the west bank of the Euphrates.

great divinity establish thou in his heart; may he not be given to sin!"* To his mother and to this son the king seems to have mainly left the care and burden of state affairs, for it is expressly said that "in the month of Nisan (March, the first month of the year), the king to Babel came not," while on the fifth day of the same month the queen-mother died "who resided in the fortified camp on the Euphrates, beyond Sippar. The king's son and his soldiers mourned for her three days, and there was weeping. In the month of Sivan (May-June), there was mourning in the land of Accad for the king's mother." The death of so important a person, who almost seems to have shared in the command of the army of defence, encamped on the northern frontier of the army, must have produced dismay and perhaps confusion, and it is not impossible that Kyros may have hastened his expedition in order to take advantage of this, to him, opportune moment. "In the month of Nisan," the chronicle continues, "Kurash, king of Parsu, collected his army and crossed the Tigris below Arbela." The following lines are too much injured to make much sense, but something must have delayed the Persian king (perhaps the occupation of Elam?), since it is only in the third month of the

---

* The author of the Book of Daniel (V., 2), makes of Belshazzar the son of Nebuchadrezzar. Should his grandmother, Queen Nitokris, really turn out to be a daughter of that king, there would be nothing amiss with the designation, which, in Oriental speech, often was and is u ed in a wide sense, for " descendant." "King" he certainly could be called, from the position he held by his father's will. Indeed, one lately published inscription shows that he had a **separate royal establishment.**

following year (Sivan of the tenth year of Nabonidus), that, " Kurash came into Accad from the land of the Elamites." Then we read "The Prefect of Erech," . . . and here the line breaks off. It is evident that Kyros met with a repulse before Erech, one of the most important cities of the empire. At all events there is no further mention of the Persians until the seventeenth year of Nabonidus, 538 B.C.

23. We have no certain information as to the manner in which Kyros spent the seven or eight years between this premature attempt and his second, successful, Babylonian campaign. He had work enough, no doubt, to fill the time—what with expeditions into the far east, building at Pasargadæ, and fortifying and improving his home-rule. As to Nabonidus, we are quite as much at fault, the cylinder which is our most trusty guide being illegible from his eleventh year to his seventeenth, *i. e.* his last. One thing is clear: he had not found, perhaps not sought, the way to reconciliation with the haughty and covetous priesthood of Babylon. On the contrary, he had done much to alienate them still more. He did, indeed, show himself in Babylon at last, and gave orders for the procession to take place: Nebo came from Borsip, and Bel "went forth." There was also a sacrifice "for peace." But at the same time he mortally offended the priests by sending for the gods of other cities and placing them in the sanctuaries of the great Babylonian patrons: "the gods of Accad, those above the atmosphere and those below the atmosphere, descended

to Babel," with the exception of those of Borsip, Kutha, and Sippar. That this sealed the king's doom, we can see from the tone assumed by the priestly scribes in the "Proclamation Cylinder" which they indited for Kyros after the fall of Nabonidus: "At this desecration," they exclaim with pious horror, "the Lord of Gods was exceedingly wroth, and all the gods inhabiting Babylon deserted their shrines." They were no longer seen at festivals and processions, for they had migrated to other congregations who had reserved places for them. In other words, the priests removed (probably under impressively mournful ceremonies and in the most public manner), the statues and images of the offended gods. The effect fully answered their purpose: "Then the people of Shumir and Accad, who had been left in darkness, prayed to Marduk to return. He granted their prayer, returned, and rejoiced the land." But not unconditionally. The god, while he restored to favor his unoffending worshippers, could not tolerate the presence of an impious ruler: "And he [Marduk] selected a king to conduct after his heart what he committed to his hands. He proclaimed the name of Kurash, king of the city of Anshan, to be king over the whole country, and to all people he declared his title. . . . To his own city of Babel he summoned him to march, and he caused him to take the road to Tintir; like a friend and benefactor he conducted his army." It is impossible to state more plainly, that the priesthood of Babylon plotted against their king, betrayed him, and called in the enemy.

24. There was, however, still another influence at work, which, for being secret, and, so to speak, underground, should not be overlooked or underrated: it was the influence of the exiled Jews. In the forty-eight years of their captivity (from 586 to 538), they had, under the guidance of their prophets, become in many ways another and a nobler people: more united, more self-contained, more firmly grounded in the pure and absolute monotheism of their religion, as formed and developed by the efforts of the great prophets. With their wealth, their strength as a compact body of many thousands inspired by one spirit, one hope, directed by one influence, with the eminent position even at court which some of their nobles seem to have attained (see the Book of Daniel), they were a power and a danger to the state. The rise of Persia must have been to them as the rising of the star of deliverance, and there can be no doubt that they either took part in the plots against Nabonidus or plotted against him on their own account, and, independently of the Babylonian priesthood, entered into negotiations with Kyros and promised him assistance and support. No other inference can be drawn from the remarkable likeness which the Hebrew documents of the time bear to the Babylonian ones. Passages like this: "Yahveh stirred up the spirit of Koresh king of Persia, that he made a proclamation . . . saying, All the kingdoms of the earth hath the Lord, the God of Heaven, given me" (Second Chronicles, XXXVI. 22, 23); and this other: "Yahveh saith of Koresh, He is my shepherd and shall perform all my

pleasure" (Isaiah XLVI. 28*), show more than an accidental coincidence in thought and wording with the line already quoted from the " Proclamation Cylinder," of Kyros: "And he [Marduk] selected a king to conduct after his heart what he committed to his hands. He proclaimed the name of Kurash, king of the city of Anshan, to be king over the whole country, and to all people he declared his title." The sequel of the two documents presents the same exact parallelism, as follows :

"Thus saith Yahveh to his anointed, to Koresh, whose right hand I have holden, to subdue nations before him . . . to open doors before him. . . . I will go before thee and make the rugged places plain. I will break in pieces the doors of brass and cut in sunder the bars of iron, and I will give thee the hidden riches of secret place . . ." (Isaiah XLV., 1-3.	" The country of Guti and all its forces he caused to bow before his feet, as well as the whole nation of blackheads (Chaldeans) whom he brought into his hand. . . . Marduk the great Lord, . . . directed his heart and hand. . . . To his own city of Babylon he summoned him to march and he caused him to take the road to Tintir ; like a friend and benefactor he conducted his enemy." (Proclamation Cylinder of Kyros.)

25. The advance of the invading forces took place from several sides. The Proclamation Cylinder speaks of them as " far-extending, of which, like the waters of the river, the numbers could not be told." The beginning seems to have been made by a rising in the lowlands by the Gulf, and Kyros himself appeared south of Babylon

Fall of Babylon, 538 B. C.

* The latter part of the Book of Isaiah, from chapter XL., is not by Isaiah, the grand old prophet and minister of Hezekiah, but by a later writer, of the time of the Captivity, whom Bible scholars have agreed to designate as " the second Isaiah."

in the month of Dumuzi (June-July), where he probably encountered a loyal army, as a battle is mentioned. At the same time his general, the Mede GOBRYAS, was conducting operations in the north. After crossing the Tigris below Nebuchadrezzar's bulwark, the so-called Median Wall, he advanced straightway against Sippar, as it was essential to gain possession of the great reservoir and the four canals. From this point the Annals-Cylinder is admirably preserved, and tells the story completely:

"The men of Accad broke out into a revolt. The soldiers took Sippar on the 14th day without fighting. Nabu-nâhid fled. On the 16th day Ugbaru [Gobryas], the governor of Gutium [the Zagros highlands, Kurdistân], and the army of Kurash, descended to Babel without fighting. Then he got Nabu-nâhid, who had been bound, into his power.* At the end of the month of Dumuzi the rebels of Guti closed the doors of the temple of Marduk, but there was nothing there for their defence, nor in the other temples; there were no weapons. In the month Arâh-Shamna " [October-November, nearly four months after the occupation], "on the third day, Kurash descended to Babel. The streets were black before him. He promised peace to the city and all within it. Ugbaru he confirmed as his viceroy, appointed governors, and from the month Kislev to the month Adar [November-March] he sent back to their shrines the gods of Accad whom Nabu-nâhid had brought down to Babel. In the dark month Arâh-Shamna, on the 11th day, . . . the king died. . . ."

From this matchless monument, whose authority is absolutely unimpeachable, supported as it is by that of the companion cylinder, we learn the capture of Babylon as it really took place, and that is a story entirely different from any given in the various

* The other cylinder, with a touch of genuine priestly spite, says: "Nabu-nâhid, the king who did not worship him, he [Marduk] delivered into the hands of Kurash."

sources to which we were compelled to trust until these late discoveries. No war, no siege, no defence, no emptying of the Euphrates into the great reservoir, no nocturnal surprise; but treason, revolt, voluntary surrender, peaceful occupation, and a triumphal entry. The one battle mentioned may be that to which Herodotus alludes (Book I., 190), but not one other point of his narrative is correct. Nabonidus was evidently delivered into the hands of Gobryas by his own treacherous subjects, probably the priests. His death on the eighth day after the arrival of Kyros has an ugly look; yet, from our knowledge of that monarch's character, suspicion of foul play scarcely can attach to him. At all events, this testimony disposes of another story, according to which the king surrendered himself into Kyros' hands, who treated him kindly and gave him a province near Persia, whither he retired, and where he peacefully spent the rest of his life. The somewhat obscure passage about the "rebels of Guti" seems to refer to a stand attempted by a faithful body of highlanders in one of the temple quarters. It is not improbable that they may have been commanded by the king's son, Belshazzar, of whom we find no mention, and that he may have perished in the desperate venture. This might account for the story in the Book of Daniel, as describing a part of the event. As for the feast, it was the season of the famous festival held in honor of the god Dumuzi, or Thammuz, in the course of his own month,* and it is not at all un-

* See "Story of Chaldea," pp. 324-326.

likely that it should have been celebrated, as a matter of religion, even at the last extremity.

26. Kyros could not linger in any one part of his empire, which was now the most extensive the world had ever seen. Yet he spent several months at Babylon, ordering, conciliating, rewarding, and doing all that the most enlightened statesmanship could dictate to establish his rule, not on the fears, but the gratitude and security of his new subjects. There is nothing that wins a people so rapidly and surely as respect shown to its religion. Kyros, therefore, did not scruple to sacrifice in the temples and to the gods of the ancient imperial city, calling himself, as well as his son KAMBUJIYA (Kambyses), the "worshipper of Marduk the great Lord," and "daily to pray to Marduk and Nebo," on behalf of himself and his son, for length of days and success. As for more solid tokens of gratitude and favor, we find no record of such, but it is easy to imagine that, in the flush of his easy victory, the conqueror could not be any thing but generous to those who had smoothed the way for him. We can infer as much from the royal magnificence with which he rewarded the Jews for their assistance. He delivered them from their bondage, bade them return to their own country and there rebuild Jerusalem and the Temple, for which purpose he gave them a grant of timber in the Lebanon, and restored to them all the sacred gold and silver vessels which Nebuchadrezzar had carried away and distributed among the temples of Babylon. He made a public proclamation to the effect that such was his pleasure, enjoining on all men to help

and further their undertaking by gifts and active assistance. In the preamble to this proclamation he speaks like a follower of Yahveh, saying that "the God of Heaven has charged him to build him a house in Jerusalem, which is in Judah," exactly as he calls himself a worshipper of Marduk, and states that "Marduk the great Lord" ordered him to repair his shrine. It does not follow that he ever professed either the Babylonian or Jewish religion, or was any thing but a Mazdayasnian himself. But the political principle on which he consistently acted was to gain his subjects' confidence and affections, and, to this end, it was absolutely necessary that he should outwardly conform to their modes of religious speech and worship when he was among them.

27. Early in the spring of the following year (537 B.C.),—at least we seem to gather as much from the mutilated end of the "Annals," Kyros departed from Babylon, leaving there his eldest son Kambyses as his viceroy. We have no information as to how exactly he occupied the next eight years. Some part of the time he must have spent at home, and we know that he deposited in his new palace at Pasargadæ most of the untold wealth which the treasuries of Sardis, Agbatana, and Babylon had yielded him. Ancient historians are not unanimous on the manner of his death, which took place in 329 B.C. It seems probable that he perished in an expedition against the MASSAGETÆ, a distant and very barbarous nomadic tribe, whose range lay in the far northeast beyond the Sea of Aral. That is the version which Herodotus gives, but, as usual, so obscured with

fables and incongruities that the narrative will not bear close inspection. No amount of fact or details, however, did we possess them, could materially add to the respect and admiration with which this most majestic and gracious figure inspired both the contemporary world and remote posterity. It is not only that he was, in the highest sense, a good king, but that he was *the first* good king we know of. He is, moreover, the first historically approved great and good man of our own race, the Aryan or Indo-European. The grandeur of his character is well rendered in that brief and unassuming inscription of his, more eloquent and proud in its lofty simplicity than all the Assyrian self-extolling, bragging annals: " I AM KURUSH THE KING, THE AKHEMENIAN."

NOTE. The unexpected discovery of the Anshan royalty, as was natural, produced a great commotion and led to some hasty and immature conclusions, which, on closer investigation, have proved unnecessary. Thus Kyros was turned into an Elamite of Turanian or Cossæan (Kasshite) stock, a polytheist and idolater too. And it was contended that his very name, with its ending in *ush* or *ash*, was unaryan, nay distinctively Cossæan. The same was asserted of the monumental name of his son, KAMBUJIYA. Yet, now that his Aryan Akhæmenian genealogy is established beyond dispute, sound policy and a wise tolerance account for his concessions to the religious feelings of conquered nations ; and as to the two names, there are not many of more undoubted and ancient Aryan origin ; they both occur in the oldest Hindu epic literature. The " KURUS " were Aryan people in Northern India, also a famous heroic race of kings ; and there was another Aryan people in the northwest corner of India, that was known under the name of " KAMBOJA." The name has survived even yet in that of a country bordering on Siam. (See principally de Harlez, "Muséon," I., 4 ; Spiegel, " Die Altpersischen Keilinschriften," 2d ed., p. 86 ; and H. Zimmer, " Alt-indisches Leben, pp. 102 ff.)

THE LATE DISCOVERIES AT SUSA.

OF all historical diggings in Western Asia, those of Susa had, next to Hamadán (Agbatana), yielded the fewest and poorest results up to 1885. Neither Mr. Loftus nor other explorers, although they knew well enough where the palaces of the Akhæmenian kings were situated, had succeeded in bringing to light any important relic, owing to the obdurate stupidity and malevolent fanaticism of the Mussulman authorities at DIZFÚL, a city built near the site of the ancient capital of Elam. Early in March, 1885, a French expedition, conducted by Mr. E. DIEULAFOY and his learned and courageous wife, arrived at the ruins, determined to attempt the impossible rather than go home disappointed; and, though they had to contend at first with the same difficulties, they were successful in the end. They were rewarded by a series of "finds" of exceptional value, which are, at this moment, being ordered and placed in the Louvre Museum, where they will form a worthy counterpart to the Sarzec collection.*

The place was easy to identify by various unmistakable landmarks. "The city of Susa," writes Mr.

* See "Story of Chaldea," p. 92.

Dieulafoy, "was cut in two by a wide river, known at present under the name of AB-KARKHA (ancient Choaspes). On the right bank were the populous quarters; on the left—temples, or at least a Ziggurat, the royal city, the citadel, and the palace, the ruins of which, entombed in an immense earth-mound, rise in the midst of the other, lesser mounds, like a steep islet from the sea; along the Karkha a few trees are growing, the last descendants of the sacred groves that were desecrated by Asshurbanipal's generals."* It is known that Dareios, son of Hystaspes (the second successor of Kyros), had Susa rebuilt and ornamented, and it was his palace for which search was made first. But it was found that this palace had been destroyed by fire, and that on top of its remains had been erected another and more sumptuous one, by his grandson, Artaxerxes, as proved by a long cuneiform inscription, containing that king's name and parentage, which ran along a magnificent frieze of painted and glazed tiles, representing striding lions (see ill. 44), and which formed the decoration of the pillared porticos. Of course the frieze was not found in its place or entire, but had to be patiently pieced together of fragments. These, however, turned up in such quantities as to allow the restoration of the frieze in a state very near completeness. A procession was thus obtained of nine of these superb animals, a work of art which was pronounced in no way inferior to the Babylonian models from which it is imitated.

In the same manner, out of fragments carefully

* See "Story of Assyria, pp. 399, 400.

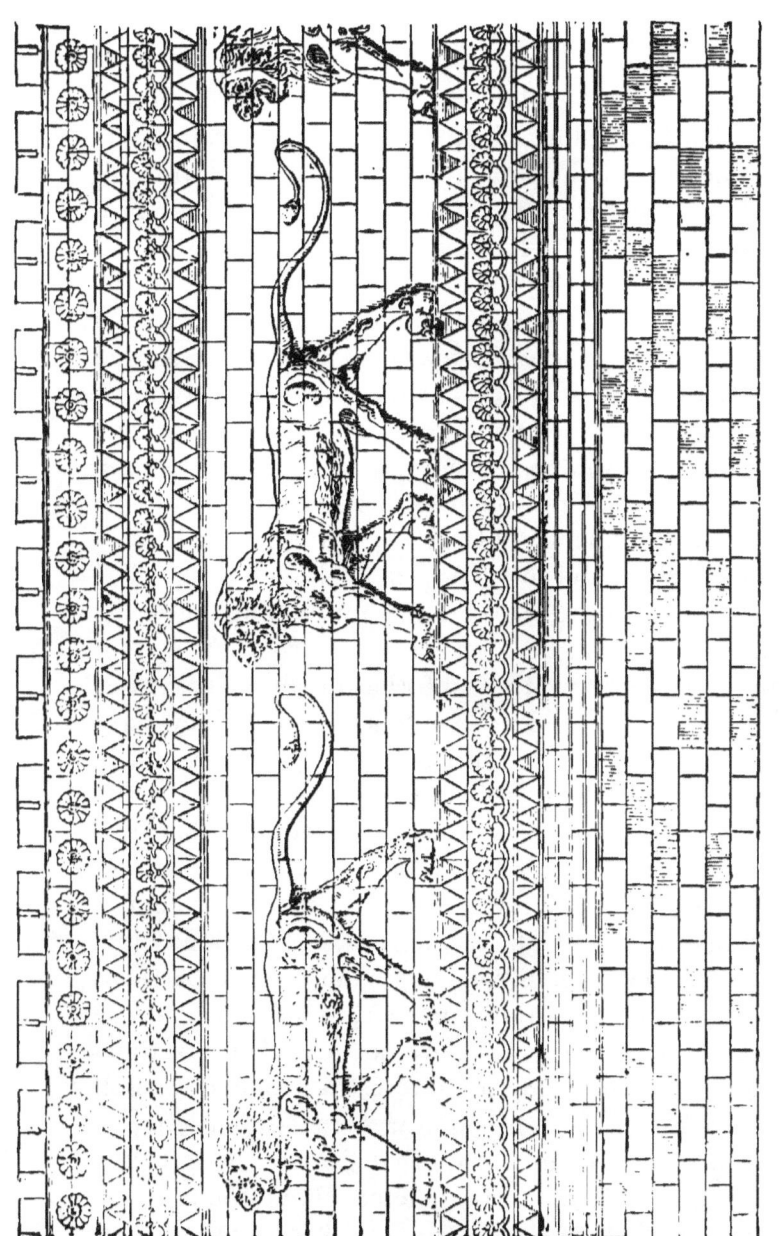

44. LION-FRIEZE, IN GLAZED TILES, AT SUSA.

(Ground—turquoise blue; lions—white, yellow, and green; inscription in white characters; Tile design below the frieze, casing the wall: gray and rose-coloured.)

collected, Mr. Dieulafoy succeeded in reconstructing another marvellous piece of work, a frieze representing archers of the royal guard. "One day," he says, "they would bring me a hand, the next a foot in a golden boot. Adding piece to piece as they fitted, I put together the feet, ankles, legs, the skirt, the body, the arm, the shoulder, and at last the head of an archer." There was a procession of them as well as of the lions. (See Frontispiece.) The costume is sumptuous to the last degree; it is the graceful and becoming "Median robe," the drapery of which, in the natural fall and softness of the folds already betrays the influence of Greek art, grafted on the conventional model of Assyrian slab-sculpture. The cut of the clothes is the same for all, but the material, or at least the design, varies, clearly showing that the archers wear the uniforms of different corps. Their hair is held by circlets of gold; they have golden bracelets at the wrist and golden jewels in their ears. Their spears have a silver call at the lower end. We know from Herodotus that this equipment belonged to the royal bodyguard of picked warriors, known by the name of "The Ten Thousand," or, "The Immortals," from their number, and because, as soon as a man died, in battle or from sickness, another forthwith took his place, so that there never were more nor less than ten thousand,—and it is highly interesting to find oneself confronted with contemporary and authentic representations of members of that famous body. Perhaps the most interesting detail about them is the fact, revealed by this discovery, that some of their uniforms were covered with scutcheon badges, woven or embroidered in the stuff, very much like those worn by the retainers of noble and royal houses in the Middle Ages. Let us hear Mr. Dieulafoy's description:

45. ENLARGED DETAIL OF THE DESIGN WOVEN INTO THE
RIGHT HAND ARCHER'S ROBES.
(See Frontispiece.)

". . . On a white ground are regularly scattered black lozenges bordered with yellow. In the middle of each lozenge is painted a white knoll bearing three towers—one yellow and two white. The design is framed by a yellow line in relief. This ornament represents, in the clearest possible manner, the citadel of Susa ; this, at least, is the conventional representation of it on the Assyrian sculptures that refer to the capture of Susa by Asshurbanipal. When the great lords of the Middle Ages had their arms embroidered or woven into the garments of their retainers, they little dreamed that they had been anticipated by the Persian monarchs !"

The "Lion-frieze" and the "Archer-frieze" are not the only specimens of Persian enamelled brick decoration brought to light at Susa. Hardly less handsome in a different way is the casing of variegated enamelled brickwork which adorned the battlemented parapet or banister of the great double stairs that led from the plain to the great court in front of the palace, in a slope so gentle, with

46. BATTLEMENTED STAIR PARAPET CASED WITH ENAMELLED BRICK-WORK, AT SUSA.

(Palace of Artaxerxes.) Compare " Battlements at Dur-Sharrukin," ill. 53 in " Story of Assyria."

steps so broad and low, that they might easily be mounted on horseback. The combinations of colors in the numerous fragments which it was Mr. Dieulafoy's good fortune to collect, seem to have been, though striking, singularly harmonious. He gives the following, as most frequently occurring:

On light blue ground, prevailing color—white, with touches of green and pale yellow.

On dark green ground, prevailing color—golden yellow, with touches of blue and white.

On black ground, prevailing color—golden yellow, with touches of pale green and white.

47. ROYAL SEAL OF THE AKHÆMENIAN KINGS.
(Found at Susa, by Mr. Dieulafoy.)

The gateways were cased in a white-and-rose-colored mosaic, above which stretched the grand lion procession.

Not the least interesting of Mr. Dieulafoy's "finds" is the royal seal of the Akhæmenian kings; not the impression alone, but the seal itself, conical-shaped, of a valuable gray, opal-like stone. The two sphinxes which seem to guard the royal medallion, plainly show, by their Egyptian character, that this seal

48. WINGED BULL AT PERSEPOLIS.
(Compare Assyrian winged bull, " Story of Chaldea," ill. 27.)

could have been adopted only after the conquest of Egypt. But the most remarkable feature about it is the figure within the winged disk, hovering above the royal effigy. It is an obvious imitation of the Assyrian Asshur-symbol, and like that symbol

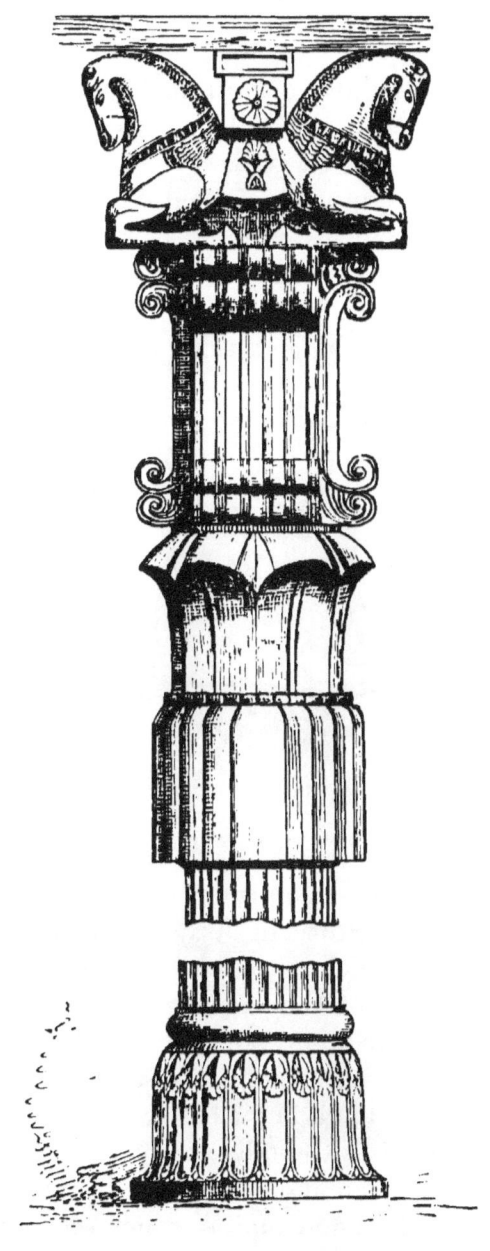

49. PERSIAN PILLAR—BASE AND CAPITAL.

is always found above or in front of the king, wherever he appears in the wall and rock-sculptures of the Akhæmenians. It is plain that they adopted it as the meetest emblem of their own supreme god Ahura-Mazda and we find it lavishly reproduced on all their monuments, be they palaces or tombs. The only difference lies in the national garb worn by the Eranian god, and the curve of the wings,

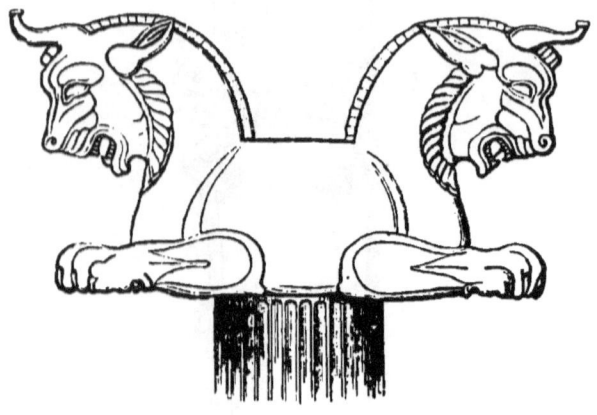

50. DOUBLE GRIFFIN CAPITAL.

which on Assyrian sculptures are straight. (Compare ill. 54 and "Story of Assyria," ill. 1 4 and 22.) We find the same alteration in the winged bulls, the majestic warders of the palace gates at PERSEPOLIS, the capital of the later Akhæmenian kings.

A column was also found at Susa, the most perfect specimen of the kind, in far better preservation than any at Persepolis, although exactly similar to the latter in the peculiar and complicated ornamentation of the upper shaft and capital, which seems to have been a distinctive and original creation of Persian art. At least nowhere else are seen the animal forms which surmount the column and support the entablature—sometimes horses, sometimes bulls, or griffins—used in just this way.

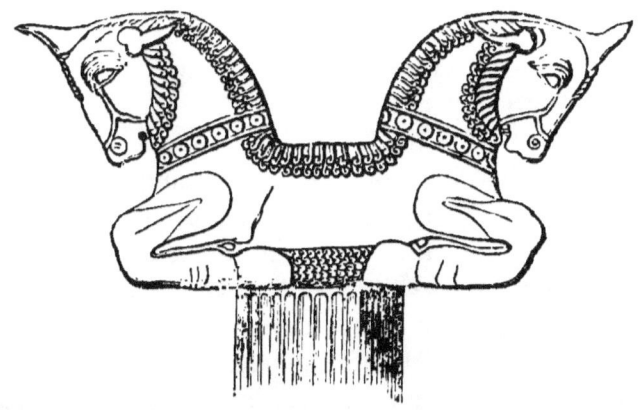

52. DOUBLE BULL CAPITAL.

XII.

KAMBYSES, 529-522 B.C.

1. KAMBYSES was the eldest son of Kyros the Great and his Persian queen, Kassandanê, and as such the undisputed heir to the crown of Persia proper and of the vast empire created by his father. One Greek writer, it is true, calls him the son of Amytis, but it is a fiction which, it is easy to see, came from a Median source. Had his mother been a foreigner, he could not have reigned, still less have succeeded so smoothly and quietly, as a matter of course. He was not a novice in statecraft, having had several years' practice as viceroy at Babylon, where several Êgibi tablets have been found, dated from that time, Kambyses being "entitled King of Babel" and Kyros "King of the Countries,"—a more comprehensive title.

2. Kambyses probably was honestly desirous of governing well and justly, and on several occasions can be shown to have tried to follow in his father's footsteps. For he was not devoid of fine qualities; but he lacked the self-control and admirable balance which made the chief greatness of his father's character. So he suffered his faults to obscure and degrade his better self, and unfortunately they were

just the faults that are most heinous and dangerous in a man armed with absolute power: ungovernable temper and suspiciousness. The former frequently carried him beyond all bounds of decency and moderation, converting even acts of justice into the enormities of a raving tyrant. Thus on one occasion, having detected one of the seven supreme judges in dishonest practices, such as taking bribes and tampering with justice, he had him flayed, ordered his chair to be covered with the skin, and compelled his son, who succeeded him in the office, to sit in that chair, when trying cases—as a warning. True, he was quick to regret his violent outbreaks; still he must have inspired more terror than love in his immediate circle, and we may well credit the report, mentioned by Herodotus, that his subjects drew this difference between him and the great Kyros, that, while they used to call the latter "father," they had no title for Kambyses but the formal one of "master." Of this feeling towards him he was sensitively aware and bitterly resented it. This unamiable nature was further poisoned by the jealousy with which he regarded his only brother, young BARDIYA,[*] whom he not unjustly suspected of being the people's favorite, and therefore looked upon as his own dangerous rival. Yet he at first acted honorably, even generously by that brother: he either gave him

[*] The Greeks give the name as SMERDIS, having probably heard "Berdis"; some call this prince TANAOXARES or TANYOXARKES, which Eranian scholars take to be a corruption for the Persian "*thanvarakhshathra*," *i. e.*, "king of the bow"; not unlikely, for we are told that Bardiya had the reputation of being the best archer and mark man among the Persians.

or confirmed him in the government of Khorasmia, Bactria, Parthia, and Karmania, *i. e.*, of nearly the whole of eastern Erân, because such had been his father's behest.

3. It is very probable that, after the fashion of Oriental politics so familiar from the history of Assyria's wars, the death of the "king of kings" was the signal for risings in some of the annexed countries, and that this fact is alluded to in Herodotus' brief statement that "Kambyses conquered over again the nations that had been conquered by Kyros." After which he began to prepare for an Egyptian campaign. Nothing could be more natural and reasonable; it was what the course of events itself brought up as the next thing to be done. The universal monarchy which evidently was the dream of Kyros, would have been incomplete without Egypt, nor was the pretence wanting to give plausible color to the aggression: for had not Amasis promised his assistance to Lydia against Persia, and been prevented from interfering only by the excessive rapidity of the conqueror's movements? and was not this a presumption that called for chastisement? It would, therefore, have been strange indeed if the new king had not turned his thoughts that way. But this was far too simple an explanation to please the ancient historians, who dearly loved an ornate story with, if possible, a thinly veiled moral to it. So we are informed that Kambyses sent to Amasis to ask for one of his daughters in marriage, and that the usurper, now well-established in the throne of the two Egypts, being unwilling to send a child of his own to a re-

mote and unknown land, and to the tender mercies of one whose violent temper may have been reported to him, bethought him of a stratagem—for to refuse point-blank would have been dangerous,—and sent to Kambyses as his own daughter, a princess of the name of NITĒTIS, a surviving daughter of his predecessor Hophra (or Apries), whom he had overthrown and supplanted. She went willingly, seeing an opening for avenging her father and family, by simply telling Kambyses of the deception practised upon him, which so enraged him, that he vowed the ruin of Egypt on the spot. The whole story is palpably improbable, if only from the fact that Nitētis must have been over forty at the time. But the Egyptians had a much neater and more plausible story of their own: they told Herodotus (who, however, was too well-informed to believe them), that Nitētis had been one of Kyros' wives, and—the mother of Kambyses. By this perversion of facts, they connected Kambyses with their own royal family, and converted the conquest into merely an armed change of dynasty, such as had occurred more than once in their history, besides making of the conqueror the avenger of his own grandfather.

4. The Egyptian campaign, although probably planned from the beginning of the new reign, could not have effect until the fourth year. It presented great difficulties, which Kambyses was wise enough not to underrate, but to meet with adequate preparations. Amasis was not a contemptible foe and had quietly done many things which made a foreign invasion a more difficult task than it

used to be. He had occupied the island of Cyprus and made friends with several Greek islands, a stroke of policy which secured him the use of considerable maritime forces, besides averting the danger of a Persian occupation which otherwise would very probably have followed the submission of the Greek cities on the sea-coast. Amasis morever was liberal-minded and, breaking through the stubborn prejudices of his people, even at the cost of a good deal of his popularity, he opened the country to the Greeks, whom he permitted to have a settlement near the mouths of the Nile, kept a body of Greek mercenaries, and even went so far as to take a wife from the Greek colony of Kyrênê. He could therefore rely on the assistance and watchfulness of his new friends from the other side of the sea. To counteract these moves, Kambyses determined to oppose fleet to fleet, Greeks to Greeks. He ordered the cities of the Phœnicians and of the Ionians to arm and man their ships and be ready to support the land army. The order was obeyed without a sign of either revolt or treason, which goes far to show that the Persian rule was a just and lenient one, at least compared to that of earlier conquerors. The Phœnician and Ionian fleets were commanded to join together just below Mount Carmel and then to proceed downwards along the coast, keeping pace with the army, which was to march along the ordinary military route. Of this a portion, amounting to several days' march, passed through a stretch of desert, the terrible wilderness of the Sinai peninsula. But Kambyses succeeded in gaining the sheikhs of the roving Bedouin tribes—

Midianites and Amalekites—whose dominion the peninsula virtually was, so that they promised not only not to molest his army on its march, but to supply it with water. It seemed as though luck would complete what prudence and foresight had so well begun, for a short time before Kambyses started on the expedition, there came to him a Greek deserter, a certain PHANÊS, who had commanded the Greek bodyguard of Amasis, and secretly left it, being discontented with something or other, to join the invaders. Amasis was well aware of the evil consequences this desertion could have for Egypt, and sent trusty men in pursuit. They tracked him as far as Lycia, where they actually captured him, but he managed to escape and gain the Persian court. He followed the king and, as Amasis had expected, made himself very useful by his knowledge of the country and the advice he was able to impart on every occasion.

5. Every thing was now ready (525 B.C.), but the king still lingered. He was leaving his empire on a dangerous expedition that would keep him away months, perhaps years. To whom should he entrust the government in his absence? The most natural and fittest person for such a trust would have been his only brother Bardiya, his heir presumptive also, as he himself was childless. But the inveterate distrust of all Oriental despots towards their own flesh and blood would not suffer him to entertain the thought. Nay, so much was that feeling intensified by his own individual temperament, jealous and suspicious to the verge of monomania, that he could not even bear to leave his brother behind; visions of

plots and usurpation harassed him continually; ruler of most of the eastern countries of Erân, i. e., nearly half the empire, whose allegiance was not very firm at best, how easily could Bardiya, the admired and beloved, incite them to open rebellion, when he would dispose of sufficient forces to overpower the other half, and seize on his absent brother's crown, perhaps without even meeting with any opposition! Smarting with the consciousness of his own impopularity, Kambyses brooded over these evil presentiments until, driven beside himself with apprehension and distrust, he sought security from fancied dangers in crime: he had Bardiya secretly assassinated. Nothing is known of how the deed was done, for the details given by the various Greek writers are contradictory, and evidently apocryphal. The only authentic record—and quite sufficient it is—we have in the great Behistûn inscription, wherein Kambyses' successor, King Dareios, makes the following brief and explicit statement:

"A man named Kambujiya, son of Kurush, of our race, he was here king before me. Of that Kambujiya there was a brother, Bardiya was his name; of the same mother and of the same father with Kambujiya. Afterwards Kambujiya slew that Bardiya. When Kambujiya had slain Bardiya, it was not known to the people that Bardiya had been slain. Afterwards Kambujiya proceeded to Egypt. . . ."

6. The campaign was short, and successful beyond expectation. While the preparations had been going on, there had been a change of rulers; the wise and wary Amasis had died, and when the Persian army reached the east-

Battle of Pelusion. Conquest of Egypt, 525 B.C.

ern mouth of the Nile, it was his son, PSAMMETIK III. (more frequently called PSAMMENIT by the Greeks), whom they encountered. There was one battle, near PELUSION, and it was final. Psammetik at once retreated to Memphis with the bulk of his army, intending to make a stand in this the holiest and most ancient city of the monarchy. Pelusion was held for a short time by another detachment, but was unable to resist the pressure of army and fleet combined. The surrender of this fortress opened Egypt to the invader; his ships now sailed up the Nile and reached Memphis before the land army, to which they afforded a most welcome and necessary support, since the Nile had to be crossed before the capital could be attacked. It would seem that the city did not offer much resistance. The citadel, indeed, with its garrison commanded by the king, did well and bravely, but was overpowered by numbers and forced to surrender. The noblest of the land fell as captives into the hands of the conqueror, and Psammetik was of the number. This virtually ended the war, and the whole country submitted almost with alacrity. An Egyptian inscription has been found which says: "When the great king, the lord of the world, Kambathet (Kambyses), came up against Egypt, all the nations of the world were with him. He made himself master of the whole land, and bade them sit down there." It may be doubted, however, whether the submission would have been as rapid and universal had the reigning house been more popular. It was not only that Amasis had been an usurper; he was not the first; and usurpers, when they flatter the national tastes and prejudices, seldom find the people's hearts obdurate against them. But Amasis had been a friend of the Greeks, had admitted them to settle in the country, and even enlisted a bodyguard of the hated and despised foreigners—all grievous sins in the eyes of the proud and bigoted Egyptians.

7. On finding himself thus almost unexpectedly master of so great a country, where every thing must have been bewilderingly strange to him and to his companions, Kambyses acted as became a son and pupil of the great Kyros, whose golden rule was: mild treatment to the vanquished, respect and toleration to their customs and religion. He treated the captive Psammetik kindly and honorably, and there was no question of sacking cities, plundering or desecrating temples, wasting plantations, and the like atrocities. The only act of severity which he enforced, was the execution of two thousand Egyptian youths, whose lives the Persians demanded, in reprisal for the massacre of the entire crew of the first ship that reached Memphis in advance of the fleet and found itself cut off from all assistance. The ordinary crew of a war-ship in those days consisted of about two hundred men, and there was nothing excessive, according to Oriental ideas, in inflicting a tenfold penalty; it was simply the fate of war. Otherwise nothing was changed or disturbed in laws, institutions, or the national life generally. The principal fortresses were garrisoned, and a Satrap appointed to maintain the peace and collect the tribute, that

was all. As to the Egyptian religion, its forms of worship must have been not only highly distasteful to a Mazdayasnian, but ludicrously absurd, especially the divine honors paid to so many animals, useful and noxious alike—the cat, the jackal, the crocodile, the ibis,—and the preservation, by means of embalming, of dead bodies, both of men and sacred animals. Yet he outwardly conformed to the religious customs of the people whose ruler he had become, and took pains to appear before them in every way as the Pharaoh, the successor of Pharaohs, and as such he is represented on a painting, kneeling in adoration before the Apis-Bull, the most sacred of all animals, reverenced as the living emblem of the One Supreme God himself. This painting still exists in one of the galleries which formed the catacombs or burying-places expressly constructed for the mummified remains of successive lines of Apis-Bulls through unnumbered centuries. The inscription informs us that the recently deceased Apis had been deposited in the resting-place prepared for him by the king Kambyses, while another inscription reports the birth of a new Apis, in the fifth year of Kambyses. The inscription quoted above (see p. 351), is a long one, engraved on the statue of an Egyptian, who held public offices under Amasis, Psammetik III., Kambyses, and Dareios, and speaks with great praise of Kambyses' zeal in religious matters and his liberality to temples and their ministers. The stories, therefore, which Herodotus transmitted of the blasphemous and sacrilegious atrocities in which that king was said to have indulged, even to the desecration of graves and the killing of the Apis-Bull with his own hand, may safely be set aside as later inventions prompted by spite against the conqueror and retailed to foreigners by ignorant or malicious guides. Greek travellers of Herodotus' time were the more likely to put faith in them, that they had themselves a mortal grudge against the Persians, and certain Persian customs must have struck them as iniquitous. Thus Herodotus is horrified at Kambyses wedding his two sisters, while we have seen that, according to the king's own religion, such unions were meritorious acts enjoined by the highest authority.

8. The most natural course for Kambyses to pursue, the conquest of Egypt once achieved and established, would have been to depart to his own lands, leaving behind governors and garrisons. But he lingered on and on, evidently possessed with an invincible repugnance to return, evincing more and more signs of mental perturbation, and yielding to unprovoked fits of murderous temper which made him a terror to his nearest kinsmen and attendants. These fits became the more frequent and ungovernable that he indulged in excessive drinking—a vice not uncommon among the Persians. It is most probable that remorse for his brother's fate was at the bottom both of his reluctance to face his own people again and of his attacks of spleen. He sought occupation in further plans of conquest, intending to carry his arms into the heart of Libya and of Ethiopia. He also meditated an expedition against Carthage, which was to be reached by sea, along the

52 RUINED PALACE AT FIRŪZABAD. CENTRAL HALL.

north coast of Africa. But the Phœnicians blankly refused to lend their ships to be used against their own colony, and as the plan could not be carried out without their assistance, it was abandoned. But he did send out a body of troops westward into the desert to take possession of the oasis held by the AMMONIANS and famous for its ancient oracle and temple known as the temple of AMMON (one of the names of the Egyptians' supreme deity), an important position for any one who wished to command the submission of the various tribes scattered between the desert and the shore. The little army never came back, nor was it ever heard of; there was a tradition among the Ammonians that it had encountered one of the terrible hot blasts of the desert and been buried in sand-drifts. Kambyses was more fortunate in his Ethiopian expedition, which he commanded in person. He went up the Nile farther than the Assyrians had ever gone, passed through the country of the Kushite Ethiopians, and actually reached the region inhabited by negroes, whose woolly hair, thick lips, and garb of skins figure among the subject nations on the sculptures of the royal palaces at Persepolis. (See ill. 54.) This fact, together with the payment of tribute, consisting in slaves and elephants' tusks, show the expedition to have been successful and to have amounted to a real conquest rather than to a passing raid. On his march back, however, and when already approaching the confines of Upper Egypt, Kambyses had to contend with the same foe as the troops sent out to Ammon, and narrowly escaped the same fate.

9. Three years had passed, and still the king tarried in Egypt; when suddenly strange and appalling news came from home. Bardiya, it was reported, the king's brother, had rebelled and proclaimed himself king. Heralds had gone forth to all ends of the empire to announce that allegiance should henceforth be paid to him and not to Kambyses. One of these heralds came to Egypt, bearing the message to the army there, unabashed by the king's presence. As Bardiya's death had been kept a profound secret and the people only thought that he lived secluded in his palace (no unusual thing in the East), no one saw any reason to doubt the news, and Kambyses found himself confronted with the reality of the fancied danger which had driven him to frenzy, but in a form which far outdid in horror his worst apprehensions: it was as though his murdered brother's ghost had risen before him and sat on his throne. Urged by his counsellors, and his kinsmen the Akhæmenian princes, he reluctantly commanded the army to set out on their homeward march. But his spirit was broken; he alone knew that the usurper must be an impostor who had in some way found out that Bardiya was dead, and took advantage of the people's ignorance of the fact to personate him. He had no hope of retrieving his fortune, for his conscience told him he deserved no better. And he had no child for whose sake to struggle and to hope, so that even should the issue be favorable, the inheritance of Kyros must pass away from his direct line, to the younger branch. True, the Persians were a loyal people, and not likely

to follow an impostor, once unmasked; but how could the wretched king effectively unmask him, save by divulging his own foul deed? Still, the good of the empire imperatively demanded that this should be done—and he resolved to humble himself and confess; but to survive such a confession was more than his proud spirit could stoop to. Besides, he was bitterly conscious that he should not be missed or mourned: was not the readiness with which his subjects, those of his own race and of the provinces, had obeyed the first call to rebellion, the best proof that he had forfeited their love and confidence, that the Hvarenô, the "awful kingly Glory" that will not stay where truth is not, had gone from him?* He had been right: it was his brother who was to them the son of the great Kyros, of him whom they had called "father"; *he* was only "the master." His long absence had done the rest. And now the liberation of the empire, the restoration of royalty, would best be entrusted to guiltless hands— nothing could prosper in those of the murderer, the "Mithra-deceiver." So he called together the noblest among the Persians who attended him, told his lamentable story with the dignified simplicity of one who already was not of this world, and bidding them, especially the Akhæmenians, repair the evil that had been done, put an end to his own life. On his young kinsman, Dareios, temporarily devolved the task of taking the army home and commanding it, until the question of succession should be duly settled.

* See above, p. 80.

53. SASSANIAN ROCK-SCULPTURES AT FIRŪZ-ABAD.

10. This is the tragedy in its grand and simple features, divested of the diffuse and conflicting statements, the puerile anecdotes of the Greek chroniclers, and viewed by the light of the great Behistûn inscription, which gives it in the following brief, but sufficiently explicit paragraph:

There are, among the Babylonian "contract-tablets," two dated September and October of "the first year of King Barziya"—ample confirmation, if such were needed, of this statement, of the universal acceptation of the usurper's claim, and of the credulity with which his self-assertion met "in the provinces."

" . . . When Kambujiya had proceeded to Egypt, then the state became wicked. Then the lie became abounding in the land, both in Persia and in Media, and in the other provinces.

"Afterwards there was a certain man, a Magian, named GAUMATA. . . . He thus lied to the state: 'I am Bardiya, the son of Kurush, the brother of Kambujiya.' Then the whole state became "rebellious." (Spring 522 B.C.) "From Kambujiya it went over to him, both Persia and Media, and the other provinces. He seized the empire. On the ninth day of the month Garmapada, then it was he seized the empire.* Afterwards Kambujiya, having killed himself, died. . . . After Gaumata the Magian had dispossessed Kambujiya both of Persia and Media, and the dependent provinces, he did after his own desire ; he became king."

* In July or August. This probably refers to the consecration or inauguration at Pasargadæ.

XIII.

DAREIOS I, THE SON OF HYSTASPES, 522-485 B.C.— FIRST PERIOD: CIVIL WARS.

1. "THERE was not a man, neither Persian nor Mede, nor any one of our family, who could dispossess that Gaumata, the Magian of the empire. The people feared him exceedingly. He slew many who had known old Bardiya. For that reason he slew them, 'lest they should recognize me that I am not Bardiya, the son of Kurush.' No one dared any thing concerning Gaumata, the Magian, until I arrived. Then I prayed to Ahura-Mazda; Ahura-Mazda brought help to me. On the tenth day of the month Bagayadish" (the first month, March–April), "then it was that I, with my faithful men, slew that Gaumata, the Magian, and the men who were his chief followers. The fort named Sikathauvatis, in the district Nisaya in Media, there I slew him. I dispossessed him of the empire. By the grace of Ahura-Mazda I became king; Ahura-Mazda granted me the empire."

Thus Dareios, in the Behistûn record. The lengthy and highly adorned narratives of the Greek historians afford a valuable commentary to this brief and pithy statement. Valuable, for overladen as they are with trumped up anecdotes, speeches of Greek invention, and facts misrepresented because not understood, they still supply us with a continuous thread of action, enabling us to make out the main features of a most dramatic incident. We may pretty safely reconstruct it as follows:

2. After Kambyses' death, his army, on the homeward march, declared in favor of the supposed Bardiya. Dareios hastened to Persia and, before deciding on a course of action, secretly wrote to the Satraps of the several provinces, to try and secure their assistance. The result was not encouraging. There seem to have really been only two on whom he could implicitly rely, besides his own father, who was Satrap in Parthia. This convinced him that it would be imprudent to proceed openly and violently, since most people believed in the usurper, and Bardiya, had he been alive, would now have been the natural and legitimate heir of his childless brother. Besides, the Magian had taken care to ingratiate himself with the provinces, by notifying them all, as soon as he assumed the sceptre, that he "granted them freedom from war-service and from taxes for the space of three years." He was therefore far from unpopular, and Dareios wisely shrank from a civil war, the issue of which would have been more than doubtful. A bold stroke, an accomplished fact—such was the only safe and practical solution, and Dareios decided on a daring deed, which would have been impossible but for certain Persian customs, on which he cleverly built his plans.

3. We have seen (see p. 279), that the Persian nation was first constituted by the fusion of several tribes—probably originally seven—under the leadership of Akhaemenes, the head of the noblest of them, the Pasargadae. But although this particular family thus became invested with hereditary royalty, great privileges were awarded to the heads of the six other

54. DAREIOS I, ON HIS THRONE, UPBORNE BY SUBJECT NATIONS, (PERSEPOLIS.)
(Note the Negro in the lower left-hand corner.

tribes or clans, who were, in fact, the king's peers and enjoyed perfect equality with him, short only of the royal power itself. They all wore the royal head-dress,—the tall *kidaris* or tiara ; they could enter the royal presence at all times, unannounced ; they were the king's companions and advisers by right of birth, and it was only from their families he could choose his first wife, his queen, as it was into their families that he married his own sons and daughters, his brothers and sisters. On this ancient and sacred custom Dareios built his simple plan. The heads of the seven tribes—he being one of them and their leader—should present themselves at the palace gates, alone, without any followers; the pretender could not possibly deny himself to them without violating a fundamental law of the empire, and he would, by so doing, arouse suspicion ; once inside the palace, their own bravery and opportunity should do the rest. The six chiefs agreed to stand by Dareios and dare the venture with him. They could take their own time to mature the plot, for one who gave himself out as a son of Kyros could not, without betraying himself, attempt any thing against the seven princes. Yet he seems to have felt some uneasiness, since, as the inscription tells us, he removed from Persia into Media, and there established himself not in the capital, Agbatana, but in a mountain castle. This removal considerably increased the difficulty and danger for the conspirators, since he was there surrounded by his brother-Magi, who, as we have seen, formed a separate and powerful class in the country. Still, the plan arranged by the seven princes could not well be altered ; indeed it became more urgent than ever that it should be carried out. They fearlessly rode up to the castle gate, Dareios pretending that he was the bringer of a message to the king from his father Hystaspes, the heir presumptive. As he had foreseen, they passed, unchallenged and unhindered by the guards. A few moments later and the usurper had ceased to live, after a brief and desperate scuffle with some attendants.* The retinue of the seven, which had been left at some distance behind, now hastened to their support and prevented a popular outbreak. This day was set apart for all coming times, to be celebrated by a festival in memory of "the slaughter of the Magian." The Greeks, utterly misunderstanding the purport of this festival, gravely asserted that a slaughter of whatever Magians were met with on the street, took place every year on the anniversary of that day, so that no Magi showed themselves out-doors as long as it lasted. Almost immediately after this feat of boldness, Dareios was proclaimed king, probably by previous agreement with his companions, and with the consent of his father Hystaspes, who continued to govern his distant province. In his great inscription he faithfully records the names of his six companions, emphasizing the fact that they were his only helpers. "These are the men who alone were there when I slew Gaumata, the Magian, who was called Bardiya. These alone are the men who were my assistants." One of them was Gobryas, his father-in-law.

* He had reigned seven months since the death of Kambyses, very nearly a year in all.

4. Thus was accomplished with astonishing ease and scarcely any bloodshed one of the most important revolutions in history. A short interval of peace now followed, during which Dareios devoted all his energies to the work of reconstruction. He tells us so, in his usual concise but comprehensive manner:

"The empire which had been taken away from our family, that I recovered. . . . I established the state in its place, both Persia and Media, and the other provinces. As it was before, so I made it. The temples which Gaumata the Magian had destroyed, I rebuilt. I reinstituted for the state both the religious chants and the worship, and gave them to the families which Gaumata the Magian had deprived of them. . . . By the grace of Ahura-Mazda I did this ; I labored until I had established our family in its place as it was before. Thus I labored, by the grace of Ahura-Mazda, that Gaumata the Magian should not supersede our family."

The mention in this passage of the Behistûn inscription of temples destroyed and rebuilt has sorely puzzled the decipherers. For it is well known that the Zoroastrian religion admits of no temples, and that its only rallying-points of worship are its *âtesh-gâhs* or fire-altars, in the open air or in unpretending, unadorned chapels.* That a Mazdayaznian, therefore, should take to himself credit for rebuilding temples seemed an unaccountable anomaly.

* The Persians *have* had temples, but at a later period, which does not come within the bounds of the present work. That period may be called that of the final decadence of pure Mazdeism. We know of temples erected to Mithra and Anâhita-Ardvi-Sûra already by King Artaxerxes, the grandson of Dareios. This was due to the influence of the Semitic and Canaanitic religions ; Mithra was transformed into a counterpart of their Baals and Molochs, and Anâhita into that of their nature goddesses—Beltis, Mylitta, Astartê, Atargatis, and the rest. She had a famous temple at Susa.

55. TOMBS OF AKHÆMENIAN KINGS AT NAKHSHI-RUSTEM. (70 FEET FROM THE GROUND).
(Sassanian sculptures at the base of the rock.)

The inconsistency, however, vanishes if we assume, with Max Duncker,* that temples not of the Persians or Medes are meant, but of the subject nations. We have seen that Kyros and, in imitation of him, his son Kambyses made it a point not only to tolerate, but personally to honor, the religions of conquered countries. It is very natural to suppose that the usurper would be uninfluenced by the dictates of sound statecraft, and, blindly following his priestly zeal, would neglect and even destroy these to him abominable seats and landmarks of heathenism. Dareios, no less naturally, immediately resumed the liberal and conciliatory policy of his house, and mentions it in his annals as a claim on the regard of a large portion of his subjects. We must remember that all the Akhæmenian monumental documents are trilingual, because addressed to three distinct races, and that, numerically, the Mazdayasnians formed the minority. We are forcibly reminded of this fact by one apparently slight detail. In the Turanian version (that which has been called the Proto-Median, or Amardian, or, more lately, Scythic), the name of Ahura-Mazda is accompanied with the explanatory clause, "the god of the Âryas." The Babylonian version speaks of "houses of the gods," an expression which excludes both Persians and Medes.

5. That Dareios himself was a Mazdayasnian, and an earnest one, of that the language used in his inscriptions leaves no shadow of a doubt. Near the Persian capital of which he was the founder, and

* Max Duncker, "Geschichte des Alterthums," vol. IV., p. 458.

which is known to us only by its Greek name, PERSEPOLIS, there is a perpendicular rock called NAKHSH-RUSTEM, in which are hewn the tombs, or rather sepulchral chambers, of Dareios and three of his immediate successors, representing the front of palaces, after the manner of the Lycian rock-tombs. (See Chap. VIII.) They are richly adorned with sculptures, among which we especially note the frieze representing a procession of dogs—the sacred animal of the Avesta; the king, standing on a platform, leaning on his bow—unstrung, for the work of life is done,—in adoration before the blazing fire-altar, the sun-disk, and the hovering emblem of Ahura-Mazda. (See ill. 56).

Of the three tombs in the row, that of Dareios alone has an inscription, which in some ways completes the record of Behistûn, having been indited several years later. It begins with the most solemn profession of faith, which affects one like the far-swelling peal of some great organ :

"A great god is Ahura-Mazda ; he has created this earth, he has created yonder heaven, he has created man, and all pleasant things for man, he has made Darayâvush king, the only king of many."

Then follows a brief review of his deeds and of his conquests, piously referred to "the grace of Ahura-Mazda." No Hebrew monotheist could be more absolute and emphatic :

"That which I have done, I have all done through the grace of Ahura-Mazda. Ahura-Mazda brought me help, till I had performed the work. May he protect me and my clan and this land. . . ."

The same statement is repeated several times in

the Behistûn annals, and though he twice qualifies it by the addition, "Ahura-Mazda *and the other gods that are*," these words have not in the original the decided polytheistic coloring that a modern rendering gives them. We know that Mazdeism admitted of divine beings subordinate to the One who is Supreme, and such, no doubt, is the meaning here. Another trait characteristic of the Mazdayasnian is the use he makes of the word "lie," which is throughout equivalent to "evil," "wickedness." After the departure of Kambyses, we are told that "the lie became abounding in the kingdom." And the word used is the Avestan "*druj*," in the more modern form "*daranga*." Towards the end of the record Dareios says: "For this reason Ahura-Mazda brought help to me, and the other gods that are, that I was not wicked, nor was I a liar ["*daraujhana*" = Avestan "*drujvan*"], nor was I a tyrant."

6. From these passages, which breathe the spirit rather of the Gâthas than of the Yasna or Vendidâd, we may conclude that King Dareios was a Mazdayasnian of the early uncorrupted school, and, with much probability, that the alterations introduced into the doctrine and ritual by the Median Magi (see p. 271) had not been adopted by the Persians. At least they do not appear to have followed the prescriptions of the Vendidâd in their treatment of the dead,—certainly not strictly. Their kings we find entombed in elaborately wrought sepulchres, not exposed to the birds. But we saw that this custom is a borrowed one, a fact betrayed by the very word "Dakhma," which originally meant "the place

of burning," showing that the early Eranians, like their brethren of India, were familiar with cremation.* Herodotus has a curious passage, from which

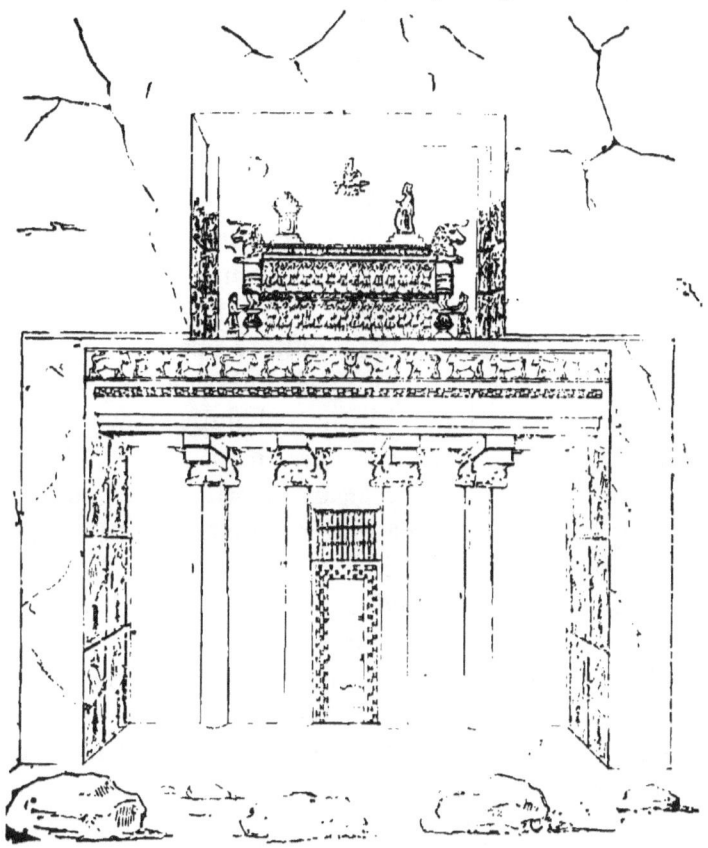

56. DETAIL OF AKHÆMENIAN TOMB.
(Compare Lycian rock-tombs, ch. viii.)

it would seem that the practice of exposing the dead was gaining ground in Persia in his time (middle of the fifth century B.C.), but in a sort of underhand

* Justi, "Geschichte des Alten Persiens," p. 88.

way, being introduced and favored—as we might expect—by the Magi:

"There is another custom which is spoken of with reserve, and not openly, concerning their dead. It is said that the body of a male Persian is never buried, until it has been torn either by a dog or a bird of prey. That the Magi have this custom is beyond a doubt, for they practise it without any concealment. The dead bodies are covered with wax and then buried in the ground."

This last practice looks very much like a concession to the Magian teachings, as a layer of wax may be considered to isolate the body and thus preservs the earth from pollution. Nor, strictly speaking, can any of the elements be polluted by a body shut up in a coffin or sarcophagus and then deposited, not in the earth itself, but in a chamber hewn in the hard, dry rock. That the Persians of Dareios' time, moreover, shunned the nearness of a corpse, as entailing impurity, we may infer from another passage of Herodotus, which tells us that this king himself, on one occasion, refused to enter Babylon through a certain gate, because above that gate, was the sepulchre of Queen Nitokris, the mother of Nabonidus, who, from some unaccountable whim, had chosen for herself that peculiar place of rest. The story may not be true, but it is significant.

7. If Dareios had hoped to avert further troubles by the swift and skilful blow which he struck at the very root of evil, in the person of the impostor Gaumata, that hope was deceived, and he was given but a very few months for the work of reconstruction which he at once undertook. The Satraps of the distant provinces had tasted the sweets of inde-

57. BUILDING KNOWN AS "RUSTEM'S TOMB," AT NAKHSHI-RUSTEM.
(Compare ill. 43).

pendence during the long absence of Kambyses and the late period of comparatively slack rule, and were loth to return under the strict control of the central authority. The populations were highly pleased with the Magian's way of governing, and the majority of them undoubtedly still believed him to be what he represented himself; so the sparks of future disturbances were by no means stamped out. A year had not elapsed, when the conflagration broke out nearly simultaneously on all points of the empire. And this unheard of thing came to pass, that every province that rebelled was led by an impostor or pretender: the success of the tragi-comedy enacted by the Magian Gaumata had borne plenteous fruits and produced a perfect epidemic of the same kind of deceit. The one reliable source of informamation for the gigantic struggle in which Darcios suddenly found himself engaged almost single-handed against adversaries that sprang up on every side of him, is of course his own narrative on the Behistûn rock; it is singularly modest and unassuming—a great contrast to the bragging of the Assyrian royal documents. We cannot do better than follow it step by step, even when not quoting from it.

8. The first to openly rebel was Elam, or Susiana. A certain ATRINA there declared himself king. At the same time a man of Babylon, NADINTABIRA by name, " thus lied to the state of Babylon: 'I am Nebuchadrezzar, the son of Nabonidus.'" The whole state of Babylon went over to him, and acknowledged him for its king. The movement at Susa appears to have been easily quelled, as all that Darcios

57. SASSANIAN SCULPTURE AT THE BASE OF THE ROCK OF NAKHSHI-RUSTEM.
(Shabúr I. receives the submission of the Roman Emperor Valerian, 260 A.D.)

says about it is this: "I went to Susiana; that Atrina was brought to me a prisoner; I slew him." Not so the rising at Babylon; it needed a real campaign to put it down. The rebel's forces were placed on the Tigris and it cost a battle for the royal army to effect a passage. Another battle was fought on the Euphrates near the capital, and, though defeated, the pretender did not surrender, but fled with a few horsemen and threw himself into Babylon, where he sustained a regular siege. Darcios records with great simplicity that he "by the grace of Ahura-Mazda, took the city and seized on the false Nebuchadrezzar," whom he put to death. This expedition occupied several months, and while he was detained in Babylonia, no less than nine countries revolted against him at once, of which he gives the list: Persia, Susiana, Media, Assyria, Armenia, Parthia, Margiana, Sattagydia, and Sakia. (See map.)

9. This second rising of Elam was of little importance, and the people themselves put it down, captured the leader and slew him. Far greater was the danger in Media, for there a man of the name of FRAVARTISH (Phraortes), a Mede, had declared himself to be "Khshatrita, of the race of Kyaxares" and called on the country in the name of its most popular national hero, the founder of its greatness. The appeal was eagerly responded to: even the Median troops which had been left at home, went over to the pretender, who was proclaimed king of Media. The rising in Sagartia was headed by a man who also gave himself out as a descendant of Kyaxares and set up an independent kingdom. But by far the

59. SASSANIAN KINGS.
(At Nakhshi-Rustem.)

worst feature in this confiscation was the defection of Persia proper; another false Bardiya appeared there, and the people accepted him. He was strong enough to initiate aggressive proceedings, by sending out troops against the satrap of the Arachosia, one of the few loyal servants of Dareios, and to bear most unflinchingly the brunt of several battles, though the result was not favorable to himself. The fortunes of Persia's lawful and heroic king may well be said to have been desperate at this juncture. Detained in a rebellious country by a siege of which the issue was doubtful, cut off from the rest of the empire, he could rely only on the troops he had with him, as he expressly says that "only those Medes and Persians who were with him remained true, and they were few in number." Yet of these few he was forced to send off two detachments to try and stay the evil in Media and in Armenia, whence the insurrection was rapidly spreading to Assyria. For in the east only two Satraps—those of Bactria and Arachosia—persisted in their allegiance, and his father, Hystaspes, did his best in his own provinces of Hyrcania and Parthia, but was unable to keep them from declaring in favor of the Median pretender. As for Dareios himself, he could not stir from Babylon, and was forced to leave his faithful friends to shift for themselves for the time. His two generals in Media and Armenia were not very successful, being too inferior in numbers to the rebel forces, and all they could do was to hold their own in strong positions, until he was able to come to their assistance.

10. Every thing now seemed to depend on the personal efforts and presence of the king. Had the capture of Babylon been delayed much longer, it is probable that the evil would have been beyond remedy. As soon as Babylon fell (September, 519 B.C.) things began to take a more hopeful aspect. The prestige of the royal presence worked wonders apart from the welcome reinforcements. Dareios first proceeded to Media, rightly considering the rising in that country the most threatening, because of the national principle it represented and the question which was at stake, really amounting to a renewal of the old contest for supremacy between Media and Persia. Phraortes boldly came forward to meet the king with an army, offering battle. His confidence was not justified by the event: he was routed and barely escaped with life. Accompanied by a few horsemen, he fled to Rhagæ, where he was captured by some troops sent in pursuit by Dareios. The cruel treatment he experienced sufficiently shows how dangerous he was deemed and how essential it was thought that he should be not only put out of the way, but degraded in the eyes of the people. "I cut off his nose, and his ears, and his tongue," says the king; "he was kept chained at my door—all the kingdom beheld him. Afterwards I crucified him at Agbatana." The same treatment was dealt to the Sagartian who claimed, like Phraortes, to be of the race of Kyaxares, and who was defeated and captured by a Median general, only that he was crucified at Arbela as an example to the Assyrian rebels. Now at last Dareios could send reinforce-

ments to his father, who, with a few troops, had bravely held the defensive, and who now gained a decisive victory over the rebels of Parthia and Hyrcania. This was in 518 B.C., and within the same year the faithful Satrap of Bactria routed those of Margiana.

11. In 517 B.C. Persia alone virtually remained in a state of insurrection. Yet the king stayed in Media, which he thought safest to control by his presence, and sent an army against the false Bardiya. Very wisely he kept his Persian troops in Media and sent the Median troops to Persia to avoid the contagious influences of national sympathies. After two battles fought in Persia the impostor was taken and executed in the summer of 517 B.C.; but his followers in Arachosia held out several months longer, and it was only in February, 516, that their leaders were at last captured and put to death. But it seemed as though as fast as threads were fastened at one end they ravelled out at the other. While the king was in Media and Persia, Babylon for the second time revolted from him in favor of a man who pretended that *he* was Nebuchadrezzar the son of Nabonidus. This new rising, however, was easily quelled by one of Dareios' generals, and the impostor was slain (January, 516 B.C.). The king meanwhile had already, in his indefatigable activity, gone to Egypt, where he put forth all his powers of conciliation to retain the affections of that important part of the empire. Egyptian monuments bear ample witness to his success, and his wise rule obtained for him a place among the great national lawgivers of the Egyp-

tians. Yet it seems that all troubles were not even yet at an end in Asia. The last column of the Behistûn inscription, though injured beyond all hope of decipherment, allows a glimpse of a third, though short-lived, rising in Elam and a war in the far east, against a Scythian people distingushed from other tribes by the name "Saki of the pointed caps." We can just make out that their chief, SAKUNKA, was taken prisoner, and probably put to death. Fortunately for Dareios, Asia Minor, the Phœnician cities, and the Ionian Greeks had not broken the peace through all these eventful years. The only attempt at rebellion was made by the Persian Satrap at Sardis, who tried to set up an independent principality for himself by uniting Lydia and Phrygia under his rule and refusing allegiance. This attempt is not mentioned in the great inscription, probably because it was not put down by force of arms, but by the assassination of the culprit, who was put to death by his own guard in obedience to a written order from the king.

12. It is the story of the almost superhuman struggle of these first years of his reign that Dareios confided to the great rock at Bagistana. The sculptured panel at the top of the inscription is a forcible illustration of the narrative. (See ill. 39.) It represents the king, protected as usual by the hovering emblem of Ahura-Mazda, and attended by two dignitaries, one of whom is Gobryas, his father-in-law, in an impetuous attitude, one foot firmly planted on the prostrate form of a man who stretches out his hands as though imploring mercy, while a proces-

sion of prisoners approaches, tied together, neck-and-neck, by one rope, and with hands bound behind their backs. These are the nine principal rebels and impostors whom it took over six years and nineteen pitched battles to overcome. They were all captured alive. The last of the band is noticeable for his pointed cap; it is the Scythian Sakunka. Short inscriptions placed above the head of each leave us no doubt about their identity. Attached to the prostrate figure is the following declaration: "This Magian, Gaumata, lied; he spoke thus: 'I am Bardiya, the son of Kurush. I am the king.'" Above the first standing figure we read: "This Atrina lied; he spoke thus: 'I am king of Susiana!'" and so on for every one.

13. In the introduction to this matchless piece of history, Dareios gives a list of the countries of which, by the grace of Ahura-Mazda, he had become king. There are twenty names. The number increases to thirty in the last of his inscriptions, that on his tomb, and includes such remote provinces towards the four quarters of the world as, in the east several districts of India (Hindush), in the west "the Ionians beyond the sea" (the people of the Greek islands, perhaps even of the Greek continent), the "Scythians beyond the sea" in the north (the people of Southern Russia), the Libyans and Kyrênians in the southwest. It stands to reason that many of these countries, situated on the extremest verge of the empire, even though visited and more or less conquered by Dareios, and by him incorporated in the list of "Satrapies," *i. e.* provinces governed by

Satraps, did not really consider themselves his obedient subjects, scarcely his vassals; but they had all felt the great king's arm, and their name must needs grace the list of "the countries that belonged to him." In his tomb-inscription there is the following effective address to his successor or any one who may behold the monument: "If thou thinkest thus; 'how many were the lands which King Darayavush ruled?'—then look on this effigy: they bear my throne, that thou mayest know them. [See ill. 39 and 54.] Then shalt thou know that the Persian man's spear reaches far, that the Persian man has fought battles far away from Persia."

XIV.

DAREIOS I. —SECOND PERIOD: YEARS OF PEACE.

1. SIX years had been absorbed by the civil wars; all the provinces needed rest, and Dareios adjourned the plans of conquest which his ambitious spirit was maturing until the wounds of the state should be healed and the growing generation should have reached manhood. For seven years he devoted himself to works of peace, and showed a genius for administration and statesmanship, such as has never since been surpassed and seldom equalled by the greatest organizers and founders of states. His system was based on the simplest principle: the greatest possible prosperity of the subject, as conducive to the greatest possible power and wealth of the state, represented by a vigilant, active, and absolute central government. The means which he used, the institutions which he created in order to achieve this great result, are startlingly modern in spirit, and even in the technical details of execution. In the first place he divided the empire into twenty provinces or "satrapies;" for, in the words of an eminent modern historian,* " the insurrections which had marred the beginning of his reign had shown him how apt a bun-

* Justi, "Geschichte des alten Persiens."

dle of countries with such utterly divergent nationalities and interests is to fall apart, and that the huge empire could be held together only by the uniform rule of a class of devoted officials, controlled and directed in all their actions by the king and his councillors." Such a class was formed of the Satraps and their subordinate officers. The king appointed them from the highest nobility of Persia, whose young sons were carefully educated for this special purpose under the king's own eyes. The power entrusted to the Satraps was very great, and an extraordinary latitude of action was very wisely allowed to those of the remote provinces, who could at any moment be called upon to face some unexpected emergency, when the delay of communication with the central authority could have dangerous and even fatal consequences. Yet they were never suffered to forget the duty that bound them on one side to the sovereign whom they represented, and on the other to the people whose welfare was given into their care. Thus a Satrap of Egypt was put to death by order of Dareios because he had presumed to coin money in his own name. The king, too, frequently undertook tours of inspection through the empire; and woe to the Satrap whose province was found in a poor condition, the people needy, oppressed, and despoiled, the fields neglected, the plantations uncared for, the villages and buildings in bad repair, while favors and honors were liberally bestowed on those who could show the master a prosperous land and contented population. As the language, religion, and national peculiarities of each country were scrupulously respected, the local customs and institutions in no case interfered with, there was nothing to prevent such a result but deliberate misrule or mismanagement on the part of the Satraps and their officials, who were accordingly held responsible.

2. Not that Dareios was at all neglectful of the interests of the crown or over-indulgent in the matter of taxation. He was, on the contrary, very keen in all that concerned the income of the exchequer—so much so, that—so Herodotus tells us—those who had called Kyros "father" and Kambyses "master," nicknamed Dareios "huckster," because "he looked to making a gain in every thing," and more especially because he introduced a system of regular taxation, instead of the voluntary gifts which his two predecessors had been content to accept from the provinces. Yet, in this, as in all things, he proceeded with real moderation, justice, and caution. He had the entire empire surveyed and every mile of ground appraised according to its capacities for production; on this valuation he based an impartially graded land-tax. It is ever to be regretted that these estimates perished, for in them we have lost the earliest known specimen of statistical work. It was probably from the original official documents that Herodotus drew his list of taxes, which is evidently genuine. We gather from it that, over and above ground-tax in gold, silver, or gold dust, most countries paid a special tribute in kind, according to their respective staple produces—horses, mules, sheep, grain, ivory, slaves, etc., besides tolls on sluices, and dues on mines, forests, and fishing. The

richest of all the provinces was that made up of
Assyria and Babylonia,—it paid by far the largest
sum, more than even Egypt and Libya. The entire income of the state is valued at about 165 millions of dollars, equal to eight times that sum at the
present rate of estimating the worth of money, yet,
at a rough calculation of the proportion between the
population and the taxation, the burden scarcely
amounted to one dollar per head.* Only Persia
proper, the royal province, was exempted from all
taxes and discharged its obligations to the head of
the state in military and civil service. Voluntary
gifts were of course expected and cheerfully offered
whenever the king came among his countrymen and
clanspeople, but as these were occasions of national
rejoicing and the king on his side was liberal with
presents, the good offices were in a way mutual and
helped to maintain the old clan-bond firm and
sacred.†

3. All these reforms and innovations, however,
fine as they were in theory, could have availed but
little in practice without some means of easy and
rapid communication between the central power and
the most outlying border-lands of the empire.
Without such means neither the Satraps nor the
subject nations could be made sufficiently to feel
their dependence on the royal authority; nor, on

* Justi, "Geschichte des alten Persiens," p. 59. He says: "600
million marks," which gives 165 million dollars, at four marks to
the dollar. Of course all such calculations are approximative.

† An ancient custom demanded that the king should give a gold-piece to each woman of Pasargadæ whenever he came to his old clan-city.

the other hand, could they enjoy the feeling of security which comes from the certainty of prompt advice and succor in emergencies. These considerations, together with others of a purely military nature—the desirability of means for the rapid and unhindered movements of troops—pointed to one great need : roads. Roads then Dareios proceeded to construct, from end to end of his empire, with the energy and thoroughness which he brought to all he undertook. One of these roads we can trace along its entire course, from Susa to the Mediterranean coastland. It did not by any means take the straightest line, for it had several purposes to serve, not the least of which was to connect the principal cities of the west and northwest, those cities which were capitals of provinces, held by Persian governors and garrisons. So the royal road from Susa went to Arbela, thence to Nineveh, thence, touching the Tigris and crossing the Euphrates, to Komana in Cappadocia, from whence, stepping across the Halys by a handsome fortified bridge, it went on through Phrygia to Sardis and the seacoast. Where it just skirts the border of Cilicia (before reaching Komana), it was protected by a garrisoned post in the shape of a gate-building. All along this literally royal highway relays were placed at regular intervals, consisting of station-houses (there were one hundred and eleven between Susa and Sardis), with saddled horses—kept night and day in readiness for any royal couriers who might come along with despatches, orders, or messages from the king. It is astonishing how quickly news and orders spread through the empire by this simple means. Dareios thus originated and instituted a real postal service; nothing was wanting to make it the exact model of our own mail—aside, of course, from the greater facilities for rapid locomotion—but to allow the public the use of the convenience, combining the service of the people and that of the state, with equal advantages to both. How long it was before this obvious and very natural step was taken we do not know. Other roads connected Susa, which, under Dareios I., became to all intents and purposes the capital of the empire, with Babylon, Damascus, and Phœnicia, with Agbatana and Rhagæ and the remote eastern provinces, branching off, near the eastern boundary, to India and to China.

4. There is no doubt that Dareios, when he endowed his empire with that prime promoter of intercourse and civilization—good roads, had the interests of commerce as much in view as political and military considerations. He gave many other proofs of his solicitude for the welfare of his subjects in this respect, and two of the grandest conceptions of modern times arose in his great mind: the necessity of uniform coinage, and the desirability of uniting the Red Sea with the Mediterranean, and thus opening a direct water-route to India, a country to which, moreover, he was the first to send an exploring expedition. He equipped for the purpose a fleet, which, after descending the Indus and emerging from its mouths into the Indian Ocean, sailed round Arabia, entered the Red Sea by the Straits of Bab-el-Mandeb, and pursued its course

northward until it came to anchor in the Bay of Suez. Having thus tested and practically established the possibility of a direct Indian route, Dareios proceeded to finish a canal, begun once on a time by Ramses II., then continued centuries later by Necho I., for the purpose of uniting the Nile with the Red Sea—consequently, indirectly, the Mediterranean with the Indian Ocean. Three granite steles have been discovered at different points of the canal, bearing sculptures and a fourfold set of inscriptions,—in Persian, Scythian, and Assyrian cuneiform, and in Egyptian hieroglyphics; on one of the steles a profile face could be made out, which appears to be an attempt at a real portrait of Dareios. This creation of three great statesmen and conquerors evidently was premature, too much ahead of the times to be generally appreciated, for the canal soon fell into neglect, and though it was cleared of the sand that choked it, and deepened some two hundred years later, it was once more, and this time finally, forgotten and disused. It was reserved for our own age to resume the work and carry it out in a new and probably indestructible form. In the introduction of a uniform gold and silver coinage Dareios was more successful; but the Persian empire was too vast, and its component provinces too many and varied in race, culture, and customs to allow of carrying out the reform to its full extent, and though he consistently tried to call in all the different local coinages by receiving them for taxes, then weighing them, smelting them down, and recoining them in the royal mint after the established standard, we do not see that Babylon, Asia Minor, Phœnicia, or Egypt ever renounced their own monetary standards.

5. Seven years—from 515 to 508 B.C.—were devoted by Dareios to works of peace. This short period sufficed him for all the innovations and reforms which turned an empire loosely composed of disconnected and incongruous elements into a compact state, the first model of modern monarchies. It was also during this interval that he began and in great part achieved the constructions which, being continued by his son and grandson, are the immortal glory of the early Akhæmenian era. We have seen that Susa was considered by foreigners and virtually was the capital of the empire, being fitted for the purpose by its ancient royal associations and especially by its vicinity to such important centres, always needing supervision, as Babylon and Agbatana, as well as to the Syrian provinces and Asia Minor. Yet Susa was by no means exclusively honored by the king's presence. It became customary for him to spend a portion of each year at the other two capitals, from motives both of policy and health, Babylon offering the inducements of a delicious winter climate, while Agbatana, cool and secluded amidst the Zagros highlands, was an incomparable resort for the summer months. But the Persian monarch could not neglect his own native state. He was bound, on the contrary, to endow it with a royal residence that should equal, if not surpass in beauty and magnificence, those of the older rival countries. So Dareios selected a favorable and appropriate site in the finest, healthiest, and most fer-

tile part of Persia proper, and set his artists and craftsmen—many of them, no doubt, Greeks from Ionia—to work, building him a palace and an audience hall worthy of his greatness. A city naturally rose around the pillared marble dwelling of royalty—the specially Persian capital which we know only under the name given to it by the Greeks, Persepolis, "the City of the Persians." What the name was in Persian, has never been known, but it is most probable that the Greek was a translation of it. This is the city which, together with its incomparable citadel of palaces, perished in the conflagration lit by Alexander's own hand, in a fit of drunken fury—a deed the eternal shame of which is scarcely balanced by the conqueror's many great qualities or excused by his extreme youth. The city must have in part survived or been rebuilt, for on its site there stood a Sassanian city, of the name of ISTAKHR. Of this, as well as of its predecessor, nothing remains but the name, and some formless rubbish—fragments of masonry, of earthed up walls, of loose brick, stone, iron—like that which alone marks the place of the once flourishing city of Bagistana at the foot of the historical rock of the same name, where Greek and Sassanian inscriptions and sculptures but poorly contrast with those of the Persian hero.

6. The Chaldeo-Assyrian architectural principle of building palaces on elevated platforms was adopted by the Persian inheritors of that ancient art; but, different therein from the Assyrians, they knew how to save labor and improve their work by making use of natural advantages and local materials. Such were

the considerations which determined the selection of the site fixed on for the new citadel. The mountains, which for some distance follow the course of the Pulwar (see p. 300), on both sides, suddenly open out towards west and east near Istakhr. The eastern spur falls off steeply and ends in a low, wide, and

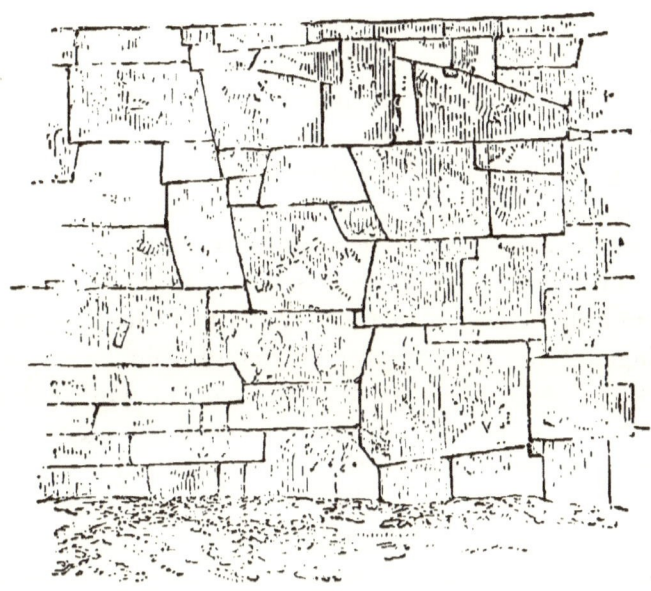

60. MASONRY OF GREAT PLATFORM AT PERSEPOLIS.

nearly flat rocky platform, in shape almost an irregular square, which invites the builder's choice. Comparatively little preliminary work was needed. The rugged and slightly sloping surface was easily converted into a triple terrace, each stage rising about twenty feet above the preceding one—a disposition which gives to the constructions an almost theatrically effective majesty, set off as they were by the dark background of the rock against which the terraces leaned, the almost perpendicular face of the mountain now known as MOUNT RACHMED. The outer edges of the platform were cut down straight to the ground, giving wall-surfaces ranging in height from fifteen to forty feet, according to the unevenness of the soil above which the first terrace rose. These surfaces were cased with blocks of marble furnished by the abundant quarries of Mount Rachmed. The construction of this casing or marble masonry, the stairways which ascend to the first terrace from the plain, and those that connect the three terraces, are, in their way, no less a wonder, as an achievement of unaided human labor, than the pyramids of Egypt or the transport of the Assyrian winged bulls and lions. The single blocks of the casing are from thirty to fifty feet in length (the depth of an average house), not less than eight feet high, and from four to six feet in thickness. Some are still longer; and although no cement or mortar has been used, such is the power of cohesion imparted by the mere tremendous weight of these huge masses, that even now the joints are scarcely perceptible to the eye, and the iron cramps which held them together in places, and which have crumbled away in the course of time, leaving only a rusty mark, are proved to have been virtually a superfluous precaution! (See ill. 60.) This is probably the most perfect existing specimen of that most ancient kind of masonry which has been called Cyclopean, and which may have been borrowed from some of the old Ionian city walls. Wherever this casing has been preserved, it has also kept its admirable polish—so perfect that the marble, to this day, reflects things like a mirror, where the surface has not been in some way injured or defaced by the barbarous and inane performances of tourists, who think they achieve immortality by scratching their worthless names on the most hallowed master-works of antiquity.

7. As to the stairs, which always strike the traveller as the most imposing feature of these grandest of ruins, they are considered the most astonishing construction of the kind in the world. There are several of them, and they are disposed rather irregularly, according to convenience. Even the principal stairway, ascending to the first terrace from the west, is not placed quite in the middle. It is a double flight, with a wide landing half-way up; there are over a hundred steps, each not quite four inches high, so wide that ten riders can commodiously mount them on horseback abreast. The whole is of marble, several steps being hewn out of one block. On the southern side there is another stairway, a single flight, somewhat steeper—thirty steps, cut out of one block! The stairs that lead from one terrace to another are constructed on the same magnificent scale, though somewhat less colossal, and not quite so gently graded as the main stairs. When the visitor has recovered from the bewildering impression hitherto produced by mere size and harmony of lines, his attention is claimed and enthralled by the profuse and exquisite ornamentation which

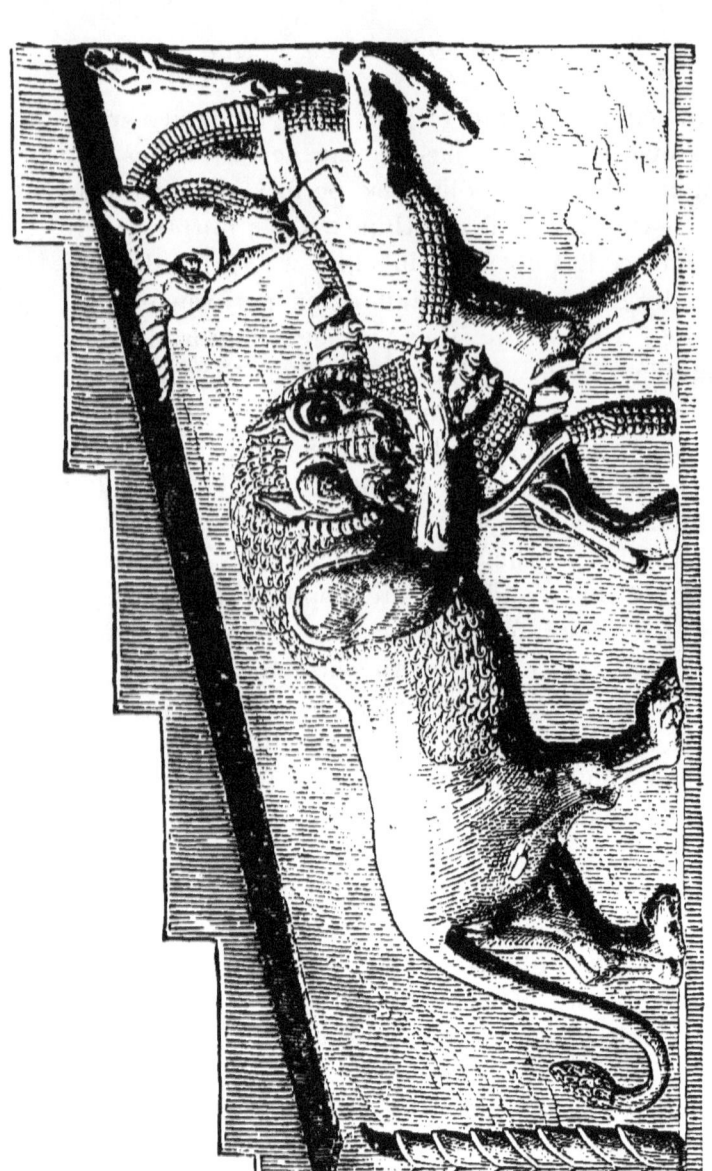

61. LION ATTACKING BULL: BAS-RELIEF REPEATED IN THE OUTER WALLS OF STAIRCASES IN THE PALACES OF DAREIOS AND XERXES AT PERSEPOLIS.

(Followed, where the widening space permits, by processions of guards. See ill. 63.)

covers every available space of the parapet and
outer stair-walls. The natural triangular panels
formed by the first few steps are everywhere filled
out with an artistic composition representing, in

62. PARAPET OF STAIR, PERSEPOLIS.

highly finished relief sculpture, that favorite group
of Oriental mythology—the fight of the Lion and
Bull, in a disposition most skilfully adapted to the
limited space, and followed, as soon as the widening
room permits, by processions of guards, while the

sculptured inside of the parapet or banisters gives the illusion of a long file of soldiers, guests, and courtiers ascending the stairs, one on every step. (See ill. 62.) The decorative effect is completed by Assyrian rosettes, and a peculiar carved pattern used in the lintels of all the doors and windows, a distinctive

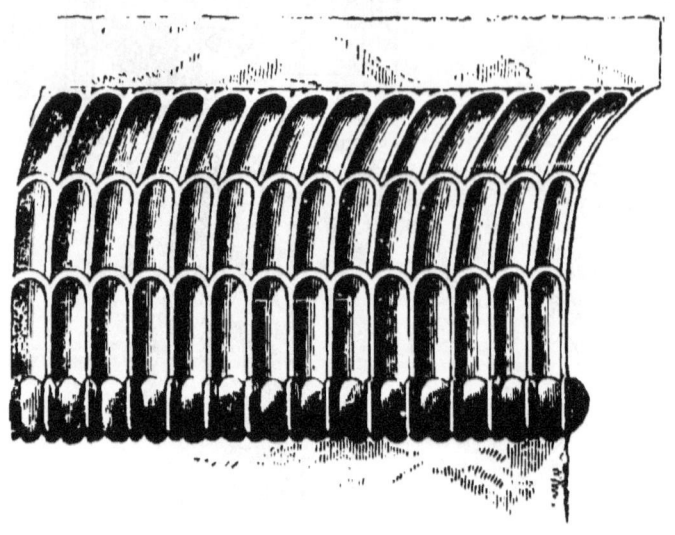

63. CARVED LINTEL OF WINDOWS AND DOORS.
(Persepolis.)

feature of Akhæmenian architectural ornamentation found also in the frieze of the palace at Firûz-abad (see ill. 52), and on the rock-sculptured façade of the royal tombs (see ill. 56).

8. In the southern terrace-wall, Dareios placed four large marble slabs, with the usual trilingual inscription, giving titles, a list of subject nations, and the customary invocation: "May Ahura-Mazda protect this land of Persia from invasion, dearth, and

64. PALACE OF DAREIOS AT PERSEPOLIS
(Actual Condition.)

lie!" (*i. e.*, evil), the exact equivalent of the Chaldean and Assyrian foundation cylinders. The Scythic inscription completes the Persian one by this statement: "Says Darayâvush the king: These great palaces have been built on this spot, where there were no palaces before." A central hall, flanked by two sets of apartments, of four rooms each, with a front entrance composed of a door and four windows opening on a porch supported by four columns, and forming at the same time the landing between the two flights of stairs,—such is the simple and harmonious arrangement which the ruins easily disclose even in their present mutilated condition. The distribution of the doors and windows is one of perfect symmetry, each entrance being in the middle of its wall, greatly differing from the Assyrian halls, where doorways were opened anywhere, near corners as often as not, apparently at random. The size and shape of the apartments, too, are very differently proportioned, quite in accordance with our modern ideas on the subject, showing that no difficulty had to be encountered in roofing the Persian palaces.[*]

9. Behind this palace, the moderate proportions of which show it to have been designed for the king's own dwelling-place, and more to the east, occupying very nearly the centre of the entire platform, is the famous Hall of the Hundred Columns, also built by Dareios I.; its size and peculiar arrangement sufficiently enlighten us on its destination: two hundred and twenty-seven feet every way, with two entrances and several windows in each wall, this magnificent building contained only one vast hall, the roof of

[*] See "Story of Chaldea," pp. 62–68.

65. ATTEMPT AT RESTORATION OF SOUTH FRONT OF PALACE OF DAREIOS AT PERSEPOLIS.
(Partly from the royal tombs, see ills. 55 and 56.)

which, of mighty cedar and cypress beams, was upborne by one hundred columns—ten rows of ten—of that peculiar and matchlessly fanciful type which is the most distinctive feature of Akhæmenian architecture. Tall and slender, they rested lightly on their inverted flower-base, carrying the raftered ceiling proudly and with ease on the strong bent necks of the animals which adorned their capitals. (See ills. 49-51). We have here the throne and audience hall, the reception and banqueting hall of the great Dareios. If nothing else, the sculptures in the eight doorways would assure us of the fact. Here we see the king seated on his throne, which is supported by rows of warriors, in the flowing Median garb or the tight-fitting Persian doublet and hose, or of figures personating subject nations. (See ill. 54.) Here he receives ambassadors or visitors bringing presents. His figure is larger than nature, to elevate him above common humanity, and the attendant who stands behind the throne with the fly-flapper wears the *paitidâna*, as though officiating before the sacred fire (see p. 114), while the master of ceremonies holds his hand before his mouth, and all who approach the royal presence keep their hands in their long sleeves in token of peaceful intentions. There again the king is presented to us as the earthly image of Ahura-Mazda, fulfilling his god-given mission of warring with and annihilating the evil creation of Angra-Mainyu, by stabbing an ugly Daêva in the shape of a monstrous composite animal, after the manner of the Chaldean wicked demons*—the "Ahrimanian Beast," as it

* See "Story of Chaldea," ills. 54 and 55, 72, 73, and 74.

66. DAREIOS FIGHTING A MONSTER—A DAÉVA OR "AHRIMANIAN BEAST."
(Persepolis, Hall of the Hundred Columns.)

has been called. At some of the entrances winged bulls mount their watch, but slightly altered from their Assyrian prototypes, (see ill. 48). It is easy to imagine the royal throne placed somewhere towards the end of the middle aisle, and the vast hall adorned and, if need be, partitioned by curtains and hangings of precious stuffs, made priceless by costly dyes and embroideries, and which, according as they were looped up or left to fall to the ground, concealed the royal majesty or allowed it to shine forth on the courtiers and guests. The rings and other appurtenances for regulating the hangings must have been somehow attached to the roof-rafters, which, like the ceiling, were almost certainly gilt; indeed, it is very likely that the inner surface of the walls may have been cased in gold plating also, after the manner of the old palaces at Agbatana; a number of short metal tacks have been found, which could scarcely have served any purpose but that of fastening such platings.

10. Pillared halls and porticos being an essentially Aryan form of architecture, there is no doubt that when Dareios built his residence at Susa he added to it a reception hall similar to that at Persepolis, and, from what the latter teaches us, we can have no difficulty in picturing to ourselves the royal banquet described in the Book of Esther, as given at that capital,—perhaps on the king's birthday, or at New-Year, the two great occasions of feasting and merry-making at the Persian court,—by Xerxes, the son of Dareios, whom the Hebrews have named Ahasuerus:

67. DOOR OF PALACE OF DAREIOS, PERSEPOLIS.

"Now it came to pass . . . that in those days, when the king Ahasuerus sat on the throne of his kingdom, which was in Shushan the palace, . . . he made a feast unto all his princes and servants ; the power of Persia and Media, the nobles and princes of the provinces, being before him. When he showed the riches of his glorious kingdom, and the honor of his excellent majesty many days. . . . The king made a feast unto all the people that were present in Shushan the palace . . . in the court of the garden of the king's palace ; where were white, green, and blue hangings, fastened with cords of fine linen and purple to silver rings and pillars of marble ; the beds [i. e., the couches or seats] were of gold and silver upon a pavement of red, and blue, and white, and black marble." And they gave them drink in vessels of gold . . . and royal wine in abundance according to the state of the king . . . " (Book of Esther, ch. I., 1-7).

11. This same Xerxes, the son of Dareios, had a palace of his own at Persepolis, of comparatively small dimensions, but his principal construction there was a fine peristyle or waiting-hall which he built at the head of the great western staircase. That such was its destination appears from the sculptures, as well as from the inscription, which calls it a "gate," and we can easily imagine some such apartment, where ambassadors, visitors, petitioners, tribute-bringers, could await the royal pleasure, processions muster and form, etc., to be a desirable and even necessary addition to the throne-and audience-hall. Behind the "gate-building" came another pair of stairs, also constructed by Xerxes, and leading up to the second terrace, on which he had erected, a little apart from his father's palace, a new reception-hall on a scale scarcely less magnificent than that of Dareios. Seventeen of the seventy-two black marble columns are still standing, though in a

68. PILLARS OF THE HALL OF XERXES.
(Black Marble. Height from base to capital—41 feet; of capital—16 feet; circumference—16 feet; 52 flutings.)

sadly mutilated condition, and bear witness to the splendor of the building, which seems to have been unenclosed by walls. The airiness of such an open colonnade would be particularly suited for summer festivals and receptions, and it may be that it was the need of a cooler audience-hall which caused this one to be built. Ruins of palaces belonging to later Akhæmenian kings, and of the same architectural type, are scattered somewhat irregularly on different points of the platform, but none are either so extensive or interesting as those we have attempted to describe.

12. It is remarkable that nothing is left standing of the masonry of the Persepolitan palaces but the doorways and windows, with their posts and lintels, all of huge marble blocks, with no vestige of walls. These ruins thus present the exact counterpart of those of Assyrian palaces, where nothing is left but the massive walls. Mr. Dieulafoy, guided by his observations and actual discoveries at Susa, as well as by examination of the rubbish at Persepolis, suggests a more than plausible reconstruction of the missing masonry:

"I think," he says, "that the Akhæmenian palaces, with the exception of the columns, doors, windows, and stairs, were built in brick cased with tiles; that these tiles, colored in two tones, light gray and a grayish rose-color,* were disposed in mosaic patterns; that the high cornice above the denticules of the entablature was ornamented with bas-reliefs in blue tiles representing bulls †; that into the composition of the outer casing of the walls there entered a certain amount of blue tile. . . . ‡

* Something like what we call "crushed-strawberry."
† Just as possibly lions or dogs.
‡ *Revue Archéologique*, Juillet, 1885.

69. GENERAL VIEW OF THE PALACE OF DAREIOS AND THE HALL OF XERXES, PERSEPOLIS.

In another place, however, Mr. Dieulafoy admits not having found many fragments of tiles at Persepolis, whence he infers that the decoration in glazed tile-work was not any thing as prevalent there as it was at Susa, where in fact *all* the ornamentation appears to have been in that material, probably in imitation of Nebuchadrezzar's palace at Babylon. In fact the near and ever open quarries of Mt. Rachmed were irresistibly suggestive of sculpture, so the sterner and more solidly magnificent Assyrian mode of decoration prevailed. Unlike the Assyrian sculptures, however, the Persian ones do not deal with historical subjects; there are no battles or sieges, no marches in distant lands, no royal hunts, or attempts at landscapes; all that meets our eye brings before us various moments of court ceremonial regulated by the strictest of etiquettes. Here we see the king on his throne, there he meets us, seemingly walking into his own palace, through its main door (see ill. 67); there again along the outer wall of the broad stair-landing, his guards are ranged in effigy as the living ones no doubt stood in the same place, day after day, presenting arms. (See ill. 65). The only alternation from court pageantry is to religious compositions, and of these the number is limited to one or two subjects of a set, unchanging type. But if Persian art was more restricted in its range of subjects, it was freer than the Assyrian in its treatment of the human figure. Sculptors and tile-painters had undoubtedly seen Greek models and had some Greek training; very likely the work was directed by Greek artists, and the influence tells in the natural handling of the draperies and the disappearance of those muscular exaggerations which are so offensive in the Assyrian reproductions of the human form.

13. A survey of the Persepolitan monuments would be incomplete without a mention of the three royal tombs cut in the rocky side of Mt. Rachmed, just behind the palaces of the living. They are in every particular similar to those at Nakhshi-Rustem, making with these seven in all, which leaves only two of the Akhæmenian kings unaccounted for. Here as there, the door in the sculptured front is a sham one, not made to open, and it has been as yet impossible to discover the real entrance to the mostly capacious sepulchral chambers behind. All we know, from Greek historians, is that the bodies were raised by means of windlasses to be deposited in their place of rest. The openings which are found at present have evidently been made by plunderers. All the tombs were found empty and robbed. As the tomb of Dareios I. is the only one that has an inscription, the others could not be identified.

XV.

DAREIOS I.: THIRD PERIOD: FOREIGN WARS.

1. THAT Dareios, after several years of peaceable and useful work, should have deliberately set out on a series of foreign wars, instead of staying at home to enjoy and let his people enjoy their hard-earned prosperity, really seems sheer perversity; unless, as has been suggested, "he felt that for a nation like the Persians war and conquest were a necessity, in order to preserve their energy and escape the danger of becoming effeminate in the enjoyment of wealth."* His thoughts turned quite naturally to the west and north. All that was to be reached in Asia being already under the Persian domination, Europe was now to be brought under it, and of course there was no lack of good reasons, commercial and political, for such a course. In the first place the Black Sea was to be converted into a Persian lake; the nations on its eastern and southern shore obeyed the rule of Susa and Persepolis, and those on the western and northern shores—the Thracians and the Scythians—should close the circle. Moreover, they were strong, independent, half-barbarous, and might become dangerous neighbors. So Dareios determined, in a vague sort of way, to go over and conquer Scythia.

* Justi, "Geschichte des alten Persiens."

He knew the way was long; so it was to Egypt or to Bactria; he knew there were some unusual obstacles—a sea arm and a great wild river: they should be bridged; as for the country and the people, he knew nothing about them, indeed,—but others had submitted, why should not they?

2. In this latter respect the Greeks had greatly the advantage of him; they did know a good deal about the Scythians and their country. The double line of their colonies which gradually extended along the shores of Thracia and Asia Minor had reached, from river to river, the mouths of the great Thracian river, the ISTER (DANUBE), and those of the numerous Scythian (now Russian) ones, along the northern shore of the Black Sea. These rivers flowed through vast and fertile lands, of which they brought the products straight into Greek hands, enlarging and enriching the Greek storehouses and commercial stations. One of these, OLBIA, at the mouth of the HYPANIS (BUG), grew into a large and luxurious city by nothing but its corn-trade and its fisheries. From all accounts, it must have held very much the place that Odessa now holds, from the same causes and in the same conditions. As Southern Russia now supplies half the world with wheat, so it did then, as far as the "world" went at the time, and the entire export trade was centred in Olbia as it now is in Odessa. The next great station was BYZANTIUM, another Greek colony, situated on the Bosporus, where Constantinople now stands. The ships that had taken their lading of corn at Olbia had to carry them out through the Bosporus, so

Byzantium held then, as it does now, the key of the entire Black-Sea trade. Some seventy years after the time of Herodotus we find from contemporary evidence that 600,000 bushels of Scythian corn went to Athens alone every year, and when Philip of Macedon, the father of Alexander, wished to starve Athens, he tried to gain possession of Byzantium. It is probably owing to the importance which the people of the vast region answering to Southern Russia had for the Greeks, both of the colonies and at home, that they took some pains to explore it, and their knowledge of it, as imparted to us by Herodotus, who himself visited Olbia and a portion of the surrounding country, is far less defective than on many much less remote places. Indeed, the descriptions of Herodotus have become more and more the base of all geographical and archæological research on the subject of ancient Russia, and where they bear on climate and the outer features of the country, they are still found amusingly correct.

3. Nothing can be truer than the general remark he makes: "The country has no marvels except its rivers, which are larger and more numerous than those of any other land. These and the vastness of the great plain are worthy of note. . . ." Then again: "The land is level, well-watered, and abounding in pasture; while the rivers which traverse it are almost equal in number to the canals of Egypt. Of these I shall only mention the most famous and such as are navigable to some distance from the sea.". He proceeds to describe the five chief rivers of that part of the world—the ISTER (DANUBE), the TYRAS

(DNIESTR), the HYPANIS (BUG), the BORYSTHENES (DNIEPR), the TANAÏS (DON), and a few more which it is not so easy to identify. The Danube he calls " of all the rivers with which we are acquainted the mightiest," and admires its volume of water swelled by so many tributaries, each itself a great river. But of the Dniepr (Borythenes), he speaks with the enthusiasm which that most beautiful and bountiful of streams has never ceased to excite in travellers or its own country people:

"Next to the Ister," he says, "it is the greatest of them all, and in my judgment it is the most productive river, not merely in Scythia, excepting only the Nile, with which no stream can possibly compare. It has upon its banks the loveliest and most excellent pasturages for cattle; it contains abundance of the most delicious fish; its water is most pleasant to the taste; its stream is limpid, while all the other rivers near it are muddy; the richest harvests spring up along its course, and, where the ground is not sown, the heaviest crops of grass; while salt forms in great plenty at the mouth without human aid, and large fish are taken in it of the sort called *antacæi* (*sturgeon*), without any prickly bones, and good for pickling."

Every word of this applies now, even to that last touch about the sturgeon, which is to our day a favorite fish for pickling. He is not less correct when he speaks of the " Woodland " which stretches by the lower course of the Dniepr, where the river divides into many arms, and which, though not to be compared in thickness with the forests of a more northern tract, presents a refreshing contrast to the absolute barrenness of the surrounding steppes; or when he places the most fertile lands higher up along the course of the river, and describes them as being settled with a nation which he calls " Husbandmen," or "Agricultural Scythians," whose pursuit was farming, and who raised most of the corn that was sold at Olbia and exported. Beyond these he places a desert region or steppe-land, ranged over by nomadic Scythians, and there, at no great distance from the river, he tells us the tombs of the Scythian kings were situated. Modern research has proved this particular also to be correct, by discovering and exploring the largest of the innumerable barrows or mounds which there cover the plain, varying its flatness with some undulation, and leading us to think that those steppes served as a burying-ground, not to the kings alone, but to the nation at large.

4. As he gets farther away from the sea-shore and the Greek settlements, his descriptions naturally become less distinct, less accurate, and at last grow quite vague and fabulous in their details. But even then a good many traits remain which are easy to recognize or, at least, to interpret. So his account of the climate, as far as his personal observation goes, is perfectly true to nature as well as amusing with the quaintness of the impression produced on a Greek by the to him unfamiliar phenomenon of a frozen ground:

"The whole district whereof we have discoursed," he says, "has winters of exceeding rigor. . . . The frost is so intense, that water poured upon the ground does not form mud, but if a fire be lighted on it, mud is produced. The sea freezes . . . At that season the Scythians make warlike expeditions upon the ice. . . . For winter there is scarcely any rain worth mentioning, while in summer it never gives over raining . . and thunder comes only in summer, when it is very heavy. . . . Horses bear the winter well, cold as it is . ."

Now there is not one word in this that does not tell. But when we come to such a passage as the following, it is not hard to say that observation has given place to hearsay:

"Above, to the northward of the farthest dwellers in Scythia, the country is said to be concealed from sight and made impassable by reason of the feathers which are shed abroad abundantly. The earth and air are full of them, and this it is which prevents the eye from obtaining any view of the region."

We are familiar through Grimm's nursery-tales with the old German snow-myth, of Frau Holla emptying her feather-beds, and so we are pleased and amused to see our dear old friend's good common-sense giving him the clue to what seemed to him at first only an absurd rumor:

"With respect to the feathers which are said by the Scythians to fill the air and to prevent persons from penetrating into the remoter parts of the continent, or even having any view of those regions, my opinion is, that in the countries above Scythia it always snows, less, of course, in the summer, than in the winter time. Now snow when it falls looks like feathers, as every one is aware, who has seen it come down close to him. These northern regions, therefore, are uninhabitable by reason of the severity of the winter; and the Scythians, with their neighbors, call the snow-flakes feathers, because, I think, of the likeness which they bear to them."

One can gather a good deal more valuable information through fanciful stories about cannibals, one-eyed men, and griffins. It is plain that the gold which the latter guard is that of the Oural mines, which certainly were known to the Greeks of Olbia and the other Black Sea colonies; and as certainly there was an overland route frequented by Greek traders; it is said that seven interpreters were needed for the journey, the way lying through nations speaking seven different languages. It is very possible that the Greeks purposely kept these things rather dark, so as not to divulge the secret of their commercial operations and the sources of their greatest profits.

5. The country of which Herodotus gives us so detailed and animated an account answers to the southern half of Russia. Of the nations which inhabited or roamed those vast and in great part wild regions, he only gives us the names as far as they were known to him, and in the Greek forms, which make foreign places and people so hard to identify; as to their manners and customs, he dismisses them mostly with this sweeping and uncomplimentary remark: "The Euxine (Black) Sea, where Dareios now went to war, has nations dwelling around it, with the one exception of the Scythians, more unpolished than those of any other region that we know of." Accordingly he devotes to the Scythians many most interesting pages. In the first place he notes that they really were named SKOLOTI, but the Greeks had got into the habit of calling them Scythians. This agrees with what we know from other sources, namely, that "Scythians" was not a race-name at all, but one promiscuously used for all remote, little known, especially nomadic peoples of the north and northeast, denoting tribes as well of Turanian as of Indo-European stock; to the latter the Scythians of Russia are now universally admitted to have belonged. He divides the nations into the "Husbandmen," the only portion of it that was settled and given to farming

(see p. 414), the "Royal Scythians," including probably the royal and noble clans, and "the wandering Scythians, who neither plow nor sow," whose country, "the whole of which is quite bare of trees," answers to the immense steppe region between the Dniepr and the Don. These nomads, like many Turanian tribes of our own day in Eastern Russia and Central Asia, followed their herds and flocks from pasture to pasture, living in wagons drawn by oxen or tents carried on wagons and easily planted into the ground. This mode of life greatly impressed Herodotus, as implying the peculiar manner of warfare, the advantages of which the Persians had just found out to their cost. Only he ascribes to premeditated wisdom what was merely a natural outcome of all the conditions of their existence.

"The Scythians," he says, "have in one respect, and that the very most important of all those that fall under man's control, shown themselves wiser than any nation upon the face of the earth. The one thing of which I speak is the contrivance by which they make it impossible for the enemy who invades them to avoid destruction, while they themselves are entirely out of his reach, unless it pleases them to engage with him. Having neither cities nor forts, and carrying their dwellings with them wherever they go; accustomed, moreover, one and all of them, to shoot from horseback, and living not by husbandry, but by their cattle, their wagons the only houses that they possess, how can they fail of being unconquerable, and unassailable even?"

6. With the appearance and costume of these ancestors of the Russians we are familiar chiefly from the marvellously beautiful and finished works of art found in a Scythian royal tomb at KERTCH, ancient PANTICAPÆON (a colony of Miletus on the

extreme eastern point of the Crimean peninsula), and consisting principally in vases of silver and electron. They are two or three hundred years later in date than the time we have arrived at, and of pure Greek workmanship; but they most certainly, and all the more faithfully, are portrayed from nature; the types they represent could not have changed in so short a time, since now, after a lapse of two thousand years, we recognize in them those of our modern Russian peasantry, where it has not been modified beyond recognition by contact with foreigners or new-fangled imported fashions. The costume too—the belted *kaftan* with its border of fur and its embroideries, the trousers struck into the soft boot (probably felt), and, in some cases, the bandaged feet—is worn, scarcely changed at all, in every Russian village. Their fondness for vapor-baths, also, though they knew them only in a rudimentary and barbarous form, has descended to the present owners of the land. As for any others of their customs, they appear savage and crude in the extreme in Herodotus' narrative, though hardly more so than those of many German and other warlike tribes in the early part of the Middle Ages. It is curious that he asserts that they took their vanquished enemies' scalps, and describes the process exactly as the American Indians have always practised it. But they must have surpassed even these in fierceness, if it is true that they not only hung the scalps to their bridle-rein, taking pride in these trophies in proportion to their numbers, but " made themselves cloaks by sewing a quantity together." "Others," we are told, " flay the right

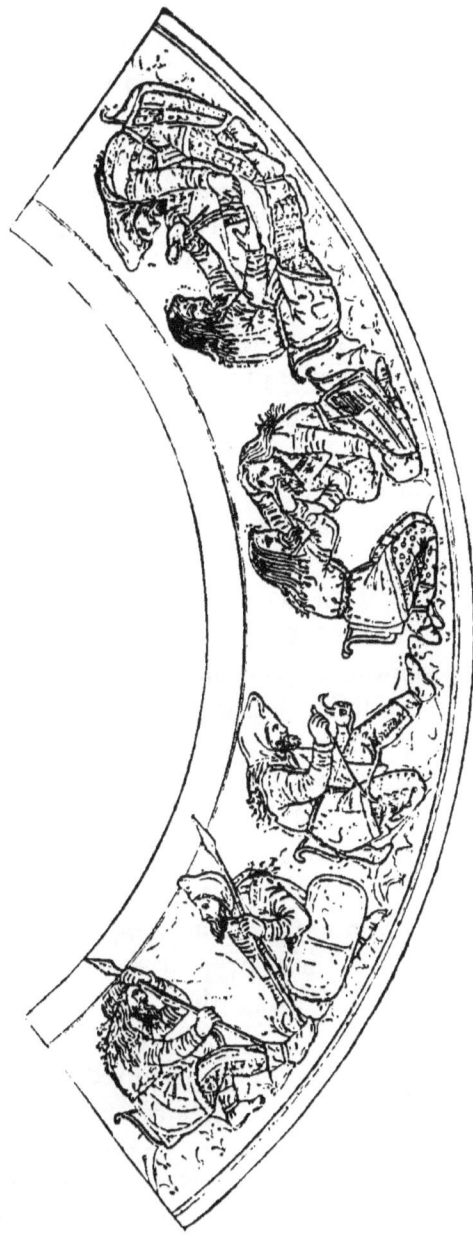

70. SCYTHIANS AFTER A BATTLE. FROM AN ELECTRON VASE OF GREEK WORKMANSHIP, FOUND IN THE ROYAL TOMB AT KERTCH (ANCIENT PANTICAPÆON).

arms of their enemies, and make of the skin which is stripped off with the nails hanging to it" (as we do of lions' and tigers' skins), "a covering for their quivers." Such things are entirely foreign and, one would think, repugnant to Greek culture, which is generally mild and temperate; yet Herodotus merely observes that "the skin of a man is thick and glossy, and would in whiteness surpass almost all other hides!" Nor does he express any horror at their way of using their enemies' skulls as drinking-cups, at feasts, receptions of guests, and other solemn occasions, after casing them on the outside with leather, and—if rich enough—lining the inside with gold. True, he remarks in one place, that "their customs are not such as he admires,"—a blame which probably is meant to cover these traits, and some others far more objectionable, because implying cruelty to the living. Such were their human sacrifices and especially the funerals of their kings. Not only they put to death and burned with him at least one of his wives and all his chief body-servants together, with his favorite horse or horses, but after a year had elapsed, strangled fifty more youths from among his best attendants, and as many of the finest horses, and disposed them around the mound, the men astride of the horses, in ghastly imitation of a mounted guard of honor. Stakes passed through the bodies maintain them in the required position.

7. Such were the country and nation which Dareios, surely somewhat lightly, determined to invade, never doubting but that he would, without any very uncommon difficulty, add it to his empire.

71. GREEK SILVER VASE, FOUND AT KERTCH (ANCIENT PANTICAPÆON).

He would on the same occasion make sure of Thracia and the Greek cities on both sides of the Bosporus and Hellespont, as well as of several Greek islands. It is said that one of his brothers entreated him to desist, and tried to make him realize the great difficulties he was going to encounter. But his mind was made up, and he sent messengers to all the Greek cities of Asia Minor, with orders to equip and man six hundred ships with three rows of oars (*trieres*), which were to sail up to the Bosporus and there to build a bridge of ships across the straits, while he himself collected the contingents of the several Asiatic nations. His army numbered 700,000 when he led it from Susa. He found all done and the fleet assembled when he arrived at the Bosporus, which he immediately crossed, leaving the bridge in the charge of part of the fleet and the Greek cities along both sides on the Bosporus, although they had but recently been conquered and annexed. He had no difficulty with the Thracians: they either submitted as he passed or had given " earth and water " to his envoys before. Only one nation, close to the Danube, attempted resistance, but was crushed by numbers. Besides, he did not go very far inland, but skirted—at a distance—the sweep of the Black Sea, accompanied and supported by the fleet. The trysting-place was the mouths of the Danube, which the ships entered, while the land army stopped, until the river was bridged, just behind the Delta, *i. e.*, the place where it separates into several branches. The ships sent by the Ionian cities were commanded by the respective tyrants of these cities, and to them Dareios entrusted the keeping of the bridge during his absence, appointing a certain time during which they were to keep faithful watch, and after which they might, if they did not see him or his army, give him up for lost and return to their homes.

8. From the moment that Dareios had crossed the Danube and plunged into the land of Scythia, which began at once on the opposite bank, everything about his movements becomes uncertain. The detailed account of his marches and countermarches in all possible directions, as given by Herodotus, lacks consistency, or rather common-sense, and can easily be seen to come through the magnifying medium of Scythian legends, not improved by Greek rendering. What we can gather with certainty is that the Scythians, after sending their families away to distant pastures and to various neighbors for safe-keeping, immediately engaged in their own peculiar mode of warfare—that warfare which Herodotus so highly admires (see p. 419), and which consisted in drawing the enemy farther and farther into the country, never actually fighting, but always harassing him, so as to wear and starve him out, without ever staking their fate on the issue of a battle. Detachments of their light infantry—and in fact they were *all* light infantry—began to show themselves three days' march from the Danube. The ponderous Persian host at once prepared for an engagement, and followed, expecting that the enemies were showing them the way to a convenient battle-ground. Thus Dareios committed his one and fatal mistake : he al-

lowed himself to be decoyed away from the seashore, and consequently cut off from retreat and supplies alike. It was long before he discovered the trick, which was continually repeated, with unvaried success, and when he did he was very far north, still pursuing an elusive, unfindable foe. The army by this time must have greatly suffered from want, not of water, but of provisions. For there were no cultivated lands to be plundered, no cities to be sacked, and the flocks and herds were kept out of the way. At length the Persians found themselves in a land of woods and marshes, by the sources of some of the great rivers. Here Herodotus gives a little incident which has a great look of genuineness about it:

> "This had gone on so long, and seemed so interminable, that Dareios at last sent a horseman to the Scythian king, with the following message: 'Thou strange man, why dost thou keep on flying before me, when there are two things thou mightest do so easily? If thou deemest thyself able to resist my arms, cease thy wanderings and come, let us engage in battle. Or if thou art conscious that my strength is greater than thine, even so shouldst thou cease to run away; thou hast but to bring thy lord earth and water, and to come at once to a conference.' To this message the Scythian king replied: This is my way, Persian. I never fear men or fly from them. I have not done so in times past, nor do I now fly from thee. There is nothing new or strange in what I do: I only follow my common mode of life in peaceful years. . . . If, however, you must needs come to blows with us speedily, look you now, there are our fathers' tombs: seek them out and attempt to meddle with them, and then we shall see whether or no we will fight with you. Till ye do this, be sure that we shall not join battle, unless it pleases us. . . . Earth and water I do not send; but thou shalt soon receive more suitable gifts.'"

9. Still the Scythians ceased to draw the Persians on, and began, instead, to harass them with unex-

pected attacks and cavalry night skirmishes. And soon came the mysteriously promised gifts.

" . . . The Scythian princes despatched a herald to the Persian camp with presents for the king. These were a bird, a mouse, a frog, and five arrows. The Persians asked the bearer to tell them what these gifts might mean ; but he made answer that he had no orders save to deliver them and to return again with all speed. If the Persians were wise, he added, they would find out the meaning for themselves. So when they heard this, they held a council to consider the matter. Dareios gave it as his opinion that the Scythians intended a surrender of themselves and all their country, both land and water, into his hands. This he conceived to be the meaning of the gifts, because the mouse is an inhabitant of the earth and eats the same food as man, while the frog passes his life in the water; the bird bears a great resemblance to the horse, and the five arrows might signify the surrender of all their power. To the explanation of Dareios, Gobryas, one of the seven conspirators against the Magian " (and the king's father-in-law), " offered another, which was as follows : ' Unless, Persians, ye can turn into birds and fly up into the sky, or become mice and burrow under-ground, or make yourselves frogs and take refuge in the fens, ye will never make your escape from this land, but die pierced by our arrows.' " *

This explanation, under existing circumstances, struck Dareios himself and all the other Persians as by far the more probable of the two ; and they lost no time in acting on the hint, if perchance it were not yet too late. Besides, they were now seized with the very reasonable fear that the Ionians might have broken faith with them, or a detachment of Scythians might have overwhelmed the keepers and destroyed the bridge. So they swiftly retraced their steps, and made for the Danube in as direct a line as they could, with their ignorance of the country.

* There is of course no proof of this story, but it is a pretty one, well in keeping, and not intrinsically improbable.

They had not now to complain of the Scythians' unwillingness to attack and fight, but were glad when they succeeded in keeping them off their track, or in deceiving them by little devices, such as keeping their tents pitched and their camp-fires burning while they stole away at dawn.

10. Meanwhile, the disaster which they dreaded was very near actually happening. Some Scythians had had a parley with the Ionian princes and urged them to "break the bridge and hasten back to their homes, rejoicing that they were free, and thanking the gods and the Scythians." The temptation was great. Here was a chance at one stroke to restore the liberties of all the Greek cities, and MILTIADES, a young Athenian nobleman, who was the chief, or rather king, of the peninsula which skirts the Hellespont on the European side, and who had but lately submitted to the Persian rule, was all for following the Scythians' advice, on patriotic grounds, thinking it a shame to miss such an opportunity of throwing off a yoke which, mild as it might be, still was a form of bondage, of slavery. The Ionian princes, at the war council which was held on the subject, were ready to join him, when the chief among them, HISTIAIOS, tyrant of Miletus, who enjoyed greater weight and influence from being the ruler of the first among the Ionian cities, reminded them that it would be entirely against their interests to break their trust. "It is through Darius," he said, "that we enjoy our thrones in our several states. If his power be overturned, I cannot continue lord of Miletus, nor ye of your cities. For there is not one of them which

will not prefer democracy to kingly rule." This argument was found so persuasive, that when the votes were collected, Miltiades saw himself alone of his opinion. It was therefore decided to hold the bridge for Dareios. Historians have praised or blamed this decision, according as they took the standpoint of patriotism and love of liberty, or of duty to a trust. It was, however, not this latter feeling, noble under any circumstances, but purely selfish considerations which influenced the Ionian princes, proving, at all events, the wisdom of Kyros' policy in placing native tyrants over the cities, then showing them favor, honor,—and trust. The newly annexed cities on the Bosporus showed more patriotic zeal, and destroyed or damaged the bridge left in their charge, so that Dareios, who was now so hotly pursued by the Scythians, even after having recrossed the Danube, that he could not shake them off on the march through Thracia, down to the very seashore, had to change his route, and cross the Hellespont on ships; nor did he feel himself safe until he reached Sardis. Thus ended this extraordinary undertaking, the only absolutely unreasonable act that can be charged to this great king. Yet his losses were not so great as his recklessness deserved; they did not amount to more than one tenth of his army. And one advantage was gained: the subjection of the Greek colonies all along the Thracian shore, the Hellespont, and the Bosporus. These latter had to pay dearly for their act of rebellion, for Dareios, as he crossed back to Asia, left a general behind, with another tenth of his army, on purpose to punish them and keep the others in obedience.

11. To the last period of Dareios' reign also belong the expeditions, at one end of the empire, into Penjâb, and at the opposite end, west of Egypt, across the desert, into the territory of Kyrênê and Barka. But neither of the expeditions was conducted personally by the king; neither were they of much importance in the general history of the times, nor had any very notable results, except that the near approach of a Persian army caused Carthage to enter into negotiations and buy herself off from a threatened invasion, by a tribute which she paid regularly for several years. Very different is the interest which attaches to the movements of the Greek cities in Ionia and the adjoining province. For there a beginning had been made, a leaven had been stirred, which was not to be quelled with the ease that the Persian king had encountered till now in his dealings with these portions of his empire. The spirit of independence shown by the northern cities had proved contagious after all, and revolts and conspiracies against the foreign rule broke out here and there. The centre and soul of these conspiracies was Miletus, whose love of liberty Histiaios had well judged. The beautiful city was besieged, taken, and destroyed almost entirely,—to the unutterable consternation of the entire Hellenic world. Her citizens were deported to the Persian Gulf, her youths and maidens taken for booty or sold for slaves, while the rebellious cities on the Hellespont were burned down. The Persian rule, as it became older, was gradually changing its character—growing heavier and harsher, and, when opposed, drifting

72. PAINTING ON GREEK VASE.

Middle row of figures: Dareios on his throne discusses with his council the Greek campaign. Lower row: The provinces of Asia do homage and bring treasure for the war. Upper row: Hellas, protected by her national deities

into ordinary Oriental cruelty. Besides, Dareios had returned home bitterly mortified and irritated by his bootless and senseless expedition into the wilds of Scythia, and gladly vented his irritation on those who displeased him. His great grudge was now against the Greeks—not those of Asia, but those across the sea, the people of Hellas. He knew that they were one nation with these rebellious colonies, that they gave them support, encouragement, and sympathy, and determined to make an end of the entire obnoxious race. Little did he dream that the mortification and losses of his Scythian campaign were as nothing to those which he was to experience at the hands of this nestful of traders, seamen, farmers, and craftsmen; that Miltiades, after being overruled by his timid and selfish compeers on the Danube, would yet satisfy his patriotic ambition, and, as the hero of Marathon, be a check on the overwhelming deluge from the East; or that not only not he himself, but his children, his children's children should ever be able to achieve the task which he now undertook, with all the caution and preparation of a wise general, indeed, but with absolute faith in its quick and easy completion.

<small>Battle of Marathon, 490 B.C.</small>

But this glorious struggle and triumph of the few lifted to superhuman heroism by an ennobling moral principle, as against the merely brutal force of numbers, does not properly belong any more to the history of the East, nor to that of remote antiquity: it is the dawn of a new star, in the West, and of times which, from their spirit, actors, and achievements, may almost be called modern. At the bottom of the new departure lies the difference between the ideals—the conception of the beauty and dignity of political and social life—set up by the Oriental and Western man: "A good master!" is the prayer and ideal of the Asiatic. "No master! Liberty at any price, as the highest good in itself!" is that of the Greek. And the Greek wins the day, for his own time and for his own race, and for future times and races to come.

INDEX.

A.

Aahmes, see Amasis.
Ab-Karkha, ancient Choaspes, river, 334.
Achæans, an early Greek nation, of Pelasgic stock, 202, 203.
Aderbeidjan, see Atropatêne.
Âdityas, a group of Aryan deities, 41.
Aêshma-Daêva, first of Daêvas, 98; see Asmodeus.
Agamtunu, see Agbatana.
Agbatana (modern Hamadân), capital of Media, 262; palace and citadel of, 263–266.
Ahasuerus, Hebrew name of Xerxes, 404.
Ahi, the Aryan Cloud-Serpent, 47.
Ahriman, see Angra-Mainyu.
Ahuna-Vairya (Parsi Honover), the most sacred and potent text, 86; its power over the fiends, 87.
Ahura-Mazda, the supreme god of Eran, meaning of the name, 61; originally a sky-god, 61, 62; his connection with Mithra, 62, 63; the chief of the Amesha-Spentas, 75; their creator, 77.
Airyâna-Vaêja, the primeval home of the Âryas, 37.
Aji-Dahâka (same as Aji), 83.
Aji, the Fiend-Serpent, 80; see Ahi.
Akhæmenes (Hakhâmanish), prince of the Pasargadæ, the founder of the Persian hereditary monarchy, 279, 286.

Akhæmenidæ, name of the dynasty founded by Akhæmenes, 279; genealogical table of the, 287.
Ako-manô, "Worst Mind," opposed to Vohu-manô, 103.
Alarodians, supplanted by Aryans in Urartu, 187.
Alexander the Great of Macedon burns down Persepolis, 27.
Alborj, see Hara-Berezaiti.
Allegory, as different from myth, 72.
Alyattês, king of Lydia, aggrandizes Lydia, 219; his war with Media, 220; makes peace with Kyaxares and marries his daughter to Kyaxares' son Astyages, 221; the greatest of the Mermnadæ, 306.
Amardians, or Mardians, one of the nomadic Persian tribes, probably un-Aryan, 278.
Amasis (Aahmes) dethrones Hophra and usurps the crown of Egypt, 307; his liberal policy obnoxious to the Egyptians, 347, 348; prepares against a Persian invasion under Kambyses, 348, 349.
Amazons, origin of the fable, 198–201.
Ameretât, see Haurvatât and Ameretât.
Amesha-Spentas, the seven "Bountiful Immortals," 74–78; the Amshaspands or archangels of the Parsis, 74.
Ammon, temple of, and expedi-

tion sent against the Ammonians by Kambyses, 355.

Amshaspands, see Amesha-Spentas.

Amytis, or Amuhia, queen of Nebuchadrezzar of Babylon, 221; the Hanging Gardens constructed for, 234.

———, daughter of Astyages of Media, probably married to Kyros, 295.

Anduan, see Anshan.

Angra-Mainyu (Ahriman), the Arch-Fiend, 88.

Anquetil Duperron, French scholar and traveller, his journey to India in search of Parsi manuscripts, 8-11; his success, 11, 12; abused by William Jones and other scholars, *ib.*; his real value, 13.

Anshan, also Anzan, Assan, and Anduan, a part of Elam, 278; occupied by the Persians, 280.

Anzan, see Anshan.

Apâm-Napât, " Son of the Waters," a name of Lightning, 45.

Apanm-Napât, a name of Atar. 80; see Apâm-Napât.

Apaosha, the Drought Fiend, his conflict against Tishtrya, 82, 83.

Apollo, the Greek Sun-god, his shrine and oracle at Delphi, 189, 210; at Miletus, 209.

Apries, see Hophra.

Aptya, see Trita.

Arabs, their conquest and oppression of Persia, 2-4.

Aramati, an Aryan deity, 76.

Ardvi-Sûra Anâhita, the celestial spring, Eranian goddess, 65.

Ardys, king of Lydia, son of Gyges, 218.

Ariaramnes (Ariyârâmana on Persian monuments), son of Teïspes and king of Persia, 280, 286.

Ariyârâmana, see Ariaramnes.

Armenians, the Aryan settlers of Urartu, 187.

Arsames (Arshama on Persian monuments), son of Ariaramnes and king of Persia, 280, 286.

Art, Persian, oldest relics of, at Pasargadæ, 303, 304; imitative, *ib.*; at Susa, 333-343; at Persepolis, 392-404; compared to Assyrian, 410.

Artaxerxes, palace of, at Susa, 334.

Artemis, temple of, at Ephesus, 209.

Aryas, primeval, 37; their nature-worship, 38-40; their Sun-Myth, 43; their Storm-Myth, 44; their ideas of sacrifice, 47-51.

Aryênis, daughter of Alyattês, married to Astyages, son of Kyaxares, 221.

Asha-Vahishta, "Perfect Holiness," one of the Amesha-Spentas, 75.

Ashavan, follower of Truth, 103.

Asia Minor, never subdued by Assyria, 186, 187; subject to Greek influences, 190, 202; Greek colonies in, 207.

Asmodeus, the Hebrew equivalent of Aêshma-Daêva, 157.

Aspahê-ashtra, an instrument of punishment in the Vendidâd, 158.

Assan, see Anshan.

Astyages (Ishtuvêgu on cuneiform monuments), son of Kyaxares, marries Aryênis, daughter of Alyattês, king of Lydia, 221; succeeds his father in Media, 224; his contemptible character, 261; dethroned by Kyros, from cylinders, 289; from Herodotus, 290; generously treated by Kyros, 296.

Asura, "Lord," by-word of Dyâus and Váruna, 40.

Asura, Sanskrit equivalent of Ahsura, 61; used in an evil sense, 100.

Âtar, Fire, connection with Ahu-

INDEX. 43*i*

ra-Mazda, 62 ; his demands on men, 79.
Âtesh-Gâh, fire altar, 118, 152.
Atharvan, one of the oldest Sanskrit names for " Lightning," 42; the son of Vâruna, 16 ; derivatives, 16.
Âthravan, the Eranian priests in the Avesta, 150, 152.
Athwya, see Thraetaôna.
Atrina, the first impostor and usurper of Elam, under Dareios I., 374 ; captured and slain, 376.
Atropatène, modern Âderbeidjân, 144 ; the country of sacred fires, 152.
Avesta, the now generally accepted name for the sacred book of the Eranians, 20 ; its component parts, 29-31.
Avesta-u-Zend, proper name of the sacred book of the Eranians, 20.
Avestan Creed, or Profession of Faith, 111.
Avestan, the now generally adopted name for the language of the Avesta, 20.
Avil-Marduk (Evil-Merodach of the Bible), son and successor of Nebuchadrezzar, 319.

B.

Babil, mound of ; uncertainty about, 233.
Babylon, walls of, built by Nebuchadrezzar, 228-230 ; the great bridge at, 231 ; the palace, 232 ; the hanging gardens, 234-238 ; temple of Bel at, 238-240; submits to Kyros, 327-328.
Babylonian Empire ; its share of the Assyrian spoils, 173.
—— customs, 242-260.
—— women, independent position of, 255-257.
Bactria, probably the country of King Vishtâspa, Zarathushtra's friend, 26.
Bagistana, see Behistûn.

Bakhdhi, capital of ancient Bactria, mentioned in the Avesta, 26.
Bakhtiyari mountains, 278.
Barashnûm, the great nine nights' purification, 136.
Bardiya (called by the Greeks Smerdis), younger son of Kyros the Great, 345 ; assassinated by order of Kambyses, 350 ; personated by an impostor, 357.
Baresma, bundle of sacred twigs, 118 ; 120 ; probably introduced by Turanian influences, 148, 149.
Barsua, see Parsua.
Behistûn or Bisutûn, ancient Bagistana ; rock of, 282 ; exploration of, by Sir Henry C. Rawlinson, 284 ; sculpture and inscriptions on the rock of, 285, 286, 360, 361, 366, 381, 382.
Bel-shar-uzzur, see Belshazzar.
Belshazzar (Bel-shar-uzzur), son of Nabonidus, 322.
Bertin, Mr. Geo., Assyriologist, 252 and 254, notes.
Bombay, city on the western coast of India, head-quarters of the Parsis, 5, 6.
Borsip, temple of Nebo at, 227.
Borysthenes, modern Dniepr, a Scythian river, described by Herodotus, 415.
Bosporus, 413 ; Dareios crosses it on a bridge of ships, 424 ; Greek cities on, rebel, 429.
Bourchier, George, English traveller and scholar, 8.
Branchidae, the hereditary priests of Apollo at Miletus, 209.
Bug, Russian river, see Hypanis.
Bunanitu, a Babylonian woman, often recurring in the Egibi tablets, 251, 256, 259, note.
Bundehesh, a Pehlevi sacred book, 32.
Burnouf, Eugène, French Orientalist ; his work on the Zoroastrian books, 14, 15.
Byzantium, a Greek colony on the

Bosporus, controls the trade of the Black Sea, 413, 414.

C.

Cappadocia, a country of Asia Minor; Hittite traces in, 198–201.
Caria, a country of Asia Minor; troops from, support Gyges, 188.
Chinvat Bridge, 95, note, 108; kept by dogs, 140; mentioned in the Gâthas, 162, 165.
Chishpaish, see Teïspes.
Choaspes, river of Susa; only water drunk by Persian kings, 318.
Cilicia, a country of Asia Minor; submits to Cyrus, 317.
Coining, invented by the Lydians, 212–217.
Corpses, impurity of, 124; how to dispose of, 124–128; pollution by, and purification, 135–137; not to be carried by one man alone, 138; how to be treated in winter, out of reach of Dakhmas, 132, 142.
Cylinder, containing proclamation of Kyros, 281–282, 327; annals of Nabonidus, 289, 328.
Cyprus, isle of, occupied by Amasis.

D.

Daëvas, demons, fiends, 64.
Daëvayasnian, meaning of the word, 95.
Dakhmas, the Zoroastrian cemeteries, 124–128; impurity of, and meritoriousness of pulling them down, 131; original meaning of the name, 370.
Danube, see Ister. Dareios crosses it on a bridge of ships, 424.
Darayâvush, see Dareios.
Dareios I., son of Hystaspes, king of Persia, successor of Kambyses II. (Darayâvush on the Persian monuments) his sculptures and inscriptions on the rock of Behistûn, 282–287; his account of Gaumata's usurpation, 361; plots against the false Bardiya, 362; with six companions attacks and slays him, 364–365; his tolerance and respect towards foreign religions, 368; his tomb at Nakhshi-Rustem, 369; himself a Mazdayasnian, 369, 370; faces and fights down rebellion in all the provinces, 372–381, institutes the satrapies, 384–386; introduces regular taxation, 386, 387; constructs roads, and founds the postal system, 387–389; unites the Mediterranean with the Red Sea, 389, 390; introduces uniformity of coinage, 390; founds Persepolis, 391; his buildings there, 392–404; invades Scythia, 422–425; his unsuccessful campaign, 425–429; prepares a campaign against Hellas, 432.
Delitzsch, Professor Friedrich, on the House of Êgibi, 246.
Delphi, shrine and oracle of Apollo at; questioned by Gyges, 189; 210.
Demavend, Mt., highest peak of the Elburz range, 64, note; Aji-Dahâk chained under, 97, note.
DESTUR, Parsi high-priest, 13, 15.
Devas, gods of light in India, 99.
Dieulafoy, Mr. E., French explorer of Susa, 319, 333–343; on the palaces at Persepolis, 408–410.
Dizfúl, a modern city near Susa, 333.
Djamaspa, a follower of Zarathusthtra, 108.
Djumdjuma, mound of,—site of the house of Êgibi, 244.
Dniepr, see Borysthenes.
Dniestr, see Tyras.
Dog, the sacred animal of the Avesta, 139; the care and respect due to it, 139–141.

INDEX. 439

Don, see Tanaïs.
Dorians, one of the Greek tribes; their descent from Epirus and Thessaly into lower Greece and the Peloponnesus, 204-207.
Dosabhai Framji Karaka, a modern Parsi writer, quoted, 4.
Druj, the Spirit of Lie, 106 :— Nasu, the corpse fiend, 93, 135; mode of purification from the, 136.
Drujvan, follower of falsehood, 103.
Dyáus, the Aryan sky-god, 40.

E.

Eclipse, battle of the, 220.
Egibi, banking house of, at Babylon, 244-250; the name probably equivalent to the Hebrew Yakûb, 246.
Elam, see Susiana.
Elburz, 64, note.
Elvend, Mt., see Mt. Orontes.
Ephesus, a Greek city in Asia Minor, temple of Artemis at, 208, 209.
Eranians, one of the great divisions of the Aryan race in Asia, 15; their migrations and hard struggles with nature, 57-59; their character, their dualism and its origin, 59, 60; their lack of imagination, 65, 66.
Ethiopians, conquered by Kambyses, 355.
Evil-Merodach, see Avil-Marduk.
Ezekiel, his prophecy about Tyre, 183; about Egypt, 184.

F.

Fars or Farsistân, see Persis.
Feridûn, Eranian hero-king, 97, note.
Fire-Worshippers, name given to the Parsis, a misnomer, 1, 6.
Frangrasyan, a Turanian ruffian, 81.

Frashaostra, a follower of Zarathushtra, 108.
Fravartish (Phraortes), the impostor and usurper of Media, under Dareios I., 376; his capture and execution, 380.
Fravashis, Spirits of the Departed, 71; supply their kindred with water, 83, 84, 154; transformed probably under Turanian influence, 155; in the Pehlevi period, 156.

G.

Ganges, great river of India, 56.
Gaokerena, or White Haoma, the celebrated Tree of Life, 65.
Garmapada, fifth month of the Persian calendar = July-August, 360.
Garô-nmâna, the Eranian Paradise, 63.
Gâthas (Songs) oldest portion of the Avesta, 24; contain Zarathushtra's own teaching, 97.
Gaumata, the Magian, an impostor; personates Bardiya, son of Kyros and usurps the crown, 360; slain by Dareios and his six companions, 365.
Gebers, see Parsis.
Gerrha, a Babylonian colony on the Arabian coast, 241.
Geush-Urvan, the guardian of cattle, 100; his petition to Ahura-Mazda, 101.
Gobryas, the Mede, a general of Kyros, occupies northern Babylonia and Babylon, 328.
―― father-in-law of Dareios I., one of the seven who slew Gaumata the Magian.
Gômêz, purification by, 136.
Gujerât, or Guzerat, a peninsula of India, 5.
Guyard, Stanislas, French Assyriologist, 146, note.
Gyges (Gugu), founder of the Lydian dynasty of the Mermnadæ, story of, 188, 189; his gifts to

the Delphic Apollo, 210; probably invented coining, 212.

H.

Hakhâmanish, see Akhæmenes.
Halévy, French Semitist, 146, note.
Halys, modern Kizil-Irmâk, a river of Asia Minor, 187.
Hamadân, see Agbatana.
Hanging gardens at Babylon, 234–238.
Haoma, the sacrificial liquor, 30; "White" or Gaokerena, 65, 118, 120.
Hara-Berezaiti, the sacred mountain of Eranian myth, 63.
Haraiti-Bareza, see Hara-Berezaiti.
Harlez, Mgr. C. de, French translator of the Avesta, his views on Turanian influences in the Avesta, 147–156.
Harpagos, a Median lord, helps Kyros to overthrow Astyages, 290; part assigned to him in the fabulous legend of Kyros' childhood, 292–293; conquers the Greek cities of Asia Minor for Kyros, 316.
Harpies, Lycian death-goddesses, 193.
Haurvatât and Ameretât, "Health and Immortality," the two last Amesha-Spentas, 76.
Hebrew affinities, in the Avesta, 156–158.
Hellas, the national common name of Greece, 202.
Hellenes, national name of the Greeks, 204.
Hellespont, crossed by Dareios in his retreat from Scythia, 429.
Hermos, a river in Lydia, 207, 312.
Herodotus, his description of Babylonian customs, 242–244.
Hindus, one of the great divisions of the Aryan race in Asia, 15.

Histiaios, tyrant of Miletus, persuades the Ionian princes to keep the bridge on the Danube for Dareios, 428.
Hittite, sanctuaries in Asia Minor, 198–201.
Hophra (Apries), king of Egypt, succeeds his father Necho II., 180; goes to the rescue of Jerusalem, but is routed and driven back, 180, 181; dethroned by Amasis, 307.
Hukairya, a peak of the Hara-Berezaiti, 65.
Huzvâresh, the Semitic part of the Pehlevi texts, 22.
Hvarenô, "Kingly Glory," 80, 81.
Hypanis, modern Bug, a Scythian river, 413; 415.
Hystaspes (Greek form of Vishtâspa), father of Dareios I., 286; was heir presumptive but never reigned, 288.

I.

Ibâ, son of Silla, a man named in the Êgibi tablets, 246.
Iddina-Marduk, son of Basha, a man named in the Êgibi tablets, 257.
Imgur-Bel, inner wall of Babylon, 230.
India, its geographical conditions and influence on the Aryan conquerors, 56–57.
Indo-Eranians, 37.
Indra, the Aryan Thunder-god. 46.
Indus, great river of India, 56.
Ionians, one of the old Greek tribes, of Pelasgic stock, 204.
Ishtuvêgu, see Astyages.
Istakhr, modern name of the site of Persepolis, 392.
Ister, modern Danube, 413, 414.

J.

Jeconiah, see Jehoiachin.
Jehoahaz, son and successor of

Josiah, submits to Necho, and is carried away captive, 171.
Jehoiakim, another of Josiah's sons, succeeds his brother Jehoahaz, 172; submits to Nebuchadrezzar, 174; dies, 176.
Jehoiachin, or Jeconiah, succeeds his father Jehoiakim, as king of Judah, and gives himself up to Nebuchadrezzar, 176.
Jeremiah, his preaching and impopularity, 175; urges submission to Nebuchadrezzar, 177-180; endures persecution, 181.
Jerusalem, taken by Nebuchadrezzar, 176; retaken and destroyed, 181-183.
Jews, carried into captivity by Nebuchadrezzar, 183; call Kyros, king of Persia, 326, 327; delivered from captivity by Kyros, 330.
Jones, William, English Orientalist, abuses Anquetil Duperron, 12; founder of Sanskrit studies, 15.
Josephus, the Jewish historian, 233.
Josiah, king of Judah, defeated by Necho at Megiddo, 171.

K.

Kambujiya, see Kambyses.
Kambyses (Kambujiya), son of Kyros the Great, at Babylon, 330; viceroy of Babylon, 331; succeeds his father, 344; his character, 344, 345; prepares for a campaign against Egypt, 346-349; has his brother Bardiya assassinated, 349, 350; invades Egypt and defeats Psammetik III. at Pelusion, 351; takes Memphis and subdues all Egypt, *ib.*; his moderate rule and respect shown to Egyptian customs and religion, 352-353; his reluctance to return to Persia and increasing mental perturbation, 354; sends an expedition against the Ammonians and himself leads one into Ethiopia, 355; receives the news of a general revolt at home and the usurpation of the throne by an impostor, 357; confesses his crime and takes his own life, 358.
Kambyses I., son of Kyros I., and king of Anshan, 280.
Kandaules, king of Lydia, story of, 188, 189.
Karkhemish, battle of, 172.
Karpans, priests of hostile religions, 108.
Kasr, mound of, the site of Nebuchadrezzar's palace, 232.
Kassandanê, Persian queen of Kyros the Great, 297.
Kava Vishtâspa, see Vishtâspa.
Kayster, a river in Asia Minor, 207.
Kertch, ancient Panticapaeon, Scythian royal tomb at, 419.
Khordeh Avesta (Lesser Avesta), a portion of the Avesta, 30; its tendency to a revival of polytheism, 161, 162.
Khrafstraghna, instrument to kill impure animals with, 115.
Khrafstras, impure creatures, 114.
Khshathra-Vairya, "Excellent Sovereignty," one of the Amesha Spentas, 75.
Kirmanshâh, modern town between Baghdad and Hamadân, 282.
Kizil-Irmâs, see Halys.
Komana, in Cappadocia, 201.
Koresh, see Kyros.
Kroisos, son of Alyattês of Lydia, 262; succeeds his father, 307; meditates war against Kyros, *ib.*; consults Greek oracles, 308; his gifts to Delphi, 309; declares war to Kyros, 310; his defeat and capture, 310-312; his attempted self-sacrifice misunderstood by the Greeks, 313-316.

Kshatrapâ, see Satrap.
Kurash, see Kyros.
Kurush, see Kyros.
Kyaxares, king of Media, founder of the Median Empire, declares war against Lydia, 219 ; makes peace, and marries his son Astyages to Aryênis, daughter of Alyattès of Lydia, 221 ; dies, 224.
Kymê, an Ionian city in Asia Minor, 201, 208.
Kyros I., son of Teispes, and king of Anshan, 280.
Kyros II., the Great (Kurush in Persian, Kurash in Assyrian, Koresh in Hebrew), king of Anshan and Persia, proclamation of, 282 ; his conquest of Media, on the cylinders, 289 ; from Herodotus, 290 ; fabulous legend of his birth and youth, 291-293 ; subdues Eastern Erân, 296, 297 ; favors the Persians, 297 ; and next to them the Medes, 298 ; builds at Pasargadæ, 300 ; conquers Lydia and captures Kroisos, 310-312 ; his generous treatment of Kroisos, 315 ; his first unsuccessful attempt against Babylon, 323 ; called by the priesthood of Babylon, 325 ; enters Babylon, 328 ; delivers the Jews, 330 ; honors Yahveh and Marduk, yet remains a Mazdayasnian himself, 330-331 ; uncertainty about his death, 331 ; his noble character, 332 ; his race undoubtedly and purely Aryan, 332, note.
Kyros, river, see Pulwar.

L.

Labashi-Marduk, son and successor of Nergal-shar-uzzur, 320.
Lacedæmon, see Sparta.
Languages, of ancient Persia (Avestan and Pehlevi), 20-22 ; of Asia Minor, 106 : of Susiana or Elam, 278 ; of the un-Aryan Persian inscriptions, 286.
Lenormant, François, on the invention of coining, on the invention of cheques and drafts, 248-250.
Lycia, a country of Asia Minor, rock tombs in, 190-193 ; submits to Kyros, 317.
Lydia, its last royal dynasty, the Mermnadæ, 188, 189 ; tombs in, 190.
Lyon, Dr. D. G., assyriologist, on "Tablets of Precedents," 255, note.

M.

Ma, a Hittite nature-goddess, her temple at Komana, 201.
Mæander, a river in Asia Minor, 207.
Magi, the Median priests, 148 ; a separate Median tribe, 268 ; probably originally un-Aryan, 269, 270 ; substituted to the Âthravans, 271 ; their political independence and power, 272.
Mandanê, supposed daughter of Astyages, and mother of Kyros the Great, 291.
Mantra (sacred text, Sanskrit), its power, 49.
Manthras, or sacred texts, when recited, 30 ; used for conjuring, 49 ; their efficacy, 86 ; against sickness, 138.
Maraphians, one of the three noblest Persian tribes, 278
Marathon, battle of, 432.
Maspii, one of the three noblest Persian tribes, 278.
Massagetæ, a barbarous people by the Sea of Aral, 331.
Mazda, see Ahura-Mazda.
Mazdayasnians, meaning of the word, 95.
Mazdeism, the religion of Zoroaster, essence of, 102-104.
Medes (Madai), under Assyrian

INDEX.   443

kings, 144; their origin and elements as a nation, 267, 268.
Median empire, its constitution, share of the Assyrian spoils, 173.
—— tribes, 267, 268.
—— wall, built by Nebuchadrezzar, 226.
Megiddo, battle of, 171.
Mermnadæ, the last native dynasty of Lydian kings, founded by Gyges, 188, 189; fall of the, 312.
Migration of the Eranians, from east to west, 57, 143; brings them under Turanian influences, 144, ff.
Miletus, the queen of Ionian cities in Asia Minor; temple of Didymæan Apollo at, 209; makes terms with Lydia, 218; with Kyros the Great, 317; revolts against Dareios, is besieged, taken, and sacked, 430.
Miltiades, the Athenian, proposes to destroy the bridge on the Danube, 423; is overruled by Histiaios and the Ionian princes, 429; wins the battle of Marathon, 432.
Mithra, the Eranian light-god, his connection with Ahura-Mazda, 62, 63; his mythical features, 67–69; his allegorical transformation, 69–73.
Mitra, the Aryan light-god, 41.
Mitra-Váruna, the Aryan duad or divine pair, 41.
Murgháb, present name of the site of Pasargadæ, 280, 300.
Myazda, offering at sacrifices, 120.
Myrina, a Greek city in Asia Minor, 208.
Mysia, a country of Asia Minor, 196; annexed to Lydia, 217.

N.

Nabonidus (Nabu-náhid), last king of Babylon, his accession, 320; his fondness for the ancient Chaldean gods and sanctuaries, 321; neglects Marduk and Nebo, and makes enemies of the Babylonian priesthood, 321, 322; betrayed by them, 325; delivered into the hands of Kyros, 328; his death, *ib.* and 329.
Nabopolassar, king of Babylon, dies, 172.
Nabu-náhid, see Nabonidus.
Nadintabira, the impostor and usurper of Babylon under Dareios I., 374; captured and slain, 376.
Nakhshi-Rustem, rock of, containing tombs of Akhæmenian kings, 369; sepulchre of Dareios at, 369, 370.
Nasu, the corpse fiend, 93; exorcised by the look of dogs, 93, 94, 135; purification from, 136; probably of Turanian origin, 150.
Návsári, a city on the western coast of India, gives refuge to the fugitive Parsis, 5.
Nebuchadrezzar, king of Babylon, defeats Necho of Egypt at Karkhemish, 172; succeeds his father Nabopolassar, 172; his campaign in Syria, 174–177; besieges and takes Jerusalem, 176; appoints Zedekiah king of Judah, 177; retakes and destroys Jerusalem, 182, 183; besieges Tyre, 184; makes peace between Lydia and Media, 221; his works of defence and embellishment in Babylonia and Babylon itself, 225–241; death of, 319.
Necho II. succeeds his father Psammetik, and plans a campaign into Asia, 170; his war in Syria, *ib.*; defeats Josiah of Judah at Megiddo, 171; is defeated by Nebuchadrezzar at Karkhemish, 172; dies, 180.
Nehavend, battle of, won by the Arabs over the Persians, 2.
Nergal-shar-uzzur (*Neriglissar*), successor of Avil-Marduk, 320.

Neriglissar, see Nergal-shar-uzzur.
Nimitti-Bel, outer wall of Babylon, 228.
Nitêtis, the Egyptian princess, story of, 347.
Nitokris, queen of Babylon, 240; mother of Nabonidus, 320; her death and mourning for her, 323; said to have chosen her sepulchre above one of the gates of Babylon, 372.

O.

Olbia, the Greek colony at the mouth of the Hypanis, 413.
Orontes, river, in Hamath, 181
—— mountain, by Agbatana (modern Hamadân), 263-264.
Ouralo-Altaic, meaning of the name, 278, note.
Ouranos, Greek equivalent of the Sanskrit Váruna, 40.

P.

Palaces, of Nebuchadrezzar at Babylon, 232, 233; at Agbatana, 263-266; at Susa, 333-343; at Persepolis, 392-411.
Panticapæon, see Kertch.
Parôdarsh (the cock), the sacred bird of the Avesta, 141.
Parsis, their small numbers, 1; their importance, *ib.*; their monotheism, 2; their settlements in India, 5; their reverence for fire, 6; their belief in a spiritual hierarchy, 7; profess themselves followers of Zoroaster, *ib.*
Parsua, or Barsua, a nation occurring in the Assyrian inscriptions, 274.
Pasargadæ, the noblest of Persian tribes, 278.
—— the clan city of the Pasargadæ, 279; ruins of Kyros, great palace at, 300; Kyros' tomb at, 300-303.

Pâzend, Eranian portion of Pehlevi texts, 22.
Pehlevi, the language of Persia in the Middle Ages, 20-22.
Pelasgi, the old Aryan stock from which the various Greek nations descended, 204.
Pelasgic, Aryan type of language, 196.
Penalties, for performing purification without being an Athravan, 116, 117; for burying a corpse, 133; for carrying a corpse alone, 137; for ill-using or killing dogs, 140; extravagant, for small offences, 158-160.
Penjâb, a part of Northern India, 5.
—— first country in India occupied by the Aryas, 38.
Persepolis, capital of the Persian kings, burned down by Alexander, 27, 342, 369, 392; Akhæmenian constructions at, 392-411; great platform, 393, 394; stairs, 395-398; palace of Dareios, 400; Hall of the Hundred Columns, 400-404; peristyle or gate-hall of Xerxes, 406; audience hall of Xerxes, 406-408; royal tombs, 411.
Persian tribes, 277-279.
Persians, an Eranian nation kindred to the Medes, and originally vassal to them, 273; their hardy nature, 276; a mixed people, as a nation, 277-279.
Persis, classical name of ancient Persia, modern Fars or Farsistân, 273; its climate and productions, 275.
Phanês, commander of Amasis' Greek body-guard, deserts to Kambyses, 349.
Pheidon of Argos, supposed by some to have invented coining, 217 note.
Phraortes, see Fravartish.
Phrygia, a country of Asia Minor, inscriptions and language of,

196; king of, sends gifts to the Delphic Apollo, 210.
Physicians, and surgeons, in the Avesta, 138, 139.
Pitris, "Fathers," Aryan spirits of the departed, 53; honors rendered them, 54.
Pognon, French Assyriologist, 146 note.
Pollution, inflicted by the presence of a corpse, 132; on the earth by burying a corpse, 133; by the Druj Nasu, 135; by carrying a corpse alone, 137.
Profession of faith, see Avestan Creed.
Psammenit, see Psammetik III.
Psammetik III. (Greek Psammenit), son of Amasis, succeeds him, 350; loses the battle of Pelusion, 351; captured at Memphis, *ib*.
Pûitika, sea, where polluted waters are purified before returning to the sea Vouru-Kasha.
Pulwar, river, ancient Kyros, flows through the valley of Murghâb, 300.
Purification, to be performed by none but Âthravans, 116, 117; prescriptions for, in the Vendidâd, 134; by *gómêz*, 136.

R.

Rachmed, mount, at Persepolis, 394; royal tombs in, 411.
Rages, a city in Media, see Rhagæ.
Rashnu, "uprightness, justice," 71; 159.
Rhagæ (Rages in the Book of Tobit), a great city in Media, 157; the seat of the "Zarathushtrotêma," 272.
Riblah, on the Orontes, a city in Hamath, 181.
Rig-Veda, the oldest of the Hindus' sacred books, 38.

S.

Sacrifice demanded by gods, 84; its efficacy, 85.
Sadyattês, king of Lydia, his war against Miletus, 218.
Sagdid ceremony, meaning and description of, 93, 94; 136; 142.
Sakunka, rebel chief of the Sakæ, taken prisoner, 381.
Sandôn, the name of the Sun-god in Lydia, 209.
Sanskrit, language and studies, 15.
Sardis, capital of Lydia, capture of, by Kyros, 312; revolt at, 317.
Sassanian dynasty, 2; restores the ancient texts, 28.
Satrap, Persian "Kshatrapâ," meaning of the word, 317, note; position and duties of, 384-386.
Scythia (south of Russia), known to the Greeks, 413; its rivers, 414, 415; its climate, 416; its people, 418; their mode of life, 419; their appearance, 420; their customs, 420-422.
Semiramis, building of Babylon attributed to, 240.
Shapûr II, king, proclaims the Avestan law, 28.
Shushan, see Susa.
Sippar, reservoir at, dug by order of Nebuchadrezzar, 225.
Skoloti, real name of the European Scythians, according to Herodotus, 418.
Smerdis, see Bardiya.
Smyrna, a Greek city in Lydia, 201; 208.
Soma, god and plant, 48.
Spaka, supposed nurse of Kyros the Great, 292; mythical significancy of the name, 294.
Sparta, one of the two chief cities of Hellas, also Lacedæmon, 312.
Spartans, make alliance with Kroisos, 308; are too late to help him, 312; defy Kyros at Sardis, 316.

Spenta-Armaiti, "Holy Piety," one of the Amesha-Spentas, 75.
Spenta-Mainyu, one of the names of Ahura-Mazda, its meaning, 74.
Spiegel, Dr. Friedrich, Eranian scholar, German translator of the Avesta, 157, note.
Spitâma, name of Zarathushtra's clan, 25.
—— son-in-law of Astyages, king of Media, 296.
Sraosha, "Obedience to the Law," 71; the chief of Yazatas, 78; 107.
Sraoshô-charana, an unknown instrument of punishment in the Vendîdâd, 158.
Suleiman range of mountains, 274.
Surât, a city on the western coast of India, gives refuge to the fugitive Parsis, 5.
Susa (Shushan) one of the capitals of the new Persian empire, 318; Akhæmenian palace at, explored by Mr. Dieulafoy, 318, 333-343.
Susiana, ancient Elam, 278; uncertain when annexed to Persia, 318.
Syennesis, king of Cilicia, helps in reconciling Alyattês and Kyaxares, 221.

T.

Tablets of precedents, the base of Babylonian law transactions, 252-256.
Taêra, principal peak of the Hara Berezaiti, 64.
Tanaïs, modern Don, a Scythian river, 415.
Tanaoxares, Tanyoxarkes, names given to Bardiya, son of Kyros the Great, 345, note.
Teïspes (Chishpaïsh on cuneiform monuments) son of Akhæmenes, the probable annexer of Anshan, 280, 286, 287.

Teredon or Tiridotis, a city built by Nebuchadrezzar at the mouth of the Euphrates, 241.
Tevâ, probably a quarter of Babylon, 322, note.
Thales of Miletus, a wise man among the Greeks, predicts an eclipse, 220.
Thermodon, a river in Asia Minor, 201.
Thracia, submits to Dareios, 424.
Thraetaôna, son of Athwya, Eranian equivalent of Sanskrit, Trita, son of Aptya, 97, note.
Tigranes I., king of Armenia, said to have been Astyages' brother-in-law, 296; friendly to Kyros, *ib.*
Tiridotis, see Teredon.
Tishtrya (the star Sirius) the chief of all the stars, 81; the giver of rain, 82; his conflict against Apaosha, the drought fiend, 82, 83.
Tombs, Lycian rock-tombs, 190-193; royal Akhæmenian, at Nakhshi-Rustem, 369, 370; at Persepolis, 411.
Trita, son of Aptya, Sanskrit equivalent of Eranian Thraetaôna, son of Athwya, 97, note.
Turanian influences on the Eranians' religion, 144-156.
Turanians, natural enemies of Eranians, 97, 98.
Tyras, modern Dniestr, a Scythian river, 414.
Tyre, siege of, by Nebuchadrezzar, 183, 184.

V.

Vara, Yima's garden, 91, 92.
Váruna, the Aryan sky-god, 40.
Vayu, the Aryan wind-god, 46.
Veda, sacred books of the Hindus.
Vendîdâd, a portion of the Avesta; meaning of the word and contents, 30; its character, 113 ff.; not strictly followed by the Per-

sians under the Akhæmenians, 370.
Vendîdâd-Sadeh, the Parsi liturgy, 8, 31.
Verethraghna (victory), 71, 73; Eranian form of "Vritrahan," 76.
Vêzaresha, the daêva who takes the souls of the wicked, 164.
Vishtâspa, or Kava Vishtâspa, King Zarathushtra's friend and disciple, 26, 102.
—— (in Greek, Hystaspes) father of King Dareios I., (see Hystaspes.)
Vispered, a part of the Avesta, contents, 30.
Vohu-Manô, "Good-Mind," one of the Amesha-Spentas, 75.
Vouru-Kasha, sea, mythical, 64.
Vritra, the Aryan cloud-fiend, 46.
Vritrahan, "Killer of Vritra," the proudest title of Indra, 46; found in the Eranian "Verethraghna," 76.

W.

West, Dr. E. W., a Pehlevi scholar.
Women, Babylonian, independent position of, 255-257.

X.

Xerxes, son of Dareios I., his constructions at Persepolis, 404-408.

Y.

Yakûb, said to be the Hebrew equivalent of Égibi, 246.
Yama, the Aryan death-god, 52; first man, 53; king of the dead, *ib*; his dogs, *ib*.

Yasna, a part of the Avesta, contents, 30.
Yazatas (good spirits), 62, 66; Yzeds of the Parsis, 78; all created by Ahura-Mazda, 161.
Yeshts, a part of the Avesta; contents and character, 31.
Yezdegerd III., last Sassanian king, 3.
Yima, his story, 89-93; his connection with the Hindu Yama, 89; his fall, 92.
Yzeds, see Yazatas.

Z.

Zaothra, holy water at sacrifices, 120.
Zarathushtra, known to classic antiquity, 2, 7, 23; was he a real person? 23; his questionable date, *ib*.; his personality as shown in the Gâthas, 24-27; was a reformer, 36; his mission and his work, 96.
"Zarathushtrotéma," the head of the Magi, 272.
Zedekiah, a son of Jehoiakin and brother of Jeconiah, appointed by Nebuchadrezzar king of Judea, 177; rebels against him, 180; barbarous treatment and captivity of, 182.
Zend, meaning of the word, 20.
Zend-Avesta, sacred book of the Eranians, 19; an incorrect name, 20.
Zohâk, a wicked usurper, a form of the mythical Aji-Dahâka, 93.
Zoroaster, see Zarathushtra.
Zoroastrians, i. e., followers of Zoroaster, persecuted by the Arab conquerors, 3, 4; their wanderings and landing in Gujerât, 4, 5.

The Gresham Press,
UNWIN BROTHERS,
CHILWORTH AND LONDON.

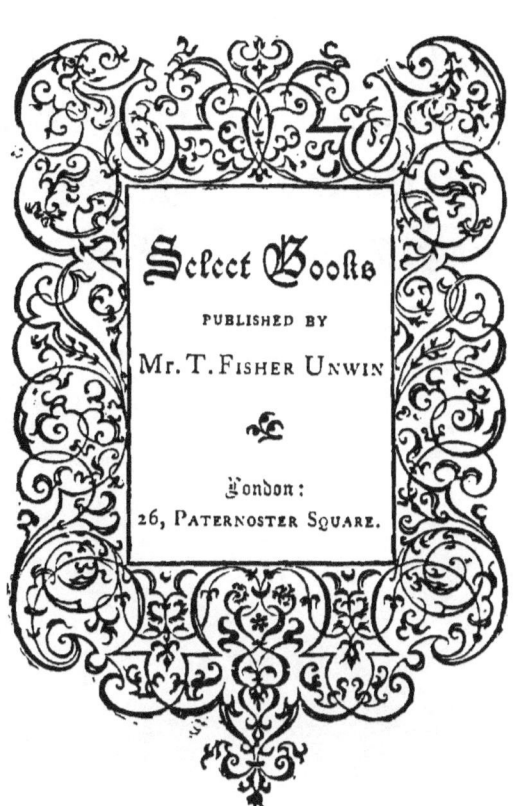

Mr. U$_{NWIN}$ *will have pleasure in sending a Specimen Copy of* The Century *or* St. Nicholas *to any address on receipt of Threepence for Postage.*

Catalogue of Select Books in Belles Lettres, History, Biography, Theology, Travel, Miscellaneous, and Books for Children.

Belles Lettres.

English Wayfaring Life in the Middle Ages (XIVth Century). By J. J. JUSSERAND. Translated from the French by LUCY A. TOULMIN SMITH. Illustrated. Second Edition. Demy 8vo., cloth, 12s.

The Author has supervised the translation, and has added fresh matter, so that the volume differs in some degree from "*La Vie Nomade.*" Many of the illustrations are taken from illuminated manuscripts, and have never been published before.

Old Chelsea. A Summer-Day's Stroll. By Dr. BENJAMIN ELLIS MARTIN. Illustrated by JOSEPH PENNELL. Second Edition. Crown 8vo., cloth, 7s. 6d.

The stroll described in these pages may be imagined to be taken during the summer of 1888; all the dates, descriptions, and references herein having been brought down to the present day.

The Twilight of the Gods. "The Purple Head," "Madame Lucifer," "The Demon Pope," "The City of Philosophers," "The Cup-bearer," "Ananda the Miracle-Worker," "The Bell of St. Euschemon," and other Stories. By RICHARD GARNETT. Crown 8vo., cloth, 6s.

The Coming of the Friars, And other Mediæval Sketches. By the Rev. AUGUSTUS JESSOPP, D.D., Author of "Arcady: For Better, For Worse," &c. Third Edition. Crown 8vo., cloth, 7s. 6d.

Contents.—I. The Coming of the Friars.—II. Village Life in Norfolk Six Hundred Years ago.—III. Daily Life in a Mediæval Monastery.—IV. and V. The Black Death in East Anglia.—VI. The Building-up of a University.—VII. The Prophet of Walnut-tree Walk.

Arcady : For Better, For Worse. By AUGUSTUS JESSOPP, D.D., Author of "One Generation of a Norfolk House." Portrait. Popular Edition. Crown 8vo., cloth, 3s. 6d.

"A volume which is, to our minds, one of the most delightful ever published in English."—*Spectator.*

"A capital book, abounding in true wisdom and humour. . . . Excellent and amusing."—*Melbourne Argus.*

The Romance of a Shop. By AMY LEVY, Author of "Reuben Sachs," &c. Crown 8vo., cloth, 6s.

The Paradox Club. By EDWARD GARNETT. With Portrait of Nina Lindon. Crown 8vo., cloth, 6s.

"Mr. Garnett's dialogue is often quite as good as his description, and in description he is singularly happy. The mystery of London streets by night is powerfully suggested, and the realistic force of his night-pieces is enhanced by the vague and Schumann-like sentiment that pervades them."—*Saturday Review.*

Euphorion : Studies of the Antique and the Mediæval in the Renaissance. By VERNON LEE. Cheap Edition, in one volume. Demy 8vo., cloth, 7s. 6d.

"It is the fruit, as every page testifies, of singularly wide reading and independent thought, and the style combines with much picturesqueness a certain largeness of volume, that reminds us more of our earlier writers than those of our own time."
—*Contemporary Review.*

Studies of the Eighteenth Century in Italy. By VERNON LEE. Demy 8vo., cloth, 7s. 6d.

"These studies show a wide range of knowledge of the subject, precise investigation, abundant power of illustration, and hearty enthusiasm. . . . The style of writing is cultivated, neatly adjusted, and markedly clever."—*Saturday Review.*

Belcaro : Being Essays on Sundry Æsthetical Questions. By VERNON LEE, Author of "Euphorion," "Baldwin," &c. Crown 8vo., cloth, 5s.

"This way of conveying ideas is very fascinating, and has an effect of creating activity in the reader's mind which no other mode can equal. From first to last there is a continuous and delightful stimulation of thought."—*Academy.*

Juvenilia : A Second Series of Essays on Sundry Æsthetical Questions. By VERNON LEE. Two vols. Small crown 8vo., cloth, 12s.

"To discuss it properly would require more space than a single number of 'The Academy' could afford. —*Academy.*

"Est agréable à lire et fait penser."—*Revue des deux Mondes.*

Baldwin: Dialogues on Views and Aspirations. By VERNON LEE. Demy 8vo., cloth, 12s.

"The dialogues are written with . . . an intellectual courage which shrinks from no logical conclusion."—*Scotsman.*

Ottilie: An Eighteenth Century Idyl. By VERNON LEE. Square 8vo., cloth extra, 3s. 6d.

"A graceful little sketch. . . . Drawn with full insight into the period described."—*Spectator.*

The Fleet: Its River, Prison, and Marriages. By JOHN ASHTON, Author of "Social Life in the Reign of Queen Anne," &c. With 70 Drawings by the Author from Original Pictures. Demy 8vo., cloth elegant, 21s. Cheaper Edition, 7s. 6d.

Romances of Chivalry: Told and Illustrated in Fac-simile by JOHN ASHTON. Forty-six Illustrations. Demy 8vo., cloth elegant, gilt tops, 18s.

"The result (of the reproduction of the wood blocks) is as creditable to his artistic, as the text is to his literary, ability."—*Guardian.*

The Dawn of the Nineteenth Century in

England: A Social Sketch of the Times. By JOHN ASHTON. Cheaper Edition, in one vol. Illustrated. Large crown 8vo., 10s. 6d.

"The book is one continued source of pleasure and interest, and opens up a wide field for speculation and comment, and many of us will look upon it as an important contribution to contemporary history, not easily available to others than close students."—*Antiquary.*

Legends and Popular Tales of the Basque

People. By MARIANA MONTEIRO. With Illustrations by HAROLD COPPING. Popular Edition. Crown 8vo., cloth, gilt edges, 6s.

"In every respect this comely volume is a notable addition to the shelf devoted to folk-lore . . . and the pictures in photogravure nobly interpret the text."—*Critic.*

Heroic Tales. Retold from Firdusi the Persian. By HELEN ZIMMERN. With Etchings by L. ALMA TADEMA. Popular Edition. Crown 8vo., cloth extra, 5s.

"Charming from beginning to end. . . . Miss Zimmern deserves all credit for her courage in attempting the task, and for her marvellous success in carrying it out."—*Saturday Review.*

Pilgrim Sorrow. By CARMEN SYLVA (The Queen of Roumania). Translated by HELEN ZIMMERN. Portrait-etching by LALAUZE. Square crown 8vo., cloth extra, 5s.

"A strain of sadness runs through the delicate thought and fancy of the Queen of Roumania. Her popularity as an author is already great in Germany, and this little work will win her a place in many English hearts."—*Standard.*

The Poison Tree : A Tale of Hindu Life in Bengal. By B. CHANDRA CHATTERJEE. Introduction by Sir EDWIN ARNOLD, M.A., K.C.S.I. Crown 8vo., cloth, 6s.

"This is a work of real genius. . . . As a picture of the social life of the Hindus it cannot but be regarded as masterly."—*British Quarterly Review.*

The Touchstone of Peril : A Tale of the Indian Mutiny. By DUDLEY HARDRESS THOMAS. Second edition. Crown 8vo., cloth, 6s.

"'The Touchstone of Peril' is the best Anglo-Indian novel that has appeared for some years."—*Times of India.*

The Amazon : An Art Novel. By CARL VOSMAER. Preface by Prof. GEORG EBERS, and Frontispiece specially drawn by L. ALMA TADEMA, R.A. Crown 8vo., cloth, 6s.

"It is a work full of deep, suggestive thought."—*Academy.*

The Temple : Sacred Poems and Private Ejaculations. By Mr. GEORGE HERBERT. New and fourth edition, with Introductory Essay by J. HENRY SHORTHOUSE. Small crown, sheep, 5s.

A fac-simile reprint of the Original Edition of 1633.

"This charming reprint has a fresh value added to it by the Introductory Essay of the Author of 'John Inglesant.'"—*Academy.*

Songs, Ballads, and A Garden Play. By A. MARY F. ROBINSON, Author of "An Italian Garden." With Frontispiece of Dürer's "Melancolia." Small crown 8vo., half bound, vellum, 5s.

"The romantic ballads have grace, movement, passion and strength."—*Spectator.*
"Marked by sweetness of melody and truth of colour."—*Academy.*

An Italian Garden : A Book of Songs. By A. MARY F. ROBINSON. Fcap. 8vo., parchment, 3s. 6d.

"They are most of them exquisite in form."—*Pall Mall Gazette.*
"Full of elegance and even tenderness."—*Spectator.*

Essays towards a Critical Method. Studies in English Literature. By JOHN M. ROBERTSON. Cr. 8vo., cloth, 7s. 6d.

The Lazy Minstrel. By J. ASHBY-STERRY, Author of "Boudoir Ballads." Fourth and Popular Edition. Frontispiece by E. A. ABBEY. Fcap. 8vo., cloth, 2s. 6d.

"One of the lightest and brightest writers of vers de société."
—*St. James's Gazette.*

Caroline Schlegel, and Her Friends. By Mrs. ALFRED SIDGWICK. With Steel Portrait. Crown 8vo., cloth, 7s. 6d.

Introductory Studies in Greek Art. Delivered in the British Museum by JANE E. HARRISON. With Illustrations. Square imperial 16mo., 7s. 6d.

"The best work of its kind in English."—*Oxford Magazine.*

Amos Kilbright: His Adscititious Adventures. With other Stories. By FRANK R. STOCKTON. 8vo., cloth, 3s. 6d.

"Mr. Stockton is the quaintest of living humorists."—*Academy.*

Gladys Fane. By T. WEMYSS REID. Fifth edition. (Unwin's Novel Series.) Small crown 8vo., 2s.

"The author of the delightful monograph on 'Charlotte Brontë' has given us in this volume a story as beautiful as life and as sad as death."—*Standard.*

Mrs. Keith's Crime. By Mrs. W. KINGDON CLIFFORD. (Unwin's Novel Series.) Second edition. Small crown 8vo., 2s.

Concerning Oliver Knox. By G. COLMORE. (Unwin's Novel Series.) Small crown 8vo., 2s.

Miss Bayle's Romance; Or, An American Heiress in Europe. By W. FRASER RAE. (Unwin's Novel Series.) Small Crown 8vo., 2s.

History.

The End of the Middle Ages: Essays and Questions in History. By A. MARY F. ROBINSON (Madâme Darmesteter). Demy 8vo., cloth, 10s. 6d.

A Series of Essays on chapters in French and Italian History—"The Claim of the House of Orleans," "Valentine Visconti," "The Convent of Helfta," "The Schism," "The French in Italy," "The Attraction of the Abyss," and other Studies.

The Federalist: A Commentary in the Form of Essays on the United States Constitution. By ALEXANDER HAMILTON, and others. Edited by HENRY CABOT LODGE. Demy 8vo., Roxburgh binding, 10s. 6d.

"The importance of the Essays can hardly be exaggerated. . . . They are undoubtedly a great work upon the general subject of political federation; and the education of no student of politics in our own country can be considered complete who has not mastered the treatise of Alexander Hamilton."—*Glasgow Mail.*

The Government Year Book: A Record of the Forms and Methods of Government in Great Britain, her Colonies, and Foreign Countries, 1889. Crown 8vo., cloth, 6s.

"Mr. Lewis Sergeant has most admirably performed his task."—*Athenæum.*
"The book fills a gap which has been frequently noticed by every politician, journalist, and economist."—*Journal des Debats.*

The Making of the Great West, 1512-1853. By SAMUEL ADAMS DRAKE. One hundred and forty-five Illustrations. Large crown 8vo., 9s.

The Making of New England, 1580-1643. By SAMUEL ADAMS DRAKE. Illustrated. Crown 8vo., cloth, 5s.

"It is clearly and pleasantly written, and copiously illustrated."
Pall Mall Budget

The Story of the Nations.

Crown 8vo., Illustrated, and furnished with Maps and Indexes, each 5s.

"L'interessante serie l'Histoire des Nations formera . . . un cours d'histoire universelle d'une très grande valeur."—*Journal des Debats.*
"The remarkable series."—*New York Critic.*
"That useful series."—*The Times.*
"An admirable series."—*Spectator.*
"That excellent series."—*Guardian.*
"The series is likely to be found indispensable in every school library."
"This valuable series."—*Nonconformist.* *Pall Mall Gazette.*
"Admirable series of historical monographs."—*Echo*

Rome. By ARTHUR GILMAN, M.A., Author of "A History of the American People," &c. Third edition.

"The author succeeds admirably in reproducing the 'Grandeur that was Rome.'"—*Sydney Morning Herald.*

The Jews. In Ancient, Mediæval, and Modern Times. By Prof. J. K. HOSMER. Second edition.

"The book possesses much of the interest, the suggestiveness, and the charm of romance."—*Saturday Review.*

Germany. By Rev. S. BARING-GOULD, Author of "Curious Myths of the Middle Ages," &c. Second edition.

"Mr. Baring-Gould tells his stirring tale with knowledge and perspicuity. He is a thorough master of his subject."—*Globe.*

Carthage. By Prof. ALFRED J. CHURCH, Author of "Stories from the Classics," &c. Second edition.

"A masterly outline with vigorous touches in detail here and there."—*Guardian.*

Alexander's Empire. By Prof. J. P. MAHAFFY, Author of "Social Life in Greece." Second edition.

"A wonderful success."—*Spectator.*

The Moors in Spain. By STANLEY LANE-POOLE, Author of "Studies in a Mosque." Second edition.

"The best, the fullest, the most accurate, and most readable history of the Moors in Spain for general readers."—*St. James's Gazette.*

Ancient Egypt. By Prof. GEO. RAWLINSON, Author of "The Five Great Monarchies of the World." Second edition.

"The story is told of the land, people and rulers, with vivid colouring and consummate literary skill."—*New York Critic.*

Hungary. By Prof. ARMINIUS VAMBÉRY, Author of "Travels in Central Asia." Second edition.

"The volume which he has contributed to 'The Story of the Nations' will be generally considered one of the most interesting and picturesque of that useful series."—*Times.*

The Saracens: From the Earliest Times to the Fall of Bagdad. By ARTHUR GILMAN, M.A., Author of "Rome," &c.

"Le livre de M. Gilman est destiné à être lu avidement par un grand nombre de gens pour lesquels l'étude des nombreux ouvrages déjà parus serait impossible.'
Journal des Débats.

Ireland. By the Hon. EMILY LAWLESS, Author of "Hurrish." Second edition.

"We owe thanks to Miss Emily for this admirable volume, in some respects the very best of 'The Story of the Nations' series as yet published."—*Nonconformist.*

Chaldea. By Z. A. RAGOZIN, Author of "Assyria," &c.

"One of the most interesting numbers of the series in which it appears."
Scotsman.

The Goths. By HENRY BRADLEY.

"Seems to us to be as accurate as it is undoubtedly clear, strong, and simple; and it will give to the reader an excellent idea of the varied fortunes of the two great branches of the Gothic nation."—THOMAS HODGKIN *in The Academy.*

Assyria: From the Rise of the Empire to the Fall of Nineveh. By ZÉNAÏDE A. RAGOZIN, Author of "Chaldea," &c.

Turkey. By STANLEY LANE-POOLE, Author of "The Moors in Spain," &c.

Holland. By Professor THOROLD ROGERS.

Mediæval France. By GUSTAVE MASSON.

Persia. By S. G. W. BENJAMIN.

Phœnicia. By CANON RAWLINSON.

Media. By Z. A. RAGOZIN.

The Hansa Towns. By HELEN ZIMMERN.

(*For further information, see "Nation Series" Catalogue*).

Biography.

Life & Times of Girolamo Savonarola. By PASQUALE VILLARI. Translated by LINDA VILLARI. Portraits and Illustrations. Two vols. Second Edition, with New Preface. Demy 8vo., cloth, 32s.

This new translation of Villari's "Savonarola" by Madame Villari contains much additional matter, and is fuller and completer than the last published Italian edition. The biography is illustrated with many portraits of famous men of the times.

Francis Bacon (Lord Verulam): A Critical Review of his Life and Character, with Selections from his Writings. By B. G. LOVEJOY, A.M., LL.B. Crown 8vo., half-bound cloth, gilt top, 6s.

"Is, perhaps, the most readable and incisive sketch of Lord Bacon's career and character that has yet been written."—*Christian Leader.*

Anne Gilchrist: Her Life and Writings. Edited by HERBERT HARLAKENDEN GILCHRIST. Prefatory Notice by WILLIAM MICHAEL ROSSETTI. Second edition. Twelve Illustrations. Demy 8vo., cloth, 16s.

"Here we find a kind, friendly, and humorous, if splenetic Carlyle; a helpful and merry Mrs. Carlyle; and a friendly and unaffected Dante Gabriel Rossetti. These characteristics, so unlike the Carlyle of the too copious memoirs, so unlike the Mrs. Carlyle, the *femme incomprise*, so unlike the Rossetti of myth, are extremely welcome."—*Daily News* (Leader).

Charles Dickens as I knew Him: The Story of the Reading Tours in Great Britain and America (1866-1870). By GEORGE DOLBY. New and cheaper edition. Crown 8vo., 3s. 6d.

"It will be welcome to all lovers of Dickens for Dickens' own sake."—*Athenæum.*

Charles Whitehead: A Critical Monograph. By H. T. MACKENZIE BELL. Cheap and Popular edition. Crown 8vo., cloth, 5s.

"Mr. Mackenzie Bell has done a good service in introducing to us a man of true genius, whose works have sunk into mysteriously swift and complete oblivion."
Contemporary Review.

Ole Bull: A Memoir. By Sara C. Bull. With Ole Bull's "Violin Notes" and Dr. A. B. Crosby's "Anatomy of the Violinist." Portraits. Second edition. Crown 8vo., cloth, 7s. 6d.

"A fresh, delightful, and charming book."—*Graphic.*

Johannes Brahms: A Biographical Sketch. By Dr. Herman Deiters. Translated, with additions, by Rosa Newmarch. Edited, with a Preface, by J. A. Fuller Maitland. Portrait. Small crown 8vo., cloth, 6s.

"An original and excellent little study of the composer."—*Saturday Review.*

The Lives of Robert and Mary Moffat.

By their Son, John Smith Moffat. Sixth edition. Portraits, Illustrations, and Maps. Crown 8vo., cloth, 7s. 6d.; Presentation Edition, full gilt elegant, bevelled boards, gilt edges, in box, 10s. 6d.; Popular Edition, crown 8vo., 3s. 6d.

"An inspiring record of calm, brave, wise work, and will find a place of value on the honoured shelf of missionary biography. The biographer has done his work with reverent care, and in a straightforward, unaffected style."
Contemporary Review.

The German Emperor and Empress:

The Late Frederick III. and Victoria. The Story of their Lives. (Being the Sixth and Popular Edition of "Two Royal Lives," 7s. 6d.) By Dorothea Roberts. Portraits. Crown 8vo., cloth, 2s. 6d.

"A book sure to be popular in domestic circles."—*The Graphic.*

Arminius Vambéry: His Life and Adventures. Written by Himself. With Portrait and Fourteen Illustrations. Fifth and Popular Edition. Square Imperial 16mo., cloth extra, 6s.

"The work is written in a most captivating manner."—*Novoe Vremya, Moscow.*

Henry Irving: In England and America, 1838-1884. By Frederic Daly. Vignette Portrait by Ad. Lalauze. Second Thousand. Crown 8vo., cloth extra, 5s.

"A very interesting account of the career of the great actor."
British Quarterly Review.

Theology and Philosophy.

The House and Its Builder, with Other Discourses: A Book for the Doubtful. By Dr. SAMUEL COX. Second Edition. Small crown 8vo., paper, 2s. 6d.; cloth, 3s.

"**Expositions.**" By the same Author. First Series. Third Thousand. Demy 8vo., cloth, 7s. 6d.

"We have said enough to show our high opinion of Dr. Cox's volume. It is indeed full of suggestion. . . . A valuable volume."—*The Spectator.*

"**Expositions.**" By the same Author. Second Series. Second Thousand. Demy 8vo., cloth 7s. 6d.

"Here, too, we have the clear exegetical insight, the lucid expository style, the chastened but effective eloquence, the high ethical standpoint, which secured for the earlier series a well-nigh unanimous award of commendation."—*Academy.*

"**Expositions.**" By the same Author. Third Series. Second edition. Demy 8vo., cloth, 7s. 6d.

"When we say that the volume possesses all the intellectual, moral, and spiritual characteristics which have won for its author so distinguished a place among the religious teachers of our time . . . what further recommendation can be necessary?"—*Nonconformist.*

"**Expositions.**" By the same Author. Fourth Series (completing the Set). Demy 8vo., cloth, 7s. 6d.

"The volume is one of the most interesting and valuable that we have received from Dr. Cox. It contains some of the strongest analytical character-sketching he has ever produced."—*Glasgow Mail.*

Present-Day Questions in Theology and Religion.
By the Rev. J. GUINNESS ROGERS, B.A. Cloth, 3s. 6d.

Contents.—I. The "Down Grade" Controversy.—II. Congregationalism and its Critics.—III. Modern Thought.—IV. Broad Evangelicals.—V. Progressive Theology.—VI. Jesus the Christ.—VII. Creed and Conduct.—VIII. Evangelical Preaching.—IX. The Church and the World.—X. Congregationalism of To-day.

The Risen Christ: The King of Men.
By the late Rev. J. BALDWIN BROWN, M.A., Author of "The Home Life," &c. Crown 8vo., cloth, 7s. 6d.

"We have again felt in reading these nervous, spiritual, and eloquent sermons, how great a preacher has passed away."—*Nonconformist.*

Christian Facts and Forces.
By the Rev. NEWMAN SMYTH, Author of "The Reality of Faith." New edition. Crown 8vo., cloth, 4s. 6d.

"An able and suggestive series of discourses."—*Nonconformist.*
"These sermons abound in noble and beautiful teaching clearly and eloquently expressed."—*Christian.*

Inspiration and the Bible: An Inquiry.
By ROBERT HORTON, M.A., formerly Fellow of New College, Oxford. Fourth and Cheaper Edition. Crown 8vo., cloth, 3s. 6d.

"The work displays much earnest thought, and a sincere belief in, and love of the Bible."—*Morning Post.*
"It will be found to be a good summary, written in no iconoclastic spirit, but with perfect candour and fairness, of some of the more important results of recent Biblical criticism."—*Scotsman.*

Faint, yet Pursuing.
By the Rev. E. J. HARDY, Author of "How to be Happy though Married." Sq. imp. 16mo., cloth, 6s. Cheaper Edition, 3s. 6d.

"One of the most practical and readable volumes of sermons ever published. They must have been eminently hearable."—*British Weekly.*

The Meditations and Maxims of Koheleth.
A Practical Exposition of the Book of Ecclesiastes. By Rev. T. CAMPBELL FINLAYSON. Crown 8vo., 6s.

"A thoughtful and practical commentary on a book of Holy Scripture which needs much spiritual wisdom for its exposition. . . . Sound and judicious handling."—*Rock.*

The Pharaohs of the Bondage and the
Exodus. Lectures by CHARLES S. ROBINSON, D.D., LL.D. Second edition. Large crown 8vo., cloth, 5s.

"Both lectures are conceived in a very earnest spirit, and are developed with much dignity and force. We have the greatest satisfaction in commending it to the attention of Biblical students and Christian ministers."—*Literary World.*

A Short Introduction to the History of
Ancient Israel. By the Rev. A. W. OXFORD, M.A., Vicar of St. Luke's, Berwick Street, Soho, Editor of "The Berwick Hymnal," &c. Crown 8vo., cloth, 3s. 6d.

"We can testify to the great amount of labour it represents."—*Literary World.*

The Reality of Religion.
By HENRY J. VAN DYKE, Junr., D.D., of the Brick Church, N.Y. Second edition. Crown 8vo., cloth, 4s. 6d.

"An able and eloquent review of the considerations on which the writer rests his belief in Christianity, and an impassioned statement of the strength of this belief." *Scotsman.*

The Reality of Faith.
By the Rev. NEWMAN SMYTH, D.D., Author of "Old Faiths in New Light." Fourth and cheaper edition. Crown 8vo., cloth, 4s. 6d.

"They are fresh and beautiful expositions of those deep things, those foundation truths, which underlie Christian faith and spiritual life in their varied manifestations."—*Christian Age.*

A Layman's Study of the English Bible
Considered in its Literary and Secular Aspects. By FRANCIS BOWEN, LL.D. Crown 8vo., cloth, 4s. 6d.

"Most heartily do we recommend this little volume to the careful study, not only of those whose faith is not yet fixed and settled, but of those whose love for it and reliance on it grows with their growing years."—*Nonconformist.*

The Parousia.
A Critical Inquiry into the New Testament Doctrine of Our Lord's Second Coming. By the Rev. J. S. RUSSELL, M.A. New and cheaper edition. Demy 8vo., cloth, 7s. 6d.

"Critical, in the best sense of the word. Unlike many treatises on the subject, this is a sober and reverent investigation, and abounds in a careful and instructive exegesis of every passage bearing upon it."—*Nonconformist.*

The Ethic of Freethought:

A Selection of Essays and Lectures. By KARL PEARSON, M.A., formerly Fellow of King's College, Cambridge. Demy 8vo., cloth, 12s.

"Are characterised by much learning, much keen and forcible thinking, and a fearlessness of denunciation and exposition."—*Scotsman.*

Descartes and His School.

By KUNO FISCHER. Translated from the Third and Revised German Edition by J. P. GORDY, Ph.D. Edited by NOAH PORTER, D.D., LL.D. Demy 8vo., cloth, 16s.

"A valuable addition to the literature of Philosophy."—*Scotsman.*

"No greater service could be done to English and American students than to give them a trustworthy rendering of Kuno Fischer's brilliant expositions."—*Mind.*

Socrates:

A Translation of the Apology, Crito, and Parts of the Phædo of Plato. 12mo., cloth, 3s. 6d.

"The translation is clear and elegant."—*Morning Post.*

A Day in Athens with Socrates:

Translations from the Protagoras and the Republic of Plato. 12mo., cloth, 3s. 6d.

"We can commend these volumes to the English reader, as giving him what he wants—the Socratic . . . philosophy at first hand, with a sufficiency of explanatory and illustrative comment."—*Pall Mall Gazette.*

Talks with Socrates about Life:

Translations from the Gorgias and the Republic of Plato. 12mo., cloth, 3s. 6d.

"A real service is rendered to the general reader who has no Greek, and to whom the two ancient philosophers are only names, by the publication of these three inviting little volumes. . . . Every young man who is forming a library ought to add them to his collection."—*Christian Leader.*

Natural Causation.

An Essay in Four Parts. By C. E. PLUMPTRE, Author of "General Sketch of the History of Pantheism," &c. Demy 8vo., cloth, 7s. 6d.

"While many will find in this volume much from which they will dissent, there is in it a great deal that is deserving of careful consideration, and a great deal that calculated to stimulate thought."—*Scotsman.*

Proverbs, Maxims, and Phrases of all Ages.

Classified subjectively and arranged alphabetically. By ROBERT CHRISTY. Two vols. Large crown 8vo., Roxburgh, gilt tops, 21s.

Travel.

Ranch Life and the Hunting Trail. By THEODORE ROOSEVELT, Author of "Hunting Trips of a Ranchman." Profusely Illustrated. Small 4to., cloth elegant, 21s.

The contents consist of the articles on Ranch Life in the Far West, which have been appearing in *The Century Magazine*, combined with much additional matter which the author has prepared for the book, rounding it out (especially in the chapters on hunting) and making it complete as a record of the ranchman's life in the cattle country, and on the hunting trail. The illustrations are the work of a ranchman, and are true to life.

Rides and Studies in the Canary Isles. By CHARLES EDWARDES. With many Illustrations and Maps. Crown 8vo., cloth, 10s. 6d.

Guatemala : The Land of the Quetzal. By WILLIAM T. BRIGHAM. Twenty-six full-page and Seventy-nine smaller Illustrations. Five Maps. Demy 8vo., cloth, £1 1s.

"A book of laborious research, keen observation, and accurate information concerning a region about which previously scarcely anything was known."
Leeds Mercury.

A Summer's Cruise in the Waters of Greece, Turkey, and Russia. By ALFRED COLBECK. Frontispiece. Crown 8vo., cloth, 10s. 6d.

The Decline of British Prestige in the East. By SELIM FARIS, Editor of the Arabic "El-Jawaïb" of Constantinople. Crown 8vo., cloth, 5s.

"A perusal of his book must do the English reader good."
Asiatic Quarterly Review.

Daily Life in India. By the Rev. W. J. WILKINS. Illustrated. Crown 8vo., cloth, 5s.

"A very able book."—*Guardian.*

Modern Hinduism : An Account of the Religion and Life of the Hindus in Northern India. By Rev. W. J. WILKINS. Demy 8vo., cloth, 16s.

"A solid addition to our literature."—*Westminster Review.*
"A valuable contribution to knowledge."—*Scotsman.*
"A valuable contribution to the study of a very difficult subject."—*Madras Mail.*

Central Asian Questions : Essays on Afghanistan, China, and Central Asia. By DEMETRIUS C. BOULGER. With Portrait and Three Maps. Demy 8vo., cloth, 18s.

"A mine of valuable information."—*Times.* [*Mail.*
"A mine of information on all 'Central Asian Questions.'"—*Allen's Indian*
"A very valuable contribution to our literature on subjects of vast and increasing interest."—*Collum's United Service Magazine.*

The Balkan Peninsula. By EMILE DE LAVELEYE. Translated by Mrs. THORPE. Edited and Revised for the English Public by the Author. Map. Demy 8vo., cloth, 16s.

"A lucid and impartial view of the situation in the East."—*St. James's Gazette.*
"Likely to be very useful at the present time, as it is one of the best books on the subject."—*Saturday Review.*

Tuscan Studies and Sketches. By LEADER SCOTT, Author of "A Nook in the Apennines," "Messer Agnolo's Household," &c. Many Full-page and smaller Illustrations. Sq. imp. 16mo., cloth, 10s. 6d.

"The sketches are of that happy kind which appeal to the learned through their style, and to the simple through their subjects."—*Truth.*

Letters from Italy. By EMILE DE LAVELEYE. Translated by Mrs. THORPE. Revised by the Author. Portrait of the Author. Crown 8vo., 6s.

"A most delightful volume."—*Nonconformist.*
"Every page is pleasantly and brightly written."—*Times.*

Miscellaneous.

Industrial Rivers of the United Kingdom. By various well-known Experts. With numerous Illustrations. Crown 8vo., cloth, 7s. 6d.

These Chapters are not confined to the commerce and industries which characterise the great rivers: the history of each stream is traced from the earliest times. The foundation of the trade and manufactures which distinguish the several ports and districts are noticed; and the improvement of the rivers and harbours, and the development of the trade and commerce, up to the latest possible period, are dealt with at length.

Crime: Its Causes and Remedy. By L. GORDON RYLANDS, B.A. (Lond.) Crown 8vo., cloth, 6s.

A treatise on crime and its causes, presenting many interesting statistics and tables on its fluctuations, and suggesting remedies and a new method of meeting it.

The Five Talents of Woman. A Book for Girls and Young Women. By the Rev. E. J. HARDY, Author of "How to be Happy though Married," &c. Sq. Imperial 16mo., cloth, 6s.; Presentation Edition, bevelled boards, gilt edges, in box, 7s. 6d.

Contents.—The Five Talents of Woman.—The Power of a Woman's Smile.—How to be a Lady.—Housewife or House-moth.—A Centre of Order.—Woman's Work: to Teach.—Between School and Marriage.—Choosing a Husband.—Helpful Wives.—The Influence of a Wife.—Pets or Pests?—Daughterfull Houses—for what?—How to be Happy though Single.—Nurses and Nursing.—Daughters and Sisters.—Woman's Letters.—Woman's Studies.—A Girl's Religion.—Woman's Recreations.

How to be Happy though Married. Small crown 8vo., cloth, 3s. 6d. Bridal Gift Edition, white vellum cloth, extra gilt, bev. boards, gilt edges, in box, 7s. 6d.

"We strongly recommend this book as one of the best of wedding presents. It is a complete handbook to an earthly Paradise, and its author may be regarded as the Murray of Matrimony and the Baedeker of Bliss."—*Pall Mall Gazette.*

"Manners Makyth Man." By the Author of "How to be Happy though Married." Popular Edition, small crown 8vo., cloth, 3s. 6d.; imp. 16mo., cloth, 6s. Presentation Edition, imp. 16mo., cloth, bevelled edges, in box, 7s. 6d.

The Theory of Law and Civil Society.

By Augustus Pulszky (Dr. Juris), Professor of Law at Budapest. Demy 8vo., cloth, 18s.

"The book is in our opinion a contribution of unusual importance to the theory of law and the state."—*Westminster Review.*

Representative British Orations.

With Introductions, &c., by Chas. K. Adams. 16mo., Roxburgh, gilt tops, 3 vols., in cloth box, 15s. The volumes may also be had without box, 13s. 6d.

"The notes are extremely useful, and contribute largely to making the work one of value to students of political history."—*Pall Mall Gazette.*

Jottings from Jail.

Notes and Papers on Prison Matters. By the Rev. J. W. Horsley, M.A., Oxon., late (and last) Chaplain of H.M. Prison, Clerkenwell. Second edition. Crown 8vo., cloth, 3s. 6d.

"The jottings are full of vivacity and shrewd common sense, and their author, amid uncongenial surroundings, has preserved a keen sense of humour."—*Echo.*

Literary Landmarks of London.

By Laurence Hutton. Fourth, revised, and cheaper edition. Crown 8vo., Illustrated cover, 2s. 6d.; cloth gilt, 7s. 6d.

"He has made himself an invaluable *valet de place* to the lover of literary London."—*Atlantic Monthly.*

About the Theatre:

Essays and Studies. By William Archer. Crown 8vo., cloth, bevelled edges, 7s. 6d.

"Theatrical subjects, from the Censorship of the Stage to the most recent phenomena of first nights, have thoroughly able and informed discussion in Mr. Archer's handsome book."—*Contemporary Review.*

English as She is Taught.

Genuine Answers to Examination Questions in our Public Schools. With a Commentary by Mark Twain. Demy 16mo., cloth, 2s.; parchment, 1s.

Mark Twain says: "A darling literary curiosity.... This little book ought to set forty millions of people to thinking."

Proverbs, Maxims and Phrases of all Ages.

Classified subjectively, and arranged alphabetically. By Robert Christy. 2 vols., half cloth, gilt tops, 21s.

"This collection is unquestionably good, and deserves every attention from the book-buyer."—*Record.*

Books for Children.

Æsop's Fables for Little Readers:
Told by Mrs. ARTHUR BROOKFIELD. Twenty-five Illustrations by HENRY J. FORD. Small 4to., cloth, 3s.6d.

"In their present shape, the fables should be very popular among the inmates of the nursery, more particularly as they are illustrated with nearly thirty clever drawings by Henry Ford, which are beautifully printed in monochrome."
—*Scottish Leader.*

Six Girls.
A Home Story. By FANNIE BELL IRVING. Illustrated by F. T. MERRILL. Crown 8vo., cloth, 5s.

"The six main characters are drawn carefully, and well differentiated. The book has many a touch of simple pathos, and many a passage of light-hearted high spirits."—*Scotsman.*

The Brownies : Their Book.
With all the Original Pictures and Poems by PALMER COX, as published in *St. Nicholas*, and with many new Pictures. Second Edition. Medium 4to., cloth, 6s.

"Never, perhaps, has a book been published better calculated to afford unlimited amusement to little people than 'The Brownies.'"—*Rock.*

New Fairy Tales from Brentano.
Told in English by KATE FREILIGRATH KROEKER, and Pictured by F. CARRUTHERS GOULD. Eight Full-page Coloured Illustrations. Square 8vo., illustrated, paper boards, cloth back, 5s.; cloth, gilt edges, 6s.

"A really charming collection of stories."—*Pall Mall Gazette.*

Fairy Tales from Brentano. Told in English by KATE FREILIGRATH KROEKER. Illustrated by F. CARRUTHERS GOULD. Popular Edition. Sq. imp. 16mo., 3s. 6d.

"An admirable translator in Madame Kroeker, and an inimitable illustrator in Mr. Carruthers Gould."—*Truth*.

In the Time of Roses: A Tale of Two Summers. Told and Illustrated by FLORENCE and EDITH SCANNELL, Author and Artist of "Sylvia's Daughters." Thirty-two Full-page and other Illustrations. Sq. imp. 16mo., cloth, 5s.

"A very charming story."—*Scotsman*.
"A delightful story."—*Punch*.

Prince Peerless: A Fairy-Folk Story-Book. By the Hon. MARGARET COLLIER (Madame Galletti di Cadilhac), Author of "Our Home by the Adriatic." Illustrated by the Hon. JOHN COLLIER. Sq. imp. 16mo., cloth, 5s.

"Delightful in style and fancy."—*Scotsman*.
"A volume of charming stories."—*Saturday Review*.

When I was a Child; or, Left Behind. By LINDA VILLARI, Author of "On Tuscan Hills," &c. Illustrated. Square 8vo., cloth, gilt edges, 3s. 6d.

"A finer girl's book could not be had."—*Scotsman*.

The Prince of the Hundred Soups: A Puppet Show in Narrative. Edited, with a Preface, by VERNON LEE. Illustrated. Cheaper edition. Square 8vo., cloth, 3s. 6d.

"There is more humour in the volume than in half-a-dozen ordinary pantomimes."—*Spectator*.

Birdsnesting and Bird-Stuffing. A Complete Description of the Nests and Eggs of Birds which Breed in Britain. By EDWARD NEWMAN. Revised and Re-written, with Directions for their Collection and Preservation; and with a Chapter on Bird-Stuffing, by MILLER CHRISTY. Crown 8vo., 1s.

The Bird's Nest, and other Sermons for Children of all Ages. By the Rev. SAMUEL COX, D.D., Author of "Expositions," &c. Second edition. Imp. 16mo., cloth, 6s.

"These beautiful discourses were addressed to children of all ages, and must have found an echo in the hearts of many youthful listeners."—*St. James's Gazette.*

Spring Blossoms and Summer Fruit;

or, Sunday Talks for the Children. By the Rev. JOHN BYLES, of Ealing. Crown 8vo., cloth, 2s. 6d.

"They are of simple and instructive character."—*Dundee Advertiser.*

Arminius Vambéry: His Life and Adventures. Written by Himself. With Introductory Chapter dedicated to the Boys of England. Portrait and Seventeen Illustrations. Crown 8vo., 5s.

"We welcome it as one of the best books of travel that our boys could have possibly placed in their hands."—*Schoolmaster.*

Boys' Own Stories. By ASCOTT R. HOPE, Author of "Stories of Young Adventurers," "Stories out of School Time," &c. Eight Illustrations. Crown 8vo., cloth, 5s.

"This is a really admirable selection of genuine narrative and history, treated with discretion and skill by the author. Mr. Hope has not gathered his stores from the highway, but has explored far afield in less-beaten tracts, as may be seen in his 'Adventures of a Ship-boy' and 'A Smith among Savages.'"—*Saturday Review.*

The Adventures of Robinson Crusoe.

Newly Edited after the Original Editions. Nineteen Illustrations. Large crown 8vo., cloth extra, 5s.

Two Little Confederates. By THOMAS NELSON PAGE. With eight full-page illustrations by E. W. KEMBLE and A. C. REDWOOD. Square 8vo., cloth, 6s.

"A charming story."—*American Traveller.*

The Century Magazine

For 1889 includes:—

The Century Gallery of Italian Masters, from the Byzantines to Tintoretto—engraved by TIMOTHY COLE from the original paintings, and accompanied by historical and critical papers by W. J. STILLMAN.

Notes and Studies in Japan. By JOHN LA FARGE, illustrated with engravings from original studies by the artist.

Ireland: Studies of its People, Customs, Landscape, Town Life, Literature and Arts.

A Series of Irish-American Stories, both humorous and pathetic; each complete in itself, but having a connected interest.

Kennan in Siberia. Mr. GEORGE KENNAN's Siberian articles, illustrated with sketches and photographs taken by GEORGE A. FROST, will contain, from November on, what the author believes to be the best and most striking of all his material.

Price 1s. 4d. Monthly; post free, 19s. a Year.

St. Nicholas,

Conducted by MARY MAPES DODGE.

AN "ALL-AROUND THE WORLD" YEAR.

St. Nicholas for 1889 tells English boys and girls of the thousands of millions of children of other countries: of French girls in their little black alpaca aprons, and German girls with their flaxen hair, and Italian boys with their dark eyes, and clever American children (the cleverest take in *St. Nicholas*), and little Chinese maidens, with their almond-eyes and long pig-tails, and woolly-headed African pickaninnies. Of the homes of all these children, of the toys of the shy Japanese, of the pine woods of the blue-eyed Norwegians, of the furs and tobogganning of the Canadians, of the gum trees and kangaroos of the Australians, of the sharks and clear blue seas of the chocolate-skinned South-Sea Islanders—in fact, of nearly everything that amuses girls and interests boys, from the nursery rhymes of the Hottentot mothers to the guns and spears that the Icelandic fathers use to kill the white bears, *St. Nicholas* means to tell its readers in Great Britain and Ireland.

Price 1s. Monthly; post free, 14s. a Year.

T. FISHER UNWIN, 26, PATERNOSTER SQUARE, LONDON, ENGLAND.

www.ingramcontent.com/pod-product-compliance
Lightning Source LLC
Chambersburg PA
CBHW020831020526
44114CB00040B/504